M. Tope
WITHDRAWN FROM
THE LIBRARY
UNIVERSITY OF
WINCHESTER
D0240510

Oxford Historical Society

VOL. LXXIII

MEDIAEVAL ARCHIVES
OF THE
UNIVERSITY OF OXFORD

PRINTED IN ENGLAND
AT THE OXFORD UNIVERSITY PRESS

MEDIAEVAL ARCHIVES

OF THE

UNIVERSITY OF OXFORD

EDITED BY THE

REV. H. E. SALTER, M.A.

FELLOW OF MAGDALEN COLLEGE, OXFORD

VOL. II

OXFORD

PRINTED FOR THE OXFORD HISTORICAL SOCIETY

AT THE CLARENDON PRESS

1921

PREFACE

THIS volume contains a roll of the Proceedings of the Justices of the Peace, holding sessions in Oxford in 1390–4 under the Statutes of Labourers; also rolls of the courts for the Assise of Bread and Ale between the years 1309 and 1351; and lastly the rolls of Proctors' Accounts 1464 to 1497. All the University Archives to the year 1485 are now in print except Registrum Aa (the Register of Congregations 1448–1463) and Registrum Aaa (the Chancellor's Register 1434–1469).

The Society has been fortunate to secure a short Introduction for the first roll from Miss B. H. Putnam, of Mount Holyoke College, Mass., U.S.A., who issued in 1908 a volume on *The Enforcement of the Statutes of Labourers* (Columbia University Studies in History, vol. xxxii), and is a well-known authority on the Statutes of Labourers and the mediaeval Justices of the Peace. It is a satisfaction that she considers that the roll, long though it is, was well worth printing. She undertook the task at a very busy time, and the thanks of the Society are due to her.

H. E. SALTER.

CONTENTS

CORRIGENDA

p. 12, l. 36, *for* Jan. 18, 1555 *read* Oct. 1, 1390.

p. 137, l. 19, *for* clematyn *read* clermatyn.

p. 152, l. 32, *for* de *read* le.

p. 158, l. 8, *for* de *read* le.

INTRODUCTION

THE STATUTES OF LABOURERS

THIS huge roll—as bulky as a Tudor Patent roll—contains the fullest proceedings before justices of the peace thus far discovered for either the fourteenth or the fifteenth century.[1] But full though the proceedings are, they relate to but one phase of the activities of the Oxford justices, namely, to their responsibilities for the enforcement of the labour laws within the City of Oxford and its suburbs.[2] The seven sessions here recorded—one in 1390, two in 1391, three in 1392, and one in 1394[3]—thus represent the most complete account hitherto known of actions on the statutes of labourers in the local courts. A comparison of these sessions with the similar ones held between 1349–59[4] shows that in the intervening thirty years there have been only slight changes in procedure. The constables do not any longer—at least in Oxford—make presentments themselves[5] but are required to produce a list of *all* labourers in their bailiwicks,[6] whether under suspicion or

[1] Cf. the extracts in Putnam, *Enforcement of the Statutes of Labourers*, app. 166–9, 197–203, 211–13, 228–9, and the lists printed in *Eng. Hist. Review*, xxviii. 321–30; xxix. 479–99. A few other rolls earlier than 1485 have since come to light and will be described in my forthcoming volume on *The Origin and Development of Sixteenth-century Treatises for Justices of the Peace.*

[2] There are in existence two sets of records of justices of the peace for the county, as distinct from the city, of Oxford; Assize Roll 717, 10–11 Richard II and Ancient Indictments 99, 13 (?) and 21 Richard II, both mentioned in the lists in the *Eng. Hist. Review.*

[3] pp. 1, 16, 67, 72, 77, 97, 116. It is puzzling to find no records for 1393; probably they were formerly in the 'baga' mentioned on p. 123.

[4] Listed in my article on Justices of Labourers in *Eng. Hist. Review*, xxi. 517–38, and described in *Statutes of Labourers*, pt. 1, ch. 1, with extracts printed in the app. To the above lists must be now added the small fragment of an Oxford roll for 1355–6, printed *infra*, pp. 125–7.

[5] Cf. *Statutes of Labourers*, 67–8, app. 201.

[6] The four city wards and the hundred and suburb outside the North Gate; e. g. pp. 20, 27, 33, 37, 39, 40, 42, 56–7.

not,[1] while in each district twelve jurors (out of a panel of eighteen) make the presentments, 'accusing' some, 'excusing' others,[2] or report that none are guilty.[3] The presence of the accused is secured through the usual writs; *venire facias, attachies, distringas, capias*, and *exigi facias*.[4] A large number admit their guilt and are in mercy, the fines being recorded,[5] while others demand a jury trial. Of the latter, some are convicted,[6] but a great many are acquitted,[7] more, I think, than in the earlier period.[8] A distinctive fact, however, about the Oxford procedure is the frequency with which the accused admit the amount received or given and leave to the justices the question as to whether it was legal;[9] the significance of this method will appear later.

As is natural in city sessions, few agricultural labourers[10] are mentioned—certainly fewer than in the earlier records for counties as a whole[11]—but the variety of crafts represented is very great, affording a vivid picture of the economic life of Oxford, and effectually disproving the old theory that the labour legislation affected chiefly workers in husbandry.[12]

A striking feature of the Oxford method of enforcing the law is the equality of treatment accorded to masters and servants. In many instances the jurors present labourers for taking 'excess' wages, adding that they 'do not know from whom',[13] but very frequently, far more so than in the earlier sessions, they give a double list, including the servants who received, and the masters who gave, the 'excess' wages.[14] As previously,[15] it appears that the guilty are permitted to give surety for each other for the payment of their penalties—

[1] pp. 2, 3.

[2] p. 78.

[3] pp. 80, 102.

[4] pp. 4, 6, 12–13, 15, 24, 25, 72–6. For mainprise, see pp. 20–1. Evidently *capias alias* and *capias pluries* are allowed (pp. 24, 25) in spite of the Statute of Labourers of 1351, 25 Edw. III, st. 2, c. 6, which permits *exigend'* after the first *capias*.

[5] pp. 5–6, 58–9.

[6] p. 62.

[7] pp. 55, 61–62.

[8] To be proved only by a statistical study.

[9] pp. 8, 69.

[10] The carters, bailiffs of husbandry, &c., are connected with the Hospital of St. John outside the East Gate; cf. e. g. p. 24.

[11] Cf. *Statutes of Labourers*, 78–81.

[12] The theory had received some slight confirmation from the preponderance of agricultural labourers noted in the cases in the upper courts between 1349 and 1377; ibid. 182–4.

[13] e. g. p. 101.

[14] e. g. pp. 40–2. If guilty, the masters sometimes pay penalties equal to those of their servants, sometimes less, and sometimes more; pp. 63, 37–8, 29.

[15] Cf. *Statutes of Labourers*, app. 207.

masters for their servants,[1] masters for other masters,[2] servants for other servants.[3] A curious instance is recorded where twelve jurors actually indict four of their own number![4]

Except for a few examples of the vague phrase 'trespass against the ordinance and statute',[5] and for one action on the compulsory service clause[6] and one on the contract clause[7] of the ordinance of 1349, the innumerable cases dealt with relate to the giving or receiving 'excess' wages or the taking of 'excess' prices.[8] Evidently, therefore, the Oxford justices of the reign of Richard II are following their predecessors in concentrating their energies on the attempt to enforce those clauses of the labour legislation that turn merely on questions of fact,[9] instead of trying to deal with the more difficult questions of law involved in the contract clause and to a lesser extent in the compulsory service clause.[10]

The roll contains such a veritable mine of information on the names, residences, and occupations of the inhabitants of Oxford in the years 1390–4, and such abundant details of rates of wages—by the day, the week, or the year—and the prices of so many commodities, that it merits the most careful study from the point of view of local and of economic history. In addition, the proceedings throw light on two important problems of the organization of the office of justice of the peace and of the administration of the labour laws connected with the legislation enacted just before the beginning of the Oxford sessions. The problems can only be indicated here; their solution will involve a thorough study of a great mass of material.

The famous statute passed at Cambridge in September 1388 contains seven chapters on labourers, beggars, rates of wages, &c., with the provision that the law is to be enforced by the

[1] p. 23. [2] p. 20.
[3] pp. 47, 94.
[4] pp. 124–5.
[5] pp. 66–7. Cf. also the fragment for 1355–6, p. 126.
[6] p. 118.
[7] Departure of a servant; p. 67; cf. also pp. 126–7.
[8] The first two, *passim*; the last less frequently, but cf. pp. 79, 86, 121, 123.
[9] Cf. *Statutes of Labourers*, 71–7. During the reign of Edw. III, many actions on the contract clause were brought in the two upper courts.
[10] Ibid. 174–9. An investigation of the subject in Year-Books and Plea Rolls for later reigns is greatly needed.

justices of the peace,[1] and one chapter on the justices, specifying the number on each commission, the amount of their salaries, the length of quarter sessions, &c.[2] Curiously enough it is not till June 28, 1390,[3] that the statute finds its way into the commission of the peace,[4] there to remain for two centuries.[5] The chapter on justices does not make any change in the organization of the sessions, and apparently it has not hitherto been noted that in the commission of 1390 the experiment was tried of naming a quorum to deal with labour cases that was larger than, and therefore distinct from, the regular quorum for felonies.[6] The second and third commissions of the peace recorded in the Oxford roll—of January 12, 1391,[7] and of October 4, 1392—[8] follow the new form almost exactly, while the first—that of September 3, 1390—accomplishes the same result in a somewhat different fashion.[9] It is, of course, obvious that under this system the justices of the peace would probably, as in Oxford, hold special sessions for labour cases and would therefore be acting precisely as if they were justices of labourers like those appointed between 1352-9, absolutely distinct from justices of the peace.[10] Even though in 1394 the form of the commission again changes and the same justices are to deal with both felonies and labour offences,[11] yet in Oxford apparently the justices continue to hold two sets of sessions, and in the administration of economic legislation during the years 1390-4 show a degree of energy that had not been witnessed since the abolition of the separate commissions

[1] 12 R. II, cc. 3-9.

[2] C. 10.

[3] Although commissions were issued in 1389; Pat. 13 R. II, pt. 1, ms. 26 d-22 d.

[4] Pat. 14 R. II, pt. 1, m. 34 d. Unfortunately, it is not possible from the printed Calendars of Patent Rolls to ascertain the form of the commission. For example, this inclusion of the Statute of Cambridge is not noted; cf. Cal. Pat. R. II, 1388-92, 341.

[5] See Lambard, *Eirenarcha*, 1602 ed., 33-40.

[6] The smaller quorum is included in the larger.

[7] pp. 16-19; cf. Pat. 14 R. II, pt. 1, m. 31 d. In Oxford, the quorum for labour cases includes all but one of the commission.

[8] pp. 97-8; cf. Pat. 16 R. II, pt. 3, m. 20 d.

[9] pp. 1-2; cf. Pat. 14 R. II, pt. 1, m. 28 d; Cal. Pat., *ut supra*, 346, in this case mentions the Statute of Cambridge. Cf. also the commission of Oct. 1 issued to six men including two of the three named on Sept. 3, Pat. 14 R. II, pt. 1, m. 33 d. The work of this later commission is not included in the roll.

[10] See p. ix, *supra*.

[11] See the Letter Patent of Aug. 11, p. 116; cf. Pat. 18 R. II, pt. 2, m. 34 d.

for labourers in 1359.[1] This voluminous Oxford roll is thus explained, but the whole subject of the successive changes in the form of the commission of the peace and of their effect on the activities of the justices throughout the country needs further investigation.

The other portion of the Statute of Cambridge to be considered here is the enactment of maximum rates of wages by the year for agricultural labourers, together with an obscurely worded reference to the wages of servants of artificers and victuallers in towns.[2] It might be assumed that these new rates by the year were intended to supersede all the old rates by the day as given in the ordinance of labourers of 1349 [3] and in the statute of 1351,[4] but since the specific rates of 1388 are stated only for agricultural labourers, it seems probable that, at least for master artisans, the previous rates must stand.[5] In any case, early in 1390, a new device was tried. The justices of the peace were commanded to proclaim rates of wages once a year,[6] taking into consideration the price of victuals, and also to limit victuallers to reasonable gains.[7] In spite of some ambiguity in phraseology, it seems clear that by this act of 1390 it was intended to repeal the previous statutory maximum rates of wages, and that until the re-imposition of a maximum limit by the act of 1445 [8] the justices were left absolutely free to determine rates as they thought best.[9] But with the exception of one assessment for Coventry

[1] Cf. art. on Justices of Labourers, *ut supra*, 525–6, 529–30; *Statutes of Labourers*, 23–4, 224.

[2] 12 R. II, c. 4.

[3] 23 Edw. III, cc. 1 and 3; described merely as the rates prevailing before this plague. The ordinance was made a statute by 2 R. II, st. 1, c. 8.

[4] 25 Edw. III, st. 2, cc. 1, 2, 3, and 4.

[5] There are many difficulties involved in this subject. For example, in view of the earlier acts, I am unable to explain the introductory statement in c. 4 of the Statute of Cambridge: 'et auxint a cause qe les lowers des ditz Laborers & Servantz nonteste mys en certeyn devant ces heures . . .'.

[6] The better reading does not justify the interpretation of 'twice yearly'.

[7] 13 R. II, st. 1, c. 8, usually referred to as the Statute of 1389, the date according to the old style. In contrast to the Statute of Cambridge, the main emphasis is now on artisans. The justices had had somewhat similar powers given them as far back as 1351; under certain special circumstances, the statutory rates of wages were to be lowered, 'solonc lafferant et discrecion des iustices'; 25 Edw. III, st. 2, c. 4.

[8] 23 Henry VI, c. 12.

[9] This view was first stated by Miss E. A. McArthur in *Eng. Hist. Review*, ix. 310–14, 554, xiii. 299–302; cf. Cunningham, *Growth of English Industry and Commerce*, 5th ed., i. 449, note 1. For a contrary opinion, see the valuable article on the Assessment of

in 1420, including wages distinctly higher than the statutory rates,[1] and one for Norfolk in 1431,[2] it has not yet been discovered whether the justices were making use of their new powers during the period of freedom from statutory control. It is therefore with peculiar interest that one turns to these Oxford sessions held so soon after the passing of the statute.

There are many references to the statutory rates,[3] or to the rates prevailing before, or just after, the pestilence.[4] There are also various phrases indicating action of the justices:—'per assignacionem iusticiariorum',[5] 'assignantur tantum recipere',[6] 'secundum ordinacionem iusticiariorum',[7] 'sicut iusticiarii ordinare vellent',[8] 'per auisamentum iusticiariorum'.[9] Moreover, a very common method adopted by the accused is that already noted; namely, they state frankly the exact amount received or given as wages, and leave to the 'discretion' of the justices the decision as to its legality.[10] For example, a servant of a tanner admits that he has had 30*s.* a year,[11] a servant of a butcher 20*s.*[12]—high rates as compared with those for agricultural labourers given in the Statute of Cambridge[13]—but both were declared legal by the justices. The latter often demand time to consider: 'datus fuit eis dies ... usque sessiones istas, eo quod iusticiarii inde medio tempore auisiarentur'.[14] In some instances they decide that they have no right to act, as in the case of a dyer: 'eo quod ars illa non potest assederi, ut eis videtur',[15] or of a stonecutter: 'quia capcio talium lathomorum non potest assederi'.[16] In other instances they are prevented from acting because the members of a craft bring into court royal charters, granting them

Wages, by R. H. Tawney in *Viertel-jahrschrift f. Sozial- und Wirthschafts-geschichte*, Band XI, Heft 3, 318, 324.

[1] *Coventry Leet Book*, ed. Miss Dormer Harris, 21. My interpretation assumes that the earlier rates were 'without meat and drink'; 25 Edw. III, st. 2, cc. 3 and 4.

[2] *Eng. Hist. Review*, xiii. 299–302. It is to be noted that this assessment was made shortly after the re-enactment of 13 R. II, st. 1, c. 8 by 6 Henry VI, c. 3.

[3] e. g. pp. 3, 26, 89.

[4] pp. 45, 95.

[5] p. 50.

[6] p. 26.

[7] p. 87.

[8] p. 85; cf. a similar phrase in a Rutland roll of 27 Edw. III; *Statutes of Labourers*, app. 200.

[9] p. 93.

[10] pp. 14, 25–6, 69, 97, 115.

[11] pp. 14, 97, 115.

[12] p. 69.

[13] According to a literal interpretation of the Statute of Cambridge, c. 4, it would be illegal to pay these servants more than 13*s.* 4*d.*, the highest rate specified for agricultural labourers.

[14] p. 97.

[15] p. 113, note 2.

[16] pp. 22, 44–5.

exemption from the jurisdiction of the justices of the peace.[1]

In view of the above evidence it seems probable that the Oxford justices had not yet formed the habit of drawing up schedules of wages, and that whenever possible they were glad to accept as legal the maximum rates already given in the various statutes of labourers.[2] But as a matter of fact (as has already been shown) the statutory rates were by no means clearly stated, except for a few classes of labourers, and in many instances were merely to be the rates that had prevailed in a given locality in normal times.[3] It is therefore natural that with their new powers under the act of 1390 the justices should feel free to exercise their 'discretion' in fixing many rates of wages and of prices, and that such rates should be accepted as legal, perhaps eventually constituting a fairly complete schedule.

Although the problem of early wage assessments is by no means solved, the evidence just described—conflicting though it is—furnishes many interesting suggestions that may eventually lead to a solution, and thus affords additional proof of the importance of these Oxford sessions.

B. H. PUTNAM.

The Introduction by Miss B. H. Putnam has explained the legal side of the roll of 1390-4. If it had been possible to keep the book in type until her Preface had been written, it would have saved me three small errors; first, the heading of the pages should be 'Statutes of Labourers' rather than 'Statute'; secondly, the first note on page 45 is incorrect, and the mention of the 'Annus XX' of Edward III is not a mistake for 'XXIII'; for the twentieth year is expressed in the Ordinance of 1349, as the standard of wages before the pestilence; thirdly, the statement on page 116, lines 30 to 32, is

[1] pp. 90, 95-6.

[2] Of course, there is nothing in the act of 1390 to prevent the acceptance of the old rates if they seemed suitable.

[3] It certainly would not be easy for the justices to obtain from the three acts of 1349, 1351, and 1388 a complete schedule of wages. Moreover, the problem is complicated by the difficulty of comparing rates of wages by the day with those by the year.

incomplete, for though the clause there mentioned[1] is omitted, its substance is inserted in an earlier sentence, and the words found on p. 18, line 22, are altered in the later commission to 'prosequi volencium audiend' & terminand', ac felonias, transgressiones & forstallarias predictas ac omnia alia superius ad determinandum non declarata ad sectam nostram tantum', &c. The later commission therefore is the same in substance as the earlier, with this difference, that in the earlier commission when cases of felony were tried either Robert Cherleton or John Hulle must be present; but in the later commission all those who try cases under the Statutes of Labourers are considered fit to judge cases of felony.

There remains to say something about the value of the roll for local history. For this purpose it should be compared with the roll for the Poll Tax of 1380, which is printed in *Oxford City Documents* (O. H. S.), pp. 1–45. In that roll the collection is by the four wards, and as the names are evidently in geographical order we have an idea where each person lived, and with the help of other records we often know the exact spot. Thus John Wadyn, smith, who appears in our record as dwelling in NE. Ward (pp. 4, 40, 78) and giving excessive wages, is found in the Poll Tax of 1380 as living near East Gate with a wife and two male servants, and by the help of the Cartulary of the Hospital of St. John we know that the actual spot was the corner of Long Wall and High Street, now occupied by Magdalen College School. In like manner John Hickes, alderman, who was of the NW. Ward in 1390–4 (pp. 12, 43, 79, 120), lived in 1380 in the same ward not far from the Castle, being a spicer, with an apprentice, four men servants, and two women servants,[2] and by the help of a New College deed we know that his house was at the corner of Queen Street and New Inn Hall Lane, immediately to the east of the church; while John Lepere, baker, of the same ward, who appears in our roll with as many as six male servants (p. 43), and was a continual offender (pp. 12, 43, 79, 119), lived in 1380 immediately on the west

[1] See the bottom of page 18 and the top of page 19.
[2] *Oxford City Documents*, p. 28.

side of the church and had five male servants and one female. In some cases a man has moved from one ward to another between 1380 and 1390, and in other cases he has more servants by the later date; but in very many cases there has been little change in either point.

We are somewhat astonished at the large number of servants, and all the more when we remember that, as we see by the Poll Tax of 1380, they were unmarried. The largest number was kept by Reginald the Tanner, who is known to have lived in Brewers Street, towards its western end. He had at least fourteen male servants and one female in 1391 (p. 9); in 1380 he had eight male servants.[1] The Poll Tax of 1380 shows that of the whole population of Oxford above the age of fifteen about a quarter were unmarried servants, who lived in their masters' houses, receiving board and clothing and a yearly wage. While the list of masters, as given in the Poll Tax, is better than in our roll, because it tells us the trade of each master, our roll is the better as regards servants, for it gives us in many cases the occupation of the servant; and we learn how many of them were brewers for their masters. Thus Reginald the Tanner, though he was a tanner by trade, as his name suggests and as is stated in our roll (p. 14), had five servants who were brewers, and in the same list (p. 10) John Shaw, who was a fishmonger, had two servants who were brewers. The rolls of the Assise of Ale which are printed in this volume show what a large number brewed ale and sold it; it was a supplementary trade which nearly every one followed; but it was becoming a specialized trade, and we have William Ottemore and John Cade described as brewers (pp. 42, 43), implying that they followed no other trade.

As Miss Putnam notices, the burgesses had no agricultural servants. Reginald the Tanner had a carter, but this would be necessary for fetching the skins from the neighbouring villages; he was not a farm carter; and there is no evidence that there were farm buildings within Oxford at any time. The Master of the Hospital of St. John alone in this roll has farm servants; but he was in occupation of more than a

[1] *Oxford City Documents*, p. 15.

hundred acres and naturally had farm servants. Even in Northgate Hundred there is no mention of masters or servants engaged in agriculture.

Where we find servants described as hosteler or tapster we may assume that their master kept an inn. In many cases we know this is the case; thus Richard Battesyn (p. 10), of the SW. Ward, no doubt was the landlord of Battes Inn, which was subsequently the Fleur de Luce; and Nicholas Saundresdone (p. 11) had a large inn on the south side of the Gild Hall.

At the Sessions of the Justices presentments were made not only of masters and servants hired by the year, but also of workmen (*operarii*) who charged in excess for a day's work. These workmen are almost entirely connected with the building trade. In 1390 there are 12 masons, 12 carpenters, 1 plumber, 9 slatters, 1 dauber, 1 waller (i.e. builder of dry walls), and 3 labourers who were probably masons' labourers. The only other occupations that occur are 1 thatcher (p. 81), 1 sawyer (p. 81), 2 brewers (p. 78) who no doubt were hired by the day to assist at the brewing of beer, and 2 coopers (pp. 39, 81) who would be hired to repair barrels and vats.

Presentments were also made, though not at the earlier sessions, of artificers who charged in excess for goods that they produced—cordwainers, tailors, skinners, tanners, smiths, a patenmaker, goldsmiths, weavers, dyers, and fourbours[1] (pp. 82, 102, 121, 123). There is nothing remarkable about the districts in which they are found, except that the number of cordwainers in Northgate Hundred is worth notice (p. 102). The Poll Tax of 1380 gives the explanation, for it shows that there was a collection of shoemakers at the corner of George Street and St. Mary Magdalen Street, and another in Parks Road opposite Wadham College. In the Poll Tax they are called *sutores*; here they are *cordewanarii*; but the names are synonymous, though cordwainer was probably the higher title.

[1] This trade, which is frequently mentioned in old deeds, is described in *N. E. D.* as the trade of 'furbishing' armour; probably it means one who sells armour.

This roll gives us the names of a few constables, an office of which it so happens that we have little information in Oxford. We learn here that there were two constables for the north suburb, probably one was for the Manor of Northgate, the other for the Godstow Manor of Bradmore, which included the greater part of the parish of St. Giles. The two manors of North and South Oseney, and the manors of Walton and Binsey must have belonged to the sessions for the county, as they do not appear in our roll; and even the north suburb does not appear in the earlier sessions of this roll.

H. E. SALTER.

UNIVERSITY ARCHIVES

STATUTE OF LABOURERS

S.E.P. Y. 15. Sept. 26, 1390

Placita tenta apud Oxoniam die Lune prox. ante festum sancti Michaelis anno regni regis Ricardi secundi post conquestum quartodecimo & diebus Veneris & Sabati extunc prox. sequentibus coram Willelmo Dageville maiore ville Oxonie & Ricardo Ouertone iustic' domini regis virtute litterarum patentium domini regis subsequencium &c., Willelmo Gerueys clerico tunc ibidem.

Dominus rex mandauit litteras suas patentes in hec uerba:—Ricardus dei gracia rex Anglie & Francie & dominus Hibernie dilecto sibi in Cristo Thome Crauele cancellario Uniuersitatis Oxonie ac dilectis & fidelibus suis Willelmo Daggeville, maiori ville sue Oxonie, & Ricardo Ouertone salutem. Sciatis quod assignauimus uos coniunctim & diuisim ad pacem nostram, necnon ad statuta apud Wyntoniam, Norhamtoniam & Westmonasterium pro conseruacione pacis eiusdem ac statuta & ordinaciones ibidem & apud Cantebrigiam de venatoribus, operariis, artificibus, seruitoribus, hostelariis, mendicantibus, & vagabundis ac aliis hominibus mendicantibus qui se nominant trauailyngmen, necnon omnia alia ordinaciones & statuta pro bono pacis nostre ac quiete, regimine & gubernacione populi nostri edita in omnibus & singulis suis articulis in villa Oxonie & suburbiis eiusdem iuxta uim, formam & effectum eorundem custodiendum & custodiri faciendum, & ad omnes illos quos contra formam ordinacionum & statutorum predictorum delinquentes inueneritis castigandum & puniendum, prout secundum formam ordinacionum & statutorum eorundem fuerit faciendum, & ad omnes illos qui aliquibus de populo nostro de corporibus suis vel de incendio domorum suarum minas fecerint ad sufficientem securitatem de pace & bono gestu suo erga nos & populum nostrum inueniendum coram uobis uenire, et si huiusmodi securitatem inuenire recusauerint, tunc eos in prisonis nostris quousque huiusmodi securitatem inuenerint saluo custodiri faciendum. Assignauimus eciam uos & duos uestrum iustic' nostros ad ea omnia & singula que contra formam ordinacionum & statutorum predictorum in uilla & suburbiis predictis attemptata fuerint & attemptari contigerit tam ad sectam nostram quam aliorum quorumcumque coram uobis prosequi vel conqueri volencium audiendum & terminandum iuxta vim & effectum ordinacionum & statutorum predictorum. Et ideo vobis & cuilibet vestrum mandamus quod circa premissa omnia & singula ad certos dies & loca quos ad hoc prouideritis intendatis, & ea audiatis & terminetis in forma predicta, facturi inde quod ad iusticiam pertinet secundum legem & consuetudinem regni nostri Anglie, saluis nobis amerciamentis & aliis ad nos inde spectantibus. Nolumus tamen quod vos, prefati maior & Ricarde, vel alter vestrum de aliquibus, que ad Cancellarium solum in dicta villa & suburbiis pertinent excercend*a*, pretextu presentis commissionis nostre in aliquo intromittatis. In cuius rei testimonium has litteras nostras fieri fecimus patentes. Teste me ipso apud Westmonasterium tercio die Septembris anno regni nostri quartodecimo. Martyn.

Sept. 3, 1390

North-Est Warde

Et super hoc preceptum est vicecomiti Oxonie quod non omitteret propter aliquam libertatem in villa Oxonie & suburbiis eiusdem quin venire faciat coram dictis iustic' dicto die Lune prox. ante dictum festum sancti Michaelis apud Oxoniam omnes constabularios del Northest Warde ville Oxonie &, preter illos, xviii liberos & legales homines eiusdem warde ad faciendum ibidem ea que eis ad tunc ex parte domini regis iniungerentur. Et quod dicti constabularii haberent tunc ibidem omnia nomina venatorum, operariorum, artificum, seruitorum, hostelariorum, mendicancium & vagabundorum & aliorum hominum mendicancium, qui se nominant trauailyngmen, imbreuiat' &c. Et quod dictus uicecomes haberet ibidem eodem die nomina dictorum constabulariorum ac xviii hominum predictorum & warantum suum &c.

Ad quem diem Lune prox. ante festum sancti Michaelis dictus uicecomes retornauit nomen constabularii predicte warde, videlicet [Iohannes] Botelstone; et quod precepit ei quod ipse apud Oxoniam dicto die l[une] haberet [omnia nomin]a venatorum, operariorum, artificum, seruitorum, hostelariorum, mendicancium & vagabundorum ac aliorum hominum mendicancium qui se nominant trauailyngmen in balliua sua. Retornauit eciam dictus uicecomes nomina dictorum xviii liberorum & legalium hominum de eadem warda. Et ulterius dictus constabularius comparuit & retornauit diuersa nomina operariorum, artificum, seruitorum, & hostelariorum de balliua sua, de quibus plures accusati fuerunt per xii de predictis xviii liberis & legalibus hominibus, quorum XII^cim ac accusatorum predictorum nomina patent inferius, videlicet de predictis [XII] Michael Salisbury, Nicholaus Porter, Iohannes Dicondawe, Ricardus Waldene, Thomas Maister, Iohannes W[ ], Thomas Babbeley, Robertus Skynnere, Iohannes Spencer de Cattestrete, Iohannes Hande glouere, Iohannes Bilburghe & Thomas Shethere, qui iurati & onerati iuxta formam dictarum litterarum patencium dicunt super [sacramentum] suum quod de dictis accusatis Iohannes Plomer plomer, Iohannes Bysshope lathomus, Iohannes Atte Shoppe, Stephanus Palmer carpentar', Nicholaus Sclattere, Iohannes Webbe wallere[1], & Willelmus Broun, Laurentius Henxeye, Simon Serle, Iohannes Sampson, Iohannes Groue & Iohannes Thacham lathomi ac Philippus Carpenter, carpentarius, ceperunt par lez iourneyes excessiue a festo sancti Michaelis archangeli ultimo preteriti usque diem confeccionis huius contra formam statutorum, set de quibus personis dictis iuratis non constat. Et ulterius predicti XII iurati [dicunt] quod omnes seruientes subscripti retenti cum magistris suis subscriptis ad deseruiendum eis a festo sancti Michaelis archangeli ultimo preteriti usque idem festum extunc proximo sequens ceperunt de dictis magistris suis excessiue contra formam statutorum, & predicti magistri sui eisdem dederunt excessiue & soluerunt, quorum magistrorum & seruientum nomina inferius aperte patent, videlicet,

Magistri	Seruitores
Michael Salesburi	Iohannes Drake Iohannes Norcote Matilda Berewyke & Robertus, seruientes eiusdem Michaelis
Daniel Sclatford	Iohannes Champyon
Ricardus Iremongere	Iohannes Clerk Petrus Dauber Iohannes Hopkyn Elena seruiens eiusdem Ricardi Iremongere
Iohannes Siluestre	Walterus & Thomas Phelip
Alicia relicta Iohannis Veyne	Iohannes Dorchestre & Matilda & Alicia
Nicholaus Nortone	Willelmus, Iohannes & Alicia
Willelmus Dageuylle	Ricardus Carpenter, Iohannes Cornysshe & Ricardus
Thomas Maister	Willelmus Cartere
Rogerus Bakere	Iohannes & Agnes

[1] Perhaps a builder of dry walls.

Iohannes Spencer	Walterus Brewere Walterus Etone brewere
Iohannes Wadyn smythe	Seruientes sui quorum nomina inferius patent
Iohannes Holewey	Iohannes Meryweder
Iuliana Garlond	Thomas Fysshwyk Iohannes Ellesfeld
Iohannes White	Iohannes Lambehythe, Radulfus, Iohannes Gersyndone, Henricus, Iohannes & Agnes
Nicholaus Kent	Thomas Tachebrooke Iohannes Hamptone Iohannes Hostiler Iohannes Abyndone & Agnes Wootton
Magister hospitalis sancti Iohannis extra portam orientalem Oxonie	Iohannes Chamberleyne Henricus Spencer Robertus Bakere Iohannes Benet, bailly Iohannes Gardyner Isabella uxor predicti Iohannis Iohannes Panter Iohannes Bristowe cartere Willelmus Louegent cartere Iohannes Couentre Walterus Swon Alicia Deye Alicia Mey

Et super hoc, isto eodem die Lune prox. ante festum sancti Michaelis preceptum est dicto uicecomiti quod non omittat p[ropter aliquam] libertatem in predictis villa & suburbiis quin venire faciat coram prefatis iustic' apud Oxoniam die Veneris tunc [proximo] futuro, videlicet die Veneris in crastino sancti Michaelis omnes & singulos accusatos predictos ad respondendum separatim domino regi de transgressionibus supradictis &c. Et ulterius isto eodem die Lune preceptum est dicto uicecomiti quod non omittat propter aliquam libertatem antedictam quin venire faciat coram predictis iustic' apud Oxoniam [dicto] die Veneris in crastino sancti Michaelis de quolibet quarterio siue custodia ville Oxonie, excepta la Northest Warde antedicta, XVIII liberos & legales homines & preter illos omnes constabularios ad faciendum ibidem ea que eis ex parte domini regis adtunc iniungentur; ita quod dicti constabularii habeant tunc ibidem omnia nomina venatorum, operariorum, artificum, laborariorum, seruientum, vagabundorum, mendicancium & omnium hominum mendicancium qui se nominant trauailyng men, videlicet quilibet constabularius in warda sua &c. inbreuiat' &c., et quod dictus uicecomes ibidem tunc habeat nomina XVIII hominum de predictis wardis, ut predictum est, imbreuiat' & preceptum suum &c. **Memb. 2**

North Est Warde, retornum inde factum per uicecomitem die Veneris in crastino sancti Michaelis anno XIIII°

Ad quem diem Veneris in crastino sancti Michaelis predictus uicecomes retornauit quod predicti Iohannes Plomer, plomer, & de lathomis antedictis videlicet Iohannes Bysshope, Willelmus Broun, Iohannes Sampson & Iohannes Groue, ac eciam de dictis carpentariis Philippus Carpenter attachiati sunt per plegium Ricardi Bristowe & Willelmi Kent qui uenerunt. Et predicti Iohannes Plomer, Iohannes Bysshope & Philippus Carpenter non potuerunt dedicere transgressiones supradictas, & posuerunt se in gracia regis, quorum fines patent, ut sequntur [*sic*], videlicet

De Iohanne Plomer per plegium Michaelis Salesbury & Petri Welyngtone xx d.

De Iohanne Bysshope per plegium Gilberti Burtone & Roberti Gybbes ii s.

De Philippo Carpenter per plegium Willelmi Gymel & Iohannis Gersyndone, fuller iii s. iiii d.

Et predicti iusticiarii certis de causis super statu & capcione dictorum Willelmi Broun, Iohannis Sampson & Iohannis Groue dederunt eis diem essendi coram eis ad proximam sessionem post sessiones istas per plegium Ade de la Ryuere & Iohannis Gersyndone, fullere.

Retornauit eciam dictus uicecomes quod de predictis magistris & seruitoribus Michael Salesbury & Matilda Berewyk seruiens eiusdem Michaelis, Daniel Sclatford, Ricardus Iremongere, Nicholaus Nortone & Alicia seruiens eiusdem Nicholai Nortone, Willelmus Dageuille, Thomas Maister, Iuliana Garlond, Iohannes Ellesfelde seruiens eiusdem Iuliane & Iohannes White attachiati sunt per plegium Henrici Porter & Iohannis Prest, qui venerunt & non potuerunt dedicere transgressiones supradictas & posuerunt se in gracia regis, quorum fines patent, ut sequuntur, videlicet

Fines de seruitoribus predictis per tempus supradictum :—

De Matilda Berewyk seruiente Michaelis Salesburi per plegium Michaelis Salesbury & Nicholai Nortone xii d.

De Alicia seruiente Nicholai Nortone per plegium Nicholai Nortone & Iohannis Marchal, fysshere viii d.
De Iohanne Ellesfelde seruiente Iuliane Garland per plegium Iohannis Bilburghe & Roberti Abyndone, skynnere, xvi s. viii d.

Fines de predictis magistris par tempus antedictum:—
De Michaele Salesbury per plegium Nicholai Nortone & Willelmi Gerueys vi d.
De Daniel Sclatford per plegium Nicholai Nortone & Iohannis White vi d.
De Ricardo Iremongere per plegium Michaelis Salesbury & Nicholai Nortone vi d.
De Nicholao Nortone per plegium Ricardi Iremongere & Michaelis Salesbury vi d.
De Willelmo Dageuill' per plegium Thome Hamptone & Willelmi Hamptone viii d.
De Thoma Maister per plegium Iohannis Hande & Walteri Raga[. . .] iiii d.
De Iuliana Garlond per plegium Ade de la Ryuere & Iohannis Bilburghe xx d.
De Iohanne White per plegium Michaelis Salesbury & Ade de la Ryuere vi d.

Retornauit eciam dictus uicecomes dicto die Veneris in crastino sancti Michaelis quod de predictis magistris, accusatis ut predicitur, videlicet Iohannes Wadyn, Rogerus Bakere, Nicholaus Kent, magister hospitalis sancti Iohannis extra portam orientalem Oxonie, Alicia relicta Iohannis Veyn, Iohannes Spencer de Cattestrete attachiati sunt per plegium Iohannis Hendene and Willelmi le Frende, qui non venerunt; ideo plegii predicti in misericordia. Et preceptum est dicto uicecomiti quod non omittat propter aliquam libertatem in dictis villa & suburbiis quin distringat predictos Rogerum, Nicholaum, magistrum dicti hospitalis, Aliciam, Iohannem Wadyn & Iohannem Spencer per omnes terras &c., ita quod nec ipsi &c., et quod de exitibus &c.; et quod habeat corpora eorum coram prefatis iusticiariis apud Oxoniam die M[ercurii] proximo post festum sancti Gregorii pape proximo futurum ad respondendum domino regi de transgressionibus antedictis &c.

Retornauit eciam dictus uicecomes dicto die Veneris in crastino sancti Michaelis quod de predictis accusatis Iohannes Siluestre attachiatus est per plegium Ricardi Calte (? Cake) & Willelmi Londe, qui venit & dicit quod non dat excessiue contra statuta &c., videlicet [non][1] dat seruientibus suis prout superius accusatur &c. & [de][1] hoc ponit se super patriam &c. Ideo preceptum est uicecomiti Oxonie quod non omittat propter aliquam libertatem in dictis uilla & suburbiis quin uenire faciat coram predictis iusticiariis apud Oxoniam die Mercurii proximo post festum sancti Gregorii pape proximo futurum in sessionibus suis proximo per ipsos iusticiarios limitatis XVIII liberos & legales homines de dicta uilla Oxonie & suburbiis eiusdem uille, qui dictum Iohannem Siluestre nulla affinitate attingant, ad faciendum iuratam illam &c.

Retornauit eciam dictus uicecomes dicto die Veneris in crastino sancti Michaelis quod de predictis accusatis Iohannes Champyone, Iohannes Clerk, Petrus Daubere, Elena seruiens Ricardi Iremongere, Walterus seruiens Iohannis Siluestre, Thomas Phelip, Iohannes Dorchestre & Matilda & Alicia seruientes Alicie relicte Iohannis Veyne, Ricardus Carpenter, Iohannes Cornysshe & Ricardus, seruientes Willelmi Dageville, Willelmus Cartere seruiens Thome Maister, Iohannes Atte Shoppe, Iohannes Holewey, & Iohannes Meryweder, Stephanus Palmere carpenter, Thomas Fysshwyk, Iohannes Lambhithe, Iohannes Gersyndone, & Radulfus, Henricus, Iohannes & Agnes seruientes Iohannis White, Thomas Tachebrook, Iohannes Hamptone, Iohannes Hostiller, Iohannes Abendone, Agnes Wottone, Nicholaus Sclattere, Walterus Brewere, Walterus Etone, Iohannes Webbe wallere, Laurencius Henxeye mason, Simon Serle masone & Iohannes Thacham masone nichil habent in dicta balliua sua per quod possint attachiari &c.; qui non venerunt; ideo preceptum est dicto uicecomiti quod non omittat propter aliquam libertatem in balliua sua &c. quin capiat omnes predictos sic ad nichil per ipsum retornatos, ubicumque inuenti fuerint in predicta balliua sua &c. Et eos saluo &c., ita quod habeat corpora eorum coram predictis iusticiariis apud Oxoniam die Mercurii proximo post festum sancti Gregorii pape proximo futurum ad respondendum domino regi de transgressionibus antedictis.

Retornauit eciam dictus uicecomes dicto die Veneris in crastino sancti Michaelis quod de predictis accusatis Iohannes Drake & Iohannes Norcote, seruientes Michaelis Salesbury, Iohannes Hopkyn seruiens Ricardi Iremongere & Willelmus & Iohannes seruientes Nicholai Nortone attachiati sunt per plegium Henrici Prat & Willelmi Kene, qui venerunt; de quibus predicti Iohannes Drake, Iohannes Norcote,

[1] Not in original.

Iohannes Hopkyn & Willelmus seruiens Nicholai Nortone submiserunt se ordinacioni statutorum & iurati sunt &c.

Et predictus Iohannes seruiens Nicholai Nortone dicit quod est tabernarius dicti Nicholai & quod capit per annum de dicto magistro suo x s., & ponit se in discrecione iusticiariorum si excessiue &c. Et super hoc datus est ei dies usque proximam sessionem &c.

Retornauit eciam dictus uicecomes quod dicti seruientes predicti magistri dicti hospitalis sancti Iohannis extra portam orientalem Oxonie, uidelicet Iohannes Chamberleyn, Henricus Spencer, Robertus Bakere, Iohannes Benet bailly, Iohannes Gardyner, Isabella uxor eiusdem Iohannis Gardyner, Iohannes Panter, Iohannes Bristowe cartere, Willelmus Louegent cartere, Iohannes Covyntre, Walterus Swon, Alicia Deye & Alicia Mey nichil habent in dicta balliua sua per quod possunt attachiari &c.; et super hoc preceptum est dicto uicecomiti quod non omittat propter aliquam libertatem in predicta balliua sua quin capiat predictos seruientes dicti magistri predicti hospitalis &c. sic ad nichil retornatos, ubicumque inuenti fuerint in predicta balliua sua &c. et eos saluo custodiat, ita quod habeat corpora eorum coram dictis iusticiariis apud Oxoniam dicto die Mercurii proximo post festum sancti Gregorii ad respondendum domino regi de transgressionibus antedictis, &c.

Memb. 3 Et ulterius isto eodem die Veneris in crastino sancti Michaelis dictus uicecomes similiter retornauit nomina omnium constabulariorum cuiuslibet quart*erii* siue custodie ville predicte, excepta la Northestwarde predicta, & quod precepit eis quod iidem constabularii, videlicet quilibet eorum haberet apud Oxoniam coram predictis iustic' isto die Veneris omnia nomina venatorum, operariorum, artificum, seruitorum, hostelariorum, mendicancium & vagabundorum, ac aliorum hominum mendicancium, qui se nominant trauaillingmen, in warda sua. Retornauit eciam dictus uicecomes nomina XVIII liberorum & legalium hominum cuiuslibet warde uille predicte, excepta la Northeste Warde antedicta. Et patet retornum dicti uicecomitis inferius simul cum retorno dictorum constabulariorum, videlicet:—

Southwest Warde

Simon Byseley constabularius ibidem isto eodem die Veneris in crastino sancti Michaelis comparuit & retornauit diuersa nomina operariorum, artificum, seruitorum & hostelariorum de balliua sua, de quibus plures accusati fuerunt per XII de predictis XVIII liberis hominibus per predictum uicecomitem de warda ista retornatis, quorum quidem xii ac omnium accusatorum predictorum de warda ista nomina patent inferius; in primis de predictis xii Thomas Whitele, Rogerus Euerard, Iohannes Walker, Ricardus Westdale, Iohannes Lolly glouere, Martinus Cole, Thomas Gryndere, Iohannes Brut, Iohannes Cook webbe, Iohannes Lyllyng, Willelmus Hembury & Iohannes Hembury qui iurati & onerati iuxt formam dictarum litterarum patencium dicunt super sacramentum suum quod de dictis accusatis in warda ista, scilicet de sclatteres Adam Sclattere, Iohannes Vente, Iohannes Marye, Ricardus Huscombe, Iohannes Coke, Henricus Slattere et Radulfus Slattere, et de lathomis Henricus Mason, Iohannes Grene & Iohannes Mason et de carpentariis Iohannes Hedyndone & de dauberes Iohannes Tymmes ceperunt par les iourneyes excessiue a festo sancti Michaelis archangeli anno regni regis nunc xiii^{o} usque idem festum prox. sequens contra formam statutorum, set de quibus personis dictis iur*atoribus* non constat. Et ulterius xii iur' predicti dicunt quod omnes seruientes subscripti retenti cum magistris suis subscriptis ad deseruiendum eis a festo sancti Michaelis dicto anno xiii^{o} usque idem festum prox. sequens ceperunt de dictis magistris suis excessiue per tempus predictum contra formam statutorum & predicti magistri sui eisdem seruientibus dederunt excessiue & soluerunt, quorum magistrorum & seruientum nomina inferius aperte patent, videlicet:—

Magistri	Seruitores[1]
Iohannes Groom, bocher	Thomas seruiens eiusdem
	Petrus Brewere
	Iohannes Brewere
	Thomas Brewere
	Thom' Brewere
	Iohannes Kudlington, brewere
	Iohannes Wodhulle
	Iohannes Wiltsshire
Reginaldus Tannere	Iohannes Galewey
	Iohannes Tannere
	Iohannes Fynyan
	Iohannes Walton
	Stephanus Cartere
	Alanus Taskere
	Thomas Hille
	Alicia seruiens predicti Reginaldi Tannere

[1] In the original the names are in four columns; the second column is headed *seruitores*, the fourth *seruientes*. The two words are evidently synonymous.

Iohannes Utteworth	Robertus Cartere Dauid seruiens eiusdem Iohannis Thomas Cony Ricardus Gosehorne Custancia Wyke Alicia Hastyngs
Iohannes Skynnere	Thomas Caunbrigg' Iohanna seruiens eiusdem Iohannis
Ricardus Battesyn	Ricardus Hosteler
Petrus Welyngtone	Iohannes Cook seruiens eiusdem Petri
Iohannes Shawe	Thomas Brewere Iohannes Brewere
Thomas Chauntour, brewere	Iohannes seruiens eiusdem Thome
Iohannes Stratford, cook	Alicia, Iohanna — seruientes eiusdem Iohannis Cook

South-Est Warde

Iohannes Gersyndone constabularius isto eodem die Veneris in crastino sancti Michaelis comparuit & retornauit diuersa nomina operariorum, artificum, seruitorum & hostelariorum de balliua sua, de quibus plures accusati fuerunt per xii de predictis xviii liberis hominibus per dictum vicecomitem de warda ista retornatis, quorum quidem xii ac omnium accusatorum predictorum de warda ista nomina patent inferius; in primis de predictis xii Iohannes Clerk fysshere, Iohannes Swanbourne, Iohannes Dentone, Iohannes Mekesburghe, Iohannes Coupere, Iohannes Rotteley, Iohannes Bedewynde, Iohannes Marchall bocher, Willelmus Prentys senior, Ricardus Kudlyngtone, Thomas Prest & Willelmus Prentys iunior qui iurati & onerati iuxta formam dictarum litterarum patencium dicunt super sacramentum suum quod de dictis accusatis in warda ista, scilicet, de lathomis Iohannes Skirwhit, Iohannes Abyndone masones et de carpentariis Andreas Carpentarius, Iohannes Shoryere carpentarius, Iohannes Carpenter, Willelmus Fyffyde carpentarii, & de laborariis par le iourne Iohannes Wottone laborer, Iohannes Staundone laborer, ceperunt par les iourneys excessiue a festo sancti Michaelis dicto anno xiii^{o} usque idem festum extunc proximo sequens contra formam statutorum; set de quibus personis, dictis iuratis non constat. Et ulterius predicti xii iurati dicunt quod omnes seruientes subscripti retenti cum magistris suis subscriptis a festo sancti Michaelis dicto anno xiii^{o} usque idem festum extunc proximo sequens ceperunt de dictis magistris suis excessiue per tempus predictum contra formam statutorum, & predicti magistri sui eisdem seruientibus dederunt excessiue & soluerunt, quorum magistrorum & seruientum nomina inferius aperte patent videlicet:—

Magistri	Seruientes
Iohannes Pope, sawyer	Willelmus Stanley
Philippus Taillour	Alicia seruiens eiusdem
Iohannes Bereford, bocher	Iohannes Walsheman
	Iuliana seruiens eiusdem I. Bereford
Elizea Goolde	Walterus seruiens eiusdem
Iohannes Stratford, cook	Robertus seruiens eiusdem
	Isabella
Iohannes Trusse, sclattere	Laurencius seruiens eiusdem
Nicholaus Saundresdone[1]	Iohannes Cosyn
	Thomas Man
	Willelmus Chestertone
	Willelmus Neville
	Rogerus Hosteler
	Iohanna Tapstere
Iohannes Clerk, fyssher	Michael Neel
	Henricus Coupere
	Isolda seruiens eiusdem
	Iohanna seruiens eiusdem

North West Ward

Iohannes Spicer constabularius ibidem isto eodem die Veneris in crastino sancti Michaelis comparuit & retornauit diuersa nomina operariorum, artificum, seruitorum & hostelariorum de balliua sua de quibus plures accusati fuerunt per XII de predictis XVIII liberis hominibus per dictum uicecomitem de warda ista retornatis, quorum quidem XII ac omnium accusatorum predictorum de warda ista nomina patent inferius; in primis de predictis XII Iohannes Charley, Iohannes Keruere, Iohannes Miltone bakere, Iohannes Bernard, Willelmus Ferour, Gilbertus Cappere, Ricardus Wenlok, Iohannes Dyue sadeler, Henricus Moyye, Henricus Chaundeler, Iohannes Colles & Ricardus Broun qui iurati & onerati iuxta formam dictarum litterarum patencium dicunt super sacramentum suum quod de dictis accusatis in warda ista scilicet de carpentariis Iohannes Malyn carpentarius, Iohannes Wiltsshire carpentarius, Thomas Bloxham & Rogerus Carpentarius & de laborariis par le iourne Willelmus Sclattere laborer & de sclatteres Ricardus[2] Waterman sclattere ceperunt par les iourneyes excessiue

[1] He occupied the Blue Boar, alias Domus Conversorum.

[2] The scribe writes 'sclatteres & Ricardus'.

a festo sancti Michaelis de anno XIII° usque idem festum extunc proximo sequens contra formam statutorum; set de quibus personis, dictis iuratis non constat. Et ulterius predicti XII iurati dicunt quod omnes seruientes subscripti retenti cum magistris suis subscriptis a festo sancti Michaelis dicto anno XIII° usque idem festum extunc proximo sequens ceperunt de dictis magistris suis excessiue per tempus predictum contra formam statutorum, & predicti magistri sui eisdem seruientibus dederunt excessiue & soluerunt; quorum magistrorum & seruientum nomina inferius aperte patent:—

Magistri	Seruientes
Iohannes Charle	Iohannes Hosteler Iohannes Brewere
Iohannes Dadyngton	Agnes seruiens eiusdem
Iohannes Hikkes alderman	Iohannes seruiens eiusdem Alicia seruiens eiusdem
Iohannes Lepere	Elena seruiens eiusdem
Iohannes Cade	Iohannes, Tibota — seruientes eiusdem

Memb. 4 Et super hoc isto eodem die Veneris in crastino sancti Michaelis preceptum est predicto uicecomiti quod non omittat propter aliquam libertatem in predictis uilla & suburbiis quin venire faciat coram predictis iusticiariis apud Oxoniam die Sabati in crastino istius eiusdem diei Veneris omnes & singulos accusatos predictos de predicta warda, vocata la South West Warde, ad respondendum separatim domino regi de transgressionibus supradictis unde, ut predicitur, accusati existunt &c. Et eciam quod non omittat propter aliquam libertatem supradictam quin venire faciat coram predictis iusticiariis apud Oxoniam die Mercurii proximo post festum sancti Gregorii pape proximo futurum omnes & singulos predictos accusatos de dictis duabus wardis, scilicet de les South Est Warde & North West Warde supradictis, ad respondendum similiter separatim domino regi de predictis transgressionibus unde, ut predictum est, accusati sunt &c.

South West Ward; retornum inde factum per uicecomitem die Veneris[1] proximo post festum Michaelis anno XIIII°

Jan. 18, 1555 Ad quem diem Sabati in crastino dicti diei Veneris proximo post festum sancti Michaelis predictus uicecomes retornauit quod de predictis accusatis de dicta warda uocata la South West Warde vide-

[1] The scribe means *Sabbati*.

licet sclatteres, Adam Sclattere, Iohannes Vente, Iohannes Marie, Ricardus Huscombe, Iohannes Coke & Henricus Sclattere attachiati sunt per plegium Iohannis Reedhod & Willelmi Gilberd qui non uenerunt. Ideo predicti plegii in misericordia. Et preceptum est uicecomiti predicto quod non omittat propter aliquam libertatem predictam quin distringat predictos Adam Sclattere, Iohannem Vente, Iohannem Marie, Ricardum Huscombe, Iohannem Coke & Henricum Sclattere per omnes terras &c., ita quod nec &c.; et quod de exitibus &c., et quod habeat corpora eorum coram predictis iusticiariis apud Oxoniam die Mercurii proximo post festum sancti Gregorii pape proximo futurum ad respondendum domino regi de transgressionibus predictis &c. Retornauit eciam dictus uicecomes quod de predictis magistris & seruitoribus Iohannes Grom bocher & Thomas seruiens eiusdem, Iohannes Tannere, seruiens Reginaldi Tannere, Ricardus Battesyn & Ricardus Hostiler seruiens eiusdem, Petrus Welyngtone & Iohannes Cook seruiens eiusdem Petri, Iohannes Shawe, Thomas Chauntour brewere, Iohannes Stratford cook ac Alicia & Iohanna seruientes eiusdem Iohannis attachiati sunt per plegium Ricardi Bate & Willelmi Prat, qui omnes uenerunt; unde dictus Iohannes Groom dicit quod dat dicto Thome seruienti suo per annum x s., & sic non dat excessiue; & quod non dat ei plus, ponit se super patriam; & predictus Thomas seruiens predicti Iohannis Groom dicit quod capit x s. per annum & non plus, & hoc [*sic*] ponit se super patriam. Et dominus Iohannes Shawe dicit quod [non][1] dedit dictis Thome Brewere & Iohanni Brewere excessiue contra statutum & hoc ponit se super patriam. Et predictus Iohannes Stratford cook dicit quod dat predicte Alicie per annum iii s. & dicte Iohanne per annum vi s.; et quod non dat plus ponit se super patriam; & dicte seruientes sue dicunt ut ipse dicit, & hoc ponunt se similiter. Ideo preceptum est dicto uicecomiti quod non omittat propter aliquam libertatem antedictam &c. quin venire faciat XVIII probos & legales homines de uilla & suburbiis predictis coram predictis iusticiariis apud Oxoniam dicto die Mercurii proximo post festum sancti Gregorii pape proximo futurum, qui dictos Iohannem Groom, Thomam seruientem eiusdem, Iohannem Shawe, Iohannem Stratford cook, Aliciam nec Iohannam seruientes eius aliqua affinitate attingant &c. ad faciendum iuratas illas &c.; et quod habeat ibidem tunc nomina eorum imbr[euiata] &c. Et dictus Thomas Chauntour

[1] Not in MS.; see also p. 7.

dicit quod Iohannes seruiens suus predictus est seruiens suus adiuuando se ad braciandum &c., & multum laborat & uigilat &c., & quod dat ei per annum x s., I tunicam cum capucio & I napirone[1] & I roket, & ponit se in discrecione iusticiariorum si excessiue contra formam statuti uel non &c.; et dictus Iohannes seruiens suus dicit quod capit de predicto magistro suo sicut idem magister suus dicit, et ponit se similiter in discrecione iusticiariorum predictorum si excessiue &c. Et super hoc datus est dies eisdem Thome & Iohanni usque dictum diem Mercurii proximo post festum sancti Gregorii &c. Et dictus Iohannes Tannere seruiens dicti Reginaldi Tannere dicit quod capit de dicto magistro suo per annum xxx s. in omnibus, & quod fuit apprenticius in arte de tann*er*e per vii annos, & quod est iam capitalis mercenarius dicti Reginaldi magistri sui, & ponit se in discrecione iusticiariorum si excessiue &c. Et super hoc datus est ei dies usque dictum diem Mercurii proximo post festum sancti Gregorii &c. Et dictus Ricardus Battesyn dicit quod Ricardus seruiens suus est hostelarius suus computaturus, & siquid perditum fuerit in hospicio suo idem Ricardus seruiens perdet, & dicit quod dat sibi per annum xx s. & I tunicam cum capucio, & ponit se in discrecione iusticiariorum si excessiue &c. Et dictus Ricardus seruiens eodem modo dicit & ponit se in discrecione ut supra &c. Et sic datus est eis dies ut supra &c. videlicet dicto die Mercurii &c. Et predicti Petrus Welyngton & Iohannes Cook seruiens suus venerunt & non possunt dedicere transgressiones predictas & ponunt se in gracia regis, quorum fines, ut inferius patet, sequntur:—

Fines

De Petro Welyngtone per plegium Ade de la Ryvere & Walteri Bone — vi d.

De Iohanne Cook seruiente Petri Welyngtone per plegium dictorum Ade de la Ryvere & Walteri Bone — xii d.

Retornauit eciam dictus uicecomes isto eodem die Sabati in crastino dicti diei[2] Veneris proximo post festum sancti Michaelis quod predicti Reginaldus Tannere & Iohannes Utteworthe attachiati sunt per plegium Ricardi Kene & Willelmi Bost & non venerunt, ideo dicti plegii in misericordia. Et preceptum est dicto vicecomiti quod non omittat propter aliquam libertatem predictam quin distringat predictos Reginaldum Tannere & Iohannem Utteworth per omnes terras &c., ita quod nec &c., et quod de exitibus &c.; et quod habeat corpora

[1] apron. [2] die, MS.

eorum coram prefatis iusticiariis apud Oxoniam dicto die Mercurii proximo post festum sancti Gregorii proximo futurum ad respondendum separatim domino regi de transgressionibus predictis &c.

Retornauit eciam dictus uicecomes isto eodem die Sabati quod predicti seruientes predicti Reginaldi Tannere, videlicet Petrus Brewere, Iohannes Harryes[1] brewere, Thomas Brewere, Thomas Brewere, Iohannes Kedlyngtone brewere, Iohannes Woodhille, Iohannis Wiltsshire, Iohannes Galewey, Iohannes Fynyan, Iohannes Waltone, Stephanus Cartere, Alanus Taskere, Thomas Hille & Alicia seruiens &c. attachiati sunt per plegium Ricardi Bristowe & Iohannis Tannere seruientis Reginaldi Tannere & non venerunt; ideo dicti plegii in misericordia. Et preceptum est dicto uicecomiti quod non omittat propter aliquam libertatem predictam quin distringat omnes predictos seruientes predicti Reginaldi, excepto predicto Iohanne Tannere, per omnes terras &c., ita quod nec &c., et quod de exitibus &c. Et quod habeat corpora eorum coram predictis iusticiariis apud Oxoniam dicto die Mercurii proximo post festum sancti Gregorii pape proximo futuri ad respondendum separatim domino regi de transgressionibus predictis &c.

Retornauit eciam dictus uicecomes isto eodem die Sabati quod predicti Iohannes Tymmes daubere & seruientes Iohannis Utteworth, videlicet Robertus Cartere, Dauid seruiens eiusdem Iohannis, Thomas Cony, Ricardus Gosehorne, Custancia Wyke, & Alicia Hastynges, ac eciam Thomas Caumbrigge & Iohanna seruientes dicti Iohannis Skynnere, Henricus Masone, Radulfus Sclattere, Iohannes Grene ac seruientes Iohannis Shawe, videlicet Thomas Brewere, Iohannes Brewere, Iohannes Masone & Iohannes Hedyndone nichil habent in dictis villa & suburbiis &c. per quod possunt attachiari. Ideo preceptum est dicto uicecomiti quod non omittat propter aliquam libertatem antedictam quin capiat predictos Iohannem Tymmes, Robertum Cartere, Dauid, Thomam Cony, Ricardum Gosehorne, Custanciam, Aliciam, Thomam Caumbrigge, Iohannam, Henricum Masone, Radulfum Sclattere, Iohannem Grene, Thomam Brewere, Iohannem Brewere, Iohannem Masone & Iohannem Hedyndone ubicumque inuenti fuerint in dictis uilla & suburbiis, & eos saluo custod*iat* &c., ita quod habeat corpora eorum coram predictis iusticiariis apud Oxoniam dicto die Mercurii proximo post festum sancti Gregorii proximo futurum ad respondendum separatim domino regi de transgressionibus predictis &c.

[1] This surname is added above the line.

Et quo ad execucionem faciendam per dictum uicecomitem uersus predictum Iohannem Skynnere, uicecomes ad istum eundem diem Sabati nullum preceptum retornauit &c.; ideo preceptum est dicto vicecomiti, sicut alias, quod non omittat propter aliquam libertatem predictam quin venire faciat coram predictis iusticiariis apud Oxoniam dicto die Mercurii proximo post festum sancti Gregorii proximo futurum predictum Iohannem Skynnere ad respondendum domino regi de transgressionibus predictis &c. Ad quem diem Mercurii &c. predictus uicecomes retornauit quod predictus Iohannes Skynnere mortuus est, prout patet inferius per returnum dicti uicecomitis dicto die Mercurii &c.

Mar. 15, 1391

Placita tenta apud Oxoniam die Mercurii prox. post festum sancti Gregorii pape anno regni regis Ricardi secundi post conquestum XIIII° & diebus Iouis, Veneris, Sabati & die Martis tunc prox. sequentibus coram Ricardo de Garstone, maiore uille Oxonie, & Ricardo Ouertone, iusticiariis domini regis virtute aliarum litterarum patencium domini regis subsequencium, Willelmo Gerueys clerico tunc ibidem.

Memb. 5

Dominus Rex mandauit litteras suas patentes in hec uerba:—

Ricardus dei gracia, rex Anglie & Francie & dominus Hibernie dilectis & fidelibus suis Thome Craule, cancellario Uniuersitatis Oxonie, Roberto Charletone, Iohanni Hulle, Ricardo Garstone maiori uille Oxonie, Iohanni Rede & Ricardo Ouerton, salutem. Sciatis quod assignauimus vos coniunctim & diuisim ad pacem nostram, necnon ad statuta apud Wyntoniam, Norhamtoniam, & Westmonasterium pro conseruacione pacis eiusdem ac statuta & ordinaciones ibidem & apud Cantebr*igiam* de venatoribus, operariis, artificibus, seruitoribus, hostelariis, mendicantibus & vagabundis ac aliis hominibus mendicantibus qui se nominant trauaillyngmen, necnon omnia alia ordinaciones & statuta pro bono pacis nostre & quiete, regimine & gubernacione populi nostri edita in omnibus & singulis suis articulis in villa Oxonie & suburbiis eiusdem, iuxta vim, formam & effectum eorundem, custodiendum & custodiri faciendum & ad omnes illos quos contra formam ordinacionum & statutorum predictorum delinquentes inueneritis castigandum & puniendum, prout secundum formam ordinacionum & statutorum eorundem fuerit faciendum, & ad omnes illos qui aliquibus de populo nostro de corporibus suis uel de incendio domorum suarum minas fecerint ad sufficientem securitatem de pace & bono gestu suo erga nos & populum nostrum inueniendum coram uobis uenire, &

si huiusmodi securitatem inuenire recusauerint tunc eos in prisonis nostris quousque huiusmodi securitatem inuenerint saluo custodiri faciendum. Assignauimus eciam uos quinque, quatuor, tres & duos uestrum iustic' nostros ad inquirendum per sacramentum proborum & legalium hominum de uilla & suburbiis predictis, per quos rei ueritas melius sciri poterit, de omnimodis feloniis, transgressionibus, forstallariis, regratariis, & extorsionibus in uilla & suburbiis predictis per quoscumque & qualitercumque factis siue perpetratis & que exnunc ibidem fieri continget, & eciam de omnibus illis qui in conuenticulis contra pacem nostram in perturbacionem populi nostri seu vi armata ierint vel equitauerint seu exnunc ire vel equitare presumpserint, & eciam de hiis qui in insidiis ad gentem nostram mahemiandum vel interficiendum iacuerint & exnunc iacere presumpserint & eciam de [hiis][1] qui capiciis & alia liberata de unica secta per confederacionem & pro manutenencia contra defensionem ac formam ordinacionum & statutorum inde ante hec tempora factorum usi fuerint & aliis huiusmodi liberata imposterum utentibus, & eciam de hostelariis & aliis qui in abusu mensurarum & ponderum ac in vendicione victualium, & eciam de quibuscumque operariis, artificibus, seruitoribus, mendicantibus & vagabundis predictis & aliis qui contra formam ordinacionum & statutorum pro communi utilitate regni nostri Anglie & populi nostri eiusdem de huiusmodi uenatoribus, operariis, artificibus, seruitoribus, hostelariis, mendicantibus & vagabundis & aliis inde factorum deliquerint vel attemptauerint in uilla & suburbiis predictis & exnunc delinquere vel attemptare presumpserint, & eciam de quibuscumque uicecomitibus, maioribus, balliuis, senescallis, constabulariis & custodibus gaolarum qui in execucione officiorum suorum erga huiusmodi artifices, seruitores, laboratores, vitellarios, mendicantes & vagabundos ac alios predictos iuxta formam ordinacionum & statutorum predictorum facienda indebite se habuerint & exnunc indebite se habere presumpserint aut tepidi fuerint, remissi vel negligentes, & exnunc tepidos, remissos, vel negligentes fore contigerit, & de omnibus aliis & singulis articulis & circumstanciis premissa omnia & singula, ac aliis contra formam ordinacionum & statutorum predictorum per quoscumque & qualitercumque factis siue attemptatis & que exnunc fieri vel attemptari contigerit qualitercumque concernentibus plenius ueritatem, & ad indictamenta quecumque coram vobis seu duobus vestrum ac aliis nuper custodibus pacis nostre & iusticiariis nostris ad huiusmodi felonias, transgressiones & malefacta in villa & suburbiis predictis

[1] Not in MS.

audiendum & terminandum assignatis uirtute diuersarum litterarum nostrarum vobis & eisdem aliis nuper custodibus pacis nostre & iusticiariis nostris in hac parte factarum facta & nondum terminata inspiciendum, & ad omnia breuia & precepta per uos & ipsos alios nuper custodes pacis nostre & iusticiarios nostros uirtute litterarum nostrarum predictarum facta & coram uobis & ipsis aliis nuper custodibus pacis nostre & iusticiariis nostris ad certos terminos futuros retornabilia ad terminos illos recipiendum & processus inde inchoatos ac processus versus omnes alios coram vobis & eisdem aliis nuper custodibus pacis nostre & iusticiariis nostris indictatos & quos coram vobis indictari contigerit quousque capiantur, reddantur vel utlagentur faciendum & continuandum. Assignauimus eciam vos quinque, quatuor, tres & duos vestrum, quorum aliquem vestrum, vos prefati Cancellarie, Roberte, Iohannes, Iohannes & Ricarde Ouertone, unum esse volumus, iusticiarios nostros ad ea omnia & singula que per huiusmodi hostelarios & alios in abusu mensurarum & ponderum ac in vendicione victualium & omnia alia que per huiusmodi operarios, artifices, seruitores, mendicantes & vagabundos contra formam ordinacionum & statutorum predictorum seu in eneruacionem eorundem in aliquo presumpta vel attemptata fuerint & attemptari contigerit, ac extorsiones & regratarias predictas tam ad sectam nostram quam aliorum quorumcumque coram vobis pro nobis vel pro se ipsis conqueri vel prosequi volencium ac transgressiones & forstallarias predictas ad sectam nostram tantum & omnia alia que virtute ordinacionum & statutorum predictorum ac aliorum ordinacionum & statutorum regni nostri Anglie per custodes pacis nostre & iusticiarios nostros huiusmodi discuti & terminari debent audiendum & terminandum, & ad eosdem operarios, artifices & seruitores per fines redempciones & amerciamenta & alio modo pro delictis suis, prout ante ordinacionem de punicione corporali huiusmodi operariis, artificibus & seruitoribus pro delictis suis exhibenda factam fieri consueuit, necnon eosdem vicecomites, maiores, balliuos, senescallos, constabularios, custodes gaolarum, venatores, vitellarios, hostelarios, mendicantes & vagabundos super hiis que contra formam ordinacionum & statutorum predictorum attemptata fuerint & attemptari continget castigandum & puniendum secundum legem & consuetudinem regni nostri Anglie ac formam ordinacionum & statutorum eorundem. Assignauimus vos eciam quinque, quatuor, tres & duos vestrum, quorum alterum vestrum vos prefati Roberte & Iohannes[1] Hulle unum esse volumus

[1] Iohanne, MS.

iusticiarios nostros ad felonias predictas & omnia alia superius ad determinandum non declarata ad sectam nostram audiendum & terminandum secundum legem & consuetudinem regni nostri Anglie ac formam ordinacionum & statutorum predictorum, prouiso semper quod si casus difficultatis super determinacione extorcionum huiusmodi coram uobis euenire contigerit, quod ad iudicium inde reddendum nisi in presencia unius iusticiariorum nostrorum de uno vel altero banco aut iusticiariorum nostrorum ad assisas in comitatu Oxonie capiendas assignatorum coram vobis minime procedatur. Et ideo vobis & cuilibet vestrum mandamus quod circa custodiam pacis ac ordinacionum & statutorum predictorum diligenter intendatis, & ad certos dies & loca quos uos quinque, quatuor, tres uel duo uestrum ad hoc prouideritis inquisiciones super premissis faciatis & premissa omnia & singula audiatis & terminetis ac modo debito & effectualiter expleatis in forma premissa, facturi inde quod ad iusticiam pertinet secundum legem & consuetudines predictas; saluis nobis amerciamentis & aliis ad nos inde spectantibus. Mandauimus enim uicecomiti nostro Oxonie quod ad certos dies & loca quos uos quinque, quatuor, tres uel duo vestrum ei scire faciatis, venire faciat coram vobis quinque, quatuor, tribus & duobus vestrum tot & tales probos & legales homines de uilla & suburbiis predictis per quos rei ueritas in premissis melius sciri poterit & inquiri; et vos, prefate Iohannes Hulle, ad certos dies & loca per uos & dictos socios vestros super hoc prefigendos breuia, precepta, processus & indictamenta, ut predictum est, coram uobis & sociis vestris nuper custodibus pacis & iusticiariis huiusmodi facta & nondum terminata, coram vobis & nunc sociis vestris predictis venire faciatis & ea inspiciatis & debito fine terminetis, sicut predictum est. Nolumus tamen quod aliquis vestrum, vos prefati Roberte, Iohannes, Maior, Iohannes & Ricarde, de aliquo premissorum que iuxta priuilegia & libertates Uniuersitatis solum corrigi & terminari debent, colore presentis commissionis in aliquo intromittatis. In cuius rei testimonium has litteras nostras fieri fecimus patentes. Teste me ipso apud Westmonasterium XII die Ianuarii anno regni nostri quartodecimo.

Jan. 12, 1391

Memb. 6

Ac dicti Willelmus Dageuille & Ricardus Ouertone recordum suum coram eis captum uirtute priorum litterarum patentium domini regis nunc superius declaratarum tenore harum litterarum venire fecerunt coram domino Ricardo de Garstone maiore ville Oxonie & Ricardo Ouertone. Et super hoc preceptum est dicto uicecomiti quod retornaret coram predictis Thoma Craule, Roberto Charletone, Iohanne Hulle, Ricardo Garstone, Iohanne Rede & Ricardo Ouertone omnia precepta ei per dictos Willelmum Dageville & Ricardum Ouertone nuper iusticiarios virtute dictarum priorum litterarum patentium domini regis directa,[1] ita quod de execucione eorundem dictis nunc iusticiariis respondeat apud Oxoniam die Mercurii proximo post festum sancti Gregorii pape proximo futurum &c.

North-Est Warde, retornum factum inde per vicecomitem die Mercurii proximo post festum sancti Gregorii anno XIIII°

Mar. 15, 1391

Ad quem diem Mercurii proximo post festum sancti Gregorii pape pretextu dicti precepti &c., dictus uicecomes retornauit quod de predictis accusatis coram predictis iusticiariis in predicta prima commissione nominatis, Rogerus Bakere, Nicholaus Kent, magister hospitalis sancti Iohannis extra portam orientalem Oxonie, Alicia relicta Iohannis Veyn & Iohannes Spencer de Cattestrete districti sunt & manucapti, viz. quilibet eorum per Iohannem Hert, Willelmum Rede, Iohannem Prat & Nicholaum Estone. Retornauit eciam de exit*ibus* terrarum cuiuslibet eorundem districtorum, preter de exitu terre dicti magistri, IIII *d.*[2] & de exitu terre predicti magistri XL *d.* De quibus districtis, ut predicitur, dicto die Mercurii proximo post festum sancti Gregorii comparuerunt videlicet Rogerus Bakere, Nicholaus Kent, magister hospitalis sancti Iohannis extra portam orientalem Oxonie & Alicia relicta Iohannis Veyne, de quibus predicti Rogerus Bakere, Nicholaus Kent & Alicia relicta &c. non potuerunt dedicere transgressiones predictas & posuerunt se in gracia regis, quorum fines patent, ut sequntur, videlicet,

De Rogero Bakere pro excessu dato per plegium Nicholai Kent & Stephani Palmere — xii d.

De Nicholao Kent pro eodem per plegium Ade de la Ryuere & Willelmi Newman — xii d.

De Alicia relicta Iohannis Veyne pro eodem per plegium Willelmi Gerueys & Iohannis Milton skynnere — vi d.

Et quo ad execucionem faciendam versus Iohannem Wadyn smyth vicecomes nullum preceptum retornavit. Ideo preceptum est dicto vicecomiti, sicut alias, quod non omittat propter aliquam libertatem predictam quin distringat predictum Iohannem Wadyn per omnes terras &c., ita quod nec ipse &c., et quod habeat corpus eius coram predictis nunc iusticiariis apud Oxoniam die Sabbati proximo post

[1] directarum, MS.
[2] In the margin 'Exit' terre Iohannis Spencer iiii d.'

festum sancti Mathei apostoli proximo futurum ad respondendum domino regi de transgressionibus predictis &c.

Et ulterius preceptum est dicto vicecomiti quod non omittat propter aliquam libertatem predictam [quin][1] venire faciat coram predictis nunc iusticiariis ad diem & locum illos omnes seruientes dicti Iohannis Wadyn pro quibus coram predictis nuper iusticiariis idem Iohannes accusatus fuit, ut supra dictum est, quorum nomina superius non declarantur &c., ita quod dictus uicecomes tunc ibidem habeat eorum nomina. Et dictus magister predicti hospitalis sancti Iohannis venit & respondit & dicit ut inferius patet, scilicet quando seruientes sui predicti respond*ent* &c.

Et predictus Iohannes Spencer de Cattestrete non venit. Ideo exitus terrarum suarum predict*arum* foris*factus* &c. Et dicti manucaptores sui in misericordia (IIII *d.*), quia ipsum non habuerunt &c. Et super hoc preceptum est dicto vicecomiti, sicut alias, quod non omittat propter aliquam libertatem predictam quin distringat predictum Iohannem Spencer de Cattestrete per omnes terras &c., ita quod nec ipse &c., et quod de exit*ibus* &c., et quod habeat corpus eius coram dictis iusticiariis apud Oxoniam die Sabati proximo post festum sancti Mathei proximo futurum ad respondendum domino regi de transgressionibus predictis &c.

Et isto eodem die Mercurii &c. predicti Willelmus Broun, Iohannes Sampson & Iohannes Grove lathomi qui per dictos iusticiarios in dicta prima commissione nominatos in ultimis sessionibus suis certis de causis super statu & capcione corundem lathomorum per certam manucapcionem habuerunt diem essendi hic isto die Mercurii, modo venerunt. Et quo ad predictos Willelmum Broun & Iohannem Groue super statu, sapientia & capcione[2] eorundem examinatos, per eorum confessionem & discrecionem iusticiariorum predictorum iidem Willelmus & Iohannes excessiue ceperunt &c., & hoc non potuerunt dedicere set posuerunt se in gracia regis; quorum fines sequntur inferius, videlicet,

De Willelmo Broun lathomo pro excessu capto per plegium Iohannis Gersyndone fullere & Henrici Faryndone — xii d.

De Iohanne Grove lathomo pro eodem per plegium Iohannis Walsyngham & Willelmi Wyndel — xii d.

Et quo ad predictum Iohannem Sampson, pro eo quod ipse est

[1] Omitted by the scribe.

[2] This word means not capacity, but salary; masters are questioned about their *donatio* and servants about their *capcio*.

magister lathomus liberarum petrarum & valde capiens[1] & subtilis in arte illa & de entaille[2] & quia capcio talium lathomorum non potest assederi cum capcione aliorum lathomorum alterius gradus & status pro altitudine discrecionis & sapiencie artis illius, per discrecionem iusticiariorum predictorum dimissus est &c.

Retornauit eciam dictus vicecomes isto eodem die Mercurii quod de predictis accusatis coram predictis iusticiariis in dicta priori commissione nominatis Iohannes Champyon, Petrus Daubere, Elena seruiens Ricardi Iremongere, Walterus seruiens Iohannis Siluestre, Thomas Phelyp, Iohannes Dorchestre & Matilda & Alicia seruientes Alicie relicte Iohannis Veyne, Iohannes Holewey, Iohannes Meryweder, Stephanus Palmere carpentarius, Thomas Fysswyk, Thomas Tachebrook, Iohannes Hamptone, Iohannes Hostiler, Iohannes Abyndone, Agnes Wottone, Walterus Etone, Iohannes Webbe wallere,[3] Laurencius Henxeye mason, Simon Serle mason & Iohannes Thacham mason non sunt inuenti in predictis villa & suburbiis &c.; qui omnes eodem die comparuerunt & non potuerunt dedicere transgressiones supradictas. Et posuerunt se in gracia regis, quorum fines patent inferius videlicet:—

De Iohanne Champyone seruiente Danielis Sclatforde pro excessu de eodem capto per plegium Stephani Palmere carpentarii & Walteri Fourbour viii d.

De Petro Daubere seruiente Ricardi Iremongere pro eodem per plegium Ricardi Iremongere & Ricardi Bristowe vi d.

De Waltero seruiente Iohannis Siluestre pro eodem de eodem per plegium Iohannis Syluestre & Ricardi Taillour de parochia sancti Petri in oriente iiii d.

De Thoma Phelyp seruiente Iohannis Siluestre pro eodem de eodem per plegium Iohannis Siluestre & predicti Ricardi Taillour iiii d.

De Iohanne Dorchestre seruiente Alicie relicte Iohannis Veyne pro eodem de eadem per plegium Iohannis Shawe & Iohannis Wodhull viii d.

De Matilda seruiente predicte Alicie relicte Iohannis Veyne pro eodem de eadem per plegium Willelmi Newman & Henrici Portere iiii d.

De Alicia seruiente predicte Alicie relicte Iohannis Veyne pro

[1] capable. [2] sculpture.
[3] ? builder of walls.

eodem de eadem per plegium Willelmi Merstone iremongere & Stephani Palmere iiii d.

De Iohanne Holewey sclattere pro excessu dato Iohanni Meryweder seruienti suo per plegium Ade Sclattere & Henrici Sclattere xii d

De Iohanne Meryweder seruiente eiusdem Iohannis Holewey pro excessu ab eodem capto per plegium Iohannis Holewey & Stephani Palmere iiii d.

De Stephano Palmere carpentario pro excessu capto per plegium Ade de la Ryuere & Nicholai Kent xii d. **Memb. 7**

De Thoma Fysshwyk seruiente Iuliane Garland pro excessu capto de eadem per plegium Iohannis Maltone & Willelmi Burtone x d.

De Thoma Thachebrook seruiente Nicholai Kent pro eodem de eodem per plegium Nicholai Kent & Iohannis Thurbarn viii d.

De Iohanne Hamptone seruiente Nicholai Kent pro eodem per plegium Iohannis White & Iohannis Gersyndone fullere viii d.

De Iohanne Hostiler seruiente Nicholai Kent pro eodem per plegium Nicholai Kent & Iohannis Bilburghe viii d.

De Iohanne Abyndone seruiente Nicholai Kent pro eodem per plegium Iohannis Otteworth & Nicholai Kent viii d.

De Agnete Wottone seruiente Nicholai Kent pro eodem per plegium Nicholai Kent & Ade de la Ryuere vi d.

De Waltero Etone brewere seruiente Iohannis Spencer de Cattestrete pro eodem per plegium Iohannis Shawe & Willelmi Gerueys viii d.

De Iohanne Webbe wallere pro excessu capto per plegium Ade de la Ryuere & Willelmi Broun vi d.

De Laurencio Henxseye masone pro eodem &c. per plegium Willelmi Broun mason & Ricardi Waterman xii d.

De Simone Serle masone pro eodem per plegium Henrici Porter & Iohannis Hembury xii d.

De Iohanne Thacham masone pro eodem per plegium Ricardi Bristowe & Iohannis Spicer xii d.

Adhuc datus est dies Iohanni seruienti Nicholai Nortone coram dictis nunc iusticiariis apud Oxoniam die sabati proximo post festum sancti Mathei apostoli proximo futurum de eo quod ipse se posuit in discrecione iusticiariorum si excessiue &c., capiendo per annum x s. &c., & est tabernarius &c.

Retornauit eciam dictus uicecomes isto eodem die Mercurii proximo post festum sancti Gregorii quod de predictis accusatis coram prefatis iusticiariis in dicta priori commissione nominatis Iohannes Clerk seruiens Ricardi Iremongere & Ricardus Carpentarius, Iohannes Cornysshe & Ricardus seruientes Willelmi Dagville, Willelmus Cartere seruiens Thome Maister, Iohannes atte Shoppe, Iohannes Lambehythe, Iohannes Gersyndone & Radulfus, Henricus, Iohannes & Agnes seruientes Iohannis White, Nicholaus Sclattere, Walterus Brewere seruiens Iohannis Spencer de Cattestrete; et eciam de dictis seruientibus predicti magistri hospitalis sancti Iohannis extra portam orientalem ville Oxonie videlicet Iohannes Chamberleyn, Henricus Spencer, Robertus Bakere, Iohannes Benet bailly, Iohannes Gardyner, Isabella uxor eiusdem Iohannis Gardyner, Iohannes Panter, Iohannes Bristowe cartere, Willelmus Louegent cartere, Iohannes Couyntre, Walterus Swon, Alicia Deye & Alicia Mey non sunt inuenti in dicta balliua sua; de quibus videlicet de seruientibus predicti magistri dicti hospitalis sancti Iohannis extra portam orientalem Oxonie videlicet Iohannes Chamberleyn, Henricus Spencer, Robertus Bakere, Iohannes Benet bailly, Iohannes Gardyner cum Isabella uxore eius, Iohannes Panter, Iohannes Bristowe cartere, Willelmus Louegent cartere, Iohannes Couyntre, Alicia Deye & Alicia Mey & eciam Ricardus seruiens Willelmi Dageville comparuerunt isto eodem die Mercurii &c., et predicti Iohannes Clerk seruiens Ricardi Iremongere, Willelmus Cartere seruiens Thome Maister, Iohannes atte Shoppe & seruientes Iohannis White videlicet Iohannes Lambehithe, Iohannes Gersyndone, Radulfus, Henricus, Iohannes & Agnes, ac Walterus Brewere seruiens Iohannis Spencer de Cattestrete & Walterus Swon seruiens magistri dicti hospitalis sancti Iohannis, ac dicti Ricardus & Iohannes seruientes Willelmi Dageville non uenerunt &c. Ideo preceptum est dicto uicecomiti, sicut alias, quod non omittat propter aliquam libertatem predictam quin capiat predictos Iohannem Clerk, Willelmum Cartere, Iohannem atte Shoppe & Iohannem Lambehithe, Iohannem Gersyndone, Radulfum, Henricum, Iohannem & Agnetem seruientes Iohannis White, Walterum Brewere seruientem Iohannis Spencer de Cattestrete & Walterum Swon ac dictos Ricardum & Iohannem Cornysshe seruientes Willelmi Dageuille ubicumque inuenti fuerint in dicta balliua sua &c.; et eos saluo custodiat ita quod eos habeat coram predictis iusticiariis apud Oxoniam die Sabati in vigilia dominice in ramispalmarum proximo future ad respondendum domino regi de transgressionibus predictis.

Mar. 18, 1391

Ad[1] quem diem Sabati dictus uicecomes retornauit quod dicti Iohannes Clerk, Willelmus Cartere, Iohannes atte Shoppe, Iohannes & Agnes seruientes Iohannis White, Ricardus & Iohannes Cornysshe seruientes Willelmi Dageville non sunt inuenti in balliua sua; qui non uenerunt. Ideo preceptum est dicto uicecomiti, sicut pluries, quod non omittat propter aliquam libertatem predictam quin capiat predictos Iohannem Clerk, Willelmum Cartere, Iohannem atte Shoppe, Iohannem & Agnetem seruientes Iohannis White, Ricardum & Iohannem Cornysshe seruientes Willelmi Dageville ubicumque inuenti fuerint in balliua sua &c.; et eos &c., ita quod habeat corpora eorum coram predictis nunc iusticiariis apud Oxoniam die Martis proximo ante festum Pasche proximo futurum ad respondendum domino regi de transgressionibus predictis &c. Et quo ad execucionem faciendam versus dictos Iohannem Lambhithe, Iohannem Gersyndone, Radulfum & Henricum seruientes Iohannis White, Walterum Brewere seruientem Iohannis Spencer de Cattestrete & Walterum Swon vicecomes nullum retornauit preceptum, & ipsi non uenerunt. Ideo preceptum est dicto uicecomiti, sicut alias, quod ipsos capiat &c., si &c., ita quod habeat corpora eorum coram dictis iusticiariis apud Oxoniam dicto die Martis ad respondendum domino regi ut supra.

Et Ricardus[2] seruiens Willelmi Dageville dicit quod conuenit cum uxore dicti Willelmi Dageville quod acciperet per annum XIII s. IIII d. & vesturam semel in anno, & dicit quod accepit nisi IX s. & vesturam, & ponit se in discrecione iusticiariorum si excessiue &c. Et habet diem usque proximam sessionem &c. Et postea venit ut inferius patet, & non potuit dedicere &c., et posuit in gracia regis.

Et Iohannes Chamberleyn seruiens predicti magistri dicti hospitalis sancti Iohannis dicit quod seruit dicto magistro suo in officio camere & precepta sua facit equitando & eundo sicut pertinet valetto facere & non intendit ad aliquod housbandrie & capit per annum XIII s. IIII d. & vesturam semel in anno tantum & ponit se in discrecione iusticiariorum si excessiue &c. Et sic per dictos iusticiarios assignatum est sibi recipere, causis predictis per se allegatis. Et quod non capit plus ponit se super patriam. Ideo preceptum est dicto vicecomiti ut inferius &c.

Et Robertus Bakere alius seruiens predicti magistri dicti hospitalis

[1] This paragraph is an addition. The scribe had left a space for the insertion, which is in different ink.

[2] The scribe returns here to Wednesday after St. Gregory's day. Two of the servants of William Dageville had the name Richard.

venit & dicit quod seruit dicto magistro suo in officio de Bakere, & ulterius facit & capit ut predictus Iohannes Chamberleyn & ponit se in discrecione iusticiariorum &c. Et sic assignatum est sibi capere &c. Et quod non capit aliter &c., ponit se super patriam. Ideo preceptum est dicto uicecomiti ut inferius.

Et Henricus Spencer dicit quod seruit dicto magistro suo in officio de Spencer, & facit ultra secundum formam loquele predictorum Iohannis Chamberleyn & Roberti Bakere, & dicit quod capit per annum sicut unus ex illis capit secundum quod predicitur, & ponit se in discrecione iusticiariorum &c. Et sic assignatur recipere &c. Et quod non capit plus ponit se super patriam. Ideo preceptum est vicecomiti ut inferius &c.

Et Iohannes Benet, bailly, dicit quod seruit dicto magistro suo hospitalis predicti sancti Iohannis in officio balliue de housbandrie, & capit per annum sicut unus ex predictis sociis suis capit, & ponit se in discrecione iusticiariorum &c. Et assignatur sic capere &c. Et quod non capit plus ponit se super patriam &c. Ideo preceptum est dicto vicecomiti ut inferius &c.

Et Willelmus Louegent cartere dicit quod capit per annum in omnibus IX s., et quod non capit ultra ponit se super patriam. Ideo preceptum est dicto vicecomiti ut inferius &c.

Et Iohannes Couyntre unus dictorum seruientum predicti magistri hospitalis predicti dicit quod non capit excessiue contra formam statuti; & hoc ponit se super patriam. Ideo preceptum est dicto uicecomiti ut inferius &c.

Et Alicia Deye & Alicia Mey dicunt quod seruiunt infirmis in dicto hospitali existentibus & multum circa eos vigilant & laborant, & dicunt quod quelibet earum capit per annum x s., & ponunt se in discrecione &c., & causa predicta per eas allegata assignantur tantum recipere per iusticiarios antedictos &c. Et quod non ceperunt plus ponunt se super patriam &c. Ideo preceptum est dicto vicecomiti ut inferius &c.

Et predictus magister predicti hospitalis sancti Iohannes isto eodem die Mercurii venit ut predicitur, & dicit quod predicti seruientes sui de se capiunt sicut ipsi allegauerunt & non alio modo. Et hoc ponit se super patriam &c. Ideo preceptum est dicto vicecomiti quod non omittat propter aliquam libertatem predictam quin venire faciat coram predictis iusticiariis apud Oxoniam die Martis proximo ante festum Pasche proximo futurum XVIII probos & legales homines de dictis villa & suburbiis &c. qui dictos magistrum hospitalis predicti & seruientes suos predictos nulla affinitate attingant &c. ad faciendum omnes iuratas predictas &c.

Et Iohannes Bristowe cartere seruiens dicti magistri hospitalis predicti venit & non potest dedicere transgr*essionem* predict*am*, & posuit se in gracia regis, cuius finis ut inferius patet sequitur videlicet:—

De Iohanne Bristowe cartere seruiente magistri hospitalis sancti Iohannis extra portam orientalem pro excessu capto de dicto magistro suo &c. per plegium Iohannis Benet de Hedyndone & Ricardi Bailly de Hedyndone xii d.

Et Iohannes Panter seruiens dicti magistri hospitalis predicti dicit quod conuenit cum predicto magistro suo de se capere per annum sicut ei liceret de eodem magistro suo recipere &c. per formam ordinacionum & statutorum predictorum & non alio modo &c.; et de hoc ponit se super patriam &c. Ideo preceptum est dicto vicecomiti ut inferius &c.

Et predicti Iohannes Gardyner & Isabella uxor sua venerunt & super eorum statu & capcione certis de causis datus est eis dies usque diem Sabbati proximo post festum sancti Mathei apostoli proximo futurum coram dictis nunc iusticiariis apud Oxoniam &c. Memb. 8

Et ulterius certis de causis datus est idem dies predicto magistro hospitalis predicti coram dictis nunc iusticiariis apud Oxoniam ad respondendum domino regi clare de accusacione super eundem magistrum affirmata, ut predicitur, causa dictorum Iohannis Bristowe, Iohannis Panter, Iohannis Gardyner & Isabelle uxoris eiusdem Iohannis Gardyner &c.

Et ulterius preceptum est dicto vicecomiti quod non omittat &c. quin venire faciat xviii probos &c. de villa Oxonie & suburbiis &c. dicto die Martis proximo ante dictum festum Pasche qui &c. ad faciendum dictam iuratam inter dominum regem & dictum Iohannem Panter &c.

South West Warde; retornum inde factum per uicecomitem die Mercurii proximo post festum sancti Gregorii anno xiiii°.

Retornauit eciam dictus uicecomes isto eodem die Mercurii proximo post festum sancti Gregorii quod de predictis accusatis coram predictis iusticiariis in dicta priori commissione nominatis videlicet de sclatteres Adam Sclattere, Iohannes Vente, Iohannes Marye, Ricardus Huscombe, Iohannes Coke & Henricus Sclattere nichil habent in dicta balliua sua per quod possunt distringi &c.; qui comparuerunt isto eodem die Mercurii & non potuerunt dedicere transgressiones predictas & posuerunt se in gracia regis; quorum fines patent ut sequitur, videlicet :—

Fines de sclatteres

De Adam Sclattere pro excessu capto per plegium Ade de la Ryuere & Nicholai Nortone x d.

De Iohanne Vente pro consimili per plegium Iohannis Aubel & Henrici Porter x d.

De Iohanne Marye pro consimili per plegium Iohannis Shawe & Iohannis Maltone x d.

De Ricardo Huscombe pro consimili per plegium Iohannis Marchall fysshere & Iohannis Clerk fysshere x d.

De Iohanne Coke pro consimili per plegium Iohannis Hembury & Rogeri Hikkes x d.

De Henrico Sclattere pro consimili per plegium Reginaldi Tannere & Ade Sclattere x d.

Et ulterius isto eodem die Mercurii venerunt Thomas Chauntour brewere & Iohannes seruiens eiusdem & Iohannes Tannere seruiens Reginaldi Tannere, qui coram predictis iusticiariis in predicta priori commissione nominatis in sessionibus suis posuerunt se in discrecione iusticiariorum super statu, donacione & capcione eorundem, prout ante patet, & qui habent diem per eosdem iusticiarios usque istum diem Mercurii &c.; modo per dictos iusticiarios in predictis ultimis litteris patentibus nominatos adhuc datus est predicto Iohanni Tannere dies, ut prius, usque proximas sessiones eorundem iusticiariorum &c. Et quo ad dictos Thomam Chauntour brewere & Iohannem seruientem eiusdem Thome super eorum donacione & capcione predictis consideratum est per dictos nunc iusticiarios quod predictus Thomas excessiue dedit &c. contra formam statut*orum* &c., et quod predictus Iohannes seruiens suus excessiue &c. recepit, & hoc non possunt dedicere, set ponunt se in gracia regis, quorum fines inferius sequntur, videlicet :—

De Thoma Chauntour, brewere, pro excessu dato Iohanni seruienti suo per plegium Iohannis Shawe & Iohannis Marchalle fysshere vi d.

De Iohanne seruiente eiusdem Thome Chauntour pro excessu capto de eodem per plegium Iohannis Marchalle fysshere & Thome Chauntour brewere viii d.

Et isto eodem die Mercurii Ricardus Battesyn & Ricardus hostiler seruiens eiusdem Ricardi Battesyn venerunt, qui per dictos iusticiarios in predicta priori commissione nominatos habuerunt diem essendi hic isto die, audituri discrecionem iusticiariorum illorum, in quam discrecionem iidem Ricardus & Ricardus super capcione eiusdem Ricardi Hostiler seruiente & donacione predicti Ricardi magistri, ut predicitur, se posuerunt &c.; et modo per discrecionem dictorum nunc iusticiariorum consideratum est quod predictus magister excessiue dedit &c.; et dictus seruiens excessiue cepit &c.; quas quidem transgressiones iidem non possunt dedicere, & ponunt se in gracia regis; quorum fines patent ut sequntur, videlicet:—

De Ricardo Battesyn pro excessu dato Ricardo seruenti suo per plegium Willelmi Melford & Iohannis Maltone viii d.

De Ricardo Hostiler seruienti Ricardi Battesyn pro excessu capto de eodem per plegium Ricardi Battesyn & Iohannis Maltone xii d.

Retoranuit eciam dictus uicecomes isto eodem die Mercurii quod predictus Iohannes Skynnere mortuus est &c., et quod Reginaldus Tannere & Iohannes Utteworthe, qui accusati fuerunt coram dictis iusticiariis in prima commissione nominatis, districti sunt & manuc*apti* quilibet eorum videlicet per Iohannem Kene, Ricardum Etone, Henricum Pate & Iohannem Est & de exitibus terre cuiuslibet eorum xii d. &c.; et super hoc iidem Reginaldus Tannere & Iohannes Utteworthe comparuerunt, & non potuerunt dedicere transgressiones supradictas, & posuerunt se in gracia regis, quorum fines patent inferius scilicet:—

De Iohanne Utteworthe pro excessu dato dictis seruientibus suis per plegium Iohannis Shawe & Iohannis Clerk fysshere x d.

De Reginaldo Tannere pro consimili facto seruientibus suis &c. per plegium Iohannis Maltone & Walteri Beenham xx d.

Retornauit eciam dictus uicecomes quod predicti seruientes Reginaldi Tannere, videlicet Petrus Brewere, Iohannes Harryes brewere, Thomas Brewere, Thomas Brewere, Iohannes Kedlyngton brewere, Iohannes Wodhull, Iohannes Wyltsshire, Iohannes Galewey, Iohannes Fynyan, Iohannes Waltone & Alicia nichil habent in dicta balliua sua, per quod distringi possunt &c., qui omnes eodem die Mercurii comparuerunt; et non potuerunt dedicere transgressiones supradictas, et posuerunt se in gracia regis, quorum fines inferius patent:—

Fines seruientum Reginaldi Tannere

De Petro Brewere seruiente Reginaldi Tannere pro excessu capto de eodem Reginaldo per plegium Reginaldi Tannere & Iohannis Maltone viii d.

De Iohanne Harryes brewere pro eodem per plegium Nicholai Nortone & Gilberti Burtone viii d.

De Thoma Brewere pro eodem per plegium Reginaldi Tannere & Ricardi Bristowe viii d.

De Thoma Brewere pro eodem per plegium Willelmi Newman & Iohannis Tannere viii d.

De Iohanne Kedlyngtone pro eodem per plegium Reginaldi Tannere & Iohannis Tannere viii d.

De Iohanne Woodhulle pro eodem per plegium Thome Chauntour brewere & Thome Gryndere vi d.

De Iohanne Wyltshire pro eodem per plegium Reginaldi Tannere & Ricardi Bristowe viii d.

De Iohanne Galewey pro eodem per plegium Iohannis Tannere seruiente Reginaldi Tannere & Iohannis Wolmongere de Oxonia viii d.

De Iohanne Fynyan pro eodem per plegium Iohannis Shawe & Reginaldi Tannere viii d.

De Iohanne Waltone pro eodem per plegium Iohannis Clerk fysshere & Ricardi Bristowe viii d.

De Alicia seruiente Reginaldi Tannere pro eodem per plegium Reginaldi Tannere & Iohannis Tannere iiii d.

Retornauit eciam dictus vicecomes predicto die Mercurii quod alii seruientes dicti Reginaldi Tannere, scilicet predicti Stephanus Cartere, Alanus Taskere & Thomas Hille nichil habent in balliua sua per quod distringi possunt; qui non venerunt; ideo preceptum est dicto vicecomiti quod non omittat propter aliquam libertatem predictam quin capiat predictos Stephanum Cartere, Alanum Taskere & Thomam Hille ubicumque inuenti fuerint in dicta balliua sua, et eos saluo custodiat, ita quod habeat corpora eorum coram predictis nunc iusticiariis apud Oxoniam die Iouis in crastino dicti diei Mercurii videlicet die Iouis proximo ante festum dominice in Ramispalmarum proximo futurum, ad respondendum domino regi de transgressionibus supradictis &c. Ad quem diem Iouis predictum predictus vicecomes retornauit quod predicti Stephanus Cartere, Alanus Taskere & Thomas Hille non sunt inuenti in dicta balliua sua &c.; qui non veuerunt. Ideo preceptum est dicto vicecomiti sicut alias, quod capiat predictos Stephanum Cartere, Alanum Taskere & Thomam Hille ubicumque inuenti fuerint in predicta balliua sua &c.; et eos saluo &c., ita quod habeat corpora eorum coram dictis iusticiariis apud Oxoniam die Sabati in vigilia dominice in ramispalmarum proximo future, ad respondendum domino regi de transgressionibus predictis &c.; ad quem diem Sabati supradictum predictus vicecomes retornauit quod predicti Stephanus Cartere, Alanus Taskere & Thomas Hille non sunt inuenti in dicta balliua sua &c.; qui non venerunt. Ideo preceptum est dicto vicecomiti, sicut pluries, quod capiat predictos Stephanum Cartere, Alanum Taskere & Thomam Hille ubicumque inuenti fuerint in dicta balliua sua &c., et eos saluo &c., ita quod habeat corpora eorum coram predictis nunc iusticiariis apud Oxoniam die Martis proximo ante festum Pasche proximo futurum ad respondendum domino regi de transgressionibus supradictis &c.

Retornauit eciam dictus vicecomes isto eodem die Mercurii proximo post festum sancti Gregorii quod de predictis accusatis coram predictis iusticiariis in predicta priori commissione nominatis, videlicet Iohannes Tymmes daubere & seruientes Iohannis Utteworth videlicet Robertus Cartere, Dauid seruiens eiusdem Iohannis, Thomas Cony, Ricardus Gosehorne, Constancia Wyke & Alicia Hastyng, ac Thomas Caumbrigge & Iohanna seruientes predicti Iohannis Skynnere, Henricus Mason, Radulfus Sclattere, Iohannes Grene, & seruientes Iohannis Shawe, scilicet Thomas Brewere & Iohannes Brewere, Iohannes Mason & Iohannes Hedyndone non sunt inuenti in dicta balliua sua &c. Et super hoc omnes isti uenerunt isto eodem die Mercurii exceptis predictis Thoma Cony, Thoma Caunbrigge & Iohanna seruiente Iohannis Skynnere, Radulfo Sclattere, Iohanne Masone & Iohanne Hedyndone qui non venerunt &c. Et isti predicti qui comparuerunt non potuerunt dedicere transgressiones predictas et posuerunt se in gracia regis, quorum fines patent ut sequntur, videlicet:— **Memb. 9**

De Iohanne Tymmes, daubere, pro excessu capto &c. per plegium Iohannis Hembury & Iohannis Partrich — vi d.

De Roberto Cartere seruiente Iohannis Utteworthe pro excessu de eodem Iohanne capto per plegium Ricardi Bristowe & Iohannis Bate — viii d.

De Dauid seruiente Iohannis Utteworth pro eodem per plegium Ricardi Bristowe & Iohannis Tannere — viii d.

De Ricardo Gosehorne seruiente Iohannis Utteworthe pro consimili per plegium Thome Chauntur brewere & Iohannis Brit — viii d.

De Constancia Wyke seruiente Iohannis Utteworthe pro eodem per plegium Iohannis Utteworthe & Iohannis Hembury — iiii d.

De Alicia Hastynge seruiente Iohannis Utteworthe pro eodem per plegium Iohannis Utteworthe & Ricardi Battesyn — iiii d.

De Henrico Masone pro excessu capto per plegium Iohannis Utteworthe & Ricardi Dyere — viii d.

De Iohanne Grene pro excessu capto per plegium Iohannis Hert & Henrici Pate vi d.

De Thoma Brewere seruiente Iohannis Shawe pro excessu de ipso Iohanne capto per plegium Willelmi Cook & Ricardi Bristowe viii d.

De Iohanne Brewere seruiente Iohannis Shawe pro eodem per plegium Iohannis Maltone & Iohannis Woddull viii d.

Et quia predicti Thomas Cony seruiens Iohannis Utteworthe, Thomas Caumbrigge, Iohanna seruiens Iohannis Skynnere, Radulfus Sclattere, Iohannes Masone & Iohannes Hedyndone non fuerunt inuenti, ut vicecomes retornauit, ut superius patet, & non comparuerunt, ideo preceptum est dicto vicecomiti, sicut alias, quod non omittat propter aliquam libertatem predictam quin capiat illos &c. ubicumque &c., ita quod habeat corpora eorum coram predictis nunc iusticiariis apud Oxoniam die Sabati in vigilia dominice in Ramispalmarum proximo future ad respondendum domino regi de transgressionibus antedictis &c.; ad quem diem Sabati predictus vicecomes retornauit quod predicti Thomas Cony seruiens Iohannis Utteworthe, Thomas Canbrigge, Iohanna seruiens Iohannis Skynnere, Radulfus Sclattere, Iohannes Masone & Iohannes Hedyndone non sunt inuenti in dicta balliua sua &c. Ideo preceptum est dicto vicecomiti, sicut pluries, quod non omittat &c. quin capiat predictos Thomam Cony seruientem Iohannis Utteworthe, Thomam Caunbrigge, Iohannam seruientem Iohannis Skynnere, Radulfum Sclattere, Iohannem Masone & Iohannem Hedyndone ubicumque inuenti fuerint in predicta balliua sua; et eos saluo custodiat &c., ita quod habeat corpora eorum coram predictis iusticiariis apud Oxoniam die Martis proximo ante festum Pasche proximo futurum ad respondendum domino regi de transgressionibus predictis &c.

Et quo ad iuratas capiendas inter dominum regem & dictos Iohannem Groom bocher & Thomam seruientem eiusdem Iohannis Groom & Iohannem Shawe & Iohannem Stratford cook & seruientes eiusdem Iohannis vicecomes nullum retornauit preceptum. Ideo predicte iurate remanent capiende &c. usque diem Martis proximum ante festum Pasche proximo futurum. Et super hoc preceptum est dicto vicecomiti, sicut alias, quod non omittat propter aliquam libertatem predictam quin venire faciat coram predictis nunc iusticiariis apud Oxoniam dicto die Martis proximo ante festum Pasche XVIII probos & legales homines de dictis villa & suburbiis qui &c., ad faciendum iuratas illas &c. Et super hoc predictis Iohanni Groom &

Thome seruienti suo, Iohanni Shawe, Iohanni Stratford cook & seruientibus eiusdem Iohannis Stratford datus idem dies ad audiendum iuratas illas &c.

South Est Warde; retornum inde factum per vicecomitem die Mercurii proximo post festum sancti Gregorii.

Retornauit eciam dictus vicecomes isto eodem die Mercurii proximo post festum sancti Gregorii quod de predictis accusatis coram predictis iusticiariis in predicta priori commissione nominatis Iohannes Abyndone lathamus & de carpentariis Andreas Carpenter, Iohannes Carpenter & Willelmus Fyffhide & Iohannes Staundone laborer attachiati sunt per plegium Iohannis Rede & Iohannis Kent, qui omnes venerunt & non potuerunt dedicere transgressiones supradictas & posuerunt se in gracia regis, quorum fines patent ut sequntur videlicet:—

De Iohanne Carpenter pro excessu capto per plegium Walteri Beenham & Willelmi Stool — xii d.

De Iohanne Abyndone masone pro excessu capto per plegium Iohannis Gersyndone & Galfridi Harley — xii d.

De Andrea Carpenter, carpentario, pro eodem per plegium Iohannis Gersyndone & Iohannis Blood — vi d.

De Iohanne Staundone, laborer, pro eodem per plegium Ade de la Ryuere & Gilberti Burtone — vi d.

De Willelmo Fyffhide, carpentario, pro eodem per plegium Willelmi Bergeveny & Nicholai Nortone — vi d.

Retornauit eciam dictus vicecomes quod de predictis magistris & seruitoribus in warda ista Iohannes Pope, sawyere, Willelmus Stanle seruiens eiusdem Iohannis Pope, Iohannes Bereford bocher, Iohannes Walssheman seruiens eiusdem, Elizea Goold, Iohannes Stratford cook, Isabella seruiens eiusdem Iohannis, Nicholaus Saundresdone, Iohannes Cosyn, Thomas Man, Willelmus Chestertone, Rogerus Hosteler, & Iohanna Tapstere seruientes eiusdem Nicholai Saundresdone, Iohannes Clerk fysshere & Isolda seruiens eiusdem Iohannis Clerk attachiati sunt per plegium Iohannis Estone & Willelmi Kene, qui omnes venerunt & non potuerunt dedicere transgressiones predictas & posuerunt se in gracia regis, quorum fines patent ut sequntur:—

Fines de seruitoribus istis per tempus predictum

De Isabella seruiente Iohannis Stratford cook pro excessu capto per plegium Willelmi Newman & Iohannis Stratford — iiii d.

De Willelmo Stanle seruiente Iohannis Pope sawiere pro excessu de ipso capto per plegium Iohannis Gersyndone & Willelmi Ottemore viii d.

De Iohanne Walssheman seruiente Iohannis Berford bocher pro eodem de eodem per plegium Iohannis Londone & Willelmi Swanbourne viii d.

De Thoma Man seruiente Nicholai Saundresdone pro consimili per plegium Henrici Porter & Iohannis Vente viii d.

De Willelmo Chestertone seruiente eiusdem Nicholai pro consimili per plegium Iohannis Forester & Iohannis Maltone viii d.

De Rogero Hosteler seruiente eiusdem Nicholai pro consimili per plegium Iohannis Forester & Thome Forsthulle x d.

De Iohanna Tapstere seruiente eiusdem Nicholai pro consimili per plegium Iohannis Gersyndone & Iohannis Maltone vi d.

De Isolda seruiente Iohannis Clerk fysshere pro eodem de eodem per plegium Iohannis Botelstone & Iohannis Groom, webbe. iii d.

Fines de predictis magistris per tempus predictum

De Iohanne Pope pro excessu dato Willelmo Stanle seruienti suo per plegium Iohannis Forester & Ricardi Bristowe vi d.

De Iohanne Bereford, bocher, pro consimili facto &c. per plegium Iohannis Forester & Thome Forsthulle viii d.

De Elizea Goolde pro consimili per plegium Willelmi Ottemore & Willelmi Swanbourne vi d.

De Iohanne Stratford, cook, pro consimili per plegium Thome Forsthulle & Thome Hamptone viii d.

De Nicholao Saundresdone pro consimili per plegium Iohannis Forester & Thome Forsthulle x d.

Memb. 10 Retornauit eciam dictus vicecomes isto eodem die Mercurii proximo post festum sancti Cregorii quod de predictis accusatis Iohannes Skirwhit, masone, Iohannes Wottone laborer, Alicia seruiens Philippi Taillour, Iuliana seruiens Iohannis Bereforde bocher, Walterus seruiens Elizee Goolde, Robertus seruiens Iohannis Stratford cook, Willelmus Neville seruiens Nicholai Saundresdone, Michael Neel & Henricus Coupere seruientes Iohannis Clerk fysshere nichil habent in dicta balliua sua per quod possunt attachiari &c. Ideo preceptum est dicto vicecomiti quod non omittat propter aliquam libertatem in dicta balliua sua, quin capiat omnes istos sic de warda ista ad nichil retornatos, ut predicitur, ubicumque inuenti fuerint in dicta balliua sua &c., et eos saluo custodiat ita quod habeat corpora eorum coram predictis nunc iusticiariis apud Oxoniam die Iouis in crastino dicti diei Mercurii, videlicet die Iouis proximo ante festum dominice in Ramispalmarum proximo futurum ad respondendum separatim domino regi de transgressionibus supradictis &c.; ad quem diem Iouis proximum ante dictam diem dominicam in Ramispalmarum predictus vicecomes retornavit quod predicti Iohannes Skirwhit, Iohannes Wottone laborer, Alicia seruiens Philippi Taillour, Iuliana seruiens Iohannis Bereford bocher, Walterus seruiens Elizee Golde, Robertus seruiens Iohannis Stratford cook, Willelmus Neville seruiens Nicholai Saundresdone ac seruientes Iohannis Clerk ſysshere, videlicet Michael Neel & Henricus Coupere, non sunt inuenti in dicta balliua sua &c.; qui non venerunt. Ideo preceptum est dicto vicecomiti, sicut alias, quod non omittat propter aliquam libertatem predictam quin capiat predictos Iohannem Skirwhit, Iohannem Wottone laborer, Aliciam seruientem Philippi Taillour, Iulianam seruientem Iohannis Bereford bocher, Walterum seruientem Elizee Goolde, Robertum seruientem Iohannis Stratford cook, Willelmum Neville seruientem Nicholai Saundresdone & Michaelem Neel & Henricum Coupere seruientes Iohannis Clerk fysshere, ubicumque inuenti fuerint in dicta balliua sua; et eos saluo &c., ita quod habeat corpora eorum coram dictis nunc iusticiariis apud Oxoniam in vigilia dominice in Ramispalmarum proximo future ad respondendum domino regi de transgressionibus predictis &c.; ad quem diem Sabati in vigilia dominice in Ramispalmarum predictus vicecomes retornauit quod predicti Iohannes Skyrwhit, Iohannes Wottone laborer, Alicia seruiens Philippi Taillour, Iuliana seruiens Iohannis Bereforde bocher, Walterus seruiens Elizee Goolde, Robertus seruiens Iohannis Stratford cook, Willelmus Neville serviens Nicholai Saundresdone & Michael Neel & Henricus Coupere seruientes Iohannis Clerk fysshere non sunt inuenti in dicta balliua sua &c.; qui non venerunt. Ideo preceptum est dicto vicecomiti, sicut pluries, quod non omittat propter aliquam libertatem predictam quin capiat predictos Iohannem Skirwhit, Iohannem Wottone laborer, Aliciam seruientem Philippi Taillour, Iulianam seruientem Iohannis Bereford bocher, Walterum seruientem Elizee Goolde, Robertum seruientem Iohannis Stratford cook, Willelmum Neville seruientem Nicholai Saundresdone & Michaelem Neel & Henricum Coupere seruientes Iohannis Clerk ſyssher si inuenti fuerint in dicta balliua sua; et eos saluo &c., ita quod habeat corpora eorum coram predictis nunc iusticiariis apud Oxoniam die Martis proximo ante festum Pasche proximo futurum, ad respondendum domino regi de transgressionibus antedictis &c.

Retornauit dictus vicecomes isto eodem die Mercurii proximo post festum sancti Gregorii eciam quod predictus Iohannes Shoriere, carpentarius, attachiatus est per plegium Iohannis Gersyndone fullere & Iohannis Bereford spicer &c., et non venit. Ideo plegii in misericordia, & preceptum est dicto vicecomiti quod non omittat propter aliquam libertatem predictam quin distringat predictum Iohannem Shoriere carpentarium per omnes terras &c., ita quod nec &c., et quod de exitibus &c., et quod habeat corpus eius coram dictis nunc iusticiariis apud Oxoniam die Martis proximo ante festum Pasche proximo futurum ad respondendum domino regi de transgressionibus predictis &c.

Retornauit eciam dictus vicecomes isto eodem die Mercurii quod dicti Philippus Taillour, Iohannes Trusse sclattere, Laurencius seruiens eiusdem Iohannis Trusse & Iohanna seruiens Iohannis Clerk fysshere attachiati sunt per plegium Iohannis Hood & Ricardi Kent, qui omnes venerunt; et de quibus predictus Philippus dicit quod ubi accusatur quod ipse excessiue contra formam statutorum dedit Alicie seruienti sue, dicit quod non dedit excessiue & hoc ponit se super patriam &c. Ideo preceptum est dicto vicecomiti ut inferius &c. Et dictus Iohannes Trusse dicit quod ubi accusatur quod ipse similiter excessiue dedit dicto Laurentio dicit quod sibi non dedit excessiue &c. Et hoc ponit se super patriam. Ideo preceptum est dicto vicecomiti, ut inferius patet &c. Et predictus Laurentius seruiens dicti Iohannis dicit quod non cepit excessiue de dicto Iohanne Trusse sicut accusatur, & de hoc ponit se similiter super patriam. Ideo preceptum est dicto vicecomiti quod &c. ut inferius &c. Et dicta Iohanna seruiens Iohannis Clerk fysshere dicit quod ubi accusatur quod ipsa excessiue cepit de dicto Iohanne magistro suo, dicit quod de ipso recepit v s. per annum; et quod non cepit plus ponit se super patriam &c. Et super hoc preceptum est dicto vicecomiti quod non omittat propter aliquam libertatem predictam quin venire faciat coram nunc iusticiariis apud Oxoniam die Martis proximo ante festum Pasche proximo futurum XVIII probos & legales homines de uilla Oxonie & suburbiis eiusdem qui dictos Philippum Taillour, Iohannem Trusse sclattere, Laurentium seruientem eiusdem Iohannis Trusse nec dictam Iohannam seruientem Iohannis Clerk fysshere aliqua affinitate atting*ant* ad faciendum iuratas illas &c. Et quod habeat ibidem tunc nomina illorum imbre*uiata* &c.

North West Warde; retornum vicecomitis inde factum die Mercurii proximo post festum sancti Gregorii, anno XIIII°

Retornauit eciam dictus vicecomes isto eodem die Mercurii proximo post festum sancti Gregorii pape quod de predictis accusatis coram prefatis iusticiariis in predicta priori commissione nominatis quod de carpentariis Iohannes Malyn carpentarius, Iohannes Wiltshire carpentarius, Thomas Bloxham carpentarius & Rogerus carpentarius, et de laborariis per le iournee Willelmus Sclattere laborer & de sclatteres Ricardus Waterman sclattere attachiati sunt per plegium Iohannis Atte Yate & Willelmi Gyu, qui omnes comparuerunt & non potuerunt dedicere transgressiones supradictas & posuerunt se in gracia regis quorum fines patent ut sequntur, videlicet:—

De Iohanne Malyn carpentario pro excessu capto per plegium Iohannis Spicer taillour & Ricardi Bristowe xii d.

De Iohanne Wiltshire carpentario pro eodem per plegium Iohannis Maltone & Willelmi Gerucys xii d

De Thoma Bloxham pro consimili per plegium Iohannis Botelstone & Michaelis Salesbury xii d.

De Rogero Carpentario pro consimili per plegium Willelmi Newman & Henrici Porter xii d.

De Willelmo Sclattere, laborer, pro consimili per plegium Iohannis Charle & Iohannis Bernard vi d.

De Ricardo Waterman, sclattere, pro consimili per plegium Iohannis Plomer, plomer, & Stephani Palmere x d.

Retornauit eciam dictus vicecomes quod de predictis magistris & seruitoribus in warda ista Iohannes Charley, Iohannes Brewere seruiens eiusdem Iohannis Charley, Iohannes Dadyngton & Agnes seruiens eius, Iohannes Hikkes alderman, Alicia seruiens eiusdem, Iohannes Lepere, Elena seruiens eiusdem, Iohannes Cade, Iohannes & Tibota seruientes eiusdem attachiati sunt per plegium Iohannis Heude & Willelmi Rote; qui omnes venerunt, & preter Iohannem Dadyngtone & Agnetem seruientem eius non potuerunt dedicere transgressiones supradictas & posuerunt se in gracia regis, quorum fines patent ut sequntur videlicet:—

Fines de seruitoribus per tempus predictum.

De Iohanne Brewere seruiente Iohannis Charley pro excessu capto de eodem magistro suo per plegium Nicholai Nortone & Iohannis Spicer x d.

De Alicia seruiente Iohannis Hikkes pro consimili per plegium Thome Forsthulle & Iohannis Spicer iiii d.

De Elena seruiente Iohannis Lepere pro consimili per plegium Iohannis Hickes & Iohannis Lepere iiii d.
De Iohanne seruiente Iohannis Cade pro consimili per plegium Iohannis Cade & Iohannis Marchall fisshere viii d.
De Tibota seruiente Iohannis Cade pro consimili per plegium Iohannis Cade & Iohannis Spicer taillour iiii d.

Fines de predictis magistris pro tempore predicto

De Iohanne Charley pro excessu dato seruienti suo predicto per plegium Iohannis Dadyngtone & Stephani Palmere vi d.
De Iohanne Hickes pro consimili per plegium Willelmi Gerueys & Willelmi Newman viii d.
De Iohanne Lepere pro consimili per plegium Iohannis Brit & Ricardi Bristowe viii d.
De Iohanne Cade pro consimili per plegium Iohannis Marchall fisshere & Thome Hamptone vi d.

Et predictus Iohannes Dadyngtone dicit quod non dedit Agneti seruienti sue excessiue contra formam statutorum, & de hoc ponit se super patriam &c.; et dicta Agnes dicit quod non recepit de dicto Iohanne magistro suo excessiue contra formam statutorum &c., et de hoc ponit se super patriam. Ideo preceptum est dicto vicecomiti quod non omittat propter aliquam libertatem predictam quin venire faciat coram prefatis nunc iusticiariis apud Oxoniam dicto die Martis proximo ante festum Pasche proximo futurum XVIII probos & legales homines de dictis villa & suburb*iis* &c., qui dictos Iohannem Dadyngtone & Agnetem nulla affinitate atting*ant* ad faciendum iuratam illam &c.

Memb. 11 Et ulterius isto eodem die Mercurii proximo post festum sancti Gregorii pape preceptum est dicto vicecomiti per dictos nunc iusticiarios in predicta posteriori commissione nominatis quod non omitteret propter aliquam libertatem predictam quin venire faciat coram dictis Ricardo de Garstone & Ricardo Ouertone apud Oxoniam die Iouis proximo ante diem dominicam in Ramispalmarum proximo futuram de quolibet quarterio siue custodia dicte ville Oxonie XVIII probos & legales homines & preter illos omnes constabularios cuiuslibet quarterii siue custodie antedict' & eciam ibidem die Sabati extunc proximo sequente XVIII probos & legales homines hundredi & suburbii extra portam borialem Oxonie & preter illos omnes constabularios hundredi & suburbii illius ad faciendum ibidem illis duobus diebus ea que eis ex parte domini regis adtunc iniungentur; et quod precipiat dictis constabulariis quod ipsi, scilicet quilibet eorum, habeant tunc ibidem omnia nomina venatorum, operariorum, artificum, seruitorum, hostelariorum, mendicancium & vagabundorum ac aliorum hominum mendicancium qui se nominant trauaillyngmen de balliua sua imbreuiata &c., et quod dictus vicecomes haberet tunc ibidem omnia nomina dictorum XVIII proborum hominum cuiuslibet quarterii siue custodie ac hundredi & suburbii predicti imbreuiata & preceptum suum &c.

Ad quem diem Iouis proximo ante dictam diem dominicam in Ramispalmarum dictus vicecomes retornauit nomina omnium constabulariorum cuiuslibet quarterii siue custodie ville predicte, & quod precepit eis quod iidem constabularii, videlicet quilibet eorum, haberent coram predictis nunc iusticiariis apud Oxoniam isto die Iouis omnia nomina venatorum, operariorum, artificum, seruitorum, hostelariorum, mendicancium & vagabundorum ac aliorum hominum mendicancium, qui se nominant trauaillyngmen, in warda sua, &c.; retornauit eciam dictus vicecomes nomina XVIII proborum hominum cuiuslibet warde ville predicte. Et patet retornum dicti vicecomitis inferius simul cum retornis constabulariorum predictorum videlicet:—

North Est Ward

[*blank*] constabularius ibidem isto eodem die Iouis comparuit & retornauit diuersa nomina operariorum, artificum, seruitorum, & hostelariorum de balliua sua de quibus plures accusati fuerunt per XII de predictis XVIII probis hominibus per dictum vicecomitem de warda ista retornatis, quorum quidem duodecim ac omnium accusatorum predictorum de warda ista nomina patent inferius; in primis de predictis XII Nicholaus Kent, Nicholaus Nortone, Michael Salesbury, Robertus Skynnere de Cattestrete, Iohannes Siluestre, Ricardus Taillour, Daniel Brewere, Henricus Freman, Ricardus Waldene, Elias Bowyere, Thomas Blount shethere & Rogerus Bakere qui iurati & onerati iuxta formam dictarum posteriorum litterarum patencium domini regis dicunt super sacramentum suum quod de dictis accusatis in warda ista scilicet de lathomis Iohannes Thaccham masone, Simon Serle, Iohannes Groue, Iohannes Sampson, Laurencius Henxeye & Willelmus Broun, & Philippus Carpenter carpentarius, Iohannes Webbe wallere, Iohannes Holewey sclatter, Iohannes Sulby coupere, Iohannes Kent laborer, Iohannes Plomer plomer ceperunt par les iourneys excessiue contra formam statutorum a tempore ultime sessionis dictorum iusticiariorum in predicta priori commissione nominatorum usque sessionem istam; set de quibus personis, dictis iuratis non constat. Et ulterius XII iurati predicti dicunt quod omnes seruientes subscripti retenti cum magistris suis subscriptis per idem tempus ceperunt de dictis magistris suis

excessiue contra formam statutorum predictorum. Et predicti magistri sui eisdem seruientibus suis dederunt excessiue per idem tempus & soluerunt quorum magistrorum & seruientum nomina inferius aperte patent, videlicet:—

Magistri	Seruitores
Iohannes Wadyn, smyth	Willelmus Smyth Thomas Fyffhide
Thomas Maister, glover	Thomas Cartere Iohannes Cartere
Willelmus Hurne cordewaner & seruientes sui	
Ricardus Iremongere	Cristina seruiens eius
Willelmus Dageville	[*five dashes*]
Willelmus Codesdone	cum seruientibus suis
Iohanna relicta Iohannis Curriour	Iohannes seruiens eiusdem

South West Warde

Iohannes Hembury constabularius ibidem isto eodem die Iouis comparuit & retornauit diuersa nomina operariorum, artificum, seruitorum & hostelariorum de balliua sua; de quibus plures accusati fuerunt per XII de predictis XVIII probis hominibus per dictum vicecomitem retornatis de warda ista, quorum quidem XII ac omnium accusatorum predictorum de warda ista nomina patent inferius. In primis de predictis XII^cim^, Galfridus Brehulle, Iohannes Walkere, Hugo Webbe, Iohannes Lyllyng, Ricardus Roos, Adam Sclattere, Iohannes Lolly glouere, Henricus Sclattere, Willelmus Bukyngham, Thomas Brewere, Dauid Bromfeld & Thomas Gryndere qui iurati & onerati iuxta formam dictarum posteriorum litterarum domini regis patencium dicunt super sacramentum suum quod de dictis accusatis in warda ista Henricus Masone masone, Willelmus Fraunkeleyn carpent*er*, Iohannes Thacham carpent*er*, Walterus Stortone carpent*er*, Henricus Sclattere, Adam Sclattere, Thomas Iowke masone & Ricardus Hudescombe sclattere ceperent par les iourneyes excessiue contra formam statutorum a tempore ultime sessionis dictorum iusticiariorum in predicta priori commissione nominatorum usque sessionem hanc; set de quibus personis, dictis iuratis non constat. Et ulterius predicti XII iurati dicunt quod omnes seruientes subscripti, retenti cum magistris suis subscriptis, per idem tempus ceperunt de dictis magistris suis excessiue contra formam statutorum predictorum. Et predicti magistri sui eisdem seruientibus suis dederunt & soluerunt excessiue per idem tempus, quorum quidem magistrorum & seruientum nomina aperte patent inferius, videlicet

Magistri	Seruitores
Iohannes Marche diere	Willelmus Newentone ser*uiens*
Ricardus Brayn diere	Thomas Herne Robertus Brewere
Iohannes Walkere bakere	Edwardus Cornysshe Gilbertus Fournour Gilim Thomas Robertus
Iohannes Utteworthe	Iohannes Abyndone Iohannes Lambourne Iohannes Penne Iohannes Harry
Petrus Welyngtone	Iohannes Benet Matilda uxor eius Iohannes Poly ser*uiens*
Simon Whelere fysshere	Margareta Tapster Iohannes Stonore
Iohannes Walsyngham	Iohannes Hosteler Iohannes seruiens hostelarii
Reginaldus Tanner	Walterus Mun brewere Willelmus Brewere Willelmus Irysshe brewere Robertus Cartere Dauid Waterman
Willelmus Hembury bakere	Willelmus Cadewyn
Thomas Forsthulle	Hugo Brewere Robertus Vyse
Willelmus Bartone	Iohannes Deryng Thomas Fourner
Iohannes Lyllyng bakere	Iohannes Caus Henricus Cornysshe Robertus
Galfridus Brehulle	Agnes Brehulle Margareta Emma
Edwardus Crook fyssher	Galfridus seruiens
Iohannes Shawe	Iohannes Dorchestre Walterus Etone brewer Cecilia Pyn
Rogerus Holme bakere	Iohannes Adam seruiens

Iohannes Strettone bakere	{ Iohannes Iolyf Gilbertus Man
Iohannes Walysshe dyere	[*blank*]

South Est Warde

Memb. 12 Iohannes Gersyndone constabularius ibidem isto eodem die Iouis comparuit & retornauit diuersa nomina operariorum, artificum, seruitorum & hostelariorum de balliua sua, de quibus plures accusati fuerunt per XII^cim de predictis XVIII^cim probis hominibus per dictum vicecomitem de warda ista retornatis, quorum quidem XII^cim ac omnium accusatorum predictorum de warda ista nomina patent inferius. In primis de predictis XII^cim Iohannes Beresford bocher, Iohannes Swanbourne, Thomas Hosebonde, Iohannes Clerk fysshere, Robertus Andrew, Iohannes Marchall fysshere, Willelmus Ottemore, Iohannes Dentone, Iohannes Mekesburghe, Thomas Hasele, Philippus Forsthulle & Iohannes Londone bocher qui iurati & onerati iuxta formam dictarum posteriorum litterarum domini regis patencium dicunt super sacramentum suum quod de dictis accusatis in warda ista Iohannes Chadde daubere cepit par les iourneyes a tempore ultime sessionis usque sessiones istas &c.; set de quibus personis, dictis iuratis non constat. Et ulterius dicti iurati dicunt quod omnes seruientes subscripti retenti cum dictis magistris suis subscriptis per idem tempus ceperunt de dictis magistris suis excessiue contra formam statutorum &c. Et dicti magistri sui eisdem seruientibus dederunt & soluerunt excessiue &c., per idem tempus, quorum quidem magistrorum & seruientem nomina aperte patent inferius.

Magistri	Seruitores
Willelmus Ottemore brewere	{ Georgius Brewere Willelmus Stanle Phinota
Willelmus York bocher	Nicholaus seruiens eius
Willelmus Swanbourne	Willelmus White
Iohannes Swanbourne	Adam Swanbourne
Iohannes Lundone	Iohannes Walssheman
Iohannes Marchall fysshere	Walterus seruiens

North West Ward

Iohannes Spicer constabularius ibidem isto eodem die Iouis comparuit & retornauit diuersa nomina operariorum, artificum, seruitorum, hostelariorum de balliua sua, de quibus plures accusati fuerunt per XII de predictis XVIII probis hominibus per dictum uicecomitem de warda ista retornatis, quorum quidem xii^{cim} ac omnium accusatorum de warda ista nomina patent inferius. Inprimis de predictis xii^{cim}, Willelmus Bergeveny, Iohannes Dadyngtone, Iohannes Cade, Iohannes Keruere, Iohannes Charle, Willelmus Hamptone chaundeler, Henricus Hamptone, Willelmus Ferour, Thomas Setertone, Henricus Moryce, Gilbertus Cappere, & Iohannes Bernard qui iurati & onerati iuxta formam dictarum posteriorum litterarum domini regis patencium dicunt super sacramentum suum quod de dictis accusatis in warda ista omnes seruientes subscripti retenti cum magistris suis subscriptis a tempore sessionis predictorum iusticiariorum in predicta priori commissione nominatorum usque sessionem hanc per idem tempus excessiue contra formam ordinacionum & statutorum de predictis magistris suis ceperunt. Et iidem magistri eisdem seruientibus per idem tempus excessiue &c. dederunt & soluerunt; quorum quidem magistrorum & seruientum nomina inferius aperte patent videlicet:—

Magistri	Seruitores
Iohannes Lepere bakere	Ricardus Smyth Ricardus Lodere Iohannes Lucas Willelmus Brasyere Robertus Frome Willelmus White
Iohannes Hikkes	Willelmus Cristemasse Willelmus Tryllyng Iohanna Gardener
Walterus Bone	Iuliana seruiens eiusdem
Iohannes Bernard, lokyere	Thomas Chilton
Iohannes Charley	Iohannes Brewere Alicia Tapstere } seruientes
Iohannes Cade, brewere	Alicia Willelmus } seruientes
Iohannes Page, bakere	Iohannes Copy Ricardus Curbache Iohannes Pany Iohannes Irelond Thomas Pylprest
Willelmus Merstone, iremongere	Alicia Dorchestre seruiens
Willelmus Wegan, ferour	Philippus Cornysshe Thomasina
Iohannes Dadyngtone	Constancia seruiens
Willelmus Iremongere	Alexander seruiens Willelmus Wyrehale
Agnes Hawuyle	Iohannes seruiens

Et super hoc isto eodem die Iouis preceptum est dicto uicecomiti quod non omittat propter aliquam libertatem predictam quin venire faciat coram predictis nunc iusticiariis apud Oxoniam die Veneris proximo ante diem dominicam in Ramispalmarum proximo futurum omnes predictos de dictis quatuor wardis coram dictis nunc iusticiariis ut predicitur accusatis ad respondendum domino regi de transgressionibus antedictis &c.

North Est Warde; retornum inde factum per uicecomitem die Veneris prox. ante diem dominicam in Ramispalmarum anno XIIII°

Ad quem diem Veneris proximo ante diem dominicam in Ramispalmarum predictus vicecomes retornauit quod de predictis lathomis accusatis de warda ista, ut predictum est, Iohannes Thacham masone, Simon Serle masone, Iohannes Groue masone, Iohannes Sampsone masone, Willelmus Broun masone & Laurentius Henxeye masone & Philippus Carpent*er* carpent*er* ac Iohannes Holewey sclattere & Iohannes Webbe wallere, Iohannes Sulby coupere & Iohannes Plomere plomere attachiati sunt per plegium Ricardi Bere & Willelmi Hereward; qui omnes comparuerunt & preter dictum Iohannem Plomer & dictum Iohannem Sampsone non potuerunt dedicere transgressiones supradictas & posuerunt se in gracia regis; quorum fines patent ut sequntur, videlicet:—

De Iohanne Thacham masone pro excessu capto per plegium Iohannis Spicer & Ricardi Bristowe viii d.

De Simone Serle masone pro consimili per plegium Henrici Porter & Iohannis Hembury viii d.

De Iohanne Groue masone pro consimili per plegium Iohannis Walsyngham & Willelmi Wyndell viii d.

De Willelmo Broun masone pro consimili per plegium Ricardi Roos & Thome Maister viii d.

De Laurencio Henxeye masone pro consimili per plegium Willelmi Broun masone & Ricardi Waterman viii d.

De Philippo Carpent*er* carpentario pro consimili per plegium Iohannis Botelstone & Stephani Palmere viii d.

De Iohanne Holewey sclattere pro consimili per plegium Ade Sclattere & Henrici Sclattere vi d.

De Iohanne Webbe wallere pro consimili per plegium Iohannis Holewey & Stephani Palmere iiii d.

Et quo ad predictum Iohannem Sampsone pro eo quod ipse est magister lathomus liberarum petrarum & valde sapien& subtilis in arte illa & de entaille & quia capcio talium lathomorum non potest assederi cum capcione aliorum lathomorum status alterius & gradus propter altitudinem discrecionis & sapiencie artis illius, per discrecionem iusticiariorum predictorum dimissus est.

Et dictus Iohannes Plomer dicit quod ipse a tempore ultime sessionis predictorum iusticiariorum in predicta priori commissione nominatorum usque sessionem hanc sicut homines de arte illa qua iam utitur, viz. de plomer, receperunt annis xx^{o} [1], xxiiii^{o}, xxv^{to} & xxvi^{to} regis Edwardi aui regis nunc & non aliter,[2] & de hoc ponit se super patriam &c. Ideo preceptum est dicto uicecomiti ut inferius &c.

Et super capcione & statu Iohannis Sulby coupere certis de causis datus est ei dies coram dictis nunc iusticiariis apud Oxoniam ad proximam sessionem eorundem iusticiariorum &c.

Retornauit eciam dictus uicecomes quod de predictis magistris & seruitoribus Iohannes Wadyn smyth & Willelmus Smyth & Thomas Fyfhide seruientes eiusdem Iohannis, Iohannes Sprount & WillelmusGodhyne & Iohannes Arundel seruientes eiusdem Iohannis Sprount, Thomas Mayster & Thomas Cartere & Iohannes Cartere seruientes eiusdem Thome Maister, Iohanna relicta Iohannis Curreour, Iohannes seruiens eiusdem Iohanne, Ricardus Iremongere & Cristiana seruiens eius attachiati sunt per plegium Willelmi Pope & Ricardi Cut; qui omnes uenerunt. Et de quibus predictus Thomas Mayster dicit quod conuenit cum predictis Thoma Cartere & Iohanne Cartere seruientibus suis quod eis daret prout liceret sibi eis dare secundum formam ordinacionum & statutorum predictorum &c., & non aliter, nec aliquid eis alio modo dedit & de hoc ponit se super patriam &c. Et dicti Thomas Cartere & Iohannes Cartere dicunt quod conuenerunt cum predicto Thoma Maister magistro quod ipsi de eo acciperent prout eis liceret recipere secundum formam ordinacionum & statutorum predictorum & non aliter, nec aliquid de eo alio modo receperunt, & de hoc ponunt se super patriam. Ideo preceptum est dicto vicecomiti, ut inferius &c.

Memb. 13

Et de quibus dictus Iohannes Wadyn smyth dicit quod conuenit cum dictis seruientibus suis quod eis daret prout sibi liceret eis dare secundum formam ordinacionum & statutorum in hoc casu prouisorum & non aliter, nec aliquid eis alio modo dedit; & de hoc ponit se super patriam &c. Et dicti Willelmus Smyth & Thomas Fyfhide

[1] The figures of the scribe seem to be confused here.
[2] The verb is omitted.

dicunt quod conuenerunt cum predicto Iohanne Wadyn magistro suo quod ipsi de eo acciperent prout eis liceret accipere secundum formam ordinacionum & statutorum predictorum & non aliter, nec aliquid de eo alio modo receperunt, & de hoc ponunt se super patriam &c. Ideo preceptum est dicto uicecomiti ut inferius &c.

Et dicti Willelmus Godhyne & Iohannes Arundell seruientes Iohannis Sprunt dicunt quod conuenerunt cum dicto Iohanne Sprunt magistro suo quod ipsi de eo acciperent prout eis liceret recipere, secundum formam ordinacionum & statutorum predictorum & non aliter, nec aliquid de eo alio modo receperunt, & de hoc ponunt se separatim super patriam &c. Ideo preceptum est vicecomiti predicto &c., ut inferius. Et dictus Iohannes Sprunt dicit ut seruientes sui predicti &c. Et de hoc ponit se super patriam &c. Ideo preceptum est dicto vicecomiti, ut inferius, &c.

Et quo ad execucionem faciendam versus predictum Willelmum Dageville, Iohannem Groue brewer & omnes alios seruientes suos, Willelmum Codestone & seruientes suos & Willelmum Herne & seruientes suos causa accusacionis antedicte, dictus vicecomes nullum preceptum retornauit &c. Ideo preceptum est dicto vicecomiti, sicut alias, quod non omittat propter aliquam libertatem in balliua sua quin venire faciat coram dictis nunc iusticiariis apud Oxoniam die Sabbati proximo post festum sancti Mathei apostoli proximo futurum predictos Willelmum Dageville & seruientes suos predictos ac dictum Willelmum Codesdone & seruientes suos & eciam Willelmum Herne & seruientes suos ad respondendum domino regi singillatim de transgressionibus antedictis &c. Et quod habeat ibidem eodem die omnia nomina seruientum illorum imbreuiat' & preceptum suum &c.

Et predicta Iohanna relicta Iohannis Curreour dicit quod dictus Iohannes seruiens suus est suus seruiens de arte seu mistera de Curreour, & dicit quod dat sibi per diem quando laborat 1 d. & prandium suum &c.; ponit se in discrecione dictorum nunc iusticiariorum &c. Et predictus Iohannes seruiens eiusdem Iohanne dicit sicut ipsa Iohanna dicit, & ponit se similiter in discrecione dictorum nunc iusticiariorum &c. Et super hoc datus eis dies coram dictis iusticiariis apud Oxoniam die sabbati proximo post festum sancti Mathei apostoli proximo futurum &c.

Et predictus Ricardus Iremongere dicit quod conuenit cum Cristiana seruiente eius quod ei daret sicut ei liceret per formam statutorum predictorum & non aliter, nec aliquid ei alio modo dedit, & de hoc ponit se super patriam. Et dicta Cristiana dicit quod ipsa cum dicto magistro suo sic conuenit scilicet quod de [eo][1] reciperet sicut ei per dicta statuta recipere liceret &c., & non aliter, nec aliquid de eo alio modo recepit, & de hoc ponit se similiter super patriam. Ideo preceptum est dicto vicecomiti quod non omittat propter aliquam libertatem predictam quin venire faciat coram dictis nunc iusticiariis apud Oxoniam die Martis proximo ante festum Pasche proximo futurum XVIII probos & legales homines de dictis vill*a* & suburb' &c, qui nec &c. ad faciendum omnes iuratas istas &c.

South West Warde. Retornum vicecomitis inde factum die Veneris proximo ante diem dominicam in Ramispalmarum anno XIIII°

Retornauit eciam dictus uicecomes isto eodem die Veneris proximo ante diem dominicam in Ramispalmarum quod de predictis accusatis coram dictis nunc iusticiariis de lathomis Henricus Masone & Thomas Iowke masone, & de carpentariis Willelmus Fraunkeleyn carpent*er*, Iohannes Thacham carpent*er* & Willelmus Storton carpent*er*, & de sclatteres Henricus Sclattere, Adam Sclattere & Ricardus Huddescombe sclattere attachiati sunt per plegium Iohannis Est & Willelmi Hende qui omnes venerunt & non potuerunt dedicere transgressiones predictas & posuerunt se in gracia regis; quorum fines patent ut sequntur, videlicet:—

De Henrico Masone pro excessu capto per plegium Iohannis Utteworthe & Ricardi Dyere	x d.
De Thoma Iowke masone pro eodem per plegium Iohannis Hembury & Rogeri Hikkes	x d.
De Willelmo Fraunkeleyn carpent*er* pro consimili per plegium Iohannis Hembury & Ade Sclattere	x d.
De Iohanne Thacham carpent*er* pro consimili per plegium Ade Sclattere & Iohannis Hembury	x d.
De Waltero Stortone carpent*er* pro consimili per plegium Ade Sclattere & Willelmi Fraunkeleyn	x d.
De Henrico Sclattere, sclattere, pro consimili per plegium Ade Sclattere & Iohannis Hembury	vi d.
De Ada Sclattere pro consimili per plegium Henrici Sclattere & Iohannis Brit	viii d.
De Ricardo Huddescombe sclattere pro consimili per plegium Iohannis Spicer & Iohannis Walkere	viii d.

[1] Omitted by the scribe.

Retornauit eciam dictus vicecomes quod de dictis magistris & seruitoribus in warda ista Ricardus Brayn, dyere, & Thomas Herne & Robertus Brewere seruientes eiusdem Ricardi Brayn, Iohannes Walkere bakere & Edwardus, Gilbertus Fournour, Gylmyn & Thomas, seruientes eiusdem Iohannis Walkere, Willelmus Hembury bakere & Willelmus Cadewyn seruiens eiusdem Willelmi Hembury, Willelmus Bartone bakere & Iohannes Deryng & Thomas Fourn*er* seruientes eiusdem Willelmi Bartone, Iohannes Lyllyng bakere & Iohannes Caus, Henricus Cornysshe & Robertus seruientes eiusdem Iohannis Lyllyng, Galfridus Brehulle & Agnes Brehulle, Margareta & Emma seruientes eiusdem Galfridi Brehulle, Simon Whelere fyshere & Margareta Tapstere seruiens eiusdem Simonis, Iohannes Shawe fysshere & Iohannes Dorchestre, Walterus Etone brewere & Cecilia Pyn seruientes eiusdem Iohannis Shawe, Iohannes Walsyngham masone & Iohannes Hostiller & Iohannes seruiens eiusdem Iohannis Walsyngham pro hostelario illo &c., Rogerus Holme bakere, Iohannes Adam seruiens eiusdem Rogeri Holm, Iohannes Strettone bakere & Iohannes Iolyf & Gilbertus Man seruientes eiusdem Iohannis Strettone attachiati sunt per plegium Iohannis Est & Willelmi Rye, qui omnes venerunt. Et de quibus dicti Ricardus Brayn dyere, Thomas Herne & Robertus Brewere seruientes eiusdem Ricardi Brayn, Iohannes Walkere bakere, Edwardus Cornysshe & Thomas seruientes eiusdem Iohannis Walker, Iohannes Lyllyng, Iohannes Caus & Henricus Cornysshe seruientes eiusdem Iohannis Lyllyng, Galfridus Brehulle & Agnes Brehulle, Margareta & Emma seruientes eiusdem Galfridi Brehulle, Simon Whelere & Margareta seruiens eiusdem Simonis, Iohannes Shawe fysshere & Iohannes Dorchestre, Walterus Etone brewere & Cecilia Pyn seruientes eiusdem Iohannis Shawe, Rogerus Holme bakere, Iohannes Adam seruiens eiusdem Rogeri Holme non potuerunt dedicere transgressiones predictas & posuerunt se in gracia regis, quorum fines patent ut sequntur, videlicet:—

Fines de seruitoribus istis per tempus predictum

De Thoma Herne seruiente Ricardi Brayn dyere pro excessu de ipso Ricardo capto per plegium Iohannis Walysshe dyere & Ricardi Brayn dyere viii d.

De Roberto Brewere seruiente dicti Ricardi Brayn pro consimili per plegium Ricardi Brayn & Thome Forsthulle viii d.

De Edwardo Cornysshe seruiente Iohannis Walkere bakere pro consimili per plegium Willelmi Gerueys & Ricardi Hende vi d.

De Thoma seruiente Iohannis Walkere pro consimili per plegium Iohannis Walkere & Iohannis Hembury viii d.
De Iohanne Caus seruiente Iohannis Lyllyng per plegium Iohannis Lyllyng & Iohannis Walkere viii d.
De Henrico Cornysshe seruiente eiusdem Iohannis Lyllyng per plegium Iohannis Walkere & Iohannis Lyllyng viii d.
De Agnete Brehulle seruiente Galfridi Brehulle pro consimili per plegium Galfridi Brehulle & Petri Welyngtone iiii d.
De Margareta seruiente eiusdem Galfridi pro consimili per plegium Galfridi Brehulle & Petri Welyngtone iiii d.
De Emma seruiente eiusdem Galfridi pro consimili per plegium Galfridi Brehulle & Petri Welyngtone iiii d.
De Margareta Tapstere seruiente Simonis Whelere pro consimili per plegium Henrici Porter & Iohannis Wodhulle iiii d.
De Iohanne Dorchestre seruiente Iohannis Shawe pro consimili per plegium Iohannis Waterman & Iohannis Shawe viii d.
De Cecilia Pyn seruiente Iohannis Shawe pro consimili per plegium Iohannis Shawe & Michaelis Turf' iiii d.
De Iohanne [*blank*] seruiente Rogeri Holme pro consimili per plegium Rogeri Holme & Iohannis Hembury viii d.

Fines de predictis magistris per tempus predictum

De Ricardo Brayn diere pro excessu dato ut supra &c. per plegium Thome Forsthulle & Iohannis Botelston vi d.
De Iohanne Walkere bakere pro consimili per plegium Iohannis Botelstone & Iohannis Blood vi d.
De Iohanne Lyllyng pro consimili per plegium Willelmi Bartone & Ricardi Roos vi d.
De Galfrido Brehulle pro consimili per plegium Petri Welyngtone & Ricardi Brayn vi d.
De Simone Whelere pro consimili per plegium Henrici Porter & Iohannis Woodhulle vi d.
De Iohanne Shawe pro consimili per plegium Willelmi Gerueys & Reginaldi Tannere vi d.
De Rogero Holme bakere pro consimili per plegium Iohannis Walkere & Iohannis Hembury vi d.

Et dicti Gilbertus Fournour & Gylmyn seruientes predicti Iohannis Walkere bakere dicunt quod quilibet eorum capit pro le Bache II d. & quod non capiunt plus ponunt se super patriam. Et dictus Iohannes Walkere dicit quod non dat eis plus, & hoc ponit se super patriam. **Memb. 14**

Ideo preceptum est vicecomiti &c., ut inferius patet &c. Et Willelmus Hembury bakere & Willelmus Cadewyn seruiens eiusdem Willelmi Hembury, Willelmus Bartone bakere & Iohannes Deryng & Thomas Fournour seruientes eiusdem Willelmi Bartone dicunt videlicet magistri quod non dederunt dictis seruientibus suis excessiue &c., & de hoc ponunt se super patriam &c. Et dicti seruientes quod non ceperunt de dictis magistris suis excessiue &c. Et de hoc ponunt se super patriam &c. Ideo preceptum est dicto vicecomiti ut inferius &c. Et dictus Robertus seruiens dicti Iohannis Lyllyng dicit quod capit per annum x s. in toto, & est seruiens eiusdem Iohannis in arte sua de bakere, & ponit se in discrecionem iusticiariorum si excessiue &c. Et sic per assignacionem iusticiariorum concessum est ei capere &c. Et dictus Iohannes Walsyngham masone dicit quod conuenit cum Iohanne Hosteler seruiente suo quod ei daret secundum id quod ei liceret dare per ordinacionem statutorum &c., & nichil ei alio modo dedit, & de hoc ponit se super patriam &c. Et dictus Iohannes Hosteler seruiens dicti Iohannis Walsyngham dicit quod sic est ut magister suus predictus dicit, & quod aliter non est nec aliter de eo aliquid cepit, ponit se super patriam &c. Ideo preceptum dicto vicecomiti ut inferius &c. Et quo ad dictum Iohannem seruientem dicti Iohannis Hosteler predicti Iohannes Walsyngham & Iohannes Hosteler dicunt quod capit per annum VI s. VIII d. & sic non excessiue, & quod non capit plus ponunt se tam mag*ister* quam seru*ientes* super patriam. Ideo preceptum est dicto vicecomiti ut inferius &c. Et dicti Iohannes Strettone bakere dicit quod non dedit dictis Iohanni Iolyf & Gilberto Man nisi secundum ordinac*ionem* statut*i*, & de hoc ponit se super patriam tam magister quam illi duo seruientes &c. Ideo preceptum est dicto vicecomiti quod non omittat propter aliquam libertatem supradictam quin venire faciat coram predictis nunc iusticiariis apud Oxoniam die Martis proximo ante festum Pasche proximo futurum XVIII probos & legales homines de dictis villa & suburbiis qui predictos magistros & seruientes de warda ista, qui se in iuratas ut predicitur posuerunt, nulla affinitate attingunt &c. ad faciendum recogniciones illas &c. Et quod habeant ibidem eodem die nomina dictorum XVIII imbreuiata & preceptum suum &c.

Retornauit eciam dictus vicecomes quod predictus Reginaldus le Tannere & seruientes sui videlicet Walterus Mun brewer, Willelmus Brewere, Willelmus Irysshe brewere, Robertus Cartere & David Waterman attachiati sunt per plegium Iohannis Herde & Willelmi

Knauet, qui omnes comparuerunt et non potuerunt dedicere transgressiones antedictas, & posuerunt se in gracia regis, & patet finis dicti Reginaldi inferius, videlicet:—

De Reginaldo Tannere pro excessu dato seruientibus &c. per plegium Ricardi Bristowe & Henrici Porter xii d.

Et ulterius isto eodem die Veneris predicti seruientes predicti Reginaldi Tannere ponunt loco suo Ricardum Bristowe ad faciendum coram dictis nunc iusticiariis fines suos pro excessibus predictis &c. unde accusati existunt, & certis de causis datus est dies dicto Ricardo Bristowe attornato eorundem seruientum ad dictos fines faciendum coram dictis nunc iusticiariis apud Oxoniam die Sabbati proximo post festum sancti Mathei apostoli proximo futurum &c.

Et ulterius dictus vicecomes retornauit isto eodem die Veneris quod dictus Iohannes Utteworthe & seruientes sui predicti, videlicet Iohannes Abyndone, Iohannes Lamburne, Iohannes Penne & Iohannes Harry attachiati sunt per plegium Iohannis Rede & Willelmi Kent, qui omnes comparuerunt. Et super hoc predictus Iohannes Utteworthe dicit quod conuenit cum dictis seruientibus separatim, videlicet quod eis daret prout sibi liceret eis dare iuxta ordinaciones & statuta in hoc casu prouisa & non aliter, nec aliquid alio modo eis nec alicui eorum dedit, & de hoc ponit se super patriam. Ideo preceptum est dicto vicecomiti ut inferius &c. Et dicti seruientes dicti Iohannis Utteworthe dicunt videlicet quilibet singulariter pro se quod est sicut magister suus predictus allegauit, & non aliter nec alio modo fecerunt ipsi nec aliquis eorum, & de hoc ponunt se super patriam &c. Ideo preceptum dicto vicecomiti quod non omittat &c. ut supra, quin venire faciat coram dictis nunc iusticiariis apud Oxoniam die Martis proximo ante festum Pasche proximo futurum XVIII probos &c. de villa & suburb*iis* predictis &c., qui nec &c., ad faciendum iuratas illas &c.

Et quo ad execucionem faciendam uersus dictos Petrum Welyntone cooke & seruientes suos, scilicet Iohannem Benet, Matildam uxorem eius & Iohannem Poly ac Iohannem Marche dyere & Willelmum Newentone seruientem eius & Edwardum Crook & Galfridum seruientem eius causa [accusa]cionis[1] predicte &c. vicecomes nullum retornauit preceptum; & qui non venerunt. Ideo preceptum est dicto vicecomiti quod non omittat propter aliquam libertatem predictam quin venire faciat illos omnes & singulos &c. coram dictis nunc iusticiariis apud Oxoniam die Sabbati proximo post festum sancti Mathei

[1] The scribe has forgotten the first six letters of this word.

apostoli proximo futurum ad respondendum domino regi separatim de transgressionibus predictis &c.

South Est Ward; retornum inde factum per vicecomitem die Veneris proximo ante diem dominicam in Ramispalmarum anno xiiii°.

Retornauit eciam dictus vicecomes isto eodem die Veneris proximo ante diem dominicam in Ramispalmarum quod de predictis accusatis coram dictis nunc iusticiariis Iohannes Chadde daubere, Willelmus Ottemore brewere, Georgius Brewere, Willelmus Stanle & Phinota seruientes eiusdem Willelmi Ottemore, Willelmus Yorke bocher & Nicholaus seruiens eiusdem Willelmi Yorke, Willelmus Swanbourne & Willelmus White seruiens eiusdem, Iohannes Swanbourne & Adam seruiens eiusdem Iohannis, Iohannes Londone & Iohannes Walssheman seruiens eiusdem Iohannis Londone, Iohannes Marchalle fysshere & Walterus seruiens eiusdem Iohannis Marchalle attachiati sunt per plegium Iohannis Hendy & Willelmi Prys, qui omnes venerunt & preter dictos Willelmum Yorke & Nicholaum seruientem eius non potuerunt dedicere transgressiones supradictas, & posuerunt se in gracia regis, quorum fines patent ut sequntur videlicet:—

Fines de seruitoribus istis per tempus predictum preter[1] de Iohanne Chadde &c.

De Iohanne Chadde daubere pro excessu capto per plegium Iohannis Gersyndone fuller & Iohannis Spicer — iiii d

De Georgio Brewere seruiente Willelmi Ottemore pro excessu capto de eodem per plegium Iohannis Utteworthe & Iohannis Swanbourne — viii d.

De Willelmo Stanle seruiente eiusdem Willelmi Ottemore pro consimili per plegium Iohannis Utteworthe & Iohannis Swanbourne — vi d.

De Phinota seruiente eiusdem Willelmi Ottemore pro consimili per plegium Iohannis Utteworthe & Iohannis Swanbourne — iiii d.

De Willelmo White seruiente Willelmi Swanbourne pro consimili per plegium Iohannis Spicer & Iohannis Lundone — vi d.

De Adam seruiente Iohannis Swanbourne pro consimili per plegium Iohannis Spicer & Iohannis Londone — viii d.

De Iohanne Walssheman seruiente Iohannis Lundone pro consimili per plegium Willelmi Gerueys & Iohannis Lundone — iiii d.

[1] 'as well as'.

De Waltero seruiente Iohannis Marchalle fysshere pro consimili per plegium Nicholai Nortone & Iohannis Blood iiii d.

Fines de dictis magistris per tempus predictum

De Willelmo Ottemore brewere pro excessu dato &c. per plegium Iohannis Swanburne & Iohannis Lundone vi d.

De Willelmo Swanbourne pro consimili per plegium Iohannis Spicer & Iohannis Lundone vi d.

De Iohanne Swanbourne pro consimili per plegium Iohannis Spicer & Iohannis Londone vi d.

De Iohanne Lundone pro consimili per plegium Iohannis Spicer & Willelmi Swanbourne vi d.

De Iohanne Marchalle fyssher pro consimili per plegium Nicholai Nortone & Iohannis Blood vi d.

Et dictus Willelmus Yorke dicit quod conuenit cum dicto Nicholao seruiente suo capiendo de illo sicut ei liceret dare per formam ordinacionum dictorum statutorum & nichil ei dedit alio modo, & de hoc ponit se super patriam. Et dictus Nicholaus dicit quod cum dicto Willelmo conuenit modo predicto & non aliter nec aliquid alio modo recepit, & de hoc ponit se super patriam. Et super hoc preceptum est dicto vicecomiti quod non omittat propter aliquam libertatem predictam quin venire faciat coram dictis nunc iusticiariis apud Oxoniam die Martis proximo ante festum Pasche proximo futurum XVIII probos & legales homines de dictis villa & suburbiis [1] qui nec &c. ad faciendum iuratas illas &c.

North West Warde; retornum inde factum per vicecomitem die Veneris proximo ante diem dominicam in Ramispalmarum, anno XIIII°.

Retornauit eciam dictus vicecomes isto eodem die Veneris proximo ante diem dominicam in Ramispalmarum quod de predictis accusatis coram dictis nunc iusticiariis Iohannes Lepere bakere & Ricardus Smythe, Ricardus Lodere, Iohannes Lucas, Willelmus Brasyere, Robertus Frome & Willelmus White seruientes eiusdem Iohannis Lepere, Iohannes Cade & Willelmus seruiens eiusdem Iohannis Cade, Walterus Boune & Iuliana seruiens eiusdem Walteri, Willelmus Wygan ferour & Thomasina seruiens eiusdem Willelmi, Iohannes Charleye & Iohannes Brewere & Alicia Tapstere seruientes eiusdem Iohannis

[1] *suburbiis* in full.

Charley attachiati sunt per plegium Ricardi Rede & Willelmi Estone, qui omnes venerunt & non potuerunt dedicere transgressiones supradictas, & posuerunt se in gracia regis, quorum fines patent ut sequntur videlicet:—

Fines de seruitoribus istis per tempus predictum

De Ricardo Smythe seruiens Iohannis Lepere pro excessu de eo capto per plegium Nicholai Nortone & Iohannis Lyllynge viii d.

De Ricardo Lodere seruiente eiusdem Iohannis pro consimili per plegium Nicholai Nortone & Iohannis Lyllynge viii d.

De Iohanne Lucas seruiente eiusdem Iohannis pro consimili per plegium Nicholai Nortone & Iohannis Lyllynge viii d.

De Willelmo Brasyere seruiente Iohannis Lepere per plegium Nicholai Nortone & Iohannis Lyllynge viii d.

De Roberto Frome seruiente Iohannis Lepere pro consimili per plegium Nicholai Nortone & Iohannis Lyllynge viii d.

Memb. 15 De Willelmo White seruiente Iohannis Lepere pro consimili per plegium Nicholai Nortone & Iohannis Lyllynge viii d.

De Willelmo seruiente Iohannis Cade pro consimili per plegium Iohannis Cade & Iohannis Walkere viii d.

De Iuliana seruiente Walteri Bone pro consimili per plegium Thome Forsthulle & Thome Hamptone iiii d.

De Thomasina seruiente Willelmi Wygan ferour pro consimili per plegium Willelmi Wygan & Iohannis Bernard iiii d.

De Iohanne Brewere seruiente Iohannis Charle pro consimili per plegium Nicholai Nortone & Iohannis Spicer xii d.

De Alicia Tapstere seruiente Iohannis Charle pro consimili per plegium Nicholai Nortone & Iohannis Spicer vi d.

Fines de magistris istis per tempus predictum &c.

De Iohanne Lepere pro excessu dato seruientibus suis predictis per plegium Nicholai Nortone & Iohannis Lyllynge vi d.

De Iohanne Cade pro consimili per plegium Thome Hamptone & Iohannis Lyllynge vi d.

De Waltero Bone pro consimili per plegium Thome Forsthulle & Thome Hamptone vi d.

De Willelmo Wygan, ferour, pro consimili per plegium Iohannis Spicer & Iohannis Bernard iiii d.

De Iohanne Charley pro consimili per plegium Nicholai Nortone & Iohannis Spicer iiii d.

Et ulterius dictus vicecomes isto eodem die Veneris proximo ante diem dominicam in Ramispalmarum retornauit eciam quod de dictis accusatis de warda ista coram dictis nunc iusticiariis Iohannes Hikkes, & Willelmus Cristemasse, Willelmus Tryllyng & Iohanna Gardyner, seruientes eiusdem Iohannis Hikkes, Iohannes Bernard lokiere, & Thomas Chiltone seruiens eiusdem Iohannis Bernard, Iohannes Page bakere & Iohannes Copy, Robertus Gurbache, Iohannes Irelond & Thomas Pylprest, seruientes eiusdem Iohannis Page, Iohannes Dadyngtone & Constancia seruiens eiusdem Iohannis Dadyngtone, Willelmus Iremongere & Alexander & Willelmus Wyrehale seruientes eiusdem Willelmi Iremongere, Philippus Cornysshe seruiens Willelmi Wygan ferour, Agnes Hawuyle & Iohannes seruiens eiusdem Agnetis attachiati sunt per plegium Iohannis Frende & Willelmi Kete, qui omnes comparuerunt. Et de quibus predictus Iohannes Hikkes dicit quod conuenit cum dictis seruientibus suis scilicet quod eis daret prout sibi liceret eis dare secundum formam ordinacionum & statutorum in hoc casu prouisorum & non aliter, nec aliquid eis alio modo dedit, & de hoc ponit se super patriam &c. Et dicti Willelmus Cristemasse, Willelmus Trillyng & Iohanna Gardyner seruientes eiusdem Iohannis Hikkes dicunt quod conuenerunt cum predicto Iohanne Hikkes magistro suo quod ipsi de eo acciperent prout eis liceret accipere secundum formam ordinacionum & statutorum predictorum & non aliter, nec aliquid de eo alio modo receperunt, & de hoc ponunt se super patriam &c. Ideo preceptum vicecomiti Oxonie ut inferius &c. Et eciam Iohannes Page bakere & Iohannes Dadyngtone dicunt, videlicet quilibet eorum separatim per se, quod ipse conuenit cum dictis seruientibus &c., scilicet quod eis daret prout sibi liceret eis dare secundum formam ordinacionum & statutorum predictorum & non aliter, nec aliquid eis alio modo dedit & de hoc ponit se super patriam &c. Ideo preceptum est dicto vicecomiti ut inferius &c. Et dicti seruientes predictorum Iohannis Page & Iohannis Dadyngtone dicunt, videlicet quilibet separatim per se, quod ipse conuenit cum predicto magistro suo quod ipse de eo reciperet prout ei precipere liceret secundum formam ordinacionum & statutorum predictorum & non aliter, nec aliquid de eo alio modo recepit, & de hoc ponit se super patriam. Ideo preceptum est dicto vicecomiti ut inferius &c. Et predictus Iohannes Barnard lokeyere dicit quod ipse non dedit Thome Chiltone seruienti suo excessiue contra formam ordinacionum & statutorum predictorum, et de hoc ponit se super patriam &c. Ideo preceptum est dicto vicecomiti ut inferius. Et dictus

Thomas Chiltone dicit quod non recepit de dicto Iohanne Bernard magistro suo excessiue contra formam ordinacionum & statutorum illorum antedictorum &c. Et de hoc ponit se super patriam &c. Ideo preceptum est dicto vicecomiti quod non omittat propter aliquam libertatem antedictam quin venire faciat coram dictis iusticiariis apud Oxoniam die Martis proximo ante festum Pasche proximo futurum XVIII probos & legales homines de dictis villa & suburbiis &c. qui dictos magistros nec seruientes suos predictos, qui ut predicitur de ista warda isto die Veneris se miserunt in iuratas predictas & posuerunt, aliqua affinitate atting*ant*, ad faciendum iuratas illas &c., idemque dies dictis magistris & seruientibus suis predictis datus est &c.

Et ulterius causa certarum materiarum allegatarum per dictos Willelmum Iremongere & Alexandrum & Willelmum seruientes eiusdem Willelmi ac Willelmum Wygan ferour & Philippum Cornysshe seruientem eiusdem Willelmi, Agnetem Hawuyle & Iohannem seruientem eiusdem Agnetis &c. datus est eis dies usque proximam sessionem iusticiariorum antedictorum &c.

Et quo ad execucionem faciendam versus dictos Aliciam seruientem Iohannis Cade, Willelmum Merstone iremongere & Aliciam Dorchestre seruientem eiusdem Willelmi pretextu accusacionis antedicte dictus vicecomes nullum isto die retornauit preceptum &c. Ideo preceptum est dicto vicecomiti, sicut alias, quod non omittat propter aliquam libertatem antedictam quin venire faciat coram dictis nunc iusticiariis ad proximas sessiones suas, videlicet die Sabbati proximo post festum sancti Mathei apostoli proximo futurum, dictos Aliciam, Willelmum & Aliciam ad respondendum domino regi de transgressionibus predictis &c.

Hundredum & suburbium extra portam borialem Oxon.

Et ulterius isto die Sabbati in vigilia dominice in Ramispalmarum dicto anno XIIII° pretextu cuiusdam precepti per dictos nunc iusticiarios dicto vicecomiti ut predicitur nuper directi, idem vicecomes retornauit nomina constabulariorum hundredi & suburbii extra portam borialem Oxonie, et quod eis precepit quod iidem constabularii haberent coram dictis nunc iusticiariis apud Oxoniam isto eodem die Sabbati omnia nomina venatorum, operariorum, artificum, seruitorum, hostelariorum, mendicancium & vagabundorum ac aliorum hominum mendicancium, qui se nominant trauaillyngmen, in balliua sua imbreuiata &c. Retornauit eciam dictus vicecomes nomina XVIII proborum & legalium hominum de hundredo & suburbio predictis &c. Et patet retornum dicti vicecomitis inferius simul cum retorno constabulariorum illorum, videlicet :—

Iohannes Screveyn & Ricardus Nortone constabularii ibidem isto eodem die Sabbati in vigilia dominice in Ramispalmarum comparuerunt & retornauerunt diuersa nomina operariorum, artificum, seruitorum & hostelariorum de balliua sua, de quibus plures accusati fuerunt per xii de predictis xviii probis hominibus per dictum vicecomitem de hundredo & suburbio istis retornatis. Quorum quidem xii ac omnium accusatorum predictorum de hundredo & suburbio istis nomina patent inferius; in primis de predictis xii, Ricardus Fulk, Ricardus Burghe, Iohannes Hunche, Iohannes Terry, Stephanus Smyth, Iohannes Lokyere, Willelmus Wodestoke, Willelmus Brehulle bakere, Simon Sadelere, Iohannes Ropere, Simon Bradeley & Iohannes Metebourne qui iurati & onerati iuxta formam dictarum posteriorum litterarum domini regis patencium dicunt super sacramentum suum quod, de dictis accusatis in hundredo & suburbio istis, de lathomis Iohannes Bloxham masone, Ricardus Frythe masone, Ricardus Nortone masone, Ricardus Prestone masone & Rogerus Meriot[1] masone; et de sclatteres Willelmus Heyne sclattere, Iohannes Aubel sclattere & Ricardus Basset, ac de carpentariis Nicholaus Carpenter & Ricardus Bekewode sawyere ceperunt par les iourneyes excessiue contra formam statutorum & ordinacionum predictorum a festo sancti Michaelis ultimo nunc preterito usque sessionem hanc; set de quibus personis, dictis iuratis non constat. Et ulterius xii iurati predicti dicunt quod omnes seruientes subscripti retenti cum magistris suis subscriptis per idem tempus ceperunt de dictis magistris suis excessiue contra formam ordinacionum & statutorum predictorum, et predicti magistri sui eisdem seruientibus suis dederunt excessiue per idem tempus & soluerunt; quorum magistrorum & seruientum nomina inferius patent, videlicet

Magistri	Seruitores :—
Alicia Hostiller	Willelmus Solond seruiens eius
Felicia Watlyngtone	Iohannes seruiens eiusdem
Ricardus Burghe, bocher	{ Iohannes Cornysshe Robertus
Willelmus Ryuel	{ Iohannes Cappelane Willelmus Frensshe Willelmus Palmes
Ricardus atte Seler	Isabella Comberdone seruiens

[1] The surname is added above the line.

Nicholaus Peion	Ricardus seruiens eiusdem
Willelmus Chyselhamptone, bochere	Robertus, Margeria } seruientes eiusdem

Et super hoc isto eodem die Sabbati in vigilia dominice in Ramis-palmarum preceptum dicto vicecomiti quod non omittat propter aliquam libertatem predictam quin venire faciat coram predictis nunc iusticiariis apud Oxoniam die Martis proximo ante festum Pasche proximo futurum omnes accusatos predictos de dictis hundredo & suburbio extra dictam portam borialem Oxonie ad respondendum domino regi de transgressionibus antedictis &c.

Memb. 16 Ad quem diem Martis proximo ante festum Pasche predictus vicecomes retornauit quod de predictis accusatis de dictis hundredo & suburbio de lathomis Iohannes Bloxham masone, Ricardus Frythe masone & Rogerus Masone, masone, & de carpentariis Nicholaus Carpenter & de sclatteres Willelmus Heyne sclattere, Iohannes Aubel sclattere & Ricardus Basset sclattere ac Ricardus Bekewode sawyere attachiati sunt per plegium Iohannis Hert & Willelmi Rede; qui omnes venerunt & non potuerunt dedicere transgressiones predictas, & posuerunt se in gracia regis, quorum fines patent ut sequntur, videlicet:—

De Iohanne Bloxham masone pro excessu capto per plegium Iohannis Scryueyn cordewanarii & Iohannis Bradele	x d.
De Ricardo Frithe masone pro consimili per plegium Ricardi Nortone & Thome Webbe	viii d.
De Rogero Masone, masone, pro consimili per plegium Ricardi Nortone & Iohannis Scryueyn	xii d.
De Ricardo Bekewode sawyere pro consimili per plegium Nicholai Carpenter & Ricardi Basset	viii d.
De Nicholao Carpenter, carpentario, pro consimili per plegium Ricardi Prestone & Willelmi Lundone	viii d.
De Willelmo Heyne sclattere pro consimili per plegium Iohannis Aubel & Ricardi Basset	viii d.
De Iohanne Aubelle sclattere pro consimili per plegium Thome Webbe & Willelmi Heynes	xii d.
De Ricardo Basset sclattere pro consimili per plegium Thome Webbe & Ricardi Nortone	viii d.

Retornauit eciam dictus vicecomes quod de predictis magistris & seruitoribus de predictis hundredo & suburbio ut predicitur accusatis Alicia Hosteler & Willelmus Solond seruiens eius, Felicia Watlyngtone,

Ricardus Burghe bochere, Iohannes Cornysshe & Robertus seruientes eiusdem Ricardi Burghe, Ricardus atte Celere, Isabella Comberdone seruiens eiusdem, Willelmus Ryuelle, Iohannes Cappelane, Willelmus Frensshe & Willelmus Palmes seruientes eiusdem Ricardi atte Celer [1], & Willelmus Chiselhamptone bochere & Robertus & Margeria seruientes eiusdem attachiati sunt per plegium Ricardi Node & Iohannis Kent qui omnes comparuerunt. Et de quibus accusatis dicti Felicia Watlyngtone, Ricardus atte Seler & Isabella Comberdone seruiens eiusdem Ricardi atte Selere non potuerunt dedicere transgressiones antedictas, & posuerunt se in gracia regis, quorum fines patent ut sequntur videlicet:—

De Felicia Watlyngtone pro excessu dato per plegium Thome Hamptone & Willelmi Ryuelle iiii d.

De Ricardo atte Selere pro consimili per plegium Willelmi Cook and Willelmi Ryuelle vi d.

De Isabella Comberdone seruiente eiusdem Ricardi pro excessu capto &c. per plegium Willelmi Cook & Willelmi Ryuelle iiii d.

Et dictus Ricardus Burghe bocher non potest dedicere quin conuenit cum dicto magistro [2] suo scilicet de se recipere & habere contra formam ordinacionum & statutorum predictorum, & posuit se in gracia regis; quorum magistri & seruientis fines patent ut sequntur videlicet:—

De Ricardo Burghe bocher pro conuencione facta cum Roberto seruiente suo, scilicet sibi dare contra formam ordinacionum & statutorum predictorum per plegium Willelmi Newman & Willelmi Hamptone vi d.

De Roberto seruiente Ricardi Burghe predicti pro conuencione secum facta contra statutum &c. per plegium Ricardi Burghe & Iohannis Cornysshe viii d.

Et ulterius predictus Ricardus Burghe bochere dicit quod dat Iohanni Cornysshe seruienti suo predicto per annum in omnibus xvi s.; et dicit quod idem Iohannes est capitalis seruiens & mercator suus in arte de Bocherie, & ponit se in discrecionem iusticiariorum si excessiue &c. Et causa predicta per discrecionem iusticiariorum predictorum consideratum est quod dictus Ricardus Burghe eosdem xvi s. det per annum &c.; et quod non dat predicto Iohanni Cornysshe ultra dictos xvi s., ponit se super patriam. Ideo preceptum est dicto vicecomiti quod non &c. ut inferius &c. Et idem Iohannes Cornysshe ponit se

[1] The scribe means *Willelmi Ryuelle*.

[2] *serviente* is meant.

similiter super patriam, quod non recipit de dicto magistro suo nisi XVI s. per annum &c. Ideo preceptum est dicto vicecomiti ut inferius.

Et dicta Alicia Hostiler dicit quod dictus Willelmus Solond seruiens suus de se capit per annum integrum x s. in omnibus, & est hostelarius suus &c. Et ponit se in discrecionem iusticiariorum &c. Et per eosdem iusticiarios consideratum est quod liceat dicte Alicie dicto Willelmo sic dare &c., videlicet quamdiu in officio & labore illo eidem Alicie sic seruit &c.; et quod eidem Willelmo similiter liceat de ea sic secundum quod predicitur accipere &c. Et quod dicta Alicia eidem Willelmo Solond non dat plus, et eciam quod dictus Willelmus Solond plus de dicto magistro [*sic*] suo non capit, ponunt se super patriam &c. Ideo preceptum est dicto vicecomiti &c., ut inferius &c.

Et dictus Willelmus Ryuelle dicit quod dat Iohanni Cappelane seruienti suo per annum XIII s. IIII d., & dicit quod est hostelarius suus & sibi de officio illo responsurus &c. Et eciam quod dat dicto Willelmo Frensshe seruienti suo per annum VI s. VIII d., & Willelmo Palmes seruienti suo predicto VIII s. per annum; et ponit se in discrecionem iusticiariorum &c. si excessiue contra formam ordinacionum & statutorum predictorum &c. Et super hoc per discrecionem dictorum nunc iusticiariorum consideratum est quod eidem Willelmo Ryuelle liceat eis sic dare &c.; & quod predictus Willelmus Ryuelle eisdem plus nec alio modo dat, nec quod ipsi seruientes aliquid ultra summas predictas recipiunt &c. tam dictus Willelmus magister quam ipsi iidem seruientes ponunt se singulariter & separatim super patriam &c. Ideo preceptum est dicto vicecomiti ut inferius &c.

Et dictus Willelmus Chyselhamptone & Margeria seruiens eiusdem Ricardi[1] non potuerunt dedicere transgressiones antedictas & posuerunt se in gracia regis, quorum fines patent ut sequntur, videlicet:—

De Willelmo Chyselhamptone bochere pro excessu dato Margerie seruienti sue per plegium Thome Hamptone & Iohannis Hembury — vi đ.

De Margeria seruiente Willelmi Chyselhamptone pro excessu de dicto magistro suo capto per plegium Willelmi Chyselhamptone & Iohannis Hembury — iiii đ.

Et quo ad accusacionem super dictum Willelmum Chyselhamptone superius affirmatam causa dicti Roberti seruientis sui, idem Willelmus dicit quod predictus Robertus seruiens suus est capitalis seruiens suus in arte sua de Bocherie, & cum denariis suis mercandizat, & multum

[1] The scribe means *Willelmi.*

laborat & multociens in nimis vili labore in arte predicta &c., & quod dat eidem Roberto per annum xx s., & ponit se in discrecionem dictorum nunc iusticiariorum si excessiue contra formam ordinacionum & statutorum predictorum &c. Et causis antedictis &c., consideratum est per dictos nunc iusticiarios quod liceat eidem Willelmo dicto Roberto sic dare & dicto Roberto sic recipere per annum dum taliter facit & agit, ut predicitur &c.; et quod dictus Willelmus nichil ultra denarios predictos predicto Roberto nec aliquid eidem alio modo dat, & quod dictus Robertus de predicto Willelmo aliquid ulterius non recipit per annum, tam dictus magister quam idem seruiens ponunt se super patriam. Ideo preceptum est dicto vicecomiti quod non omittat propter aliquam libertatem predictam quin venire faciat coram dictis nunc iusticiariis apud Oxoniam die Martis proximo ante festum Pasche proximo futurum de dictis villa & suburbio xviii probos & legales homines, qui aliquos aut aliquem aut aliquam de dictis accusatis in dictis hundredo & suburbio qui se in dictas iuratas secundum id quod predicitur posuerunt, ut predictum est, nulla affinitate atting*ant*, ad faciendum iuratas illas &c.

Retornauit eciam dictus vicecomes isto eodem die Sabbati in vigilia dominice in Ramispalmarum quod predicti Ricardus Nortone masone, Ricardus Prestone masone, Iohannes seruiens Felicie Watlyngtone, Nicholaus Peione & Ricardus seruiens eiusdem Nicholai nichil habent in balliua sua per quod possunt attachiari &c. Ideo preceptum est dicto vicecomiti quod non omittat propter aliquam libertatem in balliva sua quin capiat omnes istos, sic in parcella ista simul per dictum vicecomitem ad nichil retornatos, ubicumque inuenti fiunt[1] in balliua sua, et eos saluo custodiat &c., ita quod habeat corpora eorum coram dictis nunc iusticiariis apud Oxoniam die Sabbati proximo post festum sancti Mathei apostoli proximo futurum ad respondendum domino regi de transgressionibus antedictis &c.

Et ulterius isto eodem die Martis proximo ante festum Pasche dictus vicecomes pretextu cuiusdam precepti nuper sibi, ut superius fit mencio, directi retornauit nomina xviii proborum hominum de dictis villa & suburbiis, ad faciendum certas iuratas inter dominum regem & certas personas & partes de certis materiis prescriptis &c., & de xii^{cim} dictorum xviii hominum oneratis super iuratis subsequentibus, ut patet inferius, nomina simul cum nominibus personarum & parcium, que in iuratis illis coram dictis iusticiariis hunc diem presentem habuerunt, aperte

[1] *Sic*; but probably the scribe meant *fuerint*.

inferius patent, videlicet in primis de dictis xiicim Iohannes Lundone, Walterus Bocher, Willelmus Swanbourne, Ricardus Sherman, Iohannes Bedewynde, Thomas Waryner, Willelmus Hamptone chaundeler, Thomas Setertone, Robertus Deye skynnere, Iohannes Appelford, Henricus Moryce & Ricardus Broun, qui iurati & onerati iuxta formam materiarum in iuratis illis contentarum dicunt super sacramentum suum quod Iohannes Syluestre non dedit Thome Phelyp & Waltero seruienti suo excessiue, nec Iohannes Shawe excessiue dedit Iohanni Brewere & Thome Brewere seruientibus suis, nec Iohannes Stratford, cook, plus dedit dicte Alicie seruienti sue quam iii s., nec dicte Iohanne seruiente sue plus quam vi s. per annum, prout superius allegauit, nec Philippus Taillour excessiue dedit Alicie seruienti sue predicte, nec Iohanna seruiens Iohannis Clerk, fysshere, plus cepit de dicto Iohanne magistro suo per annum quam v s., sicut superius allegauit, nec Iohannes Dadyngtone excessiue dedit Agneti seruienti sue predicte, nec eadem Agnes de eo excessiue cepit, nec Iohannes Hikkes alderman excessiue dedit Willelmo Cristemasse, Willelmo Trillyng & Iohanne Gardener, nec conuencionem cum eis fecit nisi secundum quod ei liceret per ordinacionem statutorum &c. nec Iohannes Page bakere excessiue dedit dictis seruientibus suis scilicet Iohanni Copy, Ricardo Gurbache, Iohanni Pauy, Iohanni Irelond nec Thome Pilpreste, nisi sicut ei liceret per statuta & hoc per conuencionem, nec iidem seruientes eiusdem Iohannis Page nec aliquis eorum excessiue de dicto magistro suo ceperunt nec cepit, nisi secundum statuta & hoc per conuencionem, nec Iohannes Dadyngtone excessiue dedit Constancie seruienti sue nisi per conuencionem secundum statuta &c., nec eadem Constancia aliter de eo cepit nisi secundum quod eis liceret per ordinacionem statutorum, & hoc per conuencionem. Et sic dicti iurati dicunt quod neque predicti magistri nec eorum seruientes in aliquo contra formam ordinacionum & statutorum predictorum deliquerunt, sed omnes persone que placitauerunt verum dixerunt. Ideo consideratum est per

Memb. 17 iusticiarios predictos quod omnes illi, qui sic ut predicitur per xii dictos iuratos de accusacionibus predictis liberantur, eant quieti &c. Et ulterius dicti xii iurati dicunt quod predictus Iohannes Trusse, sclattere, excessiue dedit Laurencio seruienti suo contra formam ordinacionum & statutorum predictorum; et quod predictus Laurencius seruiens eiusdem Iohannis excessiue de ipso Iohanne Trusse cepit contra formam eorundem ordinacionum & statutorum, sicut accusati superius fuerunt &c. Et super hoc predicti Iohannes Trusse & Laurencius comparuerunt, & posuerunt se in gracia regis pro transgressione & contemptu predictis &c.; quorum fines ut inferius patet sequntur videlicet:—

De Iohanne Trusse sclattere pro excessu dato Laurencio seruienti suo unde per iuratam convictus est per plegium Iohannis Maltone & Ade Sclattere iiii d.

De Laurencio seruienti predicti Iohannis Trusse pro excessu de eodem capto unde per iuratam convictus est per plegium Iohannis Vente & Iohannis Wodhulle iiii d.

Et ulterius isto eodem die Martis proximo ante festum Pasche preceptum est dicto vicecomiti quod non omittat propter aliquam libertatem in balliua sua quin venire faciat coram dictis nunc iusticiariis apud Oxoniam die Sabbati proximo post festum sancti Mathei apostoli proximo futurum Iohannem Drake & Iohannem Norcote nuper seruientes Michaelis Salesbury, Iohannem Hopkyn seruientem Ricardi Iremongere & Iohannem seruientem Nicholai Nortone ad respondendum domino regi de eo quod ipsi accusati fuerunt, scilicet de excessu capto de dictis magistris suis, & hoc coram dictis iusticiariis in prima dictarum commissionum nominatis &c.

Et quo ad certas iuratas isto eodem die Martis inter dominum regem & quasdam personas super diuersis materiis capiendas, ut superius diuersis uicibus predicte certe persone per assignacionem dictorum iusticiariorum hunc diem presentem habuerunt, dictus vicecomes nullum retornauit preceptum. Ideo dicte iurate remanent capiende pro defectu iuratorum usque diem Sabbati proximo post festum sancti Mathei apostoli proximo futurum &c. Et super hoc preceptum est dicto vicecomiti quod non omittat propter aliquam libertatem in balliua sua quin venire faciat coram dictis iusticiariis apud Oxoniam dicto die Sabbati proximo post dictum festum sancti Mathei apostoli XVIII probos & legales homines de dictis villa & sub-urb*iis* qui dictas partes, que in iuratas illas se posuerunt, nulla affinitate attingant, ad faciendum iuratas illas &c., quarum personarum & parcium nomina ac cause & materie, pro quibus se in iuratas istas, ut predictum est, posuerunt aperte patent in precepto dicto vicecomiti directo &c., & unde ad dictum diem iurati onerati erunt &c.

Et nuper ut superius plene patet preceptum fuit dicto vicecomiti sicut pluries quod non omittat propter aliquam libertatem in balliua sua quin caperet Iohannem Wottone, laborer, Willelmum Nevyle nuper seruientem Nicholai Saundresdone de Oxonia, Michaelem Neel & Henricum Coupere nuper seruientes Iohannis Clerk fysshere de Oxonia, Stephanum Cartere & Thomam Hille nuper seruientes Reginaldi Tannere de Oxonia, Thomam Cony nuper seruientem Iohannis Utteworthe de Oxonia, Iohannem Hedyndone carpenter, Iohannem Hostiler nuper seruientem Iohannis Charlee de Oxonia, Iohannem nuper seruientem Iohannis Hikkes de Oxonia, Iohannem Kent laborer, Iohannem Clerk nuper seruientem Ricardi Iremongere de Oxonia, Iohannem Cornysshe & Ricardum nuper seruientes Willelmi Dagvile de Oxonia, Willelmum Cartere nuper seruientem Thome Maister, Iohannem nuper seruientem Iohannis White de Oxonia, Aliciam nuper seruientem Philippi Taillour de Oxonia, Iulianam nuper seruientem Iohannis Bereford de Oxonia bochere & Agnetem nuper seruientem Iohannis White de Oxonia, si &c.; et eos &c., ita quod haberet corpora eorum coram predictis iusticiariis apud Oxoniam isto eodem die Martis proximo ante dictum festum Pasche ad respondendum domino regi de diuersis excessibus &c.; unde indict*ati* sunt &c.; qui non ven*erunt* &c. Et dictus vicecomes retornauit quod non sunt inuenti in balliua sua &c. Ideo preceptum est dicto vicecomiti quod exigi faciat predictos Iohannem Wottone laborer, Willelmum Neuyle, Michaelem Neel [1] & Henricum Coupere, Stephanum Cartere, Thomam Hille, Thomam Cony, Iohannem Hedyndone, Iohannem Hosteler, Iohannem nuper seruientem Iohannis Hikkes, Iohannem Kent, Iohannem Clerke, Iohannem Cornysshe & Ricardum nuper seruientes Willelmi Dageville, Willelmum Cartere, Iohannem nuper seruientem Iohannis White, Aliciam, Iulianam & Agnetem de comitatu in comitatum [2] quousque secundum legem & cons*uetudines* regni Anglie predicti Iohannes Wottone, Willelmus Neville, Michael Neel, Henricus Coupere, Stephanus Cartere, Thomas Hille, Thomas Cony, Iohannes Hedyndone, Iohannes Hosteler, Iohannes nuper seruiens Iohannis Hikkes, Iohannes Kent, Iohannes Clerk, Iohannes Cornysshe & Ricardus nuper seruientes Willelmi Dageville, Willelmus Cartere & Iohannes nuper seruiens Iohannis White utlagentur & predicte Alicia, Iuliana & Agnes waynientur, si non comparuerunt. Et si comparuerint, tunc eas capiat et in prisona domini regis saluo custodiri faciat; ita quod habeat corpora eorum coram dictis nunc iusticiariis apud Oxoniam die Lune proximo ante festum sancti Hillarii proximo futurum ad respondendum domino regi de transgressionibus & excessibus antedictis &c.

Et ulterius predictus vicecomes retornauit isto eodem die Martis quod ubi preceptum fuit sibi, sicut pluries, capere Iohannem atte Shoppe &c., si &c., et ipsum &c., ita quod eum isto die haberet coram

[1] Neek, MS.
[2] 'from county court to county court', i.e. month after month.

dictis nunc iusticiariis apud Oxoniam &c., idem Iohannes non est inuentus in balliua sua &c.; et super hoc idem Iohannes comparuit & non potuit dedicere transgressiones predictas & posuit se in gracia regis; cuius finis patet ut sequitur, videlicet:—

De Iohanne atte Shoppe pro excessu capto per plegium Iohannis Hande glouere & Henrici Porter iiii d.

Et quo ad execucionem faciendam uersus nuper seruientes Iohannis White de Oxonia, videlicet Iohannem Lambhithe, Iohannem Gersyndone, Radulfum & Henricum ac Walterum nuper seruientem Iohannis Spencer de Cattestrete & Walterum Swon nuper seruientem dicti magistri hospitalis sancti Iohannis, ubi, ut prius fit mencio, preceptum fuit dicto vicecomiti sicut alias &c., quod non omitteret propter aliquam libertatem &c. quin ipsos caperet &c., si &c., et eos &c., ita quod haberet corpora eorum coram dictis nunc iusticiariis apud Oxoniam isto eodem die Martis ad respondendum domino regi de predictis transgressionibus &c., vicecomes nullum retornauit preceptum &c. Et ipsi non ven*erunt* &c. Ideo preceptum est dicto vicecomiti, sicut alias, quod non omittat propter aliquam libertatem predictam quin ipsos capiat &c., si &c., et eos &c., ita quod habeat corpora eorum coram predictis nunc iusticiariis apud Oxoniam die Sabbati proximo post festum sancti Mathei apostoli proximo futurum ad respondendum domino regi separatim de transgressionibus predictis &c.

Et preceptum fuit vicecomiti predicto, sicut pluries, quod caperet Alanum Taskere nuper seruientem Reginaldi Tannere de Oxonia, si &c.; et quod eum &c., ita quod eum haberet coram dictis nunc iusticiariis apud Oxoniam isto eodem die Martis ad respondendum domino regi de transgressionibus predictis; qui quidem vicecomes ad istum diem nullum retornauit preceptum &c.; qui non venit. Ideo preceptum est dicto vicecomiti sicut pluries &c. quod non omittat propter aliquam libertatem predictam quin ipsum Alanum capiat si &c., et eum &c. ita quod habeat corpus eius coram predictis nunc iusticiariis apud Oxoniam die Sabati proximo post festum sancti Mathei apostoli proximo futurum ad respondendum domino regi de transgressionibus predictis &c.

Et preceptum fuit vicecomiti sicut pluries quod caperet Thomam Caumbrigge & Iohannam nuper seruientes Iohannis Skynnere de Oxonia, Radulfum Sclattere & Iohannem Masone si &c., ita quod eos haberet coram dictis nunc iusticiariis apud Oxoniam isto eodem die Martis ad respondendum domino regi de transgressionibns predictis;

predictus vicecomes nullum retornauit preceptum. Et ipsi non venerunt. Ideo preceptum est dicto vicecomiti, sicut pluries, quod ipsos capiat si &c., et eos &c., ita quod habeat corpora eorum coram dictis nunc iusticiariis apud Oxoniam die Sabati proximo post festum sancti Mathei apostoli proximo futurum ad respondendum domino regi de transgressionibus antedictis &c.

Et preceptum fuit dicto vicecomiti, sicut pluries, quod non omitteret &c. quin caperet Iohannem Skirwhit masone, Walterum nuper seruientem Elizee Goolde & Robertum nuper seruientem Iohannis Stratford cook si &c., ita quod eos haberet coram predictis nunc iusticiariis apud Oxoniam isto eodem die Martis ad respondendum domino regi de transgressionibus predictis &c.; vicecomes nullum retornauit preceptum. Et ipsi non venerunt. Ideo preceptum est dicto vicecomiti sicut pluries quod non omittat &c. quin ipsos capiat si &c., ita quod habeat corpora eorum coram dictis nunc iusticiariis apud Oxoniam die Sabati proximo post festum sancti Mathei apostoli proximo futurum ad respondendum domino regi de transgressionibus antedictis &c.

Et preceptum fuit dicto vicecomiti quod non omitteret &c. quin distringat Iohannem Shoryere carpenter per omnes terras &c., ita quod nec &c., et quod de exitibus &c., et quod haberet corpus eius coram dictis nunc iusticiariis apud Oxoniam isto eodem die Martis ad respondendum domino regi de transgressionibus predictis &c. Et dictus vicecomes nullum retornauit preceptum &c. Et ipse non venit &c. Ideo preceptum est dicto vicecomiti quod non omittat &c. quin ipsum distringat &c. in forma predicta &c., ita quod habeat corpus eius coram dictis nunc iusticiariis apud Oxoniam die Sabati proximo post festum sancti Mathei apostoli proximo futurum ad respondendum domino regi de transgressionibus predictis &c.

Willelmus Pacche (II d.) & plegii sui in misericordia quia non sunt prosecuti versus Iohannem Sadelere de placito transgressionis contra ordinacionem seruientum &c.

Petrus Welyngtone (III d.) & plegii sui in misericordia pro consimili versus Robertum Cook &c.

Iohannes Stratford cook (III d.) & plegii sui pro consimili versus Robertum Cook &c.

Willelmus Fyffyde ponit se in gracia regis pro contemptu &c., pro rescussu facto balliuis &c., per plegium Willelmi Bergeman & Nicholai Nortone xii d.

Hugo Brehulle (II d.) & plegii sui in misericordia quia non sunt prosecuti versus Philippum Carpenter de placito transgressionis contra ordinacionem seruientum &c.

Ricardus Ragenhulle (II d.) & plegii sui in misericordia quia non sunt prosecuti versus Aliciam relictam Iohannis Veyne & Matildam seruientem eiusdem Alicie de placito transgressionis contra ordinacionem seruientum &c.

Ricardus Westerdale & plegii sui in misericordia quia non sunt prosecuti versus Iohannem Gibbes & Thomam Taillour de placito transgressionis contra ordinacionem seruientum &c.

Iohannes Marche nuper seruiens Iohannis Bereford bocher ponit se in gracia regis pro contemptu &c. eo quod a seruicio suo &c. recessit ante finem &c., sicut conuictus est per[1] recognicionem suam propriam &c.

Memb. 17 dorse
Sept. 23, 1391

Placita tenta apud Oxoniam die Sabati proximo post festum sancti Mathei apostoli anno regni regis Ricardi secundi post conquestum quintodecimo coram Ricardo de Garstone maiore ville Oxonie & Ricardo Ouertone, iusticiariis domini regis virtute predictarum posteriorum litterarum patentium domini regis &c., Willelmo Gerueys clerico tunc ibidem.

Pretextu cuiusdam precepti vicecomiti Oxonie prius per dictos iusticiarios directi idem vicecomes isto eodem die Sabati proximo post festum sancti Mathei apostoli retornauit nomina XVIII proborum hominum de dictis villa & suburbiis ad faciendum certas iuratas inter dominum regem & certas personas & partes de certis materiis, de quibus predicte persone & partes se posuerunt in iuratas illas, prout certis diebus sessionum dictorum iusticiariorum infra plenius continetur, & de certis materiis de quibus certe persone isto eodem die se posuerunt in iuratas illas, prout inferius patet &c., quorum XVIII hominum XII isto die onerati fuerunt iuxta materias predictas omnes & singulas; quorum XII oneratorum & iuratorum nomina patent in sequenti, videlicet Ricardus atte Celer, Iohannes Charley, Willelmus Codesdone, Iohannes Beaule, Iohannes Terry, Rogerus Holme, Ricardus Wyndelle, Willelmus Metebourne, Ricardus Westerdale, Michael Smyth, Thomas Wormecote & Thomas Grindere; qui dicunt super sacramentum suum quod omnes persone que se posuerunt in iuratam predict*am* coram dictis iusticiariis in predictis sessionibus suis

[1] pro, MS.

ante hunc diem presentem tam magistri quam seruientes & omnes alie veraciter dixerunt, allegando materias suas predictas de quibus accusati fuerunt ut in dictis sessionibus fit mencio &c. Ideo consideratum est per iusticiarios predictos quod eedem persone eant quiete &c.

Retornauit eciam dictus vicecomes isto eodem die Sabati pretextu cuiusdam precepti sibi prius per dictos iusticiarios directi quod Ricardus Nortone masone, Iohannes seruiens Felicie Watlyngtone, Nicholaus Pyione, Ricardus nuper seruiens eiusdem Nicholai, Iohannes Lambhythe & Willelmus nuper seruientes Iohannis White, Walterus nuper seruiens Iohannis Spencer de Cattestrete, Iohannes Masone, Iohannes Spirewhit masone, Walterus nuper seruiens Elizee Goolde, Iohannes Benet & Matilda uxor eius seruientes Petri Welyngford [*sic*], Iohannes Norcote & Iohannes Groue nuper seruiens Willelmi Dageville nichil habent in balliua sua per quod possunt attachiari nec sunt inuenti in eadem; qui omnes comparuerunt. Et de quibus Ricardus Nortone, Nicholaus Pyion, Iohannes Lambhithe & Willelmus nuper seruientes Iohannis White, Walterus nuper seruiens Iohannis Spencer de Cattestrete, Iohannes Masone, Iohannes Spirewhit, Walterus nuper seruiens Elizee Golde, Iohannes Bennet & Matilda uxor eius & Iohannes Norcote venerunt & non potuerunt dedicere transgressiones predictas, & posuerunt [se][1] in gracia regis, quorum fines patent ut sequntur videlicet:—

De Ricardo Nortone masone pro excessu capto per plegium Rogeri Bakere & Iohannis Bilburghe — xii d.

De Nicholao Pyione pro excessu dato per plegium Iohannis Hunche & Willelmi Ryuelle — vi d.

De Iohanne Lambhithe nuper seruiente Iohannis White pro consimili per plegium Iohannis White & Iohannis Forester balliui — viii d.

De Willelmo nuper seruiente Iohannis White pro consimili per plegium Iohannis White & Iohannis Forster balliui — viii d.

De Waltero nuper seruiente Iohannis Spencer de Cattestrete pro consimili per plegium Thome Waryner & Willelmi Ottemore — viii d.

De Iohanne Masone pro consimili per plegium Iohannis Walsshe, diere, & Iohannis Abyndone — viii d.

De Iohanne Sperewhit masone pro consimili per plegium Iohannis Strettone bakere & Iohannis Groom — viii d.

[1] Omitted in MS.

De Waltero nuper seruiente Elizee Golde pro consimili per plegium Willelmi Doke cook & Ricardi Bristowe viii d.

De Iohanne Norcote nuper seruiente Michaelis Salesbury pro consimili per plegium Iohannis Forester & Ricardi atte Celer viii d.

Et dictus Iohannes seruiens Felicie Watlyngtone dicit quod est magister seruiens dicte Felicie in arte de Bocherie & mercenarius suus, & capit per annum xx s. & non plus, & ponit se in discrecionem iusticiariorum &c. Et sic consideratum est quod accipiet &c.; et quod non recipit plus, ponit se super patriam.

Et Ricardus nuper seruiens Nicholai Pyione dicit quod fuit apprenticius in arte de cordewaneria & iuit ab apprenticiatu per II annos elapsos & conuenit cum dicto Nicholao pro x s. per annum in omnibus, & ponit se in discrecionem iusticiariorum &c. Et de hoc habet diem usque proximam sessionem &c. Et quod non capit plus, ponit se super patriam &c.

Et dictus Iohannes Groue dicit quod est firmarius Willelmi Dageville de brac' & reddit per annum unum certum [1], & non est seruiens, & sic dicit quod non cepit excessiue &c. Et de hoc quod ipse sic est, ponit se super patriam &c.

Et ulterius dictus vicecomes retornauit isto eodem die Sabati proximo post festum sancti Mathei apostoli quod Iohannes Spencer de Cattestrete & Iohannes Shoriere nichil habent in balliua sua per quod distringi possunt; qui eodem die comparuerunt & non potuerunt dedicere transgressiones predictas & ponunt se in gracia regis, quorum fines patent ut sequntur, videlicet.—

De Iohanne Spencer de Cattestrete pro excessu dato per plegium Iohannis Gersyndone & Iohannis Thurbarne iii d.

De Iohanne Shoryere pro excessu capto per plegium Iohannis Gersyndone & Ricardi Iremongere iiii d.

Et ulterius isto eodem die Sabati dictus vicecomes retornauit quod Alicia nuper seruiens Iohannis Cade, Willelmus Merstone iremongere & Alicia Dorchestre seruiens eiusdem Willelmi et Petrus Welyngtone cook attachiati sunt per plegium Iohannis Cost & Willelmi Kene qui omnes venerunt & non potuerunt dedicere transgressiones predictas, preter dictam Aliciam nuper seruientem Iohannis Cade &c., & ponunt se in gracia regis, quorum fines patent ut sequntur, videlicet:—

[1] i.e. a fixed rent.

De Willelmo Merstone, iremongere, pro excessu dato per plegium Willelmi Doke cook & Ricardi Bristowe vi d.
De Alicia Dorchestre seruiente pro excessu capto per plegium Willelmi Doke cook & Ricardi Bristowe iiii d.
De Petro Welyngtone cook pro excessu dato per plegium Iohannis Faukener & Thome Hamptone vi d.

Et ulterius isto eodem die Sabati dictus vicecomes retornauit quod Iohannes Wadyn smyth nichil habet per quod distringi potest; retornauit eciam nomina seruientum suorum &c. viz. Willelmum Smyth & Thomam Fyffyde; qui omnes comparuerunt. Et dictus Iohannes Wadyn dicit quod conuenit cum dictis seruientibus suis eis dare sicut ei liceret per statuta regis & non aliter, nec aliter eis dedit, & de hoc ponit se super patriam. Et dicti seruientes dicunt quod conuenerunt cum dicto Iohanne Wadyn magistro suo modo predicto, nec alio modo de eo ceperunt. Et de hoc ponunt se super patriam &c. Ideo &c. Et ulterius eodem die consideratum fuit per dictos iusticiarios & allocatum quod Willelmus Smyth predictus caperet pro anno preterito de Iohanne Wadyn xx s.; et dictus Thomas Fyffyde XIII s. IIII d.

Et quo ad capiendum Ricardum Prestone masone & Iohannem Gersyndone, Radulfum & Henricum seruientes Iohannis White, Walterum Swon nuper seruientem magistri sancti Iohannis extra portam orientalem Oxonie, Alanum Taskere nuper seruientem Reginaldi Tannere, Thomam Caumbrigge & Iohannam nuper seruientes Iohannis Skynnere, Radulfum Sclattere, Robertum nuper seruientem Iohannis Stratford cook, Iohannem Poly nuper seruientem Petri Welyngtone vicecomes nullum retornauit preceptum. Ideo preceptum est dicto vicecomiti quod ipsos capiat, ita quod eos habeat &c. apud Oxoniam coram predictis nunc iusticiariis ad proximas sessiones &c.

Et predicta Alicia nuper seruiens Iohannis Cade dicit quod capit per annum VI s. & unam tunicam & fuit cum dicto Iohanne per dimidium annum & cepit pro quantitate anni &c. & ponit se super patriam quod non capit plus, nec conuencionem fecit nisi ad voluntatem &c.

Et quo ad execucionem faciendam versus Edwardum Crook & Galfridum seruientem eiusdem Edwardi, Willelmum Herne & seruientes suos qui sibi seruierunt in primis sessionibus iusticiariorum predictorum, Iohannem & Willelmum nuper seruientes Nicholai Nortone, Iohannem Drake nuper seruientem Michaelis Salesbury, Iohannem Hopkyn nuper seruientem Ricardi Iremongere, Willelmum Dageville & seruientes ipsius Willelmi qui sibi seruierunt in primis sessionibus &c. viz. ad eos venire fecisse vicecomes nullum retornauit preceptum; qui non venerunt. Ideo preceptum est dicto vicecomiti quod execucionem versus [eos][1] faciat &c. contra proximas sessiones &c.

Et eciam ante hunc diem in aliis sessionibus, certis de causis, Iohannes seruiens Nicholai Nortone, Iohannes Gardyner & Isabella uxor eius seruientes magistri hospitalis sancti Iohannis extra portam orientalem, ac dictus magister, Iohannes Sulby coupere, Iohanna relicta Iohannis Curreour & Iohannes seruiens eiusdem Iohanne, Iohannes Tannere, Willelmus Iremongere & Alexander & Willelmus seruientes eiusdem Willelmi Iremongere ac Willelmus Wygan ferour & Philippus Cornysshe seruiens eiusdem Willelmi Wygan, & Agnes Hawuylle & Iohannes seruiens eiusdem Agnetis habent diem per iusticiarios essendi hic ad istas sessiones. Adhuc habent diem usque proximas sessiones, & ibidem inferius cause predicte plenius annotantur &c.[2]

Et quo ad capcionem corporis Roberti nuper seruientis Iohannis Stratford cook, prout vicecomes contra istum diem Sabati habuit in mandatis, vicecomes modo retornauit quod dictus Robertus non fuit inuentus &c.; qui quidem Robertus hoc eodem die comparuit, & dictus Iohannes Stratford similiter. Et dictus Iohannes Stratford dicit quod non dedit dicto Roberto nisi secundum statutum &c.; et dictus Robertus dicit quod non cepit nisi secundum statutum, & de hoc ponunt se tam magister quam seruiens super patriam. Ideo preceptum est &c. Et patet veredictum inferius prope &c.

Et ulterius per dictos iusticiarios dicti xii iurati, ut predicitur, isto eodem die Sabati onerati fuerunt de & super materiis per partes predictas isto die superius allegatis & in iuratam illam positas, qui quidem xii dicunt quod omnes persone predicte veraciter allegauerunt & dixerunt in omnibus materiis illis &c. Ideo consideratum est quod eant quiete &c.

Memb. 16 *d*

Et ubi ante hoc tempus seruientes Reginaldi Tannere coram iusticiariis posuerunt loco suo Ricardum Bristowe attornatum suum ad faciendum pro eis fines cum domino rege pro excessibus &c., qui quidem Ricardus habuit diem usque hunc diem presentem &c., qui quidem seruientes modo per dictum Ricardum fines suos faciunt ut inferius, & sic eorum nomina aperte hic patent cum eorum finibus &c.

De Waltero Mun brewere pro excessu capto per plegium Reginaldi Tannere & Ricardi Bristowe vi d.
De Willelmo Brewere pro eodem per plegium supradictum vi d.

[1] Not in MS. [2] This last sentence is an addition.

De Willelmo Irysshe brewere pro eodem per plegium supradictum vi d.
De Roberto Cartere pro consimili per plegium supradictum vi d.
De Dauid Waterman pro consimili per plegium supradictum vi d.

Jan. 8, 1392

Oxon'. Placita tenta ibidem coram Ricardo de Garstone & Ricardo Ouertone iusticiariis domini regis virtute dictarum posteriorum litterarum patencium domini regis, videlicet die Lune proximo ante festum sancti Hillarii anno regni regis Ricardi secundi xv°, Willelmo Gerueys clerico tunc ibidem.

Pretextu cuiusdem breuis domini regis vicecomiti Oxonie directi per iusticiarios predictos de exigi fac*iendo* certas personas &c. dictus vicecomes isto eodem die Lune dictum breue retornauit, in quo continetur quod certe persone utlagate existunt &c., & certe persone in eodem breui contente dictis iusticiariis diu se redd*iderunt* & inuenerunt eisdem iusticiariis securitatem essendi hic isto die ad respondendum regi de excessibus &c.; quod quidem breue cum execucione &c. huic rotulo consuitur.

[*The following two writs and the return of the sheriff are sewn on.*]

Ricardus dei gracia rex Anglie & Francie & dominus Hibernie vicecomiti Oxonie salutem. Precipimus tibi quod exigi facias Iohannem Wottone laborarium, Willelmum Nevyle nuper seruientem Nicholai Saundresdone de Oxonia, Michaelem Neel & Henricum Coupere nuper seruientes Iohannis Clerk fysshere de Oxonia, Stephanum Cartere & Thomam Hille nuper seruientes Reginaldi Tannere de Oxonia, Thomam Cony nuper seruientem Iohannis Utteworthe de Oxonia, Iohannem Hedyndone carpentarium, Iohannem Hosteler nuper seruientem Iohannis Charlee de Oxonia, Iohannem nuper seruientem Iohannis Hikkes de Oxonia, Iohannem Kent laborer, Iohannem Clerk nuper seruientem Ricardi Iremongere de Oxonia, Iohannem Cornysshe & Ricardum Carpenter nuper seruientes Willelmi Dageuyle de Oxonia, Willelmum Cartere nuper seruientem Thome Maister de Oxonia, Iohannem nuper seruientem Iohannis White de Oxonia, Aliciam nuper seruientem Philippi Taillour de Oxonia, Iulianam nuper seruientem Iohannis Bereford de Oxonia bocher & Agnetem nuper seruientem Iohannis White de Oxonia de comitatu in comitatum quousque secundum legem &

consuetudinem regni nostri Anglie predicti Iohannes Wottone, Willelmus Nevyle, Michael Neel, Henricus Coupere, Stephanus Cartere, Thomas Hille, Thomas Cony, Iohannes Hedyndone, Iohannes Hosteler, Iohannes nuper seruiens Iohannis Hikkes, Iohannes Kent, Iohannes Clerk, Iohannes Cornysshe & Ricardus nuper seruientes Willelmi Dageuyle, Willelmus Cartere & Iohannes nuper seruiens Iohannis White utlagentur & predicte Alicia, Iuliana & Agnes waynientur, si non comparuerint. Et si comparuerint tunc eos capias & in prisona nostra saluo custodiri facias; ita quod habeas corpora eorum coram dilectis & fidelibus nostris Ricardo de Garstone & sociis suis iusticiariis ad pacem in uilla Oxonie & suburbiis eiusdem conseruandam assignatis apud Oxoniam die Lune proximo ante festum sancti Hillarii ad respondendum nobis de diuersis excessibus unde indictati sunt; et unde tu ipse predictis iusticiariis apud Oxoniam die Martis proximo ante festum Pasche ultimo preterito retornasti quod ipsi non sunt inuenti in balliua tua. Et habeas ibi hoc breue. Teste, R. de Garstone maiore ville Oxonie apud Oxoniam XXI die Marcii anno regni nostri quartodecimo. Gerueys.

Ricardus dei gracia rex Anglie [&c.] vicecomiti Oxonie salutem. Cum nuper tibi precepimus quod exigi faceres Iohannem Wottone laborer, Henricum Coupere nuper seruientem Iohannis Clerk fysshere de Oxonia, Iohannem Hedyndone carpenter, Iohannem nuper seruientem Iohannis Hikkes de Oxonia, Ricardum Carpenter nuper seruientem Willelmi Dageuile de Oxonia & Willelmum Cartere nuper seruientem Thome Maister de Oxonia de comitatu in comitatum quousque secundum legem & consuetudinem regni nostri Anglie utlagarentur si non compererent, & si compererent tunc eos caperes & in prisona nostra saluo custodiri faceres, ita quod haberes corpora eorum coram dilectis & fidelibus nostris Ricardo de Garstone maiore ville Oxonie & sociis suis iusticiariis nostris ad pacem &c. in villa Oxonie & suburbiis eiusdem conseruandam assignatis apud Oxoniam die Lune proximo ante festum sancti Hillarii proximo futurum ad respondendum nobis de diuersis excessibus unde indictati sunt; quia tamen predicti Iohannes Wottone, Henricus Coupere, Iohannes Hedyndone, Iohannes nuper seruiens Iohannis Hikkes, Ricardus Carpenter & Willelmus Cartere coram predictis iusticiariis nostris comparuerunt & inuenerunt nobis sufficientem securitatem essendi coram dictis iusticiariis nostris ad diem & locum predictos ad respondendum nobis de diuersis excessibus antedictis, tibi precipimus quod de predictos Iohannem Wottone, Henricum Coupere,

Iohannem Hedyndone, Iohannem nuper seruientem Iohannis Hikkes, Ricardum Carpenter & Willelmum Cartere ulterius ad aliquem alium comitatum Oxon' exigendo, capiendo, utlagando seu in aliquo molestando occasione premissa omnino supersedeas. Et habeas ibi hoc breue. Teste R. de Garstone maiore ville Oxonie apud Oxoniam vicesimo die Decembris anno regni nostri quintodecimo

Robertus Bulloke vicecomes

Ad comitatum Oxon' tentum apud Oxoniam die Iouis xiiii^o^ die Septembris anno regni regis Ricardi secundi post conquestum Anglie quintodecimo Iohannes Wottone laborer, Willelmus Neuylle nuper seruiens Nicholai Saundresdone de Oxonia, Michael Neel & Henricus Coupere nuper seruientes Iohannis Clerke fysshere de Oxonia, Stephanus Cartere & Thomas Hille nuper seruientes Reginaldi Tannere de Oxonia, Thomas Cony nuper seruiens Iohannis Utteworthe de Oxonia, Iohannes Hedyndone carpenter, Iohannes Hosteler nuper seruiens Iohannis Charlee de Oxonia, Iohannes nuper seruiens Iohannis Hikkes de Oxonia, Iohannes Kent laborer, Iohannes Clerke nuper seruiens Ricardi Iremongere de Oxonia, Iohannes Cornysshe & Ricardus Carpenter nuper seruientes Willelmi Dageuille de Oxonia, Willelmus Cartere nuper seruiens Thome Maister de Oxonia, Iohannes nuper seruiens Iohannis White de Oxonia, Alicia nuper seruiens Iohannis Taillour de Oxonia, Iuliana nuper seruiens Iohannis Bereford de Oxonia bocher & Agnes nuper seruiens Iohannis White de Oxonia, primo exacti fuerunt secundum tenorem istius breuis, et non comparuerunt.

Ad comitatum Oxonie tentum apud Oxoniam die Iouis xii die Octobris anno supradicto predicti Iohannes Wottone, Willelmus, Michael, Henricus, Stephanus, Thomas, Thomas, Iohannes Hedyndone, Iohannes Hosteler, Iohannes nuper seruiens Iohannis Hikkes, Iohannes Kent, Iohannes Clerke, Iohannes Cornysshe, Ricardus Carpenter, Willelmus Cartere, Iohannes nuper seruiens Iohannis White, Alicia, Iuliana & Agnes secundo exacti fuerunt & non comparuerunt.

Ad comitatum Oxonie tentum apud Oxoniam die Iouis nono die Nouembris anno supradicto predicti Iohannes Wottone, Willelmus, Michael, Henricus, Stephanus, Thomas, Thomas, Iohannes Hedyndone, Iohannes Hosteler, Iohannes nuper seruiens Iohannis Hikkes, Iohannes Kent, Iohannes Clerke, Iohannes Cornysshe, Ricardus,

Willelmus, Iohannes nuper seruiens Iohannis White, Alicia, Iuliana & Agnes tercio exacti fuerunt & non comparuerunt.

Ad comitatum Oxonie tentum apud Oxoniam die Iouis septimo die Decembris anno supradicto predicti Iohannes Wottone, Willelmus, Michael, Henricus, Stephanus, Thomas, Thomas, Iohannes Hedyndone, Iohannes Hosteler, Iohannes nuper seruiens Iohannis Hikkes, Iohannes Kent, Iohannes Clerke, Iohannes Cornysshe, Ricardus, Willelmus, Iohannes nuper seruiens Iohannis White, Alicia, Iuliana & Agnes quarto exacti fuerunt secundum tenorem istius breuis, et non comparuerunt; set quidam Thomas Hertone venit & manucepit de habendo corpora eorum ad proximum comitatum ad standum recto &c.

Et ad comitatum Oxonie tentum apud Oxoniam die Iouis quarto die Ianuarii anno supradicto predicti Iohannes Wottone laborer, Willelmus Neuyle nuper seruiens Nicholai Saundresdone de Oxonia, Michael Neel, Henricus Coupere nuper seruiens Iohannis Clerke fisshere de Oxonia, Stephanus Cartere & Thomas Hille nuper seruientes Reginaldi Tannere de Oxonia, Thomas Cony nuper seruiens Iohannis Utteworthe de Oxonia, Iohannes Hedyndone carpenter, Iohannes Hosteler nuper seruiens Iohannis Charlee de Oxonia, Iohannes nuper seruiens Iohannis Hikkes de Oxonia, Iohannes Kent laborer, Iohannes Clerk nuper seruiens Ricardi Iremongere de Oxonia, Iohannes Cornysshe & Ricardus Carpenter nuper seruientes Willelmi Dageuyle de Oxonia, Willelmus Cartere nuper seruiens Thome Maister de Oxonia, Iohannes nuper seruiens Iohannis White de Oxonia, Alicia nuper seruiens Philippi Taillour de Oxonia, Iuliana nuper seruiens Iohannis Bereford de Oxonia bochere & Agnes nuper seruiens Iohannis White de Oxonia quinto exacti fuerunt secundum tenorem istius breuis. Et predicti Iohannes Wottone, Henricus Coupere, Iohannes Hedyndone, Iohannes nuper seruiens Iohannis Hikkes de Oxonia, Ricardus Carpenter nuper seruiens Willelmi Dageuyle de Oxonia & Willelmus Cartere nuper seruiens Thome Maister de Oxonia comparuerunt & tulerunt breue domini regis de supersedendo, virtute cuius breuis supersedi; quod quidem breue de supersedendo vobis mitto huic breui de exigendo consutum. Et predicti Willelmus Neuyle nuper seruiens Nicholai Saundresdone de Oxonia, Michael Neel nuper seruiens Iohannis Clerke fisshere de Oxonia, Stephanus Cartere & Thomas Hille nuper seruientes Reginaldi Tannere de Oxonia, Thomas Cony nuper seruiens Iohannis Utteworthe de Oxonia, Iohannes Hosteler nuper seruiens Iohannis Charlee de Oxonia, Iohannes Kent laborer, Iohannes Clerke nuper seruiens Ricardi Iremongere de Oxonia, Iohannes Cornysshe, Iohannes nuper seruiens Iohannis White de Oxonia, Alicia nuper seruiens Philippi Taillour de Oxonia, Iuliana nuper seruiens Iohannis Bereforde de Oxonia bochere & Agnes nuper seruiens Iohannis White de Oxonia non comparuerunt. Ideo, ad iudicium per Thomam Langenhulle & Iohannem Harpour coronatores comitatus predicti, predicti Willelmus Neuyle, Michael Neel, Stephanus Cartere, Thomas Hille, Thomas Cony, Iohannes Hosteler nuper seruiens Iohannis Charlee de Oxonia, Iohannes Kent laborer, Iohannes Clerke nuper seruiens Ricardi Irmongere de Oxonia, Iohannes Cornysshe & Iohannes nuper seruiens Iohannis White de Oxonia utlagati sunt, et predicte Alicia nuper seruiens Philippi Taillour de Oxonia, Iuliana nuper seruiens Iohannis Bereforde de Oxonia bochere & Agnes nuper seruiens Iohannis White de Oxonia wayniate sunt [1]

Et super hoc super securitatem prius dictis iusticiariis inuentam isto die comparuerunt videlicet Iohannes Wottone laborer, Henricus Coupere nuper seruiens Iohannis Clerk fysshere de Oxonia, Iohannes Hedyndone carpenter, Iohannes nuper seruiens Iohannis Hikkes, Ricardus Carpenter nuper seruiens Willelmi Dageuille de Oxonia, Willelmus Cartere nuper seruiens Thome Maister de Oxonia, qui non potuerunt dedicere transgressiones predictas & posuerunt se in gracia regis; quorum fines patent ut sequntur, videlicet :—

De Iohanne Wottone laborer pro excessu capto per plegium Henrici Markham & Ricardi Bristowe viii d.

De Henrico Coupere nuper seruiente Iohannis Clerke fysshere de Oxonia pro consimili per plegium Simonis Whelere & Ricardi Bristowe viii d.

De Iohanne Hedyndone carpenter pro eodem per plegium Thome Hamptone & Nicholai Nortone [2] x d.

De Iohanne nuper seruiente Iohannis Hickes pro consimili per plegium Iohannis Sprunt & Willelmi Gerueys viii d.

De Ricardo Carpenter nuper seruiente Willelmi Dageuille pro consimili per plegium Iohannis Maltone & Thome Hamptone viii d.

De Willelmo Cartere nuper seruiente Thome Maister pro consimili per plegium Iohannis White & Iohannis Wadyn iiii d.

[1] This return is on the back of the former writ. At this point the main record recommences.

[2] *Iohannis Forster* is written above this name.

Memorandum quod ubi certe & diuerse persone causa diuersarum materiarum superius allegatarum habuerunt diem usque istas sessiones, adhuc certis de causis habent diem usque proximas sessiones sequentes. Et eciam [ubi][1] uicecomes habuit in mandatis ad venire faciendum certas personas hic coram iusticiariis predictis ad hunc diem & eciam habuit in mandatis ad capi faciendum certas personas & illos hic ad hunc diem habendum, uicecomes nullum retornauit preceptum &c. Ideo preceptum est dicto uicecomiti quod non omittat &c. quin execucionem faciat in premissis contra sessiones proximas &c. Et iam omnes materie predicte tam ut predictum est certis de causis respectuate quam omnes materie que exequi debuissent per dictum uicecomitem plenarie annotantur in proximis sessionibus sequentibus &c.

Mar. 27-30, 1392

Placita tenta apud Oxoniam diebus Mercurii, Iouis, Veneris & Sabati in quarta septimana quadragesime anno regni regis Ricardi secundo post conquestum Anglie quintodecimo coram Ricardo de Garstone maiore ville Oxonie & Ricardo Ouertone iusticiariis domini regis virtute predictarum posteriorum litterarum domini regis &c.

Willelmo Gerueys clerico tunc ibidem.

Erga quem diem Mercurii antedictum in predicta quarta septimana quadragesime dicto anno xv^mo^ preceptum fuit per dictos iusticiarios vicecomiti Oxonie quod non omitteret propter aliquam libertatem in comitatu predicto quin venire faceret coram eisdem iusticiariis apud Oxoniam dicto die Mercurii omnes constabularios cuiuslibet warde siue quarterii ville Oxonie; et quod predicti constabularii, videlicet quilibet eorum in warda sua haberet tunc ibidem nomina omnium artificum, operariorum, laborariorum, seruientum, venatorum, mendicancium ac omnium aliorum hominum, qui se nominant trauaillyngemen, in warda sua commorancium imbreuiata &c.; et preter illos quod idem vicecomes tunc ibidem haberet de qualibet warda predicta XVIII probos & legales homines ad faciendum ibidem ea que eis ex parte domini regis per dictos iusticiarios adtunc iniungerentur; et quod idem vicecomes haberet tunc ibidem nomina dictorum constabulariorum ac XVIII hominum de qualibet warda & mandatum suum &c.

Ad quem diem Mercurii in quarta septimana quadragesime dictus vicecomes retornauit nomina omnium constabulariorum wardarum

[1] Not in MS.

predictarum, videlicet de le Northest Warde Iohannes Bilburghe & de Northwest Warde Iohannes Miltone & de le Southest Warde Iohannes Lundone & de le Southewest Warde Iohannes Hembury; et quod precepit eisdem constabulariis quod ipsi videlicet quilibet eorum in warda sua haberet tunc ibidem nomina omnium artificum, operariorum, laborariorum, seruientum, venatorum, mendicancium ac omnium aliorum hominum mendicancium qui se nominant trauaillyngemen. Retornauit eciam dictus vicecomes nomina dictorum XVIII hominum de qualibet warda dictarum quatuor wardarum. Et ulterius dicti constabularii comparuerunt & retornauerunt diuersa nomina artificum, operariorum, laborariorum & seruitorum de wardis suis scilicet quilibet eorum de balliua sua; de quibus quidam accusati fuerunt per certas iuratas separatim de dictis wardis captas & quidam excusati, et de dictis accusatis inferius plene patet, videlicet in primis,

Northe Est Warde

De XVIII liberis & legalibus hominibus retornatis per dictum vicecomitem de warda ista XII^cim^ isto eodem die Mercurii comparuerunt, quorum nomina sic patent videlicet Iohannes Bukyngham, Nicholaus Kent, Iohannes White taillour, Thomas Babbeley, Michael Salesbury, Iohannes Wadyn, Thomas Chaundeler, Thomas Botiller, Thomas Mayster, Michael Hulot, Henricus Freman & Willelmus Codesdone; quibus quidem XII^cim^ retorna facta per constabularium istius warde ostensa fuerunt, et qui quidem XII^cim^ iurati & onerati iuxta formam dictarum posteriorum litterarum domini regis dicunt super sacramentum suum quod de dictis accusatis Iohannes Thacham masone, Philippus Carpenter carpentarius, Laurencius Masone lathomus, Iohannes Holewey sclattere & Iohannes Brown laborer ceperunt per les iourneyes excessiue ab ultimis sessionibus dictorum iusticiariorum usque sessiones istas contra formam statutorum; set de quibus personis, dictis iuratis non constat. Et ulterius predicti XII iurati dicunt quod omnes seruientes subscripti, retenti cum magistris suis subscriptis ad sibi deseruiendum a festo Michaelis ultimo preterito usque idem festum proximo sequens, ceperunt excessiue per eandem conuencionem ante sessiones istas contra formam statutorum & predicti magistri sui eisdem dederunt excessiue & soluerunt, quorum magistrorum & seruitorum nomina inferius aperte patent, videlicet:—

Memb. 15 *d*

Magistri	Seruitores
Iohannes Wadyn, smyth,	Iohannes seruiens eiusdem
Michael Salesbury	Iohannes seruiens eiusdem

Dicunt eciam iurati predicti quod Ricardus Brounyng sutor vendidit sotulares & alia de arte sua excessiue; sed de quantitate rei sic vendite aut quibus personis, dictis iuratis non constat.

Northe West Warde

De XVIII liberis & legalibus hominibus retornatis per uicecomitem predictum de warda ista XII^cim isto eodem die Mercurii comparuerunt, quorum nomina sic patent, Iohannes Dadyngtone, Willelmus Iremongere, Iohannes Charle, Iohannes Keruere, Gilbertus Cappere, Thomas Seturtone, Ricardus Broun, Willelmus Hamptone chaundeler, Iohannes Lekhampstede, Henricus Moryce, Henricus More chaundeler & Willelmus Merstone; qui quidem iurati & onerati iuxta formam dictarum posteriorum litterarum domini regis, & quibus quidem XII^cim retorna facta per constabularium istius warde ostensa fuerunt, & qui XII^cim dicunt per sacramentum suum quod de dictis accusatis Rogerus Carpenter carpentarius, Iohannes Goldfynch carpentarius, Ricardus Waterman sclattere, Thomas Carpenter, Iohannes Carpenter carpentarii, Iohannes Wilts' carpentarius, Henricus Wykeham brewere, Willelmus Cokeham brewere, & Iohannes Masone lathomus ceperunt par les iourneyes excessiue ab ultimis sessionibus dictorum iusticiariorum usque sessiones istas contra formam statutorum; set de quibus personis, dictis iuratis non constat. Et ulterius predicti XII iurati dicunt quod omnes seruientes subscripti retenti cum magistris suis subscriptis a festo sancti Michaelis ultimo preterito usque idem festum proximo sequens ad sibi deseruiendum ceperunt excessiue per conuencionem illam ante sessiones istas contra formam statutorum, & dicti magistri eisdem dederunt excessiue & soluerunt; quorum magistrorum & seruitorum nomina inferius aperte patent, videlicet:—

Magistri	Seruitores
Iohannes Cade	Willelmus Bernard Tibota Tapstere
Iohannes Lepere	Lucas Fournour Willelmus Wylkyn
Iohannes Hickes	Ricardus & Willelmus seruientes
Iohannes Appelford	Alicia seruiens eiusdem
Willelmus Iremongere	Cristina seruiens eiusdem
Iohannes Charley	Robertus Brewere
Iohannes Bernard, lokyere	Iohannes & Thomas, seruientes eiusdem
Willelmus Ottemore	Willelmus Brewere Willelmus Stanley

Southe Est Warde

De XVIII liberis & legalibus hominibus retornatis per dictum vicecomitem de warda ista XIIcim isto eodem die Mercurii comparuerunt, quorum nomina sic patent, Iohannes Dentone, Iohannes Swanbourne, Iohannes Botelstone, Willelmus Prentys, Iohannes Holme, Iohannes Bereforde spicer, Robertus Andrew, Thomas Wormecote, Iohannes Grome webbe, Iohannes Dicondawe, Willelmus Ferour & Iohannes Robarde; qui onerati & iurati iuxta formam dictarum posteriorum litterarum domini regis, & quibus quidem XIIcim retorna facta per dictum constabularium istius warde ostensa fuerunt; qui dicunt neminem illorum retornatorum esse culpabilem de aliquibus articulis dictis litteris regiis contentis &c.

Southe West Warde

De XVIII liberis & legalibus hominibus retornatis per dictum vicecomitem de warda ista XIIcim isto eodem die Mercurii comparuerunt, quorum nomina sic patent, Ricardus Wyndel, Galfridus Harle, Thomas Whitele, Iohannes Walkere, Edwardus Crooke, Ricardus Westerdale, Iohannes Benet cook, Hugo Webbe, Iohannes Marche dyere, Galfridus Fullere, Rogerus Euerard & Iohannes Cook webbe; qui onerati & iurati iuxta formam dictarum posteriorum litterarum regis, & quibus quidem XIIcim retorna facta per dictum constabularium istius warde ostensa fuerunt, qui dicunt neminem illorum retornatorum esse culpabilem de aliquibus articulis dictis litteris regiis contentis &c.

Ac eciam preceptum fuit nuper per iusticiarios antedictos vicecomiti Oxonie quod non omitteret propter aliquam libertatem in balliua sua quin venire faceret coram dictis iusticiariis dicto die Iouis in quarta septimana quadragesime apud Oxoniam omnes constabularios hundredi & suburbii extra portam borialem ville Oxonie, & quod dicti constabularii haberent tunc ibidem nomina omnium artificum, operariorum, seruitorum, laborariorum, mendicancium, venatorum ac aliorum hominum qui se nominant trauaillyngemen imbreuiata; et preter illos quod idem vicecomes tunc ibidem haberet XVIII probos & legales homines hundredi & suburbii predict*orum* ad faciendum que ex parte domini regis eis iniungerentur; et quod idem vicecomes tunc ibidem haberet nomina dictorum XVIII ac constabulariorum predictorum & war*antum* suum &c.

Ad quem diem Iouis in quarta septimana quadragesime dictus vicecomes retornauit nomina omnium constabulariorum hundredi &

suburbii predict', et quod precipit eis secundum warantum suum &c., & quod execucionem fecit de dicto waranto suo ut inferius &c.

Hundredum extra portam borialem ville Oxonie

Willelmus Bakere & Iohannes Stantone constabularii comparuerunt & retornauerunt nomina artificum, operariorum, seruitorum, laborariorum, & hostellariorum de quibus plures accusati fuerunt per XII de XVIII hominibus per vicecomitem retornatis, quorum XII ac accusatorum predictorum nomina patent inferius, videlicet de predictis XII, Willelmus Ryuel, Ricardus atte Seler, Iohannes Scryueyn, Michel [*sic*] Smyth, Iohannes Tannere, Iohannes Ropere, Willelmus Whelere, Willelmus Cook, Willelmus Heynes, Thomas Webbe, Iohannes Meteburne & Willelmus Wodestoke; qui iurati & onerati iuxta formam dictarum posteriorum litterarum domini regis dicunt super sacramentum suum quod de dictis accusatis Iohannes Bloxham masone, Henricus Masone masone, Ricardus Prestone masone, Ricardus Basset sclattere, Iohannes Daubere, Iohannes Aubel sclattere, Petrus Pyrone daubere, Iohannes Stampe thecchere, Willelmus Heynes sclattere, Willelmus Stanlake masone, Nicholaus Carpenter, Ricardus Bekkewode sawiere, Ricardus Nortone masone & Rogerus Masone ac Willelmus Coupere, coupere, ceperunt par les iourneyes excessiue contra formam statutorum ab ultimis sessionibus dictorum iusticiariorum usque sessiones istas; set de quibus personis, dictis iuratis non constat. Et ulterius dicti iurati dicunt quod omnes seruientes subscripti retenti cum magistris suis subscriptis a festo sancti Michaelis ultimo preterito usque idem festum proximo sequens ad sibi deseruiendum ceperunt excessiue per conuencionem illam ante sessiones istas contra formam statutorum, & dicti magistri sui eisdem dederunt excessiue & soluerunt, quorum magistrorum & seruitorum nomina inferius aperte patent, vicelicet:—

Magistri	Seruitores
Thomas Howkyn	Iohannes Cosyn Willelmus Morley
Ricardus Burghe, bochere	Iohannes seruiens eiusdem
Willelmus Chiselhamptone	Robertus seruiens eiusdem

Dicunt eciam dicti iurati quod Iohannes Scryueyn cordewanarius, Loccus cordewanarius, Iohannes Yerdele cordewanarius, Nicholaus Metebourne cordewanarius, Iohannes Forster cordewanarius & Iohannes Mileward cordewanarius vendiderunt sotulares & alia de arte sua excessiue contra formam statutorum, set quantitatem rei vendite & quibus personis, dictis iuratis non constat.

Memb. 14 *d*

Item iurati predicti dicunt quod Willelmus Bray skynnere, Simon Sadelere sadelere, & Reginaldus Geddyng webbe excessiue ceperunt quilibet in arte sua contra ordinacionem statutorum, set de quantitate & de quibus personis iurati ignorant.

Item dicunt quod Thomas Colman webbe & Henricus & Iohannes seruientes eiusdem tam magistri dando eis excessiue quam ipsi seruientes capiendo excessiue contra ordinaciones statutorum &c.

Et ulterius ad maiorem inquisicionem ex parte domini regis de omnibus predictis retornatis, ut predicitur, & non accusatis ac pro articulis in dictis litteris contentis plenius informandis isto eodem die Iouis in quarta septimana quadragesime preceptum est dicto vicecomiti quod non omittat propter aliquam libertatem in balliua sua quin venire faciat coram dictis iusticiariis dicto die Veneris in quarta septimana quadragesime xviii de discrecioribus & probioribus hominibus ville Oxonie & eius suburbiis, qui artifices &c. nullo modo attingant &c. ad faciendum &c. Ad quem quidem diem Veneris in quarta septimana quadragesime dictus vicecomes retornauit nomina xviii^{cim} hominum &c., de quibus xii comparuerunt, quorum nomina inferius patent; qui onerati & iurati iuxta formam dictarum litterarum posteriorum domini regis, ac visis retornis predictis, dicunt quod Iohannes Ledecombe cordewanarius, Iohannes Whatele cordewanarius, Iohannes Lekhampstede cordewanarius, Iohannes Keruere cordewanarius, Philippus Forsthulle cordewanarius, Iohannes Robard cordewanarius, Thomas Waryner cordewanarius, Willelmus Codesdone & Galfridus Brehulle cordewanarii vendiderunt sotulares & alia de arte sua excessiue contra formam statutorum, set quantitatem rei uendite & quibus personis iurati ignorant. Item quod omnes sissores subscripti, videlicet Iohannes Clyuedone taillour, Iohannes Lytherpole, Iohannes White, Thomas Babbeley, Iohannes Stillyngtone, Matheus Taillour, Ricardus Waldene, Hugo Welssheman taillour, Michael Hulot, Galfridus Taillour, Henricus Moryce taillour, Walterus Burnham, Iohannes Spicer taillour, Ricardus Preyere, Robertus Andrew, Iohannes Northe, Iohannes Beaulew, Dauid Bromfeld & Willelmus Bukyngham sissores excessiue ceperunt pro nonnullis garnementis faciendis contra formam statutorum, set de quibus personis aut de numero garnementorum predictorum iurati predicti ignorant. Dicunt eciam dicti iurati quod omnes pellettarii subscripti videlicet Simon Crosse, Robertus Skynnere, Henricus Bilburghe, Willelmus Bergeueny, Iohannes Trenacle, Ricardus Kudlyngtone, Ricardus Skynnere de le southwest warde &

Iohannes Miltone excessiue ceperunt in arte sua vendendo fururas &c., & capiendo pro arte sua; set quantitatem rei vendite aut de quibus personis, iuratis predictis non constat. Dicunt eciam iurati predicti quod omnes ar ifices subscripti videlicet Carolus Goldsmyth aurifaber, Henricus Faryndon cellar*ius* [1], Willelmus Webbe textor, Willelmus Fourbour fourbour, Willelmus Waget sellar*ius*, Iohannes Westone cellar*ius*, Iohannes Dyne cellar*ius*, Iohannes Gybbes dyere, Iohannes Spyrewhit masone, Iohannes Staundone laborer, Gilbertus Cokermouth pathyere [2], Iohannes Goldsmyth aurifaber, Iohannes Ferour ferour, Iohannes Tannare tannere, Walterus Carpenter carpentarius, Ricardus Westerdale dyere, Iohannes Marche dyere, Ricardus Brayn dyere, Ricardus Hudescombe tegulator & Reginaldus Tannere tannere scilicet omnes artifices predicti quilibet in arte sua excessiue cepit & vendidit contra formam statutorum, set quantitatem capcionis aut rei vendite dicti iurati ignorant. Et dicti Iohannes Spirewhit masone, Iohannes Stauntone laborer & Gilbertus Cokermouth excessiue ceperunt de diuersis hominibus ab ultimis sessionibus dictorum iusticiariorum usque sessiones istas par les iourneyes; set de quibus personis, dictis iuratis non constat; quorum quidem iuratorum nomina hec sunt, videlicet Iohannes Forster, Iohannes Bukyngham, Nicholaus Nortone, Willelmus Iremongere, Iohannes Marchall fysshere, Willelmus Swanbourne, Iohannes Bereforde spicer, Ricardus Wyndel, Rogerus Maddok, Thomas Whitele, Iohannes Charley & Henricus Freman. Dicunt eciam iurati predicti quod omnes seruientes subscripti retenti cum magistris suis subscriptis a festo sancti Michaelis archangeli ultimo preterito usque idem festum proximo sequens per conuencionem illam excessiue & contra ordinaciones &c. ante sessiones istas de eisdem magistris suis ceperunt & iidem magistri eisdem seruientibus suis excessiue dederunt contra formam statutorum &c.; quorum quidem magistrorum ac seruitorum nomina inferius aperte patent, videlicet:—

Magistri	Seruitores
Iuliana Gerland	Iohannes seruiens eiusdem
Iohannes Forster	Thomas seruiens eiusdem
Iohannes Miltone skynnere	Willelmus Hostiller Matilda Tapstere
Iohannes Walsshe dyere	Thomas Dyere
Iohannes Marche dyere	Iohannes Chamberleyn

[1] i. e. sellarius.

[2] i. e. *pavyere*: s. v. *pathing*, N. E. D.

Iohannes Utteworthe	Iohannes Forster Walterus Wiltsshire Iohannes Harry Iohannes Abyndone
Ricardus Battesyn	Iohannes Hostiller
Iohannes Shawe	Iohannes Dorchestre
Reginaldus Tannere	Petrus Brewere Willelmus Brewere Ricardus Waterman
Willelmus Iremongere	Cristina seruiens eiusdem [1]
Nicholaus Spicer	Thomas Fysshewik Willelmus Chestertone
Iohannes Clerk fysshere	Willelmus Cleue
Ricardus Westerdale diere	Willelmus seruiens eiusdem
Ricardus Brayn diere	Iohannes seruiens eiusdem
Iohannes Faukoner	Iohannes seruiens eiusdem Alexander Brewere Iohannes Befford
Thomas Forsthulle	[*blank*] Brewere
Iohannes Merstone	Iohannes Somertone hostillarius
Iohannes Walsyngham	Iohannes Hostiller

Et super hoc isto eodem die Iouis in quarta septimana quadragesime preceptum est vicecomiti Oxonie quod non omittat propter aliquam libertatem in balliua sua quin venire faciat coram predictis nunc iusticiariis apud Oxoniam dicto die Veneris in predicta quarta septimana quadragesime omnes & singulos accusatos predictos ad respondendum separatim domino regi de transgressionibus & excessibus predictis &c.

North Est Warde. Retornum inde factum per vicecomitem die Veneris in quarta septimana quadragesime anno xv^{mo}

Ad quem diem Veneris in quarta septimana quadragesime predictus vicecomes retornauit quod de predictis accusatis Iohannes Thacham masone, Laurencius Masone & Iohannes Holewey sclattere attachiati sunt per plegium Ricardi Haryng & Willelmi Est, qui omnes comparuerunt, et non potuerunt dedicere transgressiones predictas. Et posuerunt se in gracia regis, quorum fines patent ut sequntur:—

Fines

De Iohanne Thacham masone pro excessu capto per plegium Iohannis Bereforde spicer & Henrici Hamptone viii d.

[1] This line is crossed out and 'quia alibi ut plene patet ante' written.

De Laurencio Masone latamo pro eodem per plegium Iohannis Bilburghe & Iohannis White taillour viii d.
De Iohanne Holeway sclattere pro consimili per plegium Michaelis Salesbury & Iohannis Coupere viii d.

Retornauit eciam dictus vicecomes quod de dictis magistris & seruientibus quod Michael Salesbury & Iohannes seruiens eius, Iohannes Wadyn smyth & Iohannes seruiens eiusdem, attachiati sunt per plegium Iohannis Hert & Willelmi Kene qui comparuerunt, & de quibus Michael Salesbury & Iohannes seruiens eiusdem non potuerunt dedicere transgressiones predictas, set posuerunt se in gracia regis, quorum fines patent ut sequntur videlicet :—
De Michaele Salesbury pro excessu per plegium Thome Hamptone & Iohannis White iiii d.
De Iohanne seruiente Michaelis Salesbury pro excessu capto per plegium Thome Hamptone & Iohannis White vi d.

Et dictus Iohannes Wadyn dicit quod conuenit cum dicto Iohanne seruiente suo quod ei daret sicut iusticiarii ordinare uellent & aliter non, & de hoc ponit se super patriam &c. Et dictus Iohannes seruiens eiusdem Iohannis Wadyn dicit quod conuenit cum predicto magistro suo quod de eo acciperet sicut iusticiarii ordinare uellent &c. Et aliter non &c. Et de hoc ponit se super patriam &c.

Et quo ad venire faciendum Philippum Carpenter carpentarium, Iohannem Broun laborer & Ricardum Brounyng cordewanarium &c. idem vicecomes iam retornauit quod ipsi nichil habent, & ideo preceptum est dicto vicecomiti quod non omittat &c., quin eos &c., ita quod illos habeat coram &c. ad proximas sessiones &c., eo quod ipsi iam non uenerunt &c.

Et quo ad execucionem faciendam versus Iulianam Gerlaund & Iohannem seruientem eiusdem, Iohannem Forester & Thomam seruientem eius vicecomes nullum retornauit preceptum. Ideo preceptum est &c. contra proximas sessiones &c.

North West Warde. Retornum inde factum per vicecomitem die Veneris in quarta septimana quadragesime anno xv^{mo} **Memb. 13** *d*

Retornauit eciam dictus vicecomes isto eodem die Veneris in quarta septimana quadragesime quod de predictis accusatis de warda ista Rogerus Carpenter carpentarius, Iohannes Goldfynche carpentarius, Iohannes Lekhampstede cordewanarius, Iohannes Whatele cordewanarius, Ricardus Waterman sclattere, Iohannes Thacham carpentarius, Iohannes Wiltshire carpentarius, Rogerus Waryn brewere, Henricus Wykeham brewere, Willelmus Cokham brewere attachiati sunt per plegium Ricardi Kent & Iohannis Herde, qui omnes comparuerunt in propriis personis suis preter Rogerum Carpenter qui venit per Willelmum Masone de Eynesham attornatum suum coram dictis iusticiariis rec*eptum*. Et preter Iohannem Lekhampstede non potuerunt dedicere transgressiones supradictas. Et ponunt se in gracia regis, quorum fines patent ut sequntur, videlicet in primis:—

De Rogero Carpenter carpentario pro excessu capto per plegium dicti Willelmi Masone de Eynesham & Thome Hamptone viii d.

De Iohanne Goldfynche carpentario pro consimili per plegium Willelmi Iremongere & Henrici Moryce viii d.

De Iohanne Whatele cordewanario pro consimili per plegium Iohannis Lekhampstede & Philippi Forsthulle viii d.

De Ricardo Waterman sclattere pro consimili per plegium Iohannis Miltone skynnere & Roberti Purdy viii d.

De Iohanne Thacham carpentario pro consimili per plegium Iohannis Bernard & Iordani Penket viii d.

De Iohanne Wiltshire carpentario pro consimili per plegium Iohannis Bernard & Iordani Penket viii d.

De Rogero Waryn brewere pro consimili per plegium Willelmi Doke cook & Willelmi Hamptone vi d.

De Henrico Wykeham brewere pro consimili per plegium Iohannis White taillour & Iohannis Bilburghe vi d.

De Willelmo Cokeham brewere pro consimili per plegium Iohannis Bernard & Elie Bowyere vi d.

Et dictus Iohannes Lekhampstede cordewanarius dicit quod non vendidit sotulares & alia de arte sua excessiue contra formam statuti &c.; et de hoc ponit se super patriam &c.

Retornauit eciam dictus vicecomes isto eodem die Veneris in quarta septimana quadragesime quod de predictis magistris & seruientibus Iohannes Cade & Willelmus Bernard & Tibota Tapstere seruientes eiusdem, Iohannes Lepere & Lucas Fournour & Willelmus Wylkyn seruientes eiusdem Iohannis Lepere, Iohannes Hickes, Ricardus & Willelmus seruientes eiusdem Iohannis Hickes, Iohannes Appelford & Alicia seruiens eiusdem, Iohannes Miltone skinnere & Willelmus Hosteler & Matilda Tapstere seruientes eiusdem, Willelmus Iremongere & Cristina seruiens eiusdem, Iohannes Charley & Robertus Brewere seruiens eiusdem, Willelmus Ottemore & Willelmus Brewere & Willelmus Stanle seruientes eiusdem attachiati sunt per plegium

Ricardi Honte & Willelmi Etone, qui omnes comparuerunt; et de quibus dicti Iohannes Cade & Willelmus Bernard seruiens eius, Iohannes Appulford & Alicia seruiens eiusdem Iohannis non potuerunt dedicere transgressiones supradictas. Et posuerunt se in gracia regis, quorum fines patent ut sequntur, videlicet in primis:—

Fines de magistris

De Iohanne Cade pro excessu dato per plegium Ricardi Burghe & Ricardi Bristowe iiii d.

De Iohanne Appulford pro consimili per plegium Iohannis Miltone skynnere & Henrici Porter iiii d.

De Willelmo Iremongere pro consimili per plegium Thome Hamptone & Iohannis Bilburghe vi d.

De Iohanne Charley pro consimili per plegium Iohannis Miltone skynnere & Willelmi Hamptone chaundeler iiii d.

De Willelmo Ottemore pro consimili per plegium Thome Hamptone & Henrici Faryndone iiii d.

Fines de seruitoribus

De Willelmo Bernard seruiente Iohannis Cade pro excessu capto per plegium Ricardi Burghe & Ricardi Bristowe vi d.

De Alicia seruiente Iohannis Appulford pro consimili per plegium Iohannis Miltone skynnere & Henrici Porter iiii d.

De Cristina seruiente Willelmi Iremongere pro consimili per plegium Thome Hamptone & Henrici Porter iiii d.

De Roberto Brewere seruiente Iohannis Charley pro consimili per plegium Iohannis Miltone skynnere & Willelmi Hamptone chaundeler vi d.

De Willelmo Brewere seruiente Willelmi Ottemore pro consimili per plegium Henrici Faryndone & Willelmi Ottemore vi d.

De Willelmo Stanley seruiente Willelmi Ottemore pro consimili per plegium Thome Hamptone & Henrici Porter vi d.

Et ulterius predictus Iohannes Cade dicit quod dat dicte Tibote Tapstere seruienti sue VIII s. per annum &c., et non plus, & de hoc ponit se super patriam; & dicta Tibota eodem modo allegat ex parte sua; et de hoc ponit se super patriam &c. Et Iohannes Lepere dicit quod dat Luce Fournour & Willelmo Wylkyn secundum ordinacionem iusticiariorum &c., & sic cum eis conuencionem &c., et aliter non. Et de hoc ponit se super patriam &c. Et dicti Lucas & Willelmus Wylkyn eodem modo ex parte sua allegant & dicunt &c., et de hoc ponunt se [super][1] patriam &c. Et Iohannes Hickes dicit quod dat Ricardo seruienti suo XIIII s. per conuencionem & Willelmo seruienti suo x s., & non aliter, et de hoc ponit se super patriam &c. et dicti Ricardus & Willelmus seruientes dicti Iohannis Hickes pro se ipsis separatim allegant & dicunt modo quo magister suus predictus allegauit & dixit. Et quod sic est & aliter non, ponunt se super patriam &c. Et Iohannes Miltone skynnere dicit quod dat Willelmo Hosteler seruienti suo per annum XIII s. IIII d. & non plus nec cum eo conuenit pro alt*era*[2] summa nec Matilde seruienti sue nisi IIII s. pro dimidio anno &c., et de hoc ponit se super patriam. Et dicti seruientes eiusdem Iohannis dicunt quod est ut magister allegauit; et de hoc ponunt se super patriam &c.

Et ulterius dictus vicecomes retornauit isto eodem die Veneris in quarta septimana quadragesime quod predicti Thomas Carpenter, Iohannes Carpenter carpentarii, & Iohannes Masone ac Iohannes & Thomas seruientes Iohannis Bernard lokyere nichil habent in balliua sua per quod possunt attachiari &c. Ideo preceptum est dicto vicecomiti quod non &c. quin &c., ita quod eos habeat &c. ad proximas sessiones &c. ad respondendum &c., eo quod ipsi iam non uenerunt &c.; et quo ad execucionem faciendam versus Iohannem Bernard lokyere nullum retornauit preceptum; ideo preceptum est &c. ut supra contra proximas sessiones &c.

South Est Warde; retornum inde factum per uicecomitem die Veneris in quarta septimana quadragesime anno xv^mo

Retornauit eciam dictus vicecomes isto eodem die Veneris in quarta septimana quadragesime quod de predictis accusatis de warda ista Iohannes Sperewhit masone, Philippus Forsthulle cordewaner, Iohannes Stauntone laborer, Iohannes Robard cordewaner, Gilbertus Cokermouth pathyere, Ricardus Kudlyngtone skynnere, Nicholaus Spicer, Thomas & Willelmus Chestertone seruientes eiusdem Nicholai Spicer, Iohannes Clerk fysshere & Willelmus Cleue seruiens eiusdem Iohannis Clerk fysshere & Iohannes Ferour attachiati sunt per plegium Thome Wenge & Nicholai Kene qui omnes in propriis personis suis comparuerunt preter Nicholaum Spicer, qui comparuit per Iohannem Maltone attornatum suum coram predictis iusticiariis ante rec*eptum* &c. Et de quibus predicti Iohannes Spirewhit masone, Iohannes Stauntone laborer, Gilbertus Cokermouth & Iohannes Ferour non

[1] Omitted by the scribe. [2] Or alt*iori*.

potuerunt dedicere transgressiones predictas, et posuerunt [se][1] in gracia regis; quorum fines patent ut sequntur, videlicet in primis:—

De Iohanne Spirewhit masone pro excessu capto per plegium Iohannis Lundone & Iohannis Bereford spicer viii d.

De Iohanne Stauntone laborer pro consimili per plegium Iohannis Chadde & Willelmi Prentys viii d.

De Gilberto Cokermouth pro consimili per plegium Iohannis Bilburghe & Iohannis Marchall bochere viii d.

De Iohanne Ferour fabro pro consimili per plegium Thome Prest & Iohannis Marchall fysshere viii d.

Et ulterius predictus Nicholaus Spicer per dictum attornatum suum dicit quod dat dictis Thome Fysshwyke & Willelmo Chesterton secundum ordinacionem statut*orum* & non aliter; et de hoc ponit se super patriam &c. Et dicti seruientes sui dicunt quod accipiunt de dicto magistro suo secundum ordinacionem &c., et non aliter, & de hoc ponunt se super patriam. Ideo preceptum est vicecomiti ut inferius. Et dictus Philippus Forsthulle cordewanarius & Iohannes Roberd cordewanarius dicunt quod ipsi nullos sotulares nec aliqua alia de arte sua alicui vendiderunt contra statut*um* prout superius accusatur; et de hoc ponit se super patriam. Ideo preceptum est vicecomiti ut inferius. Et dictus Iohannes Clerke fysshere [dicit][1] quod ipse dedit dicto Willelmo Cleue seruienti suo secundum statutum, viz. secundum ordinacionem XIIII s. & aliter non. Et de hoc ponit se super patriam. Et dictus Willelmus Cleue dicit quod accipit de dicto magistro suo XIIII s., et non plus, & de hoc ponit se super patriam. Ideo preceptum est vicecomiti Oxonie quod non omittat &c., quin venire faciat coram dictis iusticiariis ad proximas sessiones XVIII probos & legales homines de villa Oxonie & suburbiis eiusdem ad faciendum iuratas illas &c., et qui nec &c.

Et ulterius isto eodem die Veneris in quarta septimana quadragesime Iohannes Londone & Iohannes Marche seruiens suus coram dictis iusticiariis comparuerunt, & cognouerunt quod fecerunt conuencionem &c. contra statutum. Et ponunt se inde in gracia regis, set nichil solutum fuit &c.; quorum fines patent ut sequntur, in primis:—

De Iohanne Londone quia fecit conuencionem cum Iohanne Marche seruiente suo, videlicet quod ei daret contra ordinacionem statuti, per plegium Nicholai Nortone & Willelmi Hamptone iiii d.

[1] Not in MS.

De Iohanne Marche seruiente Iohannis Lundone pro eodem per plegium supradictum iiii d.

Et ulterius dictus Ricardus Cudlyngtone dicit quod non debet coram dictis iusticiariis iustificari, quia dicit quod pellettarii habent quandam cartam a regibus Anglie eis concessam quod debent coram magistris de arte illa iustic*iari* &c.; et petit quod nichil ei fiat de iustic' illa &c. causa carte sue predicte &c. Et sic habet diem usque ad proximas sessiones ad demonstrandum cartam illam &c.

Memb. 12 *d*

Et ulterius ubi preceptum fuit vicecomiti Oxonie quod venire fecisset hic coram iusticiariis isto eodem die predictos Iohannem Gybbes dyere, Robertum Andrew taillour, Iohannem Northe taillour, Iohannem Trendale skynnere, Iohannem Beaule taillour, Thomam Waryner cordewaner, Iohannem Goldsmythe, Iohannem Ledecombe cordewaner, Willelmum Codesdone cordewaner, Iohannem Clyueden taillour, Iohannem Lytherpole, Iohannem White taillour, & omnes alios sissores videlicet Thomam Babbeley, Iohannem Styllyngtone, Matheum Taillour, Ricardum Waldene, Hugonem Welssheman, Michaelem Hulot, Galfridum Taillour, Henricum Moryce, Walterum Burnham, Iohannem Spicer & Ricardum Preyere & eciam omnes pellettarios subscriptos videlicet Simonem Crosse, Robertum Skynnere, Henricum Bilburghe, Willelmum Bergeueny & Iohannem Miltone; et omnes artifices subscriptos viz. Carolum Goldsmythe aurifabrum, Ricardum Hudescombe sclattere, Reginaldum Tannere, Iohannem Keruere cordewanarium & Henricum Faryndone cellar*ium*, Willelmum Webbe webbe, Willelmum Fourbour fourbour, Willelmum Waget cellar*ium*, Iohannem Westone cellar*ium*, Iohannem Dyne cellar*ium*, Ricardum Westerdale diere, Iohannem Marche diere, Ricardum Brayn diere, ad respondendum domino regi de excessibus &c. dictus vicecomes nullum retornauit preceptum. Ideo preceptum est dicto vicecomiti sicut alias quod non omittat propter aliquam libertatem &c., quin venire faciat omnes illos ad proximas sessiones &c. ad respondendum &c.

South West Warde. Retornum inde factum per vicecomitem in quarta septimana quadragesime anno xv^{mo}, videlicet die Sabati[1]

Retornauit eciam dictus vicecomes isto eodem die Veneris in quarta

[1] The last three words are an addition. Perhaps the business of this ward was begun on the Friday and concluded on the Saturday.

septimana quadragesime quod de predictis accusatis de warda ista Walterus Carpenter carpentarius, Iohannes Dacham carpentarius, Iohannes Utteworthe & Iohannes Abyndone & Iohannes Harry seruientes eiusdem Iohannes Utteworthe, Iohannes Faukoner & Iohannes seruiens eiusdem Iohannis Faukoner, Iohannes Befford & Alexander seruientes eiusdem Iohannis Faukoner, Galfridus Brehulle cordewaner, Ricardus Battesyn & Iohannes Hostiller seruiens eiusdem Ricardi, Iohannes Merstone & Iohannes Somertone seruiens suus & hostellarius &c., Iohannes Shawe & Iohannes Dorchestre seruiens suus, Reginaldus Tannere & Petrus Brewere, Willelmus Brewere & Ricardus Waterman seruientes eiusdem Reginaldi attachiati sunt per plegium Iohannis Kene & Willelmi Ace qui omnes comparuerunt; et de quibus predicti Walterus Carpenter, Iohannes Dacham, Iohannes Utteworthe, Iohannes Harry & Iohannes Abyndone seruientes eiusdem Iohannis, Iohannes Faukoner ac Iohannes, Iohannes Besseford & Alexander seruientes eiusdem Iohannis Faukoner, Iohannes Shawe & Iohannes Dorchestre seruiens eiusdem Iohannis Shawe, Reginaldus Tannere, Petrus Brewere, Willelmus Brewere & Ricardus Waterman seruientes eiusdem Reginaldi non potuerunt dedicere transgressiones supradictas, et posuerunt se in gracia regis, quorum fines patent ut sequntur, videlicet in primis:—

De Waltero Carpenter carpentario pro excessu capto per plegium Henrici Porter & Willelmi Newman — viii d.

De Iohanne Dacham pro consimili per plegium Walteri Stortone carpenter & Henrici Porter — viii d.

De Iohanne Utteworthe pro excessu dato per plegium Iohannis Shawe & Iohannis Faukoner — iiii d.

De Iohanne Harry seruiente Iohannis Utteworthe pro excessu capto per plegium Iohannis Shawe & Iohannis Faukoner — vi d.

De Iohanne Abyndone seruiente Iohannis Utteworthe pro consimili per plegium Iohannis Shawe & Iohannis Faukoner — vi d.

De Iohanne Faukoner pro excessu dato per plegium Iohannis Utteworthe & Willelmi Bergeueny — iiii d.

De Iohanne seruiente eiusdem Iohannis Faukoner pro excessu capto per plegium Iohannis Utteworthe & Willelmi Bergeueny — vi d.

De Iohanne Besseford seruiente dicti Iohannis Faukoner pro consimili per plegium Iohannis Utteworthe & Willelmi Bergeueny — vi d.

De Alexandro seruiente Iohannis Faukoner pro consimili per plegium Iohannis Utteworthe & Willelmi Bergeueny vi d.
De Iohanne Shawe pro excessu dato per plegium Iohannis Utteworthe & Iohannis Faukoner iiii d.
De Iohanne Dorchestre pro excessu capto per plegium Iohannis Utteworthe & Iohannis Faukoner vi d.
De Reginaldo Tannere pro excessu dato per plegium Thome Hamptone & Henrici Faryndone viii d.
De Petro Brewere seruiente dicti Reginaldi pro excessu capto per plegium Thome Hamptone & Henrici Faryndone vi d.
De Willelmo Brewere seruiente dicti Reginaldi pro consimili per plegium Thome Hamptone & Henrici Faryndone vi d.

Et de quibus predictis isto die comparentibus Galfridus Brehulle cordewanarius dicit quod non vendidit sotulares nec aliqua alia de arte sua contra statutum sicut accusatus est. Et de hoc ponit se super patriam. Ideo preceptum est vicecomiti ut inferius &c. Et predictus Ricardus Battesyn dicit quod non dat Iohanni Hostellario sua contra statutum. Et de hoc ponit se super patriam &c. Et dictus Iohannes Hosteller dicit ut magister suus &c. Et de hoc ponit se super patriam &c. Ideo preceptum est &c. Et dictus Iohannes Merstone dicit quod non dat Iohanni Somertone hostellario suo nisi XIII s. IIII d.; et de hoc ponit se super patriam. Et dictus Iohannes Somertone similiter. Ideo preceptum est dicto vicecomiti quod non omittat propter aliquam libertatem in balliua sua quin venire faciat &c. XVIII &c., videlicet ad proximas sessiones &c., qui nec &c. ad faciendum iuratas predictas.

Et ulterius ubi preceptum fuit dicto vicecomiti quod venire fecisset coram dictis iusticiariis ad diem hunc Iohannem Walsshe & Thomam Dyere seruientem eiusdem Iohannis, Iohannem Tannere, Ricardum Skynnere, Dauid Bromfeld taillour, Ricardum Westerdale dyere & Willelmum seruientem eiusdem Ricardi Westerdale, Iohannem Marche dyere & Iohannem Chamberleyn seruientem eiusdem Iohannis, Ricardum Brayn diere & Iohannem seruientem eiusdem, Martinum Cole & Robertum seruientem eiusdem Martini, Thomam Forsthulle & Iohannem Brewere seruientem eiusdem Thome, Willelmum Bokyngham taillour, Iohannem Walsyngham & Iohannem Hostiller seruientem eiusdem Iohannis Walsyngham, Iohannem Forester & Walterum Wiltshire seruientes I. Utteworthe ad respondendum domino regi de diuersis excessibus, unde ut superius patet accusati sunt, vicecomes nullum retornauit preceptum. Ideo preceptum est dicto vicecomiti sicut alias quod non omittat propter aliquam libertatem in comitatu Oxonie quin venire faciat coram dictis iusticiariis ad proximas sessiones omnes illos &c.

Et ulterius isto eodem die comparuerunt Iohannes Smyth & Robertus seruiens Martini Cole; et de quibus predictus Iohannes dicit quod est seruiens in arte fabri & capit per septimanam vi d.; et dictus Robertus dicit quod est seruiens dicti Martini in arte de Bakere & capit per conuencionem &c. a festo Natalis domini usque festum sancti Michaelis proximo sequens x s.; de capcione quorum hominum auisiandum est inter iusticiarios &c. contra proximas sessiones &c. Et super hoc in proximis sessionibus sequentibus per auisamentum iusticiariorum consideratum est quod dictus Iohannes capiat per septimanam ut supra. Et quod dictus Robertus similiter ut supra. Et in eisdem sessionibus dictus Robertus ponit se super patriam quod non cepit plus &c.

Hundredum extra portam borialem ville Oxonie. Retornum inde factum die Sabati in quarta septimana quadragesime anno xv^mo^ per vicecomitem Oxonie.

Retornauit eciam dictus vicecomes isto eodem die Sabati in quarta septimana quadragesime quod de predictis accusatis de hundredo isto Ricardus Nortone masone, Willelmus Chyselhamptone bochere & Robertus seruiens eiusdem, Iohannes Yerdele cordewaner, Nicholaus Metebourne cordewaner, Iohannes Forester cordewaner, Iohannes Milleward cordewaner, Willelmus Coupere coupere & Rogerus Masone attachiati sunt per plegium Ricardi Hert & Iohannis Staumpe, qui omnes comparuerunt in propriis personis suis, preter dictum Rogerum Masone qui comparuit per Willelmum Masone de Eynesham attornatum suum coram dictis iusticiariis ante recept*um*. Et preter dictos Willelmum Chyselhamptone & Robertum seruientem eiusdem Willelmi & dictum Willelmum Coupere non potuerunt dedicere transgressiones supradictas; et posuerunt se in gracia regis, quorum fines patent ut sequntur videlicet in primis:—

De Ricardo Nortone masone pro excessu capto per plegium Ricardi Brayn & Ricardi Prestone viii d.

Memb. II *d*

De Iohanne Yerdele cordewanario pro consimili per plegium Iohannis Bradele & Iohannis Milnere viii d.

De Nicholao Metebourne cordewanario pro consimili per plegium Iohannis Yerdele & Iohannis Bradele viii d.

De Iohanne Forester cordewanario pro consimili per plegium Iohannis Muleward & Iohannis Bradele viii d.

De Iohanne Muleward cordewanario pro consimili per plegium Iohannis Forester & Iohannis Bradele viii d.

De Rogero Masone, masone, pro excessu capto per plegium Thome Hamptone & Willelmi Masone de Eynesham viii d.

Et ulterius predictus Willelmus Chyselhamptone dicit quod non dedit dicto Roberto seruienti suo contra statutum &c. Et de hoc ponit se super patriam &c. Et eciam idem Robertus dicit quod non cepit de dicto magistro contra statuta & de hoc ponit se super patriam. Ideo preceptum est vicecomiti Oxonie quod non omittat propter aliquam libertatem in balliua sua quin venire faciat coram dictis iusticiariis apud Oxoniam ad proximas sessiones &c. XVIII &c. qui nec &c.

Retornauit eciam dictus vicecomes isto eodem die Sabati in quarta septimana quadragesime quod de predictis accusatis in hundredo isto Iohannes Scryueyn cordewanarius, Willelmus Braye skynnere, Simon Sadelere, Loccus Cordewaner, Thomas Howkyn, & Iohannes Cosyn & Willelmus Morley seruientes eiusdem Thome Howkyn, Iohannes Bloxham masone, Henricus Masone, Ricardus Burghe bochere & Iohannes seruiens eiusdem Ricardi, Ricardus Prestone masone, Iohannes Daubere, Iohannes Aubel sclattere, Petrus Perone daubere, Iohannes Staumpe thecchere, Thomas Colman webbe, Henricus & Iohannes seruientes eiusdem Thome, Reginaldus Geddyng webbe, Willelmus Heynes sclattere, Willelmus Stanlake masone, Reginaldus Geddyng webbe,[1] Nicholaus Carpenter carpentarius & Ricardus Bekwode sawyere comparuerunt omnes in propriis personis suis preter Thomam Howkyn, qui comparuit per Willelmum Newman attornatum suum coram dictis iusticiariis ante recept*um*. Et predicti Loccus Cordewaner, Iohannes Bloxham masone, Henricus Masone, Ricardus Prestone masone, Iohannes Daubere, Iohannes Aubel sclattere, Iohannes Staumpe thecchere, Willelmus Heynes sclattere, Willelmus Stanlake masone, Nicholaus Carpenter carpentarius & Ricardus Bekwode sawyere non potuerunt dedicere transgressiones supradictas & ponunt se in gracia regis, quorum fines patent ut sequntur, videlicet in primis:—

De Locco Cordewanario pro excessu capto per plegium Willelmi Bray & Simonis Sadelere viii d.

[1] This repetition must be a mistake.

De Iohanne Bloxham masone pro consimili per plegium Ricardi Burghe & Henrici Masone viii d.
De Henrico Masone pro consimili per plegium Iohannis Miltone skynner & Iohannis Scryueyn viii d.
De Ricardo Prestone masone pro consimili per plegium Ricardi Dyere & Ricardi Nortone viii d.
De Iohanne Daubere pro consimili per plegium Nicholai Carpenter & Thome Colman viii d.
De Iohanne Aubel sclattere pro consimili per plegium Thome Colman & Willelmi Masone viii d.
De Iohanne Staumpe thecchere pro consimili per plegium Ricardi Burghe & Iohannis Lundone bochere viii d.
De Willelmo Heynes sclattere pro consimili per plegium Willelmi Stanlake & Ricardi Burgh viii d.
De Willelmo Stanlake masone pro consimili per plegium Nicholai Carpenter & Ricardi Bekwode viii d.
De Nicholao Carpenter pro consimili per plegium Willelmi Stanlake & Ricardi Bekwode viii d.
De Ricardo Bekkewode sawyere pro consimili per plegium Nicholai Carpenter & Willelmi Stanlake viii d.

Et dictus Simon sadelere dicit quod capit pro arte sua &c. sicut homines ceperunt ante primam pestilenciam &c., videlicet annis regni regis Edwardi aui regis nunc [*blank*] & ante; et non aliter; & de hoc ponit se super patriam. Ideo preceptum vicecomiti ut inferius &c. Et dictus Thomas Howkyn dicit per dictum attornatum suum quod dat Iohanni Cosyn seruienti suo per annum XIII s. IIII d. & non plus, et dicto Willelmo Morley X s. per annum; et iidem seruientes dicunt ut magister suus dicit; et de hoc tam magister quam seruientes ponunt se super patriam. Ideo preceptum vicecomiti ut inferius &c. Et dictus Ricardus Burghe bochere dicit quod dat Iohanni seruienti suo per annum XVI s. & non plus; et idem dicit quod non accipit plus; et tam magister quam seruiens de hoc ponunt se super patriam. Ideo preceptum est vicecomiti ut inferius &c. Et dictus Petrus Perone daubere dicit quod non capit excessiue; et de hoc ponit se super patriam. Ideo preceptum est vicecomiti &c. Et dictus Iohannes Scryueyn dicit quod ipsi[1] cordewanar*ii* Oxonie h*abent* quandam cartam domini regis &c. Et supponit quod iusticiarii predicti causa eiusdem carte ipsum iustificare uolunt &c. Et super hoc habet diem usque proximas

[1] ipse, MS.

sessiones ad ostendendum cartam illam &c. Et Willelmus Braye skynnere dicit similiter quod magistri de arte sua habent quandam cartam a domino rege eis concessam quod iustificari debent per magistros artis sue &c., et sic supponit quod dicti iusticiarii ipsum iustificare uelint &c. Et habet diem usque proximas sessiones &c. Et quo ad venire faciendum Ricardum Basset sclattere & Iohannem Skynnere, vicecomes Oxonie qui inde unum warantum habuit iam ad istum diem nullum retornauit warantum &c. Ideo preceptum est dicto vicecomiti quod non omittat propter aliquam libertatem in balliua sua quin venire faciat predictos Ricardum Basset & Iohannem Skynnere &c. ita quod sint coram dictis iusticiariis ad proximas sessiones &c. Et quo ad capcionem dictorum Thome Colman webbe, Henrici & Iohannis seruientum eiusdem Thome & Reginaldi Geddyng webbe pro arte sua, iusticiarii nondum auisantur. Ideo habent diem usque proximas sessiones &c.

Et quo ad capiendum Ricardum Prestone masone & Iohannem Gersyndone, Radulfum & Henricum seruientes Iohannis White, Walterum Swon nuper seruientem magistri sancti Iohannis extra portam orientalem Oxonie, Alanum Taskere nuper seruientem Reginaldi Tannere, Thomam Caumbrigge & Iohannam nuper seruientes Iohannis Skynnere, Radulfum Sclattere & Iohannem Poly nuper seruientem Petri Welyngtone, vicecomes nullum retornauit preceptum. Ideo preceptum est &c.

Et quo ad execucionem faciendam versus Edwardum Crook & Galfridum seruientem eiusdem Edwardi, Willelmum Herne & seruientes suos qui sibi deseruierunt in primis sessionibus iusticiariorum predictorum, Iohannem & Willelmum seruientes Nicholai Nortone, Iohannem Drake nuper seruientem Michaelis Salesbury, Iohannem Hopkyn nuper seruientem Ricardi Iremongere, Willelmum Dageuille & seruientes ipsius Willelmi qui deseruierunt in primis sessionibus iusticiariorum predictorum, videlicet ad eos venire fecisse, vicecomes nullum retornauit preceptum, & qui non venerunt. Ideo preceptum dicto vicecomiti quod execucionem versos eos faciat contra proximas sessiones &c.

Et eciam [quoniam][1] ante hunc diem in aliis sessionibus certis de causis Iohannes seruiens Nicholai Nortone, Iohannes Gardyner & Isabella uxor eius seruiens magistri hospitalis sancti Iohannis extra portam orientalem Oxonie, ac eciam dictus magister hospitalis pre-

[1] Not in MS.

dicti, Iohannes Sulby coupere, Iohanna relicta Iohannis Curreour & Iohannes seruiens ciusdem Iohanne, Iohannes Tannere, Willelmus Iremongere & Alexander & Willelmus seruientes eiusdem Willelmi Iremongere, Willelmus Wygan ferour & Philippus Cornysshe seruiens Willelmi Wygan & Agnes Hawuyle & Iohannes seruiens eiusdem Agnetis habuerunt diem per dictos iusticiarios essendi hic ad sessiones istas, adhuc habent diem ad proximas sessiones &c. Et sciendum quod hec est materia pro qua dictus Iohannes seruiens Nicholai Nortone habuit diem usque sessiones &c., videlicet pro eo quod ipse allegauit coram iusticiariis quod fuit tabernarius predicti Nicholai, & quod capit de eo per annum x s., & ponit se in discrecionem iusticiariorum &c.; et eciam super statu & capcione dictorum Iohannis Gardyner & Isabelle uxoris eius datus fuit eis dies coram dictis iusticiariis usque sessiones istas, eo quod iusticiarii inde medio tempore auisiarentur. Et eciam dies datus fuit dicto magistro usque sessiones istas eo quod ipse responderet domino regi clare de accusacione super eundem magistrum affirmata ut predictum est, causa dictorum Iohannis Bristowe, Iohannis Panter, Iohannis Gardyner & Isabelle uxoris eiusdem Iohannis Gardyner. Et eciam dicto Iohanni Sulby coupere super statu & capcione eiusdem &c. Et eciam dicta Iohanna Curreour allegauit quod Iohannes seruiens suus predictus est de mistera de curreour & dat sibi quando laborat I d. & prandium per diem &c. Et sic ponit se tam domina quam seruiens in discrecionem iusticiariorum &c. Et dictus Iohannes Tannere posuit se in discrecionem iusticiariorum de eo quod ipse fuit apprenticius per VII annos in arte de tannere & iam capit per annum XXX s. &c., & causa certarum materiarum allegatarum per dictos Willelmum Iremongere, Alexandrum & Willelmum seruientes eiusdem Willelmi Iremongere, Willelmum Wygan ferour & Philippum Cornysshe seruientem eiusdem Willelmi Wygan, Agnetem Hauuyle & Iohannem seruientem eiusdem Agnetis, viz. super capcione & statu eorundem, datus fuit eis dies ut predictum est &c.

Placita tenta apud Oxoniam die Lune in festo sancti Martini episcopi anno regni regis Ricardi secundi post conquestum sextodecimo & diebus Martis, Mercurii & die Iouis extunc proximo sequentibus coram Thoma Somersete maiore ville Oxonie & Ricardo Ouertone iusticiariis domini regis virtute litterarum patencium domini regis subsequencium. Willelmo Gerueys clerico tunc ibidem.

Memb. 10 *d*.

Nov. 11, 1392

Dominus Rex mandauit litteras suas patentes in hec uerba:—

Ricardus dei gracia rex Anglie & Francie & dominus Hibernie dilectis & fidelibus suis Radulfo Ruderythe cancellario Uniuersitatis Oxonie, Roberto Charltone, Iohanni Hulle, Thome Somersete maiori ville Oxonie, Iohanni Rede & Ricardo Ouertone salutem. Sciatis quod assignauimus [&c. as in the letters patent of Jan. 12, 1391] . . . patentes. Teste me ipso apud Oxoniam quarto die Octobris anno regni nostri sextodecimo. Martyn.

Ac dicti Ricardus de Garstone & Ricardus Ouertone recordum suum coram eis captum virtute ultimarum litterarum domini regis patencium predictarum eis directarum & superius declaratarum, tenore harum litterarum venire fecerunt coram dictis Thoma Somersete maiore ville Oxonie & Ricardo Ouertone. Et super hoc preceptum est dicto vicecomiti quod retornaret coram predictis Radulfo Ruderythe, Roberto Charltone, Iohanne Hulle, Thoma Somersete, Iohanne Rede & Ricardo Ouertone omnia precepta ei per dictos Ricardum de Garstone & Ricardum Ouertone nuper iusticiarios virtute dictarum ultimarum litterarum domini regis patencium eis direct', ita quod de execucione eorundem dictis nunc iusticiariis respondeat apud Oxoniam istis presentibus sessionibus nunc sequentibus &c.

Et ulterius preceptum est dicto vicecomiti per predictos nunc iusticiarios quod non omittat propter aliquam libertatem in comitatu Oxonie quin venire faciat coram dictis nunc iusticiariis apud Oxoniam die Lune in festo sancti Martini episcopi proximo futuro omnes constabularios cuiuslibet warde ville Oxonie, & eciam omnes constabularios hundredi extra portam borialem ville Oxonie, et quod dicti constabularii videlicet quilibet eorum in warda sua ac balliua habeat tunc ibidem nomina omnium venatorum, operariorum, artificum, seruitorum, hostelariorum, mendicancium & vagabundorum ac aliorum hominum mendicancium, qui se nominant trauaillyngemen, in warda sua & balliua commorancium imbreuiata &c., et preter illos quod idem vicecomes habeat tunc ibidem de qualibet warda antedicta ac de hundredo predicto XVIII probos & legales homines ad faciendum tunc ibidem ea que ex parte domini regis per dictos nunc iusticiarios iniungentur. Et quod dictus vicecomes habeat ibidem nomina dictorum constabulariorum ac XVIII hominum de qualibet warda ac hundredo antedictis & preceptum suum &c.

Memb. 9 *d*

Ad quem diem Lune in festo sancti Martini predictus vicecomes retornauit nomina dictorum constabulariorum wardarum & hundredi predictorum, que nomina inferius patent, et quod precepit eisdem constabulariis secundum tenorem precepti antedicti. Retornauit eciam dictus vicecomes nomina dictorum xviii hominum de qualibet warda & hundredo predict*o*. Et ulterius dicti constabularii comparuerunt & retornauerunt prout vicecomes predictus eis preceperat. De quibus quidam accusati fuerunt per certas iuratas separatim de dictis wardis & hundredo captas, prout inferius plene patet, videlicet in primis

North West Warde

Iohannes Miltone skynnere constabularius ibidem isto eodem die Lune in festo sancti Martini retornauit diuersa nomina artificum, operariorum, seruitorum & hostelariorum de balliua sua; de quibus plures accusati fuerunt per xii de predictis xviii liberis hominibus per dictum vicecomitem de warda ista retornatis; quorum quidem xii ac accusatorum predictorum nomina patent inferius. In primis de predictis xii Iohannes Dadyngtone, Willelmus Iremongere, Iohannes Cade, Willelmus Merstone iremongere, Ricardus Brown, Iohannes Keruere, Thomas Setertone, Iohannes Ledecombe, Iohannes Bernard, Henricus Morys, Willelmus Hamptone chaundeler & Willelmus Coltone; qui iurati & onerati iuxta formam dictarum litterarum patencium domini regis dictis nunc iusticiariis ultimo directarum dicunt super sacramentum suum quod seruientes subscripti, retenti cum magistris suis subscriptis, ceperunt excessiue de dictis magistris suis citra ultimas sessiones iusticiariorum predictorum &c. contra formam statutorum, & dicti magistri sui eisdem seruientibus dederunt excessiue contra formam ordinacionum &c. per tempus predictum &c.; quorum magistrorum & seruientum nomina inferius patent &c., videlicet in primis

Magistri	Seruientes
Iohannes Dadyngtone	Katerina seruiens eiusdem
Willelmus Iremongere	Cristina seruiens eiusdem

North Est Warde

Iohannes Bilburghe constabularius ibidem isto eodem die Lune in festo sancti Martini retornauit diuersa nomina operariorum, artificum, seruitorum & hostelariorum de balliua sua; de quibus plures accusati fuerunt per xii de predictis xviii probis & legalibus hominibus per dictum vicecomitem de warda ista retornatis; quorum quidem xii ac omnium accusatorum predictorum de warda ista nomina inferius patent; in primis de predictis xii Iohannes Forster, Iohannes White taillour, Iohannes Syluestre, Willelmus Codesdone, Daniel Brewere, Thomas Mayster, Michael Hulot, Iohannes Wadyn, Willelmus Waget, Thomas Chaundeler, Henricus Freman & Thomas Blount, qui onerati & iurati iuxta formam dictarum ultimarum litterarum domini regis patencium dicunt per sacramentum suum quod de dictis accusatis de warda ista Thomas Carpenter carpentarius, Iohannes Thacham latomus, Hugo Drake laborarius, Philippus Carpenter carpentarius, Willelmus Broun lathomus, Iohannes Webbe daubere, Laurencius Masone latomus, Iohannes Holeway sclattere & Iohannes Plomer plomer ceperunt excessiue par lez iourneyes citra ultimas sessiones contra formam statutorum; set de quibus personis, dictis iuratis non constat. Et ulterius predicti iurati dicunt quod omnes seruientes subscripti retenti cum magistris suis subscriptis &c. ceperunt excessiue de eisdem magistris suis citra ultimas sessiones &c. contra formam ordinacionum &c., et iidem magistri sui eisdem seruientibus excessiue dederunt per idem tempus &c., quorum magistrorum & seruientum nomina inferius aperte patent, videlicet in primis

Magistri	Seruientes
Ricardus magister hospitalis sancti Iohannis extra portam orientalem Oxonie	Iohannes Bortyntone Henricus Spencer Robertus Bakere
Nicholaus Kent	Thomas Brewere Iohannes Brewere Thomas Cartere
Iohannes White, taillour	Henricus Brewere Robertus Brewere Iohannes Hamptone brewere
Nicholaus Nortone	Willelmus Hosteler Iohannes Tauerner
Iohannes Forester	Iohannes Somertone hosteler Alicia Tapstere
Iuliana Gerland	Iohannes Ellesfelde Thomas Man
Rogerus Sherman, bakere	Amicia Katerina } seruientes eiusdem
Iohannes Sprunt	Henricus Brewere Iohannes Brewere Iohannes Brewere Willelmus Brewere

Thomas Maister	Dauid Cartere
Daniel Statford [*sic*], brewere	Petrus Brewere Patricius de Hibernia
Michael Salesbury	Ricardus Brewere Iohannes Brewere

South Est Warde

Ricardus Polaghan constabularius ibidem isto eodem die Lune in festo sancti Martini retornauit diuersa nomina operariorum, artificum, seruitorum & hostelariorum de balliua sua; de quibus plures accusati fuerunt per XII de predictis XVIII liberis hominibus per dictum vicecomitem de warda ista retornatis, quorum quidem XII ac omnium accusatorum predictorum nomina inferius patent; in primis de predictis XII, Iohannes Swanbourne, Iohannes Dentone, Iohannes Botelstone, Iohannes Marchall fysshere, Willelmus Ferour, Philippus Forsthulle, Robertus Andrew, Iohannes Roberd, Iohannes Lundone, Thomas Wormecote, Iohannes Groom webbe & Iohannes Marchalle bocher, qui iurati & onerati iuxta formam dictarum ultimarum litterarum patencium domini regis dictis nunc iusticiariis directarum dicunt per sacramentum suum quod de dictis accusatis de warda ista Iohannes Wottone laborer, Iohannes Sawyere, Iohannes Chadde laborer, Iohannes Carpenter carpentarius & Lucas Sclattere sclattere ceperunt excessiue par lez iourneyes citra ultimas sessiones iusticiariorum predictorum continue contra formam statutorum &c.; set de quibus personis, dictis iuratis non constat. Et ulterius predicti iurati dicunt quod omnes seruientes subscripti retenti cum magistris suis subscriptis citra ultimas sessiones continue usque istas presentes sessiones excessiue ceperunt de dictis magistris suis & iidem magistri eisdem seruientibus excessiue dederunt contra formam ordinacionum & statutorum &c.; quorum magistrorum ac seruientum nomina inferius aperte patent, videlicet in primis

Magistri	Seruientes
Iohannes Swanbourne	Adam seruiens eiusdem
Willelmus Swanbourne	Willelmus White Katerina seruiens eiusdem
Nicholaus Spicer	Iohannes Hosteler Iohannes Langenhulle Willelmus Chestertone Georgius Brewere Iohanna Tapstere
Ricardus Roos	Henricus seruiens eiusdem

Iohannes Clerk fysshere	Thomas Bonde Iohannes Wodeward Nicholaus Wodeward Cristiana
Thomas Marchall ferour	Thomas Parnefeld Bartholomeus seruiens eiusdem

South West Warde

Simon Whelere constabularius ibidem isto eodem die Lune in festo sancti Martini retornauit diuersa nomina operariorum, artificum, seruitorum & hostelariorum de balliua sua, que retorna ostensa fuerunt xii hominibus de predictis xviii liberis hominibus per dictum vicecomitem de warda ista retornatis, quorum quidem xii nomina inferius patent, videlicet Iohannes Faukoner, Iohannes Walkere, Rogerus Holme, Ricardus Wyndelle, Iohannes Lolly, Edwardus Crook, Iohannes Cook webbe, Iohannes Hembury, Martinus Cole, Reginaldus Tannere, Iohannes Strettone bakere & Iohannes Benet; qui iurati & onerati iuxta formam dictarum litterarum patencium domini regis ultimo dictis nunc iusticiariis directarum dicunt per sacramentum suum neminem illorum retornatorum de warda ista esse culpabilem de aliquibus articulis dictis litteris regiis contentis &c.

Hundredum extra portam borialem Oxonie

[*Blank*], constabularii ibidem, isto eodem die Lune in festo sancti Martini retornauerunt diuersa nomina operariorum, artificum, seruitorum & hostelariorum de balliua sua, de quibus plures accusati fuerunt per xii de predictis xviii liberis hominibus per dictum vicecomitem de hundredo isto retornatis; quorum quidem xii ac omnium accusatorum predictorum nomina inferius patent; in primis de predictis xii, Ricardus atte Celer, Willelmus Ryuelle, Iohannes Steyntone, Iohannes Lokyere, Iohannes Suttone webbe, Thomas Webbe, Willelmus Heynes, Iohannes Terry, Willelmus Wodestoke, Willelmus Chyselhamptone, Ricardus Nortone & Willelmus Brehulle, qui iurati & onerati iuxta formam dictarum ultimarum litterarum patencium domini regis dicunt per sacramentum suum quod de dictis accusatis in hundredo isto cordewanarii subscripti, videlicet Ricardus Haywarde, Willelmus Sylcoke, Iohannes Scryueyn, Iohannes Yerdesle, Nicholaus Metebourne, Lodowicus Cordewaner, Iohannes Cherhey, Iohannes Forster & Iohannes Muleward citra ultimas sessiones continue usque istas sessiones vendiderunt sotulares & alia de arte sua

Memb. 8 *d*

excessiue contra formam ordinacionum & statutorum &c., set de quantitate rei sic vendite aut quibus personis, dictis iuratis non constat. Item dicunt quod Stephanus Smyth, Michael Smyth & Iohannes Smyth fabri ceperunt excessiue in arte sua per tempus predictum contra formam statutorum predictorum, set de quibus personis aut de quantitate dicte capcionis dictis iuratis non constat. Item dicunt quod Ricardus Basset sclattere, Iohannes Aubel sclattere, Petrus Perone laborer, Iohannes Staumpe thecchere, Reginaldus Geddynge laborer, Iohannes Forster daubere, Iohannes Irysshe laborer, Nicholaus Carpenter carpentarius, Iohannes Carpenter carpentarius, Ricardus Prestone masone, Willelmus Stanlake masone, Iohannes Bloxham masone & Henricus Masone masone ceperunt excessiue per tempus predictum par lez iourneyes contra ordinacionem &c., set de quibus personis, dictis iuratis non constat. Item dicunt dicti iurati quod Thomas Howkyn dedit Waltero Brewere seruienti suo per tempus predictum excessiue contra formam ordinacionum & statutorum &c.; et quod idem Walterus excessiue de dicto magistro suo cepit per tempus predictum contra formam ordinacionum & statutorum predictorum &c.

Et super hoc preceptum est dicto vicecomiti quod non omittat propter aliquam libertatem in comitatu predicto quin venire faciat coram predictis nunc iusticiariis apud Oxoniam hac instanti die Martis proximo post festum sancti Martini proximo futurum omnes accusatos predictos in hac presenti sessione, secundum quod predictum est &c., ad respondendum domino regi separatim de excessibus & transgressionibus predictis &c.

North Weste Warde; retornum inde factum per uicecomitem die Martis proximo post festum sancti Martini anno xvi°

Ad quam diem Martis proximo post festum sancti Martini predictus uicecomes retornauit quod de predictis accusatis de warda ista Iohannes Dadyngtone & Katerina seruiens eiusdem & Willelmus Iremongere & Cristiana seruiens eiusdem attachiati sunt per plegium Willelmi Kene & Iohannis Hore; qui omnes comparuerunt & non potuerunt dedicere transgressiones predictas; et posuerunt se in gracia regis, quorum fines patent ut sequntur, videlicet in primis:—

De Iohanne Dadyngtone pro excessu dato per plegium Michaelis Salesbury & Iohannis Swanbourne iiii d.

De Katerina seruiente Iohannis Dadyngtone pro excessu capto per plegium Michaelis Salesbury & Iohannis Swanbourne iiii d.

De Willelmo Iremongere pro excessu dato per plegium Michaelis Salesbury & Iohannis Northwode iiii d.

De Cristiana seruiente Willelmi Iremongere pro excessu capto per plegium Michaelis Salesbury & Iohannis Northwode iiii d.

North Est Warde; retornum inde factum per uicecomitem die Martis proximo post festum sancti Martini anno xvi°

Retornauit eciam dictus uicecomes isto eodem die Martis proximo post festum sancti Martini quod de predictis accusatis de warda ista Thomas Carpenter, Iohannes Thacham, Hugo Drake laborer, Philippus Carpenter, Willelmus Broun masone, Iohannes Webbe daubere, Laurencius Masone & Iohannes Plomer attachiati sunt per plegium Iohannis Redy & Willelmi West, qui omnes comparuerunt preter dictum Thomam Carpenter, qui per Willelmum Stauertone attornatum suum comparuit. Et preter dictos Iohannem Thacham & Hugonem Drake laborer non potuerunt dedicere transgressiones supradictas, & posuerunt se in gracia regis, quorum fines patent ut sequntur videlicet in primis:—

De Thoma Carpenter pro excessu capto per plegium Iohannis Botelstone & Thome Waryner iiii d.

De Philippo Carpenter pro consimili per plegium Michaelis Salesbury & Danielis Sclatford vi d.

De Willelmo Broun masone pro consimili per plegium Iohannis Forester nuper balliui ville Oxonie & Henrici Faryndone vi d.

De Iohanne Webbe daubere pro consimili per plegium Laurencii Masone & Iohannis Chadde vi d.

De Laurencio Masone pro consimili per plegium Iohannis Plomer & Iohannis Webbe daubere vi d.

De Iohanne Plomer pro consimili per plegium Willelmi Iremongere & Michaelis Salesbury vi d.

Et predicti Iohannes Thacham & Hugo Drake dicunt quod non ceperunt excessiue contra ordinacionem statuti &c.; et de hoc ponunt se super patriam. Ideo preceptum vicecomiti, ut inferius &c.

Retornauit eciam dictus vicecomes quod [de][1] dictis magistris & seruientibus Ricardus magister hospitalis sancti Iohannis extra portam orientalem Oxonie & Iohannes Bortyntone, Henricus Spencer & Robertus Bakere seruientes eiusdem magistri, Nicholaus Kent & Thomas Brewere, Iohannes Brewere & Thomas Cartere seruientes

[1] Not in MS.

eiusdem Nicholai, Iohannes White taillour & Henricus Brewere, Robertus Brewere & Iohannes Hamptone brewere, seruientes eiusdem Iohannis White, Iuliana Gerland & Iohannes Ellesfeld & Thomas Man seruientes eiusdem, Rogerus Shereman bakere & Amisia & Katerina seruientes eiusdem, Iohannes Spront & Henricus Brewere, Iohannes Brewere & Iohannes Brewere & Willelmus Brewere seruientes eiusdem Iohannis Spront, Thomas Maister glouere & Dauid Cartere seruiens eiusdem, Nicholaus Nortone, Willelmus Hosteler & Iohannes Tauerner seruientes eiusdem, Iohannes Forster & Iohannes Somertone hostelarius, & Alicia Tapstere, Daniel Sclatford brewere & Petrus Brewere & Patricius de Hibernia seruientes eiusdem, Michael Salesbury & Ricardus Brewere & Iohannis Brewere seruientes eiusdem attachiati sunt per plegium Iohannis Kene & Ricardi Kent; et de quibus predictus Ricardus magister & seruientes sui predicti per Willelmum Stauertone attornatum suum comparuerunt et omnes alii in propriis personis suis comparuerunt, preter Iulianam Gerland & servientes suos predictos qui per Willelmum Hamptone venerunt; et de quibus predicti Ricardus magister & seruientes sui predicti ac Rogerus Sherman & Amicia seruiens eiusdem Rogeri & Iohannes Spront & Henricus Brewere seruiens eiusdem Iohannis Spront, & Thomas Maister & Dauid Cartere seruiens eiusdem Thome, Iohannes Forester & Iohannes Somertone hostelarius & seruiens eiusdem Iohannis Forester, Daniel Sclatford[1] & Patricius de Hibernia seruiens eiusdem Danielis, Michael Salesbury & Ricardus seruiens eiusdem Michaelis non potuerunt dedicere transgressiones predictas, & ponunt se in gracia regis, quorum fines patent ut sequntur, videlicet in primis:—

Fines de magistris

De Ricardo magistro hospitalis sancti Iohannis extra portam orientalem Oxonie pro excessu dato per plegium Iohannis Botelstone & Thome Waryner	vi d.
De Rogero Sherman bakere pro consimili per plegium Nicholai Kent & Willelmi Sergeant	iiii d.
De Iohanne Spront pro consimili per plegium Thome Hamptone & Iohannis Swanbourne	vi d.
De Thoma Maister glouere pro consimili per plegium Iohannis Trenacle & Thome Hamptone	iiii d.
De Iohanne Forester pro consimili per plegium Iohannis Northwode & Willelmi Palmere	iiii d.

[1] Scatford, MS.

De Daniele Sclatford[1] pro consimili per plegium Michaelis Salesbury & Rogeri Sherman bakere iiii d.

De Michaele Salesbury pro consimili per plegium Willelmi Iremongere & Ricardi Broun iiii d.

Fines de seruientibus

De Iohanne Bortyntone seruiente Ricardi [magistri][2] hospitalis sancti Iohannis &c. pro excessu capto per plegium Iohannis Botelstone & Thome Waryner vi d.

De Henrico Spencer seruiente eiusdem magistri pro consimili per plegium Iohannis Botelstone & Thome Waryner vi d.

De Roberto Bakere seruiente eiusdem magistri pro consimili per plegium Iohannis Botelstone & Thome Waryner vi d.

De Amicia seruiente Rogeri Sherman bakere pro consimili per plegium Ricardi Bristowe & Willelmi Gerueys iiii d.

De Henrico Brewere seruiente Iohannis Spront pro consimili per plegium Thome Hamptone & Iohannis Swanbourne vi d.

De Dauid Cartere seruiente Thome Maister glouere pro consimili per plegium Thome Maister & Henrici Porter iiii d.

De Iohanne Somertone seruiente Iohannis Forester pro consimili per plegium Iohannis Northwode & Willelmi Palmere vi d.

De Patricio de Hibernia seruiente Danielis Statford [*sic*] pro consimili per plegium Michaelis Salesbury & Rogeri Bakere vi d.

Memb. 7 *d*

De Ricardo Brewere seruiente Michaelis Salesbury pro consimili per plegium Willelmi Iremongere & Ricardi Broun vi d.

Et ulterius omnes dicti magistri de warda ista, qui superius pro excessu dato aliquibus de seruientibus suis prescriptis isto die finem fecerunt, allegant & dicunt separatim isto eodem die coram dictis iusticiariis quod non dederunt reliquis seruientibus suis prescriptis excessiue contra ordinacionem &c., prout accusantur, ut superius patet, nec aliquam conuencionem cum eis fecerunt nisi secundum formam ordinacionum &c. Et de hoc ponunt se separatim super patriam &c. Ideo preceptum est dicto uicecomiti ut inferius &c. Et eciam omnes predicti reliqui seruientes eorundem magistrorum separatim allegant quod est sicut dicti magistri sui superius allegauerunt & non aliter, & de hoc ponunt se singillatim super patriam. Ideo preceptum est dicto vicecomiti ut inferius &c. Et insuper omnes alii magistri de

[1] Scatford, MS. [2] Not in MS.

ista warda isto die comparentes, ut predicitur, similiter allegant & dicunt separatim quod non dederunt dictis seruientibus suis excessiue contra formam ordinacionum &c. prout superius accusantur &c. nec aliquam conuencionem cum eis fecerunt nisi secundum ordinaciones &c. ; et de hoc ponunt se singillatim super patriam. Ideo preceptum est dicto vicecomiti ut inferius &c. Et similiter omnes seruientes istorum ultimorum magistrorum predictorum de warda ista comparentes isto eodem die, ut premittitur, allegant & dicunt separatim quod est sicut iidem magistri sui allegauerunt & dixerunt & non aliter. Et de hoc similiter ponunt se singillatim super patriam &c. Ideo preceptum est dicto vicecomiti, ut inferius &c.

Et quo ad execucionem faciendam uersus Iohannem Holeway sclattere superius accusatum dictus vicecomes nullum retornauit preceptum. Ideo preceptum est dicto uicecomiti sicut alias quod uenire faciat dictum Iohannem coram iusticiariis predictis apud Oxoniam die Mercurii proximo nunc sequente ad respondendum domino regi de transgressione predicta &c.

South Est Warde. Retornum inde factum per vicecomitem Oxon' die Martis proximo post festum sancti Martini anno xvi°

Retornauit eciam dictus vicecomes isto eodem die Martis proximo post festum sancti Martini quod de predictis accusatis de warda ista Iohannes Wottone laborer, Iohannes Sawyere laborer, Iohannes Chadde laborer, Iohannes Carpenter & Lucas Sclattere attachiati sunt per plegium Iohannis Hende & Willelmi Kent, qui omnes comparuerunt. Et de quibus predicti Iohannes Wottone, Iohannes Sawyere & Iohannes Chadde non potuerunt dedicere transgressiones predictas, & ponunt se separatim in gracia regis, quorum fines patent, ut sequntur, videlicet in primis:—

De Iohanne Wottone laborer pro excessu capto per plegium Nicholai Kent & Iohannis Bilburghe	vi d.
De Iohanne Sawyere laborer pro consimili per plegium Hugonis Hayles & Thome Hamptone	vi d.
De Iohanne Chadde laborer pro consimili per plegium Iohannis Forester, nuper balliui uille Oxonie, & Michaelis Salesbury	vi d.

Et predicti Iohannes Carpenter & Lucas Sclattere dicunt quod non ceperunt excessiue &c. prout accusantur superius &c. Et de hoc ponunt se super patriam &c. Ideo preceptum est dicto vicecomiti ut inferius &c.

Retornauit eciam dictus vicecomes isto eodem die Martis quod de predictis magistris & seruientibus superius de warda ista accusatis Willelmus Swanbourne & Willelmus White seruiens eiusdem, Iohannes Swanbourne & Adam seruiens eiusdem, Nicholaus Spicer & Iohannes Hosteller, Iohannes Langenhulle, Willelmus Chestertone, Georgius Brewere & Iohanna Tapstere seruientes eiusdem Nicholai Spicer, & Iohannes Clerk & Thomas Bonde, Iohannes Wodward & Cristiana seruientes eiusdem Iohannis Clerk, Iohannes Marchall ferour, Thomas Parnefeld & Bartholomeus seruientes eiusdem Iohannis Marchall attachiati sunt per plegium Iohannis Hood & Ricardi Speek, qui omnes comparuerunt in propriis personis preter Nicholaum Spicer, qui per Iohannem Maltone attornatum suum venit; et de quibus predicti Iohannes Swanbourne & Adam seruiens eiusdem & Nicholaus Spycer & Iohannes Langenhulle seruiens eiusdem, & Iohannes Marchall ferour & Bartholomeus seruiens eiusdem Iohannis non potuerunt dedicere transgressiones predictas, & ponunt se singillatim in gracia regis, quorum fines patent ut sequntur, videlicet in primis:—

Fines de magistris.

De Iohanne Swanbourne pro excessu dato per plegium Iohannis Spront & Willelmi Sergeant iiii d.

De Nicholao Spicer pro consimili per plegium Thome Hamptone & Iohannis Maltone vi d.

De Iohanne Marchall ferour pro consimili per plegium Iohannis Miltone skynnere & Ricardi Brayn iiii d.

Fines de seruientibus.

De Ada seruiente Iohannis Swanbourne pro excessu capto per plegium Iohannis Spront & Willelmi Sergeant vi d.

De Iohanne Langenhulle pro consimili per plegium Iohannis Maltone & Henrici Porter vi d.

De Bartholomeo seruiente Iohannis Marchall ferour pro consimili per plegium Iohannis Marchall & Ricardi Polaghan iiii d.

Et ulterius omnes dicti magistri de warda ista qui superius pro excessu dato aliquibus de seruientibus suis prescriptis isto die finem fecerunt, allegant & dicunt separatim isto eodem die coram dictis iusticiariis quod non dederunt reliquis seruientibus suis prescriptis excessiue contra formam ordinacionum &c. prout accusantur, ut superius plenius patet, nec aliquam conuencionem cum eis fecerunt nisi secundum formam ordinacionum &c. Et de hoc ponunt se separatim super patriam &c. Ideo preceptum est dicto vicecomiti ut inferius &c. Et eciam omnes predicti reliqui seruientes eorundem magistrorum separatim allegant quod est sicut dicti magistri sui superius allegauerunt & non aliter; et de hoc ponunt se separatim super patriam. Ideo preceptum est dicto vicecomiti ut inferius &c. Et insuper omnes alii magistri de ista warda, isto die comparentes ut predicitur, similiter allegant & dicunt separatim quod non dederunt dictis seruientibus suis excessiue contra formam ordinacionum &c. prout superius accusantur &c., nec aliquam conuencionem cum eis fecerunt nisi secundum ordinacionem &c.; et de hoc ponunt se singillatim super patriam. Ideo preceptum est dicto vicecomiti ut inferius &c. Et similiter omnes seruientes istorum ultimorum magistrorum predictorum de warda ista comparentes isto eodem die ut premittitur allegant & dicunt separatim quod est sicut magistri sui allegauerunt & dixerunt & non aliter. Et de hoc similiter ponunt se separatim super patriam. Ideo preceptum est dicto vicecomiti ut inferius &c.

Et quo ad execucionem faciendam versus Willelmum Swanbourne & Katerinam seruientem eiusdem, Ricardum Roos & Henricum seruientem eiusdem Ricardi, vicecomes nullum retornauit preceptum. Ideo preceptum est dicto vicecomiti quod &c. venire faciat predictos Willelmum Swanbourne & Katerinam seruientem eiusdem, Ricardum Roos & Henricum seruientem eiusdem coram dictis iusticiariis apud Oxoniam hac instanti die Mercurii proximo post festum sancti Martini ad respondendum domino regi de excessibus & transgressionibus predictis &c.

Hundredum extra portam borialem ville Oxonie; retornum inde factum per vicecomitem isto die Martis proximo post festum sancti Martini anno xvi°

Retornauit eciam dictus vicecomes isto eodem die Martis proximo post festum sancti Martini quod de predictis accusatis de hundredo isto isti cordewanarii, videlicet Ricardus Haywarde, Willelmus Silkoke, Iohannes Scryueyn, Iohannes Yerdesley, Nicholaus Metebourne, Lodowicus Cordewaner, Iohannes Forester & Iohannes Muleward, & de fabris Michael Smyth & Stephanus Smyth; et de sclatteres Ricardus Basset & Iohannes Aubel, & Thomas Howkyn & Willelmus Brewere seruiens eiusdem Thome; et de laborariis Petrus Pyrone, Iohannes Staumpe thecchere & Iohannes Forester daubere, et de carpentariis Nicholaus Carpenter & Iohannes Carpenter; et de latomis Willelmus Stanlake, Iohannes Bloxham & Henricus Masone attachiati sunt per plegium Hugonis Est & Iohannis Calfe qui omnes comparuerunt &, preter dictos Iohannem Scryueyn, Thomam Hokyn

Memb. 6 *d*

& Willelmum Brewere seruientem eiusdem Thome, Iohannem Staumpe & Iohannem Bloxham masone, non potuerunt dedicere transgressiones predictas, & ponunt se in gracia regis, quorum fines patent ut sequntur, videlicet in primis :—

De Ricardo Hayward cordewaner pro excessu capto per plegium Iohannis Bradele & Stephani Smyth viii d.

De Willelmo Sylkoke cordewaner pro consimili per plegium supradictum viii d.

De Iohanne Yerdesle cordewaner pro consimili per plegium supradictum viii d.

De Nicholao Metebourne cordewaner pro consimili per plegium supradictum viii d.

De Lodowico Corueyser[1] cordewaner pro consimili per plegium supradictum viii d.

De Iohanne Forester cordewaner pro consimili per plegium supradictum viii d.

De Iohanne Muleward cordewaner pro consimili per plegium supradictum viii d.

De Stephano Smythe fabro pro consimili per plegium Ricardi Basset & Willelmi Wrasteler viii d.

De Michaele Smythe fabro pro consimili per plegium Ricardi Basset & Willelmi Wrasteler viii d.

De Ricardo Basset sclattere per plegium Iohannis Faukoner & Henrici Porter viii d.

De Iohanne Aubel sclattere pro consimili per plegium Iohannis Steyntone & Gilberti Burtone viii d.

De Petro Pirone laborario pro consimili per plegium Willelmi Stanlake masone & Iohannis Carpenter de southe est warde ville Oxonie vi d.

De Iohanne Forester daubere pro consimili per plegium Willelmi Stanlake masone & Iohannis Carpenter de south est warde Oxonie vi d.

De Nicholao Carpenter carpentario pro consimili per plegium Thome Hokyn & Iohannis Scryueyn viii d.

De Iohanne Carpenter carpentario pro consimili per plegium Thome Hokyn & Iohannis Scryueyn viii d.

De Willelmo Stanlake latamo pro consimili per plegium Petri Pyrone & Iohannis Forester laborer viii d.

[1] N.B.

De Henrico Masone lathomo pro consimili per plegium Thome Hokyn & Iohannis Bradele viii d.

Et ulterius predictus Thomas Hokyn dicit quod non dedit Willelmo Brewere seruienti suo contra ordinacionem &c.; et de hoc ponit se super patriam. Et dictus Willelmus Brewere dicit quod non recepit excessiue contra ordinacionem &c. de dicto magistro suo &c.; et de hoc ponit se super patriam &c. Ideo preceptum est dicto vicecomiti ut inferius &c.

Et dicti Iohannes Scryueyn cordewaner, Iohannes Stampe thecchere & Iohannes Bloxham masone dicunt quod non ceperunt excessiue contra ordinacionem &c.; et de hoc ponunt se separatim super patriam &c. Ideo preceptum est vicecomiti ut inferius &c.

Et retornauit eciam dictus vicecomes quod predicti Iohannes Cherhey cordewaner, Reginaldus Geddyng, Iohannes Irysshe laborer & Ricardus Prestone masone & Iohannes Smythe nichil habent in balliua sua per quod possunt attachiari; et illi non venerunt &c. Ideo preceptum est dicto vicecomiti quod non omittat propter aliquam libertatem in balliua sua quin capiat omnes illos &c., si &c.; et eos &c., ita quod habeat corpora eorum coram iusticiariis predictis apud Oxoniam die Mercurii proximo futuro post dictum festum sancti Martini ad respondendum domino regi de transgressione predicta &c.

Et ulterius isto eodem die Martis proximo post festum sancti Martini preceptum est dicto vicecomiti quod non omittat &c. quin venire faciat coram dictis nunc iusticiariis apud Oxoniam dicto die Mercurii proximo post dictum festum sancti Martini omnes & singulos accusatos predictos in omnibus sessionibus predictis, qui per processum attachiandi sunt & adhuc ad responsum suum super accusacionibus illis non venerunt &c. Et eciam quod capiat omnes & singulos accusatos predictos qui per processum contra eos superius habitum capiendi sunt & adhuc ad responsum suum de accusacionibus predictis non venerunt &c., quod habeat corpora eorum coram dictis nunc iusticiariis ad diem & locum predictos ad respondendum separatim domino regi de transgressionibus predictis &c.

Ad quem diem Mercurii proximo post festum sancti Martini predictus vicecomes retornauit quod predicti Philippus Carpenter carpentarius, Iuliana Gerland & Iohannes seruiens eiusdem Iuliane, Iohannes Forester nuper balliuus Oxonie & Thomas seruiens eiusdem, Thomas Carpenter carpentarius, Iohannes Masone lathomus, Robertus Anderewe taillour, Iohannes Northe taillour, Thomas Waryner cordewaner,

Iohannes White taillour, Thomas Babbeley taillour, Ricardus Waldene taillour, Walterus Burnham taillour, Iohannes Spicer taillour, Robertus Skynnere pelliparius, Willelmus Bergeueny pelliparius, Iohannes Miltone pelliparius, Iohannes Tannere tannarius, Ricardus Skynnere, David Bromfelde taillour, Ricardus Brayn dyere & Iohannes seruiens eiusdem Ricardi, Martinus Cole bakere & Robertus seruiens eiusdem Martini, Thomas Forsthulle, Iohannes Walsyngham & Iohannes seruiens eiusdem, Iohannes Utteworthe & Iohannes Forester & Walterus Wilshire seruientes eiusdem Iohannis Utteworthe, Iohannes Scryueyn cordewaner, Ricardus Basset sclattere, Petrus Welyngtone & Iohannes Poly seruiens eiusdem Petri, Edwardus Crook & Galfridus seruiens eiusdem Edwardi, Iohannes Marche dyere pro dando excessu Iohanni Chamberleyn seruienti suo. Iohannes White taillour & Henricus seruiens eiusdem attachiati sunt per plegium Iohannis Dere & Willelmi Kent; qui omnes comparuerunt, et de quibus predicti Philippus Carpenter carpentarius, Iohannes Forester nuper balliuus ville Oxonie, Iohannes Masone lathomus, Thomas Forsthulle & Ricardus Basset sclattere non potuerunt dedicere transgressiones supradictas, et posuerunt se separatim in gracia regis, quorum fines patent ut sequntur videlicet in primis :—

De Philippo Carpenter carpentario pro excessu capto per plegium Iohannis Forester nuper balliui Oxonie & Willelmi Newman vi d.

De Iohanne Forester nuper balliuo ville Oxonie pro excessu dato per plegium Gilberti Burtone & Willelmi Hamptone iiii d.

De Iohanne Masone lathomo de le Northwestwarde pro excessu capto per plegium Iohannis Benet cook & Rogeri Geffrey viii d.

De Thoma Forsthulle pro excessu dato per plegium Thome Hamptone & Nicholai Norton iiii d.

De Ricardo Basset sclattere pro excessu capto per plegium Iohannis Faukoner & Henrici Porter vi d.

Memb. 5 *d*

Et omnes alii qui isto eodem die Mercurii proximo post festum sancti Martini comparuerunt, ut predictum est, allegauerunt & dixerunt separatim videlicet quilibet per se quod non sunt culpabiles nec aliquis eorum culpabilis de accusacionibus predictis unde ut predictum est accusati existunt; et de hoc ponunt se super patriam separatim &c. Ideo preceptum est dicto vicecomiti quod non omittat propter aliquam libertatem in balliua sua &c. quin venire faciat coram dictis nunc iusticiariis apud Oxoniam die Iouis proximo post festum sancti Martini proximo futuro xviii probos & legales homines de villa Oxonie & suburbio eiusdem qui aliquas personas predictas, que se posuerunt in aliquas iuratas predictas nondum determinatas, aliqua affinitate &c. ad faciendum omnes iuratas illas &c. Et super hoc dicto die Iouis proximo post festum sancti Martini predictus vicecomes virtute dicti precepti sui retornauit nomina xviiicim proborum hominum secundum tenorem dicti precepti sui &c.; de quibus xii comparuerunt videlicet Iohannes Lolly, Iohannes Rottele, Iohannes Hembury, Walterus Wheton', Willelmus Prentys, Iohannes Milet, Thomas Prest, Vrinus Taillour, Iohannes Haseley, Iohannes Strettone, Iohannes Smyth skinnere, Henricus More chaundeler, qui onerati & iurati secundum formam & tenorem dictarum ultimarum litterarum domini regis patencium dictis nunc iusticiariis directarum, ac demonstratis eisdem iuratis omnibus materiis & accusacionibus predictis &c., dicunt super sacramentum suum quod omnes predicte persone que se in iurat*as* ill*as* posuerunt secundum quod predictum est bene & veraciter allegauerunt & dixerunt &c. et in nullo culpabiles existunt. Ideo consideratum est &c. quod eant quiete &c. Et quo ad execucionem faciendam versus alios predictos accusatos, videlicet de capiendo Iohannem Broun laborer de la Northest Warde pro excessu capto, Ricardum Brounyng cordewanarium pro sotularibus &c. venditis excessiue, & de venire faciendo Thomam seruientem Iohannis Forester nuper balliui[1] Oxonie pro excessu de eodem Iohanne capto, & de capiendo Iohannem Carpenter carpentarium de la Northweste Warde ac Iohannem & Thomam seruientes Iohannis Bernard lokyere pro excessu capto de eodem Iohanne Bernard, & de venire faciendo eundem Iohannem Bernard pro excessu dato eisdem &c., & Iohannem Gybbes[2] diere pro excessu capto in arte sua, ac omnes alios artificiarios subscriptos pro excessibus captis in artibus suis, videlicet Iohannem Trenacle skynnere, Iohannem Beawlew taillour, Iohannem Goldsmyth aurifabrum, Iohannem Ledecombe cordewaner, Willelmum Codesdone cordewaner, Iohannem Clyuedone taillour, Iohannem Lytherpole taillour, Iohannem Stillyngtone taillour, Matheum Welssheman taillour, Hugonem Walssheman (*sic*) taillour, Matheum Hulot taillour, Galfridum Taillour, Henricum Moryce taillour, Ricardum Preuere taillour ac Simonem Crosse skynnere, Henricum Bilburghe skynnere, Carolum Goldsmythe

[1] He was bailiff for the year ending Michaelmas 1389.

[2] Added above the line 'non fiat ulterior execucio versus istum Iohannem Gybbes per discrecionem iusticiariorum, eo quod ars illa per eos non potest assederi, ut eis uidetur'.

aurifabrum, Ricardum Hudescombe sclattere, Reginaldum Tannere tannarium, Iohannem Keruere cordewanarium, Henricum Faryndone sadelere, Willelmum Webbe textorem, Willelmum Fourbour fourbour, Willelmum Waget sadeler, Iohannem Westone sadeler, Iohannem Dyne sadeler, Ricardum Westerdale dyere & Willelmum seruientem eiusdem, videlicet qui Ricardus Westerdale excessiue dedit dicto Willelmo seruienti suo &c., et qui idem Willelmus excessiue cepit &c. ac Iohannem Marche diere pro excessiue recipiendo in arte sua & Iohannem Chamberleyne seruientem eiusdem Iohannis Marche pro excessu recipiendo &c., ac dictos Ricardum Westerdale[1] diere, & Ricardum Brayn[2] diere pro excessiue capiendo in arte illorum, ac Iohannem Walysshe, dyere & Thomam Dyere seruientem eiusdem videlicet magistrum pro excessu dando & seruientem pro excessu recipiendo, & Iohannem Brewere seruientem Thome Forsthulle pro excessu ab eo capto, Willelmum Bukyngham taillour pro excessu recipiendo in arte illa, & Iohannem seruientem Iohannis Walsyngham pro excessu ab eodem capto, ac Iohannem Skynnere skynnere pro excessu in arte &c., ac de capiendo Ricardum Prestone masone, Iohannem Gersyndone, Radulfum & Henricum nuper seruientes Iohannis White taillour, Walterum Swon nuper seruientem magistri sancti Iohannis extra portam orientalem Oxonie, Alanum Taskere nuper seruientem Reginaldi Tannere, Thomam Caunbrigge & Iohannam nuper seruientes Iohannis Skynnere, dictos seruientes pro excessiue recipiendo, ac Radulfum Sclattere sclattere, ac de venire faciendo Willelmum Herne & seruientes suos qui sibi deseruierunt in primis sessionibus intratis in isto rotulo, & Iohannem & Willelmum nuper seruientes Nicholai Nortone ac Willelmum Dageville & seruientes suos qui sibi deseruierunt in predictis primis sessionibus, ac Iohannem Drake nuper seruientem Michaelis Salesbury & Iohannem Hopkyn nuper seruientem Ricardi Iremongere, qui se submiserunt ordinacioni statutorum &c., vicecomes antedictus nullum retornauit preceptum &c. Ideo preceptum est dicto vicecomiti ut inferius.

Et eciam ante hunc diem in aliis sessionibus certis de causis Iohannes Gardyner & Isabella uxor eius seruientes magistri hospitalis sancti Iohannis extra portam orientalem Oxonie, ac eciam dictus magister, Iohannes Sulby coupere, Iohanna relicta Iohannis Curreour & Iohannes seruiens eiusdem Iohanne, Iohannes Tannere, Willelmus Iremongere ac Alexander & Willelmus seruientes eiusdem Willelmi

[1] Above the line is written 'non fiat ulterior execucio'.

[2] Above the line is written 'non fiat ulterior execucio causa ut supra'.

Iremongere, Willelmus Wygan ferour & Philippus Cornysshe seruiens eiusdem Willelmi Wygan & Agnes Hawuyle & Iohannes seruiens eiusdem Agnetis habuerunt diem per dictos iusticiarios essendi hic ad sessiones istas &c., scilicet quod iusticiarii auisari uoluerunt super statu & capcione dictorum Iohannis Gardyner & Isabelle uxoris eius, & de eo quod dictus magister hospitalis antedicti clare responderet iam istis sessionibus domino regi super accusacione super eundem magistrum affirmata, ut predictum est, causa dictorum Iohannis Bristowe, Iohannis Panter, Iohannis Gardyner & Isabelle uxoris eius, et eciam pro capcione dicti Iohannis Sulby coupere, et eciam de eo quod dicta Iohanna Curreour allegauit quod ipsa dedit dicto Iohanni seruienti suo qui est de mistera de curreour, quando laborat, per diem I d. & prandium, que se posuit in discrecio*nem* iusticiariorum & seruiens similiter, et eo quod dictus Iohannes Tannere ponit se in discrecio*nem* iusticiariorum de eo quod ipse fuit apprenticius per VII annos in arte de tannere & iam capit per annum XXX s. &c., & eciam quia iidem iusticiarii auisari uoluerunt super statu, donacione & capcione dictorum Willelmi Iremongere & Alexandri & Willelmi seruientum eiusdem Willelmi Iremongere, ac dicti Willelmi Wygan ferour & Philippi Cornysshe seruientis eiusdem Willelmi Wygan, & dicte Agnetis Hawuyle & Iohannis seruientis eiusdem Agnetis, & Ricardi Kidlyngtone skynnere, Willelmi Braye skynnere & Thome Colman webbe & Henrici & Iohannis seruientum eiusdem &c., modo consideratum est per dictos iusticiarios quod liceat dicte Iohanne relicte Iohannis Correour dicto Iohanni seruienti suo dare & sibi seruienti recipere forma predicta &c., et eciam dicto Iohanni Tannere recipere sicut ante dictum est &c.; et ulterius omnibus aliis prescriptis, preter magistro sancti Iohannis, datus est dies adhuc causis antedictis usque proximas sessiones &c. coram predictis iusticiariis &c.; et dictus magister hospitalis antedicti mortuus est, prout alibi per dictum uicecomitem certificatur & testatur &c.; et eciam datus est dies adhuc Willelmo Coupere super statu & capcione eiusdem ut supra &c.

Et ubi preceptum fuit dicto vicecomiti quod venire faciat Iohannem Holewey sclattere, Willelmum Swanbourne & Katerinam seruientem eiusdem Willelmi, Ricardum Roos & Henricum seruientem eiusdem Ricardi ad hunc diem Mercurii coram dictis iusticiariis ad respondendum domino regi de excessu &c., vicecomes nullum retornauit preceptum. Ideo preceptum est dicto vicecomiti ut inferius.

Et ubi preceptum fuit dicto vicecomiti quod caperet Iohannem Cherheye cordewanarium, Reginaldum Geddynge, Iohannem Irysshe laborer, Ricardum Prestone masone & Iohannem Smyth &c., ita quod eos haberet hic hac instanti die Mercurii predicti ad respondendum regi de excessibus &c., idem uicecomes nullum retornauit preceptum; ideo preceptum fuit dicto vicecomiti sicut &c., quod non omitteret propter aliquam libertatem &c. quin execucionem faciat versus omnes accusatos predictos & non de materiis unde accusati fuerunt aliquo modo deliberatos, contra proximas sessiones &c. secundum tenorem precepti sui sibi inde directi &c.; qui nulla precepta inde sibi directa ad aliquas sessiones iusticiariorum de pace in dicta villa Oxonie & eius suburb*io* apud Oxoniam tentas ante festum Natalis domini anno xviii° regis nunc retornauit &c. Ideo preceptum est dicto uicecomiti ad ultimas sessiones tentas ante dictum festum Natalis domini quod execucionem faciat versus omnes predictos accusatos erga proximas sessiones tenendas post dictum festum Natalis domini &c. Et ulterius ad quaslibet sessiones iusticiariorum &c. datus est dies illis predictis accusatis positis in auisamento iusticiariorum super materiis unde accusati fuerunt, scilicet usque dictas proximas sessiones iusticiariorum, tenendas apud Oxoniam post dictum festum Natalis domini &c.

Memb. 4 *d*

Sept. 15, 1394

Placita tenta apud Oxoniam die Martis in crastino Exaltacionis sancte crucis anno regni regis Ricardi secundi post conquestum xviii^mo^ & die Mercurii extunc proximo sequente coram Ricardo de Garstone maiore ville Oxonie & Ricardo Ouertone & Willelmo Gerueys iusticiariis domini regis virtute litterarum patencium domini regis subsequencium.

Dominus rex mandauit litteras suas patentes in hec uerba:—Ricardus dei gracia rex Anglie & Francie & dominus Hibernie dilectis & fidelibus suis Roberto Alyngtone cancellario Uniuersitatis Oxonie, Roberto de Cherltone, Iohanni Hulle, Ricardo Garstone maiori ville Oxonie, Willelmo Wylicotes, Iohanni Rede, Ricardo Ouertone & Willelmo Gerueys salutem. Sciatis [&c. as in the Letters Patent of Jan. 12, 1391, omitting after the sentence which ends *statutorum eorundem* the words *Assignavimus ... statutorum predictorum*]. Teste me ipso apud Westmonasterium xi° die Augusti anno regni nostri decimo octauo.

Memb. 3 *d*

Ac dicti Thomas Somersete & Ricardus Ouertone recordum suum coram eis captum virtute ultimarum litterarum domini regis patencium predictarum eis directarum & superius declaratarum tenore harum litterarum venire fecerunt coram dictis Ricardo de Garstone maiore ville Oxonie, Ricardo Ouertone & Willelmo Gerueys. Et super hoc preceptum est dicto vicecomiti quod retornet coram predictis Roberto Alyngtone, Roberto de Cherltone, Iohanne Hulle, Ricardo de Garstone, Willelmo Wylicotes, Iohanne Rede, Ricardo Ouertone & Willelmo Gerueys omnia precepta ei per dictos Thomam Somersete & Ricardum Ouertone nuper iusticiarios virtute dictarum ultimarum litterarum domini regis patencium eis directarum, ita quod de execucione eorundem dictis nunc iusticiariis respondeat apud Oxoniam istis presentibus sessionibus nunc sequentibus &c.

Et ulterius preceptum est dicto vicecomiti per dictos nunc iusticiarios quod non omittat propter aliquam libertatem in balliua sua quin venire faciat coram dictis nunc iusticiariis apud Oxoniam die Martis in crastino Exaltacionis sancte crucis proximo futuro omnes constabularios de le Northwest Ward ville predicte; et quod dicti constabularii haberent tunc ibidem nomina omnium venatorum, operariorum, artificum, seruitorum, hostelariorum, mendicancium & vagabundorum ac aliorum hominum mendicancium, qui se nominant trauaillyngmen, in dicta warda commorancium imbreuiata &c., et preter illos quod idem vicecomes habeat tunc ibidem de dicta warda XVIII probos & legales homines ad faciendum tunc ibidem ea que eis ex parte domini regis per dictos nunc iusticiarios iniungentur; et quod dictus vicecomes tunc habeat ibidem nomina dictorum constabulariorum ac XVIII[cim] hominum predictorum imbreuiata & preceptum suum &c.

Ad quem diem Martis in crastino Exaltacionis sancte crucis predictus vicecomes retornauit nomen constabularii warde predicte, quod nomen inferius patet; et quod precepit eidem constabulario secundum tenorem precepti sui antedicti. Retornauit eciam dictus vicecomes nomina dictorum XVIII hominum de warda predicta &c. Et ulterius dictus constabularius comparuit & retornauit prout vicecomes predictus ei preceperat ut patet inferius &c.

North Est Warde

Iohannes Bilburghe constabularius ibidem isto eodem die Martis in crastino Exaltacionis sancte crucis retornauit diuersa nomina operariorum, artificum, seruitorum & hostellariorum de balliua sua; que retorna ostensa fuerunt XII[cim] hominibus de predictis XVIII[cim] liberis & probis hominibus per dictum vicecomitem de warda ista retornatis, quorum quidem XII[cim] nomina inferius patent, videlicet Thomas Waryner, Iohannes Dyne, Michael Hulot, Matheus Taillour, Iohannes Holme, Thomas Maister, Daniel Sclatford, Iohannes Wadyn, Thomas Babbeley, Carolus Goldsmyth, Robertus Abyndone & Stephanus

Palmere, qui iurati & onerati iuxta formam dictarum litterarum patencium domini regis ultimo dictis nunc iusticiariis directarum dicunt per sacramentum suum neminem illorum retornatorum de warda ista esse culpabilem de aliquibus articulis dictis litteris regiis contentis &c. Ideo &c.

Die[1] Martis proximo post festum Exaltacionis sancte Crucis videlicet in crastino eiusdem festi anno XVIII^{mo} regni regis Ricardi secundi venit coram iusticiariis domini regis ad pacem in villa Oxonie & eius suburbio conseruandam assignatis Matheus Ruthyn taillour de Oxonia & peciit seruicium Cristiane Henxseye alias Trewelove existentis in presencia iusticiariorum que renuit seruire, que fatebatur se esse natam ante primam pestilenciam per decem annos & amplius, & per sacramentum dicti Mathei ac Thome Waryner & Michaelis Hulot probatum existit quod eadem Cristiana fuit vagrans ac vagabunda, non de mercatura uiuens, nec certum excercens artificium, nec habens unde de suo proprio uiuens, nec terram propriam circa cuius culturam se occupare poterit, nec alteri seruiens. Ideo committatur prisone quousque securitatem inuenerit de seruiendo ut supra &c.

Et ulterius preceptum est dicto vicecomiti quod non omittat &c. quin venire faciat coram dictis nunc iusticiariis apud Oxoniam die Mercurii proximo futuro post dictum festum Exaltacionis sancte crucis omnes constabularios de lez Northwestwarde, Southwestwarde & Southestwarde ville predicte ac hundredi & suburbii extra portam borialem ville antedicte; et quod ipsi haberent tunc ibidem videlicet quilibet eorum de warda sua ac balliua nomina omnium venatorum, operariorum, artificum, seruitorum, hostelariorum, mendicancium & vagabundorum ac aliorum hominum mendicancium qui se nominant trauaillyngmen in dicta warda & balliua sua separatim commorancium imbreuiata &c.; et preter illos quod idem uicecomes haberet tunc ibidem de qualibet warda antedicta & de hundredo predicto XVIII probos & legales homines ad faciendum tunc ibidem ea que eis ex parte domini regis per dictos nunc iusticiarios iniungentur; et quod dictus vicecomes haberet tunc ibidem nomina dictorum constabulariorum ac XVIII hominum de qualibet warda & hundredo antedicto imbreuiata & preceptum suum &c.

Ad quem diem Mercurii proximo post festum Exaltacionis sancte crucis predictus vicecomes retornauit nomina dictorum constabulario-

[1] This paragraph is on a loose piece of parchment which has been stitched to the margin of the roll.

rum wardarum ac hundredi & suburbii predicti que nomina inferius patent; et quod precepit eisdem constabulariis secundum tenorem precepti sui antedicti. Retornauit eciam dictus vicecomes nomina dictorum XVIII hominum de qualibet warda & hundredo predicto, et ulterius dicti constabularii comparuerunt & retornauerunt prout vicecomes eis preceperat; de quibus quidam accusati fuerunt per certas iuratas separatim de dictis wardis & hundredo captas prout inferius plene patet, videlicet in primis:—

[North West Warde

Iohannes Bernard constabularius ibidem isto eodem die Mercurii proximo post festum Exaltacionis sancte Crucis retornauit diuersa nomina artificum, operariorum, seruitorum & hostellariorum de balliua sua, de quibus plures accusati fuerunt per XII de predictis XVIII liberis hominibus per dictum vicecomitem de warda ista retornatis, quorum quidem XII ac accusatorum predictorum nomina patent inferius; in primis de predictis XII Iohannes Spicer, Iohannes Whitheed, Willelmus Hampton chaundeler, Willelmus Ottemore, Iohannes Keruere, Henricus Moryce, Iohannes Cade, Willelmus Bakere, Walterus Burnham, Henricus More chaundeler, Ricardus Iremongere & Willelmus Merstone, qui iurati & onerati iuxta formam dictarum litterarum patencium domini regis dictis nunc iusticiariis ultimo directarum dicunt super sacramentum suum quod seruientes subscripti retenti cum magistris suis subscriptis ceperunt excessiue de dictis magistris suis citra ultimas sessiones iusticiariorum predictorum &c. contra formam statutorum, & dicti magistri sui eisdem seruientibus dederunt excessiue contra formam ordinacionum &c., per tempus predictum &c., quorum magistrorum & seruientum nomina inferius patent &c. uidelicet in primis:—

Magistri	Seruientes
Henricus Taillour	Willelmus Hunte
Iohannes Lepere	Ricardus Wylkyn Iohannes Tal' Lucas Robertus Forster Iohannes Tempul Helena uxor eius
Ricardus Shutteford	Iohannes Pole
Iohannes Whitheed, goldsmyth	Iohannes Farltone
Willelmus Hamptone, chaundeler	Iohannes Diere

Iohannes Charley	Willelmus Editha
Iohannes Bernard	Thomas Chiltone
Iohannes Lekhampstede	Willelmus Iohannes Edmundus Alicia
Iohannes Keruere	Iohannes
Iohannes Hikkes	Ricardus Brewere Agnes
Walterus Burnham	Iohannes Bolle
Walterus Boon	Alicia Iuliana
Symon Shereman	Iohannes Holewey Andreas Holewey Agnes Fortes
Willelmus Irmongere	Alexander Iohannes Chaundeler Willelmus Wyrehale Cristiana
Iohannes Hauyle	Robertus
Willelmus Ottemore	Iohannes Thomas
Walterus Skynnere	Walterus Iohannes Ricardus

Dicunt eciam dicti XII iurati quod de dictis accusatis de warda ista Iohannes Tymmes laborer, Rogerus Carpenter carpentarius, Ricardus Waterman sclattere, Iohannes Wiltshire carpentarius, Willelmus Sclattere, Iohannes Sclattere, Willelmus Cookham laborer, Rollandus Carpenter, Dauid Mowere, Walterus Masone & Iohannes Martyn, masone, ceperunt excessiue par les iourneyes citra ultimas sessiones contra formam statutorum, set de quibus personis dictis iuratis non constat.

Southwest Warde

Iohannes Benet constabularius ibidem isto eodem die Mercurii proximo post festum Exaltacionis sancte Crucis retornauit diuersa nomina artificum, operariorum, seruitorum & hostellariorum de balliua sua, de quibus plures accusati fuerunt per XII de dictis XVIII liberis hominibus per dictum vicecomitem de warda ista retornatis, quorum quidem XII ac accusatorum predictorum nomina patent inferius; in primis de predictis XII, Iohannes Faukener, Rogerus Holme, Iohannes

Memb. *2 d*

Cook webbe, Iohannes Walkere, Ricardus Brayn, Willelmus Veysy, Galfridus Fullere, Reginaldus Tannere, Iohannes Dyere, Thomas Chauntour, Willelmus Bartone & Petrus Brembre qui iurati & onerati iuxta formam dictarum litterarum patencium domini regis dictis nunc iusticiariis ultimo directis dicunt super sacramentum suum quod de dictis accusatis de warda ista Agnes Pilprest kempstere, Hugo Burbage cordewaner, Ricardus Hodescombe sclattere, Henricus Plomer, Querne Pekkere, Iohannes Vente sclattere, Iohannes Thacham carpenter, Walterus Carpenter, Iohannes Marye sclattere, Willelmus Groom bocher, Ricardus Plomer plumbarius, Andreas Tauerner, Thomas Sawyere, Laurencius Masone & Dauid Bromfeld taillour omnes preter dictos Hugonem Burbage, Willelmum Groom bocher, Ricardum Plomer, Andream Tauerner & Dauid Bromfeld ceperunt excessiue par lez iourneyes citra ultimas sessiones iusticiariorum predictorum continue contra formam statutorum &c.; set de quibus personis, dictis iuratis non constat; et quod dictus Hugo Burbage citra ultimas sessiones continue usque istas sessiones vendidit sotulares & alia de arte sua excessiue contra formam ordinacionum & statutorum &c.; set de quantitate rei sic vendite aut quibus personis, dictis iuratis non constat; et quod dictus Willelmus Groom vendidit carnes excessiue contra formam ordinacionum &c., set de quantitacione (*sic*) dicte capcionis excessiue dictis iuratis non constat; et quod dictus Ricardus Plomer excessiue cepit pro arte sua facienda contra &c., set de quibus personis aut de quantitate capcionis dictis iuratis non constat; et quod dictus Dauid Bromfeld excessiue cepit pro nonnullis garnementis faciendis contra formam statutorum &c., set de quibus personis aut de numero garnementorum predictorum iurati predicti ignorant. Et ulterius dicti iurati dicunt quod omnes seruientes subscripti retenti cum magistris suis subscriptis a festo sancti Michaelis ultimo preterito usque idem festum proximo sequens ad sibi deseruiendum ceperunt excessiue per conuencionem illam ante sessiones istas contra formam statutorum, & dicti magistri sui eisdem dederunt excessiue & soluerunt; quorum magistrorum & seruitorum nomina inferius aperte patent, videlicet:—

Magistri	Seruientes
Iohannes Bristowe, taillour	Rogerus
Thomas Welles, taillour	Matheus Uuan
Willelmus Bukingham, taillour	Robertus Willelmus

Galfridus Brehulle	Agnes
Willelmus Bartone	Robertus
Iohannes Faukener, brewere	Iohannes Barwe Iohannes Spaldyng
Iohannes Walkere	Thomas
Iohannes Shawe, senior	Iohannes Willelmus
Iohannes Merstone	Ricardus Hosteller
Iohannes Otteworthe, brewere	Willelmus Polhampton Robertus Rede Willelmus Hayle Robertus Cartere Dauid Cartere
Iohannes Lyllyng, pistor	Iohannes Gryndere Willelmus Bonde Rogerus Potager Iohannes Lodelowe Iohannes Exceter Alicia Howel
Thomas Smart	Ricardus
Willelmus Veysy, brewere	Patricius
Reginaldus Tannere	Willelmus Baggeley Dauid Waterman
Iohannes Walsyngham	Thomas Alicia Helena
Thomas Forsthulle, tauerner & brewere	Walterus Ricardus Iohannes

Southest Warde

Iohannes Rotteley constabularius ibidem isto eodem die Mercurii proximo post festum Exaltacionis sancte Crucis retornauit diuersa nomina artificum, operariorum, seruitorum & hostellariorum de warda sua, de quibus plures accusati fuerunt per xii de dictis xviii liberis hominibus per dictum vicecomitem de warda ista nominatis & retornatis, quorum quidem xii ac accusatorum predictorum nomina patent inferius; in primis de predictis xii, Iohannes Stabelere, Iohannes Gersyndone, Willelmus Ferour, Philippus Forsthulle, Iohannes Northe, Iohannes Trenacle, Iohannes Bereford iunior, Willelmus York, Iohannes Botelstone, Iohannes Holme, Iohannes Groom webbe & Thomas Waryner, qui iurati & onerati iuxta formam dictarum litterarum patencium domini regis dictis nunc iusticiariis directarum dicunt super sacramentum suum quod de dictis accusatis de warda ista Lucas Sclattere sclattere, Hugo Sclattere, Iohannes Wottone laborer, Iohannes Sperewhit masone, Iohannes Pope sawyere, Andreas Carpenter carpentarius, Thomas Coty daubere, Iohannes Chadde daubere, Iohannes Staundene daubere, Iohannes Slyforde masone, Iohannes Trusse sclattere, Laurencius Sclattere, Edmundus Hauteruyle & Thomas Masone masone ceperunt excessiue par lez iourneyes citra ultimas sessiones contra formam statutorum, set de quibus personis dictis iuratis non constat; et quod Gerardus Patynmakere vendidit patenes & alia de arte sua excessiue citra ultimas sessiones contra statuta; set de quantitate rei sic vendite aut quibus personis, dictis iuratis non constat; et quod omnes seruientes subscripti retenti cum magistris suis subscriptis a festo sancti Michaelis ultimo preterito usque ad festum proximo sequens ad sibi deseruiendum ceperunt excessiue per conuencionem illam ante sessiones istas contra formam statutorum; et dicti magistri sui eisdem dederunt excessiue & soluerunt; quorum magistrorum & seruitorum nomina inferius aperte patent videlicet:—

Magistri	Seruientes
Iuliana Grasiere	Philippus Chaundeler
Hugo Benet	Willelmus Herberfeld Ricardus Toucestre Edwardus Iohanna Abbot
Iohannes Clerk, fysshere	Iohannes Langenhulle Ricardus Katerina
Iohannes Ferour	Warinus Hopyr
Iohannes Lundone	Iohannes Marche
Nicholaus Spicer	Henricus Gale Iohannes Bessord Willelmus Parfey Iohannes Mascote Iohannes Smart Iohanna Tauerner
Simon Whelere	Iohannes Stonere

Ulterior execucio facta uersus accusatos superius & inferius in rotulo isto contentos sequitur & continetur in aliis rotulis in baga qua iste rotulus residet contentis

Hundredum extra portam borialem Oxonie

[*blank*] constab*ularii* ibidem isto eodem die Mercurii proximo post

festum Exaltacionis sancte Crucis retorn*auerunt* diuersa nomina artificum, operariorum, seruitorum & hostellariorum de hundredo isto, de quibus plures accusati fuerunt per xii de dictis xviii liberis hominibus per dictum vicecomitem de hundredo isto nominatis & retornatis; quorum quidem xii ac accusatorum predictorum nomina patent inferius; in primis de predictis xii, Willelmus Ryuelle, Ricardus atte Seler, Willelmus Cook, Willelmus Bakere, Iohannes Terry, Iohannes Lokyere, Willelmus Tewe, Edmundus Gray, Walterus Ormesby, Thomas Webbe, Iohannes Aubel & Iohannes Sautere, qui iurati & onerati iuxta formam dictarum litterarum patencium domini regis dictis nunc iusticiariis ultimo directarum dicunt super sacramentum suum quod de dictis accusatis de hundredo isto & suburbio omnes fabri subscripti videlicet Michael Smythe, Iohannes Smythe, Stephanus Smythe, & Willelmus Smythe ceperunt excessiue de diuersis hominibus in arte sua, set de quibus personis aut de quantitate capcionis ignorant; et quod subscripti sutores videlicet Iohannes Scryueyn, Ricardus Hayward, Willelmus Shrouesbury, Petrus Flemmyng, Iohannes Yerdeley, Nicholaus Metebourne, Petrus Metebourne, Iohannes Forester & Iohannes Mele[ ] vendiderunt sotulares & alia de arte sua excessiue contra formam ordinacionum & statutorum &c.; set de quantitate rei sic vendite aut quibus personis, dictis iuratis non constat; et quod omnes lathami subscripti videlicet Henricus Masone, Ricardus Nortone, Willelmus Stanlake & Willelmus Masone ceperunt excessiue in arte sua facienda; et quod laborarii subscripti videlicet [ ] Forester, Iohannes Cherchey, Petrus Perone & Iohannes Stampe ceperunt excessiue par lez iourneyes citra ultimas sessiones de diuersis hominibus contra ordinaciones &c.; set de quibus personis, dictis iuratis non constat; et eciam dicunt dicti iurati quod omnes seruientes subscripti retenti cum magistris suis subscriptis a festo sancti Michaelis ultimo preterito usque idem festum proximo sequens multi eorum & aliqui eorum per certum tempus tempore eiusdem a[nni] [1] ceperunt excessiue de dictis magistris suis per eadem tempora, et iidem magistri eisdem seruientibus excessiue dederunt contra formam statutorum &c.; quorum magistrorum ac seruientum nomina inferius aperte patent:—

Memb. 1 *d*

Magistri	Seruientes
Thomas Hokyn	Willelmus seruiens eius
Ricardus atte Seler	{ Iohannes Cartere Ricardus Wygan

[1] Uncertain.

Willelmus Ryuel	Iohannes Cappelane Willelmus Loughteberghe
Willelmus Coke	Thomas Halywelle
Willelmus Chyselhamptone	Iohannes seruiens eius
Willelmus Bakere	Willelmus seruiens eius
Iohannes Steyntone	Iohannes seruiens eius
Iohannes Hunche	Iohannes seruiens eius
Iohanna Burghe	Iohannes Cosyn
Alicia Hostiller	Willelmus seruiens eius
Willelmus Haynes	Ricardus seruiens eius
Willelmus Daggeuyle	Iohannes seruiens eius Ricardus seruiens eius

Et sciendum est quod ulterior execucio facta uersus dictos accusatos patet alibi ut superius prope fit mencio.

FRAGMENT OF A ROLL OF 1355

THE following fragment of a roll for the court held under the Statute of Labourers is preserved in the University Archives among the rolls of the Assise of Bread and Ale. It is in very bad condition and one side is illegible. It shows that the penalties were rather heavier in 1355 than under Richard II. Twyne saw this document among the Town Archives and gives its heading in Twyne MS. iv. 140.

Sept. 4, 1355, to Sept. 29, 1356

Extracte finium, exituum & amerciamentorum coram Cancellario Universitatis Oxonie & maiore eiusdem ville iustic' domini regis ad ordinationem & statutum de operariis, artificibus, [& serui]entibus dudum editas in villa Oxonie & suburb' eiusdem custodiendas & custodiri faciendas assignatis, videlicet a quarto die Septembris anno regni regis E. III. post conquestum vicesimo nono, regni vero sui Francie xvio, usque ad festum sancti Michaelis tunc proximo sequens anno xxx.

De Roberto Reynold webbe de fine pro excessu per plegium Willelmi Fencote ii s.

De Iohanne Cade webbe pro eodem per plegium Walteri le Seriaunt ii s.

De Willelmo seruiente eiusdem Iohannis per plegium dicti Iohannis Cade vi d.

De Egidio seruiente dicti Iohannis per plegium eiusdem Iohannis vi d.
De Simone le Brewer pro eodem per plegium [ ] Hertwelle ii s.
De Felicia uxore Thome Ha .... pro eodem per plegium Walteri le Seriaunt iii d.
De Margaria la Kembestere per plegium Roberti Lyskard iii d.
De Willelmo Woderde webbe per plegium Walteri le Seriaunt ii s.
De Ricardo de Wyttenham seruiente eiusdem Willelmi pro eodem per plegium dicti Willelmi vi d.
De Iohanne Ber .... seruiente Iohannis Wyndesore pro eodem per plegium Thome de Kyngestone vi d.
De Philippo Burtone pro eodem per plegium Iohannis le ...... vi d.
De Hugone Musselwyke regratar*io* pro eodem per plegium Walteri le Seriaunt xii d.
De Willelmo Bache skynnere pro eodem per plegium Ricardi Salesbiry vi d.
De Agnete Mersdew shuppestere pro eodem per plegium eiusdem Ricardi iii d.
De Iohanne Capul curreour pro eodem per plegium Willelmi May xii d.
De Willelmo seruiente eiusdem Iohannis pro eodem per plegium predicti Iohannis viii d.
De Willelmo Bonde, taillour, pro eodem per plegium Nicholai Kyng vi d.
De Waltero le Thechere quia non est prosecutus uersus Hugonem de Yeftele de placito transgressionis contra statutum [1] [ ]

. . . .

De eodem Thoma et dictis plegiis quia idem Thomas non est prosecutus uersus Galfridum de Lodewelle de placito transgressionis contra statutum vi d.
De Iohanne de Stodle & Matill' uxore eius & Willelmo le Northerne & Roberto Hafunte plegiis suis de prosecutione quia non sunt prosecuti uersus Ioh' de Abendone de placito consimili vi d.
De Hugone filio Iohannis le Brewere quia recessit a seruicio

[1] Seven lines obliterated by gall.

Petri le Panyter infra terminum sine licencia & causa racionabili per plegium eiusdem Petri xii d.
De Henrico le Porter balliuo hundredi extra portam borealem [ ]
De Iohanne le Mareschal quia cepit salarium excessiuum per plegium Ricardi de Salesbury xii d.
De Iohanne Kelyngworth, coupere, pro eodem per plegium Roberti Mauncel xviii d.
De Adam Bedeford pro excess' fact' per plegium Ricardi Salisbury ii s.
De Ricardo Coutone pro eodem per plegium Thome le Couk xii d.
De Thoma le Flecchere pro eodem per plegium predicti Thome le Couk xii d.
De Iohanne . . . . skynnere pro eodem per plegium Ricardi Coutone ii s.
De Roberto le Cobelere pro eodem per plegium predicti Ricardi Coutone iii d.
De Iohanne le Chapman, upholdere, pro eodem per plegium Iohannis Atte Noke vi d.
De Petro le Taillour de Cattestret pro eodem per plegium Iohannis le Chapman xviii d.
De Thoma [ ] weynton, braciante, pro eodem per plegium Margerie de Stanlake xii d.
De Henrico Wantyng glouer pro eodem per plegium Iohannis Coke, taillour [1] vi d.

[1] The roll is torn off here. The dorse continues the list of fines but is illegible.

THE ASSISE OF BREAD AND ALE

1309–1351

The next part of this volume consists of the records of courts that were held in Oxford between the years 1309 and 1351. The courts were in connexion with the assise of bread, the assise of ale, and the assay of weights and measures. After the riot of St. Scolastica's day the Chancellor had supreme control of all these courts, but these records, being of an earlier period, are not properly described as University archives. In common with the rest of the contents of Pyx Y, they seem to have been the property of Twyne, and he gives extracts from them in Twyne MSS., vol. iv, p. 139; and as that which precedes and that which follows in that volume is taken from the Town archives, it is probable that these rolls were there at that time. They may have been given to Twyne when the Gild Hall was cleared to make room for the officials of King Charles I.

The rolls are kept in one bundle and are mixed, but for convenience we have given the rolls of the assise of bread apart from the rolls of the assise of ale. Although the two franchises were never separate, and he who had the assise of ale had also the assise of bread, yet there were separate rolls for the two assises. The court for the trying of bread was held twelve or more times a year, while the court for the assise of ale was held but twice. In a few cases it will be found that the fixing of the price of ale is entered on the roll of the assise of bread, but in all cases the roll of amercements for breach of the assise of ale is distinct, so that it has been possible to separate the rolls as they deal either with bread or with ale.

In the Middle Ages there were various methods to protect the interests of the purchaser; for at that time competition by itself was ineffective to secure cheapness and honest work in things that were manufactured. As a general rule each trade gild had the supervision of the work of its members and appointed officers to search the shops and test the work that was offered for sale, while the price to be charged was fixed by the gild as a whole. This was the method of the cordwainers, glovers, skinners, and other such corporations in Oxford. In the reign of Richard II another method came into use, and the court which was held under the Statute of Labourers had power to punish manufacturers who charged an excessive price for their goods. In the case of meat and fish, officers were appointed by the town every year to examine the quality of what was offered in the market, with power to forfeit that which was unfit, but they had no power to settle the price. In the case of bread and ale, articles of general consumption, the price was fixed, the quality was tested, and penalties were inflicted by the community as a whole in courts that were held from time to time for this special purpose, and the proceeds belonged to him who had the Court Leete or View of Frankpledge.

The method by which the price of bread and ale was to be fixed was laid down in a Statute called 'Assisa panis et cervisie' which is printed in *Statutes of the Realm*, vol. i, pp. 199, 200. The word *assisa*, which is used in many ways, means originally something fixed, and here it means the fixed price of bread and ale. The Statute is often attributed to the year 1267, but is really of uncertain date; and in any case it is certain that the assise was much older. Professor Cunningham has shown that it was in existence before 1200 (*Growth of English Industry*, i. 501); and the Statute which is assigned to 1267 was nothing more than recognizing what existed already, and ordaining that the same scale should be used throughout the realm. It was laid down that the price of ale was to vary according to the price of grain; but in the case of bread the price never varied, but the weight of the loaf varied according to the price of wheat. The method will be easily grasped from the following documents, if it is remembered that bread was weighed with troy weight, and that in that scale you may either reckon 20 pennyweights to the ounce and 12 ounces to the pound, or 12 pennyweights to the shillingweight and 20 shillingweights to the pound.

Attached to the rolls of the assise of bread and ale is the following document, written in a hand of about the year 1400. It is practically a reproduction of what is given in the 'Assisa panis et cervisie' printed in the *Statutes of the Realm*.

E.S.P. Y. 16

Quando quarterium frumenti venditur pro xii d., tunc wastellus de quadrante ponderabit vi lib. xvi sol.; panis autem de coketto de eodem blado & de eodem boletello ponderabit plus quam wastellus ii s., et de blado minoris precii ponderabit plus quam wastellus v s.; panis autem de simenello ponderabit minus quam wastellus ii s. quia coctus. Panis autem de treit de quadrante ponderabit ii wastellos; panis uero integer de frumento ponderabit unum coket & dim.; panis de omnibus ponderibus[1] ii cokettos.

Quando quarterium frumenti venditur pro xviii d. tunc wastellus de quadrante ponderabit iiii li. x s. viii d.

Pro ii s.	lxviii s.	Pro vii s. vi d.	xviii s. i d. ob.
„ ii s. vi d.	liiii s. iiii d.	„ viii s.	xvii s.
„ iii s.	xlviii s.	„ viii s. vi d.	xvi s.
„ iii s. vi d.	xlii s.	„ ix s.	xv s.
„ iiii s.	xxxviii s.	„ ix s. vi d.	xiiii s. iiii d. ob. q.
„ iiii s. vi d.	xxx s.	„ x s.	xiii s. vii d. q.
„ v s.	xxvii s. ii d. ob.	„ x s. vi d.	xii s. xi d. q.
„ v s. vi d.	xxiiii s. viii d. q.	„ xi s.	xii s. iiii d. q.
„ vi s.	xxii s. viii d.	„ xi s. vi d.	xii s. ix d.
„ vi s. vi d.	xx s. xi d.	„ xii s.	xi s. iiii d.
„ vii s.	xix s. v d.		

Et sciendum est quod in ista assisa potest pistor lucrari in quolibet quartorio frumenti (ut probatum est per pistores domini regis) iii d., furfur suum, & duos pan*es* de furnagio, & quatuor seruientibus i d. ob., & duobus garcionibus ob. q.; in sale ob., in busca iii d.; in boletello locando ob.; sciendum est etiam quod non mutatur assisa panis nisi pro vi d. crescentibus & decrescentibus, & hoc pro quarterio frumenti vendito.

Pistor cum inveniatur panis suus de quadrante in defectu ponderis ii s. vel infra amercietur, & si numerum illum excedat subeat iudicium pillorie & non remittetur iudicium delinquenti neque pro auro neque pro argento.

It is worth while to give four more documents of the same kind which have never been printed, to throw light on the various kinds of bread that are mentioned in the following rolls. The first is taken from Twyne MS. iv. 134, being copied by Twyne from the Red Book of Oxford, which has long been lost. This Red Book seems to have been put together during the years 1330 to 1380, and, as this entry in the Red Book was borrowed from London, its date may be somewhat early in the fourteenth century. It is valuable as settling what was the nature of the bread called *clermatyn*.

Ex rubro libro ciuitatis Oxonie fol. 70; desumpt' ex parvo nigro libro[2] Lundon' circa finem, in Gilda Aula.

[1] An error for *bladis*. The same error occurs in *Munim. Acad.* i. 180, taken from Registers B and C. Probably our document was copied from one of those registers or from a common source.

[2] This volume is referred to in *Muni-*

Incipit assisa panis et ceruisie.

Quando quarterium frumenti venditur pro xii d., tunc panis de quadrante de wastello ponderabit vi lib. xvi s.; panis autem de coketo de eodem blado et eodem bultello ponderabit plus quam wastellus ii s., et de blado minoris precii ponderabit plus quam wastellus v s.; panis autem de simello [*sic*] ponderabit minus quam wastellus ii s. quia coctus; panis uero integer de frumento ponderabit unum cokettum et dimidium; panis uero de trayt[1] ponderabit duos wastellos; panis uero de omnibus bladis ponderabit duos cokettos. Et sciendum est quod panis ryngatus, hoc est cribratus, idem quod clermatyn, ponderabit unum wastellum et dimidium; panis uero integer de frumento ponderabit unum cokettum et dimidium maioris ponderis ut supra; panis uero de omnibus bladis ponderabit duos cokettos maioris ponderis.[2]

Quando quarterium frumenti venditur pro 18 d. tunc wastellum de quadrante ponderabit iiii li. x s. viii d.

[Then follows the same list of prices as above.]

Nota quod quando quarterium frumenti venditur pro 12 d., tunc wastellus de quadrante ponderabit equaliter vi lib. xvi sol., et tunc valebit bussellum frumenti i d. ob., qui faciunt VI quadrantes, et ergo habebimus de bussello VI wastellos ponderantes in uniuerso xl lib. xvi sol.; sic igitur operandum est; detur certum precium busselli quodcunque volueris; postea videatur quod quarta possunt abstrahi a predicto bussello et in tot dividatur hec summa xl lib. xvi sol.; et pondus wastelli patebit. Verbi gracia valeat bussellum iiii d. Quot quarta possunt sumi a iiii d.? Constat quod XVI quarta. Tunc ergo dividatur hec summa xl lib. xvi sol. per XVI, et tunc XVI^ma^ pars erit pondus wastelli, viz. li solidos.

Nota cuiuscunque pretii bussellum frumenti fuerit, siue maioris siue minoris, semper omnes wastelli de uno bussello, siue sint plures siue pauciores, ponderabunt equaliter xl lib. xvi sol.

Note marginales ibidem:—

Panis levis qui dicitur pouf[3] mercatorum debet esse de eodem bultello et pondere quo wastellus est.

Panis dominicus,[4] qui dicitur demeyne, debet ponderare quantum wastellus de quadrante excepto pondere ix d. per suam coctionem.

menta Gildhalle (Rolls Series), i. 353 *n.*, where it is stated that it is no longer in existence.

[1] In *Liber Albus Gildhalle London*, iii, p. 411 (Rolls Series), *trait* is called *panis bissus*.

[2] This paragraph mentions seven kinds of bread of which the most expensive was simnel; then wastell, coket, clermatyn, whole-meal, trait, bread of mixed grain. In *Liber Albus Gildhalle London*, iii, p. 423 (Rolls Series), one kind of bread is called 'bunne'. Was this wastel (= gasteau)? *Turte bread* seems to be distinct from *trait* (ib. iii. 413) and to be the same as whole-meal bread.

[3] Twyne writes 'pous', but it is 'pouf' in the Liber Albus of London, fol. 215 A (*Munimenta Gildhallae*, i. 353, Rolls Series), where these two paragraphs occur. It was also called French bread.

[4] In *Munimenta Gildhallae London*, ii, p. 783 (Rolls Series), it is shown that *panis dominicus* is sometimes identical

Si quarterium frumenti crescit de uno denario, tunc panis de obolo decrescit in pondere de xii d.

Si quarterium frumenti vilescit de uno denario, tunc panis de obolo crescit in pondere de xii d.

Et nota quod quilibet panis debet temptari, dum fuerit calidus, per assaiam factam Lundonie.

Lucrum pistoris.

Sciendum est quod pistor potest lucrari in quolibet quarterio frumenti prout probatum est per pistorem domini regis iiii d. et furfur suum et II panes ad furnagium, et tribus servientibus iii ob.; in carbonibus ob.; in gest[1] ob.; in sale ob.; in busca ii d.; in bultello locato ob.[2]

Assisa ceruisie.

Quando quarterium frumenti venditur pro iii solidis aut xl denariis et hordeum pro xx denariis aut ii solidis, et quarterium avene pro xvi denariis, tunc debent et bene possunt braceatores in civitate vendere II lagenas ad i d., et extra III lagenas ad i d.; et quando in burgo III lagene venduntur ad i d., tunc extra burgum possunt et debent vendere IIII lagenas ad i d.; et sciendum quod non mutatur assisa ceruisie nisi pro xii d. crescentibus uel decrescentibus in venditione quarterii bladi, nec mutatur assisa panis nisi pro vi denariis crescentibus vel decrescentibus in venditione quarterii frumenti.

Iudicium Pillorie.

Si pistor aut braceatrix convicti fuerint quod dictas assisas panis et cervisie non observaverint, primo, secundo, tercio amercientur secundum quantitatem delicti, hoc est quotiescumque pistor defecerit in pondere panis de quadrante citra ii s. vi d., amercietur ut dictum est; et si excedat ii s. vi d. debet subire iudicium pillorie sine aliqua redempcione pecunie. Et si pluries deliquerint et castigari noluerint, paciantur iudicium corporis, scilicet pistor collistrigium et braceatrix tribuchetum vel castigatorium.

Incipit Marescalcia domini regis de penis ordinatis. Ibidem fol. 72.

Assisa panis secundum quod continetur in marescalcia domini regis eis liberata teneatur secundum venditionem frumenti scilicet melioris, secundi et tertii; tam wastellum quam alii panes ponderentur cuiuscumque generis sicut supradictum est per mediam venditionem frumenti; et tunc non mutatur assisa sine pondus nisi per sex denarios crescentes uel decrescentes in venditione quarterii frumenti; et pistor, cum panis suus de quadrante inveniatur in defectu ponderis ii sol. vi d. et infra numerum illum amercietur; et si numerum illum excedat, subeat iudicium pillorie, et non remittatur iudicium delinquenti neque pro auro neque pro argento;

with *simnel*. But in *The Little Red Book of Bristol*, ii, p. 237, the two are distinct, and here it seems to be less valuable than simnel.

[1] yeast.

[2] A different version of this paragraph may be found in *Munimenta Gildhallae London*, ii, p. 107 (Rolls Series).

et quilibet pistor habeat signum suum proprium super quodlibet genus panum suorum; et si pistor convictus fuerit in ponderacione panis sui et predictas assisas non observaverit primo, secundo et tercio amercietur secundum quantitatem delicti, si non grave fuerit delictum; et si graviter deliquerit pluries et castigari noluerit, patiatur iudicium corporis sui scilicet pilloriam; et sciendum est quod pistor non debet subire iudicium pillorie nisi excedat numerum ii solidorum et vi denariorum in defectu panis de quadrante. Pilloria siue collistrigium et tumberellum continue habeantur debite fortitudinis ita quod delinquentes exequi possunt iudicium sine corporali periculo.

Assisa vini secundum assisam domini regis observetur, scilicet sextarium ad xii d., et si tabernarius assisam illam excesserit hospitium eius per maiorem et ballivos claudatur et non permittatur ei vinum vendere donec a domino rege licenciam obtineat.

Assisa cervisie secundum venditionem bladi de quo fit braseum statuatur, proclametur et observetur; et braceatrix non accrescat quadrantem in lagena nisi pro xii d. crescentibus in quarterio brasei, nec decrescat quadrantem in lagena nisi pro xii d. decrescentibus, et qui assisam cervisie fregerit primo, secundo, tercio amerciantur et quarto sine redemptione subeant iudicium tumberelli.

The next document is taken from Registrum A of the University Statutes, fol. 98^{v}, the handwriting being of about 1350. It is of interest because it is in English and for other reasons.

[ ][1] ferthyng wastel shall weye as þe assise is y wryten.[2] And the ferþyng white sowr' loff[3] shall weye more þan þe wastell by ii s. And þe ferþyng symnel shal weye lasse þan þe wastell by ii s. for hit is y soden. And þe ferþyng frensh[4] lof shall weye as moche as þe symnel. And a ferþyng temsed[5] lof shal weye a ferþyng wastell and half. And a ferþyng lof of furth ryiȝt[6] whete shall weye a ferþyng white sowr' lof and half. And a ferþyng traite lof shal weye to ferþyng wastell. And a ferþyng lof of alle kyn corne shal weye to white sowr' loaves.

By[7] this assise the baker gene[8] in euery quarter of whete, as it is

[1] The record is much obliterated by the use of gall, but there is a transcript in Twyne MSS., xiv. 112, which was made before the writing was injured. The first letter looks like O, and is so read by Twyne. Possibly it is D, representing the word *The*.

[2] The assise precedes in the original.

[3] Sour bread or sour loaf is supposed to mean 'leavened'; see N. E. D., *sour*.

[4] In the previous document 'pouf' bread, which is supposed to be the same as French bread, is to be of the same weight as wastell; here it is to be of the same weight as simnel, and in the *Little Red Book of Bristol*, ii. 237, it is lighter than simnel.

[5] Temse is a sieve; this is *panis cribratus* of the previous record.

[6] 'forth right' means entire wheat; *panis de integro frumento*. Twyne gives *ryght*, but as far as the original can be read it seems to be spelt as above.

[7] This paragraph is illegible in the original, and is taken from Twyne.

[8] Must mean 'gains'.

proued by the kinges bakers, iii d. and his bran & II loves to ye[1] owne hir and for a hyne i d. ob. and for a grome ob. & in salt ob. and in berne[2] ob., in candell ob. and in wode iii d. This is proued by y° kinges statutes.

The next comes from the same Registrum A, fol. 82ᵛ, and from what precedes and follows it must be of about 1388; it is of value because it gives the names *toutsayn* and *dynglerouncy*.

Pondera panis. Memorandum quod panis Clermatyn debet ponderare wastellum et dimidium; item Toutsayn excedet panem Clermatyn quadrant*atum* per iii s.; item Dynglerouncy ponderabit duos coketos; item panis equinus excedet Dynglerouncy in quadrante per ii s. vi d.

The same record, word for word, is found in a formulary preserved at the Bishop's Registry at Peterborough, fol. 129; the volume was drawn up about 1400 by John Snappe who was Vice-Chancellor at Oxford in 1397, and was probably copied by him from the Register at Oxford.

The fourth and last record is mainly of importance for the pictures that it gives. It is Douce Charter 62 (in the Bodleian) of about the year 1450, giving a table to show the variation of the weight of the loaf according to the variation of the price of corn. It is in five columns, each having a picture at the top: the first column has a picture of 'The saks with mele'; the second has 'The Wastel', a circular flat cake with a pattern round the edge; the third has 'The ferthyng wyght loff'; the fourth has 'The halpeny wete loff'; the fifth 'The pese loff'. The loaves are represented with straight sides, as if baked in a tin, but whether the tin was round or square is not clear from the picture. At the foot of the table is written:—'Thys ys yᵉ syse of al maner of brede; what greyne of corn so evyr yt be, yt schal be weyd aftyr yᵉ ferthyng wastel; for yᵉ semnel weyzeth lasse and yᵉ wastel be ii^s by cause of yᵉ ferthyng[3]; and yᵉ ferthyng wyght lofe schal wey more than yᵉ wastel be ii^s be cause of yᵉ brayng[4]; and yᵉ halpeny wete lofe schal wey III ferthyng wythe loffis; and yᵉ lofe of almaner corne schal wey II ob. wyth lofys; and the baker schal be alowyed in yᵉ crafte for fornage iiiᵈ, for wode iiiᵈ, for II pagys i d. ob., for salt ob.,

[1] Perhaps Twyne misread the original. It may have been 'to the oven hire'. In the Latin it is *ad furnagium*.

[2] i. e. barme (= yeast).

[3] 'seithyng' must be meant; see below.

[4] To *bray* is to pound; but this makes no satisfactory sense.

for barme ob., for candel ob., for ye teydogge[1] ob.; an al ye brenne to awantage. And thys ys ye statuyt of Wenchester.'[2]

In the following rolls we have ten names of different kinds of bread; wastell, coket, clermatyn, panis integer de frumento, panis de omni blado, simnel, tusseyn (toyseyn, touseyn), treyt, paindemain, panis albus; but of these *paindemain* (which is only mentioned once) is generally identified with *simnel*, *tusseyn* (as will be shown) is the same as *panis integer*, and we may assume that *panis albus* is another name for *coket*; the list, therefore, is reduced to seven kinds of bread. We will take them in their order according to their value.

The most valuable bread[3] was simnel. According to the assise list simnel, wastell, and coket were made of the same white flour, but a farthing simnel was to be two shillings lighter than a farthing wastell and four shillings lighter than a farthing coket. We are told that the simnel might fairly be lighter than the wastell 'quia coctus', that is, because it was boiled as well as baked. This is how cracknel biscuits are made, and the picture of a simnel in 'The Boke named The Assyse of Bread'[4] is not unlike a large cracknel.

Next in value comes wastell. In one place in our rolls the name is spelt Gastel, and the word is no doubt the same as *gâteau*. As wastell and simnel are treated as though they would normally be of the same weight, and simnel is known to have been some kind of cake, we may assume (even apart from the name) that wastell was not plain break, like coket, but a cake. Probably the English for wastell was cake-bread; and the description of cake-bread in the *N. E. D.*, 'bread made in flattened cakes', answers to the picture of a wastell which is to be found in 'The Boke named The Assyse of Bread' and in the Douce MS. that is mentioned above.

The third is coket, of which there were two kinds, according as it was made of the best or second-best flour. A farthing coket of the former kind weighed two shillings more than a farthing wastell, of the

[1] In the Latin version 'in boletello locando obolum': the word must mean *boulting cloth*, but it is not in *N. E. D.*

[2] The Statute of Winchester of 1285, as printed in *Statutes of the Realm*, i. 96–8, contains nothing about bread and ale; the Statutum de Pistoribus, printed there, i. 202, 203, has sometimes been attributed to 1285 (ib. 202 *n.*), but reference seems to be to the Assise of Bread, printed i. 199, 200, which is usually assigned to 1267.

[3] According to the list given in *The Little Red Book of Bristol*, vol. ii, p. 237, more valuable than *simnel* was *panis Francicus*; but that list is of little value; it is inaccurate in many points.

[4] Printed in black letter about 1525, and reproduced in facsimile by E. W. Ashbee; it translates the Latin assise 'symnell shall wey lesse than the wastel by two shillings bycause of the sethynge'.

latter kind five shillings more. The name coket had disappeared by the beginning of the sixteenth century, and in the list of bread in 'Arnold's Chronicle' and in 'The Boke named The Assyse of Bread' it is called White Bread. It is likely enough that this name was in use in the Middle Ages as well, for in our rolls the scribe occasionally speaks of *panis albus*, and Blancpain was a family name in Oxford at the beginning of the thirteenth century.

The fourth bread is clermatyn, which was to weigh half as much again as wastell. It is not mentioned in the first and fifth of the lists printed above, which we assign to about 1400 and 1450, but it is mentioned in the other three lists, which are earlier; and they explain what its nature was. It is described as *panis ryngatus, hoc est cribratus*, or *temse bread*, so that it may be identified with *cribble bread*.[1] It seems that after the grain had been ground the baker sifted it to obtain white flour; first he sifted out the bran, then the next coarsest which was sometimes called treat, treit, or treyt, now often known as pollard; and thirdly he sifted out what is now called sharps or toppins and was at one time called cribble. From the finest flour was made coket, from cribble was made clematyn, and from treyt was made panis de treyt. There is no mention of this bread in the sixteenth or following centuries.[2]

The fifth bread is *panis integer de frumento*, which was to weigh half as much again as coket. There were, as we have said, two kinds of coket, and, according to the Assise, it was the heavier coket that should supply the standard, but in 'The Boke named The Assyse' the lighter coket is taken. In that book, and in John Powell's *Assize of Bread* which was often reprinted between 1650 and 1714, the English for *panis integer* is wheaten bread, i. e. bread made of the whole grain.

Sixth is treyt, trait, or trete, which weighed twice as much as wastell. It is often assumed that *treyt* is the same as *turte* bread, but this seems to be a mistake. In the *White Book of London* (Rolls Series), vol. iii, p. 411, it will be seen that tourte is identical with whole-meal bread, and that treyt is a cheaper kind. The best account of the word is in

[1] Bread called 'cribel' is mentioned at Leicester in 1352 (*Records of the Borough of Leicester*, vol. ii, p. 89). In the Vellum Book of Leicester (*E. H. R.* xiv, p. 504) *panis cribelatus* weighed half as much again as wastell.

[2] A writer of 1552 speaks of bread called 'chete bread, raunged bread or cribel bread'; see *N. E. D.*, s.v. *chete*. Ranged or ringed means sifted. At Leicester 'rynge bread' was *treit* not *clermatin* (*E. H. R.* xiv, p. 504). As both breads were made from what had been sifted out, the name *ringatus* could be used of either.

the *N. E. D.*, s.v. Treat. It is mentioned as early as the statute which is generally assigned to the year 1267, but in our rolls it is only mentioned three times, and it is omitted in 'The Boke named the Assyse of Bread'.

Last comes *panis de omnibus bladis*, bread made of mixed grain; it weighed twice as much as the coket. In 'The Boke named the Assyse of Bread' and other printed tables of the assise of bread, it is called Household Bread.

In addition there is one mention of *paindemain*; but all the authorities are agreed that this is another name for simnel. There is more difficulty over the bread which is called tusseyn, toyseyn, or touseyn, and occurs sixteen times. The word cannot be found in the dictionaries, and all that can be said is that it is not identical with clermatyn, treit, or bread of mixed grain, for they are mentioned by the side of tusseyn, but that in no case where tusseyn occurs is there any mention of *panis integer* or whole-meal bread.

In the fourth of the lists printed above there is mention of Toutsayn bread, which was to weigh three shillings more than clermatyn. Now this will be correct if Toutsayn is the same as *panis integer*. For this bread was to weigh a coket and a half, whereas clermatyn was a wastell and a half. Now as there was a difference of two shillings between a coket and a wastell, there would be a difference of three shillings between Toutsayn and clermatyn.

Dynglerouncy, which occurs in the same list as Toutsayn, was evidently the same as Household Bread, or Pese Loaf, or Bread of Mixed Grain.

The relative popularity of these kinds of bread and the size of loaf which was in most request can be deduced from the facts which are given in the rolls of the assise. In 163 cases there was a defect of weight in wastell; in 161 cases it was the farthing wastell, and in only two cases the halfpenny wastell. In 199 cases the coket was too light, and, if the one case of *panis albus* is added, the total is 200; all of these refer to the halfpenny coket loaf, with the exception of six which are the farthing coket. Clermatyn is mentioned 78 times, of which 72 are the halfpenny clermatyn; in the case of the other six the size of the loaf is not given. Of *panis integer* we have 41 cases, and if we add the 16 cases of *tusseyn* the total is 57; of these 42 were halfpenny loaves, 12 were penny loaves, and three are not fully described. *Treyt* is mentioned only three times, and in each case a halfpenny loaf. Bread of mixed grain or household bread occurs 33 times, in two cases a farthing loaf, in 18 cases a halfpenny loaf, in six cases a penny loaf, and in seven cases the description is incomplete. Simnel, the dearest bread, occurs only 14 times, 13 of them being the farthing simnel and one the halfpenny.

About the custody of the assise of bread and ale there was a long dispute between the Town and the University; beginning in 1248 it did not end until 1355. The interests of the Town and the University were not the same; for those who transgressed in the matter of bread or ale were Townsmen, and their fellow burgesses were unwilling to enforce the penalties that were due. In 1248, 'for the tranquillity and benefit of the University', the King granted (among other privileges) that, whenever the burgesses had a trial of bread and ale, notice was to be given to the Chancellor and Proctors of the University on the previous day, that they might be present, if they wished, either in person or by deputy.[1] In 1255 this grant was repeated, and it was laid down that bread and ale should be tried twice in the year.[2] In 1285 Edward I issued a writ, stating that by the grant of Henry III all bread and ale that was found to be contrary to the assise was to be forfeited to the King, and that, as the Mayor and Bailiffs did not exact this penalty duly, it was to be collected in future by the Constable of the Castle, who would answer for it at the Exchequer.[3] This writ is surprising, partly because it makes no mention of amercements such as we find on the rolls of the assise, but only of forfeited bread and ale, and partly because we should have assumed that what was forfeited as well as the amercements belonged not to the King but to the burgesses in right of their fee-farm of the City. But the writ, if it was ever carried into effect, was short-lived and was repealed on March 18, 1301, when the Sheriff was commanded to cause the assise of bread and ale to be kept in the presence of the Proctors of the University or their deputies as often as is necessary, as the Constable of the Castle no longer attends to the assise.[4] Three years earlier than this we have a complaint of the University that they had been granted the privilege of making trial of the ale once a year, but the burgesses would not allow it.[5] There is no evidence that the University had received such a privilege, and it must be remembered that in the Middle Ages many wild claims were made without foundation. In 1305, and again in 1311, the University complained that the assise was not properly

[1] *Univ. Archives* (O. H. S.), i. 19.
[2] Ib. i. 20.
[3] *Munim. Civ. Oxon.* (O. H. S.), p. 1.
[4] *Cal. of Fine Rolls*, 1272–1307 p. 439.
[5] *Univ. Archives*, i. 79.

observed, the penalties not being duly exacted;[1] and it is mentioned in 1311 that when a baker was adjudged to stand in the pillory, he was allowed to do no more than go up on the scaffold and then come down again, whereas he should have been fixed in the pillory for an hour.[2] In 1315 the University complained that the punishment of the tumbrel was not enforced on brewers, as the statute required.[3] On March 4, 1318, the King committed to Richard Damory the forfeiture of bread and ale in Oxford at a rent of £5 a year; but no doubt the court was held as heretofore by representatives of the Town and University. In 1320 the University complained that the penalties due to bakers and brewers were remitted *in favorem delinquentium*, and petitioned that the Chancellor might have a duplicate of the roll of offences.[4] This seems to have been carried out, and two of our rolls of the assise of ale are indentures, showing that they were drawn up in duplicate. The University also complained of the juries that were selected to give decisions about the price of wheat and other matters connected with the assise, and asked that the Chancellor and the Mayor should together choose the juries.[5] On March 20, 1324, the King made an important grant by which the custody of the assise, together with its profits, was granted to the Chancellor and the Mayor jointly, this grant to hold good during the King's pleasure;[6] and on the death of Edward II it was renewed by his son in 1327[7] and again on March 18, 1336.[8] On April 12, 1336, the King renewed his grant, making it perpetual.[9] A deed of 1339 shows that there was friction between the Mayor and the Chancellor, the one refusing to be present at the time and place fixed by the other;[10] and in 1355, after the riot of St. Scholastica, the custody of the assise was granted to the Chancellor alone. In 1461 the annual payment of £5 for the assise was reduced to one penny.[11] It may be added that the profits of the assise of bread and ale were a perquisite of the Chancellor, or of the Chancellor and Proctors; there is no mention of them in the accounts of the University.

It was natural enough that when the burgesses of Oxford were deprived of the profits of the assise of bread and ale, they desired a remission of part of their fee-farm. In 1324 they petitioned the King for a reduction of £5, and the King ordered the Treasurer and

[1] *Munim. Civ. Oxon.*, pp. 6, 15.
[2] Ib., p. 22.
[3] Ib., p. 29.
[4] Ib., p. 35, and *Univ. Archives*, i. 101.
[5] *Univ. Archives*, i. 103.
[6] Ib. i. 107.
[7] *Cal. of Fine Rolls*, p. 18.
[8] *Univ. Archives*, i. 127.
[9] Ib. i. 129.
[10] Ib. i. 135.
[11] Ib. i. 251.

the Barons of the Exchequer to make search concerning the justice of the claim; it seems, however, that owing to the disturbances of the time nothing was done, and when Edward III ascended the throne the burgesses renewed their demand.[1] Thereupon the King ordered the Treasurer and the Barons of the Exchequer to examine into the matter. Nothing more is reported until in 1352 the burgesses once more urged their claim,[2] and after an inquiry it was found that their fee-farm rent ought to be reduced £5. As many of our rolls do not specify the amercements that were levied, we do not know how much the assise of bread was worth; but the roll of 11 Ed. III shows that in that year the amercements and the forfeited bread were of the value of £4 10*s.*, and, if the amercements for ale are added, the total must have been nearly £10. No doubt there were some expenses of the court, but the profits must always have been well over £5.

Bread might be defective in two ways, either in quality or in weight, and our rolls show that each offence was punished in a special way. If the bread was of bad quality it was forfeited, and apparently was sold for what it would fetch, but no amercement was levied; this is a conclusion drawn from the entry in our rolls, viz. that on April 28, 1326; there was no defect (in weight), but horsebread was forfeited worth 7*d.* In all cases where a monetary fine is imposed, it is because the bread was defective in weight. On the other hand, if the bread was defective in weight it does not seem to have been forfeited; thus on October 31, 1337, there were four cases in which coket bread was defective, but in the schedule of bread that was forfeited that day there is no coket. Again on April 5, 1315, loaves of the value of ninepence were declared to be defective in weight, but the value of forfeited bread for that day was 2¼*d.* It may be objected that it can hardly have been the custom that a loaf should be sold in the open market as of full weight, after it had been proved that it was of insufficient weight; but it may have been that the loaf was broken, so that it could not be sold, and then was left in the hands of the baker for his private use.

The roll of 11 Ed. III is particularly valuable because it gives not only the names of the offenders but also the amounts they had to pay. The penalties are called either *misericordia* or *finis*; a close inspection will show that in most cases a *finis* comprises more than one *misericordia*, but as far as can be seen this does not apply to all the cases; thus on May 19, 1338, William de Brehulle pays a fine, though it is

[1] *Cal. of Close Rolls* (1327–1330), p. 17.

[2] *Munim. Civ. Oxon.*, pp. 120–4.

his first offence. The roll of 17 Ed. II gives the amercements in some cases but not in all, and does not distinguish between fines and amercements. When the offence was often repeated, the punishment was the pillory, in which case there was no amercement as well. The punishment of the pillory seems to have been often inflicted on a festival, e.g. St. Paul's day (see court of November 23, 1325), St. Frideswide's day (see court of September 14, 1314). The final and worst punishment was to be compelled to abjure the trade of baking for a year and a day.

Memb. 2 Rotulus temptacionum panis factorum coram Iohanne de Dokelingtone, Andrea de Pyrie & Willelmo de B[ourgh][1] custodibus assise panis & ceruisie in villa Oxonie per commissionem domine Margarete, regine Anglie, in presencia magistrorum Thome de [Awn][2]geruilla & Iohannis de Erdesholpe[2] deputatorum per cancellarium Uniuersitatis ad huiusmodi temptaciones superuidendas in villa predicta.

[Oct. 17. 1309] Temptacio panis facta die Veneris proxima ante festum sancte Frideswyde virginis anno regni regis Edwardi filii regis Edwardi [tercio] per sacramentum Iohannis Wyth, Thome de Mortone, Iohannis de Couele & Roberti de la Bache iuratorum super venditione frumenti die Sabbati proxima precedente in [mercato ville] predicte; qui dicunt per sacramentum suum quod die Sabbati predicto quarterium melioris frumenti se vendebatur pro octo solidis, secundi melioris pro septem solidis & vi den., et tercii melioris pro septem solidis.

Panis quadr' de wastello Michaelis le Chapman de Wodestoke inventus in manibus Iohannis de Harwedone deficit in pondere — xviii d.

Panis obolotus de Coketo Hugonis de Eynesham deficit in pondere — iii s.

Panis ob. de consimili Ade de Tademerton deficit in pondere — ii s.

Panis ob. de consimili Willelmi de Chippenham deficit in pondere — xx d.

[1] Restored from Twyne, iv. 139.

[2] It would be a natural assumption that these two were the proctors for the year, but it seems that it was not so. On Oct. 27, 1309, Bricius de Scharstede is named as one of the proctors (Bp. Dalderby's Register, Inst. fol. 154). Of the burgesses mentioned, John de Dokelington was mayor, and William de Bourgh was one of the bailiffs for 1309; Andrew de Pyrie was probably an alderman; he had been mayor in 1297. The profits of the Town of Oxford were part of the dowry of Queen Margaret.

Panis ob. de consimili Ade de Eynesham deficit in pondere ii s.
Panis ob. de consimili Ricardi de Bloxham deficit in pondere ii s.
Panis ob. de Clermatin Ade de Eynesham deficit in pondere ii s.
Panis ob. de consimili Ade de Tademertone deficit in pondere iii s.
Panis ob. integer de frumento Galfridi de Couele deficit in pondere ii s.
Panis ob. de omni blado Roberti fil. Henrici le Gaoler deficit in pondere iii s.
Panis ob. de consimili Iohannis le Furner extra portam borialem Oxonie deficit in pondere iii s.

Temptacio panis facta die Martis proxima post festum Omnium Sanctorum anno regni regis E. tercio per sacramentum Nigelli de Godwynestone, Roberti de la Bache, Simonis le Barber, Willelmi de Puseye, Iohannis de Couele & Iohannis de Couesgraue; qui dicunt quod die Mercurii & Sabbati proxima precedente quarterium melioris frumenti se vendebatur pro viii s., secundi melioris pro vii s. vi d., et tercii melioris pro vii s. [Nov. 4, 1309]

Panis quad. de wastello Reginaldi Lickepipin inventus in manu Simonis de Wortone deficit in pondere vii d.
Panis obol' de coketto Edmundi de Rollendright def. in pondere xviii d.
Panis obol' de consimili Ade de Tilhurst deficit in pondere xv d.
Panis obol' de consimili Iohannis de Thomele deficit in pondere iii s. Et quia compertum fuit per recordum curie quod defectus iste est quartus defectus panis ipsius Iohannis preter alios minutos defectus, ideo adiudicatur iudicio pilloric; & habet iudicium.
Panis ob. de consimili Ricardi de Bloxham def. in pondere xviii d.
Panis ob. de consimili Iohannis de Leye def. in pondere xviii d. et fecit finem pro ii s.
Panis ob. de consimili Ade de Tademertone def. in pondere xviii d.
Panis ob. de consimili Roberti le Skinnere def. in pondere xii d.
Panis ob. de consimili Willelmi Broun junioris def. in pondere xii d.
Panis ob. de integro Iuliane Edward def. in pondere xviii d.

Panis ob. de omnibus Henrici Grym def. in pondere xviii d.
Panis ob. de consimili Iuliane Edward def. in pondere xviii d.

[Nov. 22, 1309] Temptacio panis facta die Sabbati proxima post festum sancti Edmundi regis anno regni regis E. tercio per sacramentum Thome de Mortone, Thome Somer, Iohannis de Wintonia, Iohannis Stene, Willelmi de Wodeford & Ricardi de Gloucestria iuratorum qui dicunt per sacramentum suum quod die Mercurii proxima precedente quarterium melioris frumenti se vendebatur pro viii s., secundi melioris pro vii s. vi d., et tercii melioris pro vii s.

Panis qua. de wastello inventus in manibus Emme Broun def. in pondere ix d.
Panis ob. de coketto Iohannis de Thomele deficit in pondere ii s.
Panis ob. de clermatin Roberti filii Henrici le Gaoler def. in pondere iii s. vi d.

[Dec. 23] Temptacio panis facta die Martis prox. post festum sancti Thome Apostoli anno r. r. E. tercio per sacramentum Gilberti de Winchecombe, Willelmi de Puseye, Iohannis de Couele, Iohannis de Hampstede, Laurencii le Gaunter & Iohannis de Odyham iuratorum, qui dicunt per sacramentum suum quod die Sabbati prox. precedente quarterium melioris frumenti se vendebatur pro viii s., secundi melioris pro vii s. vi d. et tercii melioris pro vii s.

Panis qua. de wastello inventus in manibus Willelmi le Spicer deficit in pondere xii d.

[Jan. 17, 1310] Temptacio panis facta die Sabbati prox. post festum sancti Hillarii anno r. r. E. tercio pro sacramentum Thome de Mortone, Iohannis le Saucer, Roberti de la Bache, Iohannis de Shireburne, Iohannis de Couele & Nigelli de Godwynestone iuratorum, qui dicunt quod die Mercurii prox. precedente quarterium melioris frumenti se vendebatur pro viii s., secundi melioris pro vii s. vi d., & tercii melioris pro vii s.

Panis qua. de wastello inventus in manu Ricardi de Uptone def. in pondere viii d.
Panis qua. de wastello inventus cum Agnete Cary def. in pondere vi d.
Panis ob. de coketto Hugonis Godestre def. in pondere ii s. vi d.
Panis ob. de eodem Willelmi Broun iunioris def. in pondere xii d.
Panis ob. de clermatin Hugonis Godestre def. in pondere xii d.

Temptacio panis facta die Veneris proxima post festum sancti Gregorii pape anno r. r. E. tercio per sacramentum Walteri de Wycoumbe, Reginaldi Iues, Ade de Spalding, Willelmi le Deveneys, Roberti de Bache & Iohannis de Couele iuratorum, qui dicunt per sacramentum suum quod diebus Sabbati & Mercurii proximo preteritis quarterium melioris frumenti communiter se vendebatur pro viii s., secundi melioris pro vii s. vi d. & tercii melioris pro vii s. [Mar. 13, 1310]

Panis ob. de simenello Radulfi de Wittencye def. in pondere x s.
Panis quad. Willelmi de Godestowe de simenello def. in pondere ii s.
Panis qua. de Wastello inventus in manu Iohannis Batts def. in pond. xvi d.
Panis qua. de eodem Michaelis de Wodestoke inventus in manu Isolde de Aynho deficit xviii d.
Panis ob. de coketto Iohannis le Longe pistoris def. in pondere xii d.
Panis ob. de eodem Ade de Tilhurst def. in pondere ii s.
Panis ob. de eodem Elene le Mareschal def. in pondere ii s. vi d.
Panis ob. de eodem Ade de Tademertone def. in pondere ii s. vi d.
Panis ob. de eodem Willelmi Broun iunioris def. in pondere ii s. vi d.
Panis ob. de eodem Willelmi de Wythulle def. in pondere ii s.
Panis ob. de eodem Walteri le Wyse def. in pondere iii s. vi d.
Panis ob. de eodem Hugonis Godestre def. in pondere ii s. vi d.
Panis ob. de eodem Roberti de Quenyntone def. in pondere ii s. vi d.
Panis ob. de clermatin Ade de Tademertone def. in pondere xviii d.
Panis ob. de consimili Elene le Mareschall def. in pondere iii s.
Panis ob. de omnibus bladis Willelmi de Stoford def. in pondere vi s. vi d.
Panis ob. de consimili Willelmi de Hasele def. in pondere xii s.
Panis ob. de consimili Iohannis de Tiwe pistoris def. in pondere iiii s.

Temptacio panis facta die Veneris in festo sancti Cuthberti episcopi anno r. r. E. tercio per sacramentum Willelmi de Colesburne, Thome le Irmongere, Willelmi de Puseye, Iohannis de Odyham, Thome de Mortone & Ricardi de Cosingtone iuratorum; qui dicunt per sacra- [Mar. 20, 1310] mentum suum quod diebus Sabbati & Mercurii proximo precedentibus melius frumentum se vendebatur pro viii s. viii d., secundum melius pro viii s. & tercium melius pro vii s. viii d.

Panis qua. de simenello Radulfi de Witteneye def. in pondere ii s.
Panis qua. de wastello inventus in manu Gilberti de Waltham def. x d.
Panis qua. de eodem Roberti le Chapman de Wodestoke inventus cum Emma Perceval deficit vi d.
Panis qua. de eodem inventus in manu Rogeri le Flexman def. vi d.
Panis ob. de coketto Iohannis de Thomele def. xv d.
Panis ob. de clermatin Ricardi de Bloxham def. xviii d.
Panis ob. de eodem Radulfi de Witteneye def. iii s.
Panis ob. de integro Iohannis de Tiwe def. iiii s.
Panis ob. de omni blado Willelmi de Hasele def. ii s.
Panis denarr[atus] de consimili Ricardi atte Huthe def. iii s. vi d.
Panis denarr' de consimili Henrici de Yftele pistoris inventus cum Iohanne le Taillur def. iii s. vi d.

Memb. 2 [May 31,] 1310 Ponderacio panis facta die Sabbati proxima post festum Ascencionis domini anno r. r. E. tercio per sacramentum Thome de Mortone, Nigelli de Godwynestone, Iohannis de Couele, Radulfi de Haylle, Iohannis de Caumpedene sutoris & Thome Somer iuratorum qui dicunt quod die Mercurii proxima precedente quarterium melioris frumenti se vendebatur pro x s., secundi melioris pro ix s. vi d., et tercii melioris pro viii s. viii d.

Panis ob. de coketto Ade de Eynesham def. in pondere xviii d.
Panis ob. de consimili Willelmi de Stoford def. ii s.
Panis ob. de clermatin Ricardi de Bloxham def. iii s. vi d.
Panis denarr' de integro Ricardi de Tiwe de parochia Omnium Sanctorum def. iii s.
Panis denarr' de consimili Nicholai atte Huthe def. iii s.
Panis denarr' de consimili Galfridi de Couele def. x s.
Panis denarr' de consimili Iuliane Edward def. x s.

[June 6,] 1310 Temptacio panis facta die Sabbati in vigilia Pentecostes anno prenotato per sacramentum Ricardi de Mortone, Thome Somer, Thome de Mortone, Roberti de la Bache, Willelmi Attenoke & Henrici le Lumenur iuratorum qui dicunt per sacramentum suum quod die Mercurii proxima precedente quarterium melioris frumenti se vendebatur pro x s., secundi melioris pro ix s. vi d., & tercii melioris pro ix s.

Panis qua. de wastello inventus in manu Willelmi Bagard coci def. iii s. vi d.
Panis ob. de coketto Iohannis de Thomele deficit xviii d.
Panis ob. de consimili Willelmi de Thomele deficit xv d.
Panis denarr' de integro Galfridi de Couele deficit iiii s.
Panis denarr' de consimili Iohannis de Tiwe deficit viii s. vi d.
Panis denarr' de omnibus Willelmi de Bartone deficit ii s.
Panis denarr' de consimili Iohannis de Tiwe deficit ix s.

Temptacio panis facta die Mercurii proxima post festum sancti Barnabe apostoli anno predicto per sacramentum Radulfi de Haille, Willelmi de Miltone, Willelmi le Bocbynder, Iohannis de Couele, Thome le Irmongere, & Roberti le Coupere iuratorum qui dicunt per sacramentum suum quod die Sabbati proxima precedente melius frumentum se vendebatur pro x s., secundum melius pro ix s. vi d., & tercium melius pro ix s. [June 17,] 1310

Panis obolotus de omni blado Iohannis de Tiwe deficit in pondere ii s. et quia compertum est per recordum huius rotuli quod idem Iohannes pluries transgressor fuit contra assisam panis, ideo consideratum est quod idem Iohannes subeat iudicium pillorie & habet iudicium.
Panis ob. de omni blado Henrici le Gaoler def. v s.
Panis ob. de consimili Alicie de Adewell def. iiii s.
Panis ob. de consimili Iohannis de Harwedone def. iii s.
Panis ob. de consimili Isabelle Withefd [*sic*] def. iiii s. vi d.
Iohannes filius Henrici le Gaoler in misericordia quia furn*at* panem pro equis falsum & incongruum & extra omnimodam assisam.

Temptacio panis facta die Mercurii prox. ante festum sancti Kenelmi regis anno r. r. E. quarto per sacramentum Reginaldi Iues, Roberti de la Bache, Nigelli de Godwynestone, Radulfi de Cockeswelle, Iohannis de Coucle & Thome de Mortone iuratorum super venditione frumenti; qui dicunt per sacramentum suum quod die Sabbati proxima precedente melius frumentum se vendebatur pro ix s. vi d., secundum melius pro ix s. et tercium melius pro viii s. vi d. [July 15,] 1310

Wodestoke:

Panis qua. de wastello Roberti Gaderecold de Wodestoke def. in pondere	xii d.
Panis qua. de consimili Ricardi de Sulyhulle de Wodestoke def. in pond.	xii d.
Panis qua. de consimili Hikkedale Persun de Wodestoke def. in pond.	xii d.
Panis qua. de consimili Roberti le Chapman de Wodestoke def. in pond.	xii d.
Panis qua. de consimili Ricardi Hete de Wodestoke def. in pond.	xii d.
Panis qua. de consimili Philippi Croume de Wodestoke def. in pond.	xii d.
Panis ob. de coketto Elene le Mareschal deficit	ii s.
Panis ob. de consimili Willelmi de Emyntone deficit	ii s.
Panis ob. de consimili Iohannis de Thomele def.	xii d.
Panis ob. de consimili Walteri de Burcestria def.	iii s.
Panis ob. de consimili Nicholai de Emyntone def.	xii d.
Panis ob. de consimili Ade de Tilhurst def.	xviii d.
Panis ob. de clermatin Walteri le Wyse def.	ii s.
Panis ob. de consimili Walteri de Burcestria def.	ii s.
Panis ob. de consimili Willelmi Broun iunioris def.	xviii d.
Panis ob. de consimili Willelmi de Emyntone def.	ii s.
Panis ob. de consimili Roberti de Gryndere def.	xii d.
Panis ob. de integro frumento Thome Toky def.	v s.
Panis ob. de consimili Agnetis del Bachous def.	xviii d.
Panis ob. de consimili Galfridi de Couele def.	iii s.
Panis ob. de consimili Ricardi de Tiwe de parochia Omnium Sanctorum def.	ii s.
Panis ob. de omni blado Henrici le Gaoler def.	iii s.
Panis ob. de consimili Alicie de Adewelle def.	iii s.
Panis ob. de consimili Henrici filii Radulfi de Witteneye def.	iiii s.

Panis denarr' de consimili Iohannis de Tiwe deficit in pondere x s., unde postea fecit finem pro dimidia marca.

Mem. quod Philippus de Mixebury respond[ebit] de xii s. x d. ob. de panibus forisfactis a principio anni usque huc.

Temptacio panis facta die Mercurii proxima post festum sancti Egidii abbatis anno r. r. E. quarto per sacramentum Willelmi de Colesburne, Gilberti de Winchecoumbe, Thome de Mortone, Thome le Irmongere, Nigelli de Godwynestone & Galfridi de Grauntpount iuratorum; qui dicunt per sacramentum suum quod diebus Sabbati & Dominice[1] proximo precedentibus melius frumentum se vendebatur pro viii s., secundum melius vii s. vi d., & tercium melius pro vii s. **[Sept. 2, 1310]**

Panis qua. de wastello Roberti Gaderecold de Wodestoke inventus cum Alot' la Hokestere deficit in pondere xii d.
Panis qua. de wastello Iohannis Petitpas de Walingford def. ii s.
Panis ob' de coketto Roberti de Burcestria def. in pondere xviii d.
Panis ob. de consimili Walteri de Burcestria def. in pondere iii s.
Panis ob. de clermatin Willelmi de Thomele def. in pondere xviii d.
Panis ob. de consimili Willelmi Broun iunioris def. in pondere xviii d.
Panis ob. de consimili Walteri de Burcestria def. in pondere iii s.
Panis denarr' de integro Willelmi de Stoforde def. in pondere v s.

Temptacio panis facta die dominica proxima ante festum sancti Michaelis anno r. r. E. quarto per sacramentum Radulfi de Cockeswelle, Thome le Irmongere, Roberti de Wyleby, Radulfi de Haylle, Ricardi le Grasier & Thome de Wycoumbe iuratorum, qui dicunt per sacramentum suum quod diebus Mercurii & Sabbati proximo precedent' melius frumentum se vendebatur pro vii s. vi d., secundum melius pro vi s. viii d., et tercium melius pro vi s. **[Sept. 27, 1310]**

Panis ob. de wastello Iohannis de Thomele deficit in pondere v s. vi d.
Panis ob. de eodem Ade de Tademertone def. iii s.

Wodestoke:
Panis qua. de wastello Ricardi Persun de Wodestoke def. xvi d.
Panis qua. de consimili Gilberti le Spencer de eadem def. xii d.
Panis qua. de consimili Michaelis le Chapman def. xii d.
Panis qua. de consimili Ricardi King deficit xii d.
Panis qua. de eadem Hugonis de Kent deficit x d.
Panis qua. de consimili Thome King deficit xii d.

[1] On markets on Sundays during harvest, see *Munim. Civ. Oxon.* (O. H. S.), p. 110.

Panis ob. de coketto Henrici de Neubotle deficit iiii s.
Panis ob. de consimili Iohannis de Horspath deficit v s.
Panis ob. de consimili Ricardi de Bloxham deficit ii s.
Panis ob. de consimili Alicie de Rufford def. ii s.
Panis ob. de consimili Roberti de Burcestria def. ii s. vi d.
Panis ob. de consimili Elene le Mareschal def. xviii d.
Panis ob. de consimili Ade de Tademertone deficit iii s.
Panis ob. de consimili Willelmi de Emyntone def. iii s.
Panis ob. de consimili Willelmi de Eynesham def. iii s. vi d.
Panis ob. de consimili Matillidis Loud deficit ii s.
Panis ob. de consimili Iohannis le Longe def. iiii s.
Panis ob. de consimili Willelmi de Thomele def. ii s.
Panis ob. de consimili Hugonis le Coupere def. iiii s. vi d.
Panis ob. de clermatin Elene le Mareschal. def. iii s.
Panis ob. de consimili Roberti de Burcestria def. iiii s.
Panis ob. de consimili Matillidis Loud def. ii s.
Panis ob. de consimili Willelmi de Eynesham def. iiii s.
Panis ob. de consimili Ade de Tilhurst def. iii s.
Panis ob. de consimili Iohannis le Long def. iiii s.
Panis ob. de consimili Alicie de Rufford def. ii s.
Panis ob. de consimili Ade de Tademertone def. iiii s. vi d.
Panis ob. de consimili Willelmi de Thomele def. xviii d.
Panis ob. de consimili Nicholai de Westone def. iii s.
Panis ob. de integro Galfridi de Couele def. iiii s.
Panis ob. de consimili Radulfi de Stockenechirche def. iii s.

On a schedule stitched on

Summa totalis panum forisfactorum a die sancti Michaelis anno r. r. E. tercio usque ad festum sancti Michaelis anno eiusdem quarto xv s. iii d.; unde Philippus de Mixeburi respond[et]. De quibus idem Philippus soluit I. Cementario pro factura del Waryng apud molendina x s. viii d.; de quibus ballivi respond[ebunt] de medietate vel v s. iiii d. Item soluit pro pane & vino expendendis [in] aula communi x d. Et sic remanent iii s. ix d., de quibus Andreas de Pyria resp' de ii s. ix d.; et sic Philippus debet firmario xii d., balliui v s. iiii d., & Andreas de Pyria ii s. ix d.

On the back of the schedule

Tastatores ceruisie anno VII°, Walterus de Burncestre, Thomas de Croydon, Robertus le Grinder, Adam de Denton, iurati.

Temptacio panis facta die Lune proxima ante festum apostolorum Simonis & Iude anno r. r. E. filii regis E. quarto per sacramentum Thome Somer, Gilberti de Winchecoumbe, Iohannis de Couele, Nigelli de Godwynestone, Iohannis de Caumpedene sutoris & Simonis de Fencote iuratorum qui dicunt per sacramentum suum quod die Mercurii proxima precedente melius frumentum se vendebatur in mercato Oxonie pro viii s., secundum melius pro vii s. vi d., et tercium melius pro vii s. Memb. 3 [Oct. 26, 1310]

Panis ob. de integro Galfridi de Couele deficit in pondere xii d.

Panis Iohannis Stene inventus cum Reginaldo le Taillur, cuius panis furn[atus] fuit extra omnem assisam; ideo consideratum est quod quantum inveniri poterit de predicto furn[o] sit forisfactum.

Panis ob. de coketto Thome le Warde deficit in pondere x s.

Temptacio panis facta die Iouis proxima post festum Omnium Sanctorum anno predicto per sacramentum Willelmi de Colesburne, Roberti de Watlingtone, Thome Somer, Willelmi de Puseye, Thome le Irmongere & Iohannis de Odyham iuratorum qui dicunt per sacramentum suum quod die Sabbati proxima precedente quarterium melioris frumenti se vendebatur pro viii s., secundi melioris pro vii s. vi d., et tercii melioris pro vii s. [Nov. 5, 1310]

Panis ob. de coketto Iohannis de Thomele deficit in pondere ii s. vi d. et quia prius fuit in pillorio, ideo consideratum est die Veneris proxima sequente in plena curia quod abiuret ministerium pistorie per unum annum & unum diem; et abiurauit.

Panis ob. de coketto Iohannis le Longe deficit xviii d.

Panis ob. de integro Galfridi de Couele def. vii d.

Panis ob. de consimili Willelmi le Workman def. v s.

Panis ob. de consimili Willelmi filii Iohannis le Palse de Brehulle def. vi s.

Temptacio ceruisie facta die Veneris proxima post festum sancte Katerine virginis anno supradicto per sacramentum Radulfi de Cockeswelle, Thome Somer, Roberti de Wyleby, Ade de Spalding, Ricardi de Cosington, Iohannis de Wyntonia, Roberti de Drihulle, Iohannis de Colesburne, Iohannis le Webbe, Nicholai [ ], Willelmi de Thomele carnificis & Iohannis Buffard carnificis XII iuratorum ad inquirendum super communi vendicione bladi facta in [Nov. 27, 1310] villa Oxonie duobus diebus mercat[i] precedentibus videlicet frumenti, ordei & auenarum; qui dicunt per sacramentum suum quod duobus diebus mercat[i] predictis quarterium melioris frumenti se vendebatur pro viii s., secundi melioris pro vii s. iiii d., et tercii melioris pro vi s. viii d.; quarterium vero ordei se vendebatur pro v s.; et quarterium avenarum pro ii s. viii d. Et [secundum istam] temptacionem consideratum est in plena curia quod braciatrices in Oxonia vendant in cuua lagenam bone ceruisie pro i d. et qua., et in doleo pro i d. & obolo.

[Dec. 15, 1310] Temptacio panis facta die Martis proxima post festum sancte Lucie virginis anno r. r. E. quarto per sacramentum Thome de Mortone, Roberti de la Bache, Willelmi de Puseye, Iohannis de Couele, Willelmi atte More, & Iohannis le Webbe iuratorum, qui dicunt per sacramentum suum quod diebus Sabbati & Mercurii proximo precedentibus quarterium melioris frumenti se vendebatur pro vii s. viii d., secundi melioris pro vii s., et tercii melioris pro vi s. viii d.

Panis qua. de wastello Ricardi Persun de Wodestoke def. in pondere — xii d.
Panis qua. de consimili Roberti le Walshe de eadem def. in pond. — xx d.
Panis qua. de consimili Gilberti le Spencer de eadem def. in pondere — x d.
Panis qua. de consimili Iohannis le Sawyer de eadem def. in pond. — xii d.
Panis ob. de coketto Edmundi de Rollendright deficit in pondere — iii s.
Panis ob. de consimili Thome Toky deficit in pondere — xviii d.
Panis ob. de consimili Willelmi de Chippenham def. in pondere — xii d.
Panis ob. de consimili Thome filii Iohannis de Horspath def. in pond. — xii d.
Panis ob. de clermatin Henrici de Gaoler def. in pondere — v s.
Panis ob. de integro Thome de Dorkecestria def. in pondere — viii s.
Panis denarr' de omni blado Willelmi de Whitele def. in pondere — vi s.

[Jan. 9, 1311] Temptacio panis facta die Sabbati proxima post festum Epiphanie domini anno r. regis E. quarto per sacramentum Willelmi de Puseye,

Willelmi de Whatele, Iohannis de Gunwardeby, Thome le Cotiller, Iohannis de Loughteburghe & Henrici le Mareschal iuratorum; qui dicunt per sacramentum suum quod diebus Mercurii & Sabbati proximo precedentibus melius frumentum se vendebatur pro vii s. viii d., secundum melius pro vii s., et tercium melius pro vi s. viii d.

Panis qua. de wastello Willelmi de Kent de Wodestoke def. xii d.
Panis ob. de coketto Roberti de Gryndere def. xviii d.
Panis ob. de clermatin Ade de Tilhurst def. xii d.
Panis ob. de integro Radulfi de Stockenechirche def. iii s.
Panis denarr' de consimili Iuliane Edward deficit ii s. vi d.

Temptacio panis facta die Iouis in crastino sanctorum Fabiani & Sebastiani anno r. r. E. quarto per sacramentum Thome de Mortone, Roberti de la Bache, Nigelli de Godwynestone, Thome le Irmongere, Roberti de Wyleby & Iohannis de Couele iuratorum; qui dicunt per sacramentum suum quod die Sabbati proxima precedente melius frumentum se vendebatur pro viii s., secundum melius pro vii s. viii d., et tercium melius pro vii s. [Jan. 21, 1311]

Panis ob. de coketto Iohannis de Leye def. ii s.
Panis ob. de consimili Ade de Tademertone def. v s.
Panis ob. de integro Henrici le Gaoler deficit viii s. et quia compertum est per inspeccionem rotulorum istorum quod predictus Henricus pluries transgressor fuit contra assisam, ideo die Veneris proxima sequente in plena curia adiudicatur pillorie; et habet iudicium.

Temptacio panis facta die Mercurii proxima ante festum sancti Valentini martiris anno predicto per sacramentum Thome de Mortone, Roberti de Wyleby, Thome Somer, Nigelli de Godwynestone, Willelmi de Miltone & Willelmi de Whatele iuratorum; qui dicunt per sacramentum suum quod die Sabbati proxima precedente melius frumentum se vendebatur pro viii s. ii d., secundum melius pro vii s. viii d., et tercium melius pro vii s. [Feb. 10, 1311]

Panis ob. de coketto Willelmi de Emyntone def. in pondere xii d.

Temptacio panis facta die Martis proxima post festum Annunciacionis beate Marie virginis anno predicto per sacramentum Thome Somer, Radulfi de Cockeswelle, Thome de Mortone, Iohannis Atteyate, Nigelli de Godwynestone & Roberti de Bowes iuratorum; qui dicunt [Mar. 30, 1311] per sacramentum suum quod die Sabbati proxima precedente communis vendicio melioris frumenti se fecit in mercato pro viii s., secundi melioris pro vii s. vi d., et tercii melioris pro vii s.

Panis qua. de simenello Iohannis le Mattere de Wodestoke def. xviii d.
Panis qua. de eodem Henrici filii Radulfi de Wittene def. xx d.
Panis qua. de wastello Thome King de Wodestoke def. xviii d.
Panis qua. de consimili Roberti le Walsshe de eadem def. xviii d.
Panis qua. Philippi Croume de eadem deficit ii s.
Panis qua. Edithe le Chapman de eadem def. xiiii d.
Panis ob. de coketto Willelmi de Chippenham deficit xii d.
Panis ob. de consimili Thome de Eynesham def. xii d.
Panis ob. de consimili Iohannis de Leye def. xiiii d.
Panis ob. de consimili Edmundi de Rollendri' def. ii s.
Panis ob. de clermatin Willelmi de Chippenham def. iii s.
Panis ob. de consimili Ade de Eynesham def. xviii d.

[Apr. 20, 1311] Temptacio panis facta die Martis proxima ante festum sancti Georgii martiris anno predicto per sacramentum Iohannis atte Yate, Thome le Irmongere, Ricardi le Grasiere, Ricardi de Edrope, Iohannis le Ferrur & Ricardi de Cosingtone, qui dicunt per sacramentum suum quod die Sabbati proxima precedente vendicio melioris frumenti communiter se fecit in mercato pro vii s. vi d., secundi melioris pro vii s., et tercii melioris pro vi s. viii d.

Panis ob. de coketto Willelmi Broun senioris def. in pondere xviii d.
Panis ob. de consimili Walteri de Burcestria def. in pondere xviii d.
Panis ob. de clermatin Iohannis de Leye def. in pondere xviii d.

[July 3, 1311] Temptacio panis facta die Sabbati proxima post festum apostolorum Petri & Pauli anno predicto per sacramentum Willelmi de Puseye, Gilberti de Westone, Gilberti de Winchecoumbe, Galfridi de Grauntpont, Thome le Irmongere & Ricardi le Grasiere iuratorum qui dicunt per sacramentum suum quod diebus Mercurii & Sabbati proximo precedentibus melius frumentum se vendebatur pro vii s., secundum melius pro vi s. vi d., et tercium melius pro vi s.

Panis qua. de wastello Thome King de Wodestoke def. in pondere xviii d.

Panis qua. de consimili Michaelis le Chapman def. ii s. iiii d.
Panis qua. de consimili Edythe le Chapman def. xii d.
Panis qua. de consimili Roberti le Chapman def. xii d.
Panis qua. de consimili Ricardi King deficit xii d.
Panis qua. de consimili Gilberti le Spencer deficit xii d.
Panis qua. de consimili Willelmi de Kent deficit xvi d.
Panis ob. de coketto Hugonis Toky deficit iii s. vi d.
Panis ob. de consimili Walteri de Burcestria def. ii s. vi d.
Panis ob. de consimili Willelmi Broun iunioris def. iiii s. vi d.
Panis ob. de consimili Iohannis de Horspath def. ii s. vi d.
Panis ob. de consimili Alicie de Rufford def. ii s. vi d.
Panis ob. de consimili Ade de Tademertone def. ii s. vi d.
Panis ob. de consimili Edmundi de Rollendright def. iiii s. vi d.
Panis ob. de clermatin Alicie de Rufford def. v s.
Panis ob. de consimili Hugonis Toky deficit iii s.
Panis ob. de consimili Willelmi de Emyntone def. v s.
Panis ob. de consimili Ade de Tademertone def. xviii d.
Panis ob. de consimili Iohannis de Horspathe def. iiii s. [dorse]
Panis ob. de consimili Henrici de Neubotle def. iiii s.
Panis ob. de consimili Roberti de Burcestria def. iiii s. iiii d.
Panis ob. de consimili Walteri de Burcestria def. iiii s. iii d.
Panis ob. de integro Iuliane Edward deficit ii s.
Panis denarr' de consimili Radulfi de Stockenechirche def. x s.
Panis ob. de omni blado Thome le Warde deficit xii d.
Panis ob. de consimili Iohannis de Thornburghe def. ii s.

Temptacio panis facta die Sabbati prox. ante festum sancti Petri quod dicitur ad uincula anno r. regis E. quinto per sacramentum Iohannis de Couele, Nigelli de Godwynestone, Roberti de la Bache, Thome Somer, Thome le Irmongere & Willelmi de Puseye iuratorum qui dicunt quod die Mercurii proxima precedente quarterium melioris frumenti se vendebatur in mercato pro vi s. iiii d., secundi melioris pro v s. viii d., et tercii melioris pro v s. iiii d. [July 31, 1311]

Panis qua. de wastello Iohannis le Sawyer def. xviii d.
Panis ob. de coketto Willelmi Broun iunioris def. iii s.

Ponderacio panis facta die dominica proxima ante festum sancti Bartholomei apostoli anno r. regis E. quinto per sacramentum Iohannis de Staundene, Nigelli de Godwynestone, Iohannis Prest carnificis, [Aug. 22, 1311]

Iohannis Bisshop, Iohannis de Hampsted & Iohannis de Odyham iuratorum, qui dicunt quod die Mercurii proxima precedente quarterium melioris frumenti se vendebatur pro v s., secundi melioris pro iiii s. vi d., et tercii melioris pro iiii s.

Panis ob. de coketto Roberti de Burcestria def. in pondere iii s.
Habet iudicium
Panis ob. de consimili Walteri de Hereford def. xii d.
Panis ob. de consimili Willelmi Broun iunioris def. v s.

[Oct. 15, 1311] Temptacio panis facta die Veneris proxima post festum Translacionis sancti Edwardi regis anno predicto per sacramentum Thome de Mortone, Roberti de la Bache, Iohannis Atteyate, Willelmi de Puseye, Gilberti de Westone, Willelmi Attemore & Thome le Irmongere iuratorum qui dicunt per sacramentum suum quod die Mercurii proxima precedente melius frumentum se vendebatur pro iiii s. x d., secundum pro iiii s. vi d. & tercium pro iiii s. ii d.

In ista temptacione nullus invenitur defectus.

[Nov. 3, 1311] Temptacio panis facta die Mercurii in crastino Animarum anno r. regis E. quinto per sacramentum Thome Somer, Roberti de la Bache, Nigelli de Godwynestone, Thome de Mortone, Galfridi de Henxey, Simonis de Wortone & Iohannis Atteyate iuratorum qui dicunt per sacramentum suum quod die Sabbati proxima precedente quarterium melioris frumenti se vendebatur pro v s. ii d., secundi melioris pro iiii s. viii d. et tercii melioris pro iiii s. iiii d.

Panis qua. de wastello Roberti le Walsshe de Wodestoke def. xviii d.
Panis qua. de consimili Ricardi Persun def. xii d.
Panis ob. de clermatin Willelmi Broun iunioris def. iiii s. vi d.; habet iudicium; habuit iudicium die Lune in vigilia sancti Andree anno predicto
Panis ob. de integro Iohannis de Brehulle def. ii s.

[Nov. 5, 1311] Temptacio ceruisie facta die Veneris proxima post festum Omnium Sanctorum anno predicto per sacramentum Thome Somer, Radulfi de Cockeswelle, Iohannis de Staundene, Iohannis Stene, Ricardi de Cosintone, Roberti de Wyleby, Iohannis de Saunford parmentar, Gilberti de Winchecoumbe, Iohannis le Ta[uern]er, Thome de Croydon, Willelmi de la More & Gilberti de Westone iuratorum ad inquirendum super communi vendicione bladi facta Oxonie duobus diebus mercati proximo precedentibus videlicet frumenti, ordei & auenarum; qui dicunt per sacramentum suum quod duobus diebus mercati predictis quarterium melioris frumenti se vendebatur pro v s. iiii d., secundi melioris pro iiii s. viii d., et tercii melioris pro iiii s. iiii d.; quarterium uero melioris ordei pro iii s. viii d. & secundi melioris pro iii s. [iiii d.]. Et quarterium melioris auene pro ii s. & alterius melioris pro xxii d.; et secundum istam temptacionem consideratum est quod brac[iatrices] in Oxonia uendant [lagenam bon]e ceruisie in cuuis pro ob. & qua., et in doleis pro i d., et sic proclamatum.

Temptacio panis facta die Martis in festo sancti Thome apostoli anno predicto per sacramentum Thome Somer, Iohannis Atteyate, Thome le Irmongere, [ ] Glouc', Willelmi de la More & Walteri de Swyneshulle iuratorum qui dicunt per sacramentum suum quod die Sabbati proxima precedente quarterium melioris frumenti se vendebatur pro v s. iiii d., secundi melioris pro v s., et tercii pro iiii s. iiii d. **[Dec. 21, 1311]**

Panis qua. de wastello Edithe le Chapman deficit in pondere x d.
Panis qua. de consimili Roberti le Walshe deficit in bonitate & pondere x d.
Panis ob. de coketto Willelmi de Emyntone deficit ii s. (fecit finem pro vi d.)
Panis ob. de consimili Thome Godestre def. ii s. vi d. (fecit finem pro xii d. & pac')
Panis ob. de consimili Agnetis le Pyper def. ii s. (condonatur)

Ponderacio panis facta die Martis in festo Conuersionis sancti Pauli anno predicto per sacramentum Ricardi de Mortone, Thome de Mortone, Ricardi de Edrope, Iohannis de Gunwardeby, Willelmi de Puseye, Henrici de Edrope, Ricardi de Cosintone, Iohannis de Worthe & Iohannis de Coucle iuratorum, qui dicunt quod die Sabbati proxima precedente melius frumentum se vendebatur pro v s., secundum melius pro iiii s. vi d., & tercium pro iiii s. **[Jan. 25, 1312]**

In ista temptacione nullus invenitur defectus.

Ponderacio panis facta die Sabbati proxima ante festum sancti Gregorii pape anno predicto per sacramentum Roberti de la Bache, Gilberti de Winchecoumbe, Thome [ ], Iohannis Stene, **[Mar. 5, 1312]**

Henrici de Caumpedene, Gilberti de Westone & Willelmi le Teynturer iuratorum, qui dicunt per sacramentum suum quod die Mercurii proxima [precedente melius] frumentum se vendebatur pro iiii s. x d., secundum melius pro iiii s. vi d., et tercium pro iiii s. iiii d.

Panis qua de simenello Radulfi de Wittene deficit in pondere ii s.; fecit finem pro ii s.

Panis [ ] de consimili Roberti de Bokingham deficit xii d.
Panis [ ] de clermatin Roberti de Bokingham deficit v s. vi d. } fecit finem pro xii d.

Panis [ ] de consimili Hugonis de Bartone deficit iiii s. vi d.

[Apr. 25, 1312] [Ponderacio panis facta] die Martis in festo sancti Marcii [*sic*] evangeliste anno predicto per sacramentum Thome de Morton, Iohannis de Wintonia, Ricardi de Gloucestria, Iohannis [,] Henxey, Ricardi de Stratford, Ricardi de Edrope, & Iohannis Semere iuratorum qui dicunt per sacramentum suum quod die Sabbati proxima precedente melius frumentum se vendebatur pro iiii s. viii d., secundum pro iiii s. iiii d., et tercium pro iiii s.

Panis qua. de wastello Henrici Horn deficit ii s. vi d.
Panis qua. de consimili Iohannis le Sawyer def. viii d.
Panis qua. de consimili Edithe le Chapman def. xviii d.
Panis qua. de consimili Iohannis de Goseford def. xviii d.
Panis qua. de consimili Ricardi King deficit ii s.
Panis qua. de consimili Hugonis de Kent deficit ii s. vi d.
Panis ob. de coketto Ade de Tademertone deficit iiii s.
Panis ob. de consimili Willelmi de Chippenham def. iii s.
Panis ob. de clermatin Henrici de Stanlake def. ii s. vi d.
Panis ob. de consimili Ade de Tademertone def. ii s. vi d.
Abiurauit ministerium pistorie die Veneris prox. seq. per unum annum & unum diem
Panis ob. de consimili Radulfi de Wittene deficit vi s.

[May 31, 1312] Ponderacio panis facta die Mercurii proxima post festum sancti Augustini episcopi anno predicto per sacramentum Thome Somer, Roberti de la Bache, Thome de Mortone, [ ], Iohannis Atteyate & Willelmi de la More iuratorum qui dicunt per sacramentum suum quod die Sabbati proxima precedente melius frumentum se vendebatur pro iiii s. viii d., secundum melius pro iiii s. iiii d., & tercium pro iiii s.

Panis qua. de wastello Henrici Horn deficit xii d.[1]
Panis qua. de consimili Roberti le Chapman def. xii d.
Panis qua. de consimili Iohannis le Sawyer def. xii d.
Panis ob. de coketto Willelmi de Chippenham def. iiii s.
Panis ob. de integro Iuliane Edward def. ii s. vi d.

Ponderacio panis facta die Sabbati prox. post festum sancti Petri Aduincula anno r. r. E. sexto per sacramentum Radulfi de Cockeswelle, Thome de Mortone, Iohannis Atteyate, Ricardi de Stratford, Ade de Tilhurst & Iohannis de Longeworth iuratorum; qui dicunt per sacramentum suum quod die Mercurii proxima precedente melius frumentum se vendebatur pro v s., secundum melius pro iiii s. vi d., & tercium melius pro iiii s. ii d. [Aug. 5, 1312]

Panis qua. de wastello Roberti le Walshe de Wodestoke deficit in bonitate & in pondere [ ]
Panis ob. de coketto Walteri de Eynesham deficit ii s.

Ponderacio panis facta die Sabbati in crastino sancti Hugonis episcopi anno r. r. E. sexto per sacramentum Thome Somer, Iohannis Atteyate, Nigelli de Godwynestone, Ricardi de Edrope, Thome de Croydon & Thome de Mortone iuratorum, qui dicunt per sacramentum suum quod die Mercurii proxima precedente melius frumentum se vendebatur pro iiii s. [ ]d., secundum melius pro iiii s. vi d., & tercium pro iiii s. [Nov. 18, 1312]

In ista temptacione nullus inuentus fuit defectus.

Ponderacio panis facta die Sabbati in crastino Concepcionis beate Marie uirginis anno predicto per sacramentum Thome Somer, Thome de Mortone, Roberti de la Bache, Iohannis de Odiham, Ricardi de Edrope, Nigelli de Godwynestone & Iohannis de Colesburne iuratorum qui dicunt quod die Mercurii prox. precedente melius frumentum se vendebatur pro iiii s. x d., secundum melius pro iiii s. vi d., & tercium pro iiii s. ii d. [Dec. 9, 1312]

Panis ob. de coketto Iohannis de Thomele def. xviii d.; condonatur.

Temptacio ceruisie facta die Lune prox. post festum Concepcionis beate Marie virginis anno r. r. E. sexto per sacramentum Ade de [Dec. 11, 1312]

[1] There is something in the margin opposite this name, probably 'Wodestoke'.

Spalding, Thome Somer, Iohannis Stene, Ricardi de Cosingtone, Willelmi de la More, Iohannis le Tauerner, Ricardi de Hethrop, Gilberti de Westone, Ricardi le Cha, Willelmi de Stourtone, Iohannis le Webbe & Roberti de Puyntle iuratorum ad inquirendum & presentandum communem venditionem bladi duobus diebus mercati proximo precedentibus; qui presentant per sacramentum suum quod duobus diebus mercati predictis quarterium melioris frumenti se vendebatur pro iiii s. x d., secundi melioris pro iiii s. vi d., & tercii pro iiii s. ii d.; et quarterium melioris ordei se vendebatur pro iii s. viii d. & alterius melioris pro xl d.; quarterium meliorum avenarum se vendebatur pro ii s. vi d. & alterius melioris pro ii s. iiii d.; et secundum istam temptacionem consideratum est quod braciatrices in Oxonia vendant lagenam bone ceruisie in cuuis pro ob. & qua., & in doleis pro i d. & non ulterius, & sic proc[lamatum est].

[Mar. 14, 1313] Ponderacio panis facta die Mercurii prox. ante festum sancti Gregorii pape anno predicto per sacramentum Thome Somer, Iohannis de Couele, Thome de Mortone, Roberti de la Bache, Iohannis de Odyham, Ricardi de Gloucestria, Ricardi de Cosintone, Ricardi de Edrope, Radulfi de Haille, Iohannis de Wintone, Ricardi de Stratforde & Gilberti Westone iuratorum; qui dicunt quod die Sabbati prox. precedente melius quarterium frumenti se vendebatur pro v s. ii d., secundum pro iiii s. viii d., & tercium pro iiii s. vi d.

Panis ob. de clermatin Willelmi de Wyghthulle deficit in pondere ii s. (xii d.)
Panis ob. de integro Iuliane Edward def. ii s. vi d. (xviii d.)

[Jan. 20, 1313] Ponderacio panis facta die Sabbati in festo sanctorum Fabiani & Sebastiani anno r. r. E. sexto per sacramentum Ricardi de Mortone, Iohannis Atteyate, Thome de Mortone, Ricardi de Uptone, Iohannis de Odyham & Ricardi de Stratford iuratorum; qui dicunt per sacramentum suum quod die Mercurii prox. precedente melius quarterium frumenti se vendebatur pro v s., secundum melius pro iiii s. vi d., & tercium pro iiii s.

Panis ob. de coketto Henrici de Ocle def. ii s.
Panis ob. de clermatin Henrici de Ocle def. ii s.
Panis ob. de integro Iuliane Edward def. v s.

[Nov. 5, 1313] Ponderacio panis facta die Lune proxima post festum Omnium Sanctorum anno r. r. E. septimo per sacramentum Iohannis Atteyate, Thome de Mortone, Thome le Hirmongere, Iohannis de Odiham,

Nicholai de Glettone, & Willelmi le Teinturer iuratorum; qui dicunt super sacramentum suum quod die Sabbati proxima precedente melius quarterium frumenti se vendebatur pro v s. vi d., secundum melius pro v s., & tercium pro iiii s. vi d.

Panis ob. de coketto Walteri de Burncestria def. iii s. (xii d.)
Panis ob. de consimili Henrici de Rollendricht def. ii s. (vi d.)
Panis ob. de consimili Iohannis de Horspath def. xviii d. (xii d.)
Panis ob. de clermatin Hugonis le Coupere def. ii s. vi d. (xii d.)
Panis ob. de consimili Walteri de Burncestria def. ii s. (supra)

Ponderacio panis facta die Iouis in vigilia sancti Andree apostoli anno r. r. E. septimo per sacramentum Thome de Mortone, Thome le Irmongere, Ade de Dentone, Radulfi de [ ], Iohannis de Coumbe & Walteri de Swyneshulle iuratorum; qui dicunt per sacramentum suum quod die Sabbati proxima precedente melius quarterium frumenti se vendebatur pro v s. vi d., secundum melius pro iiii s. viii d., & tercium pro iiii s. ii d. [Nov. 29, 1313]

In ista temptacione nichil inuentum fuit in defectu.

Temptacio ceruisie facta die Veneris in festo sancti Andree apostoli anno r. r. E. septimo per sacramentum Thome Somer, Ade de Spalding, Ricardi de Uptone, Iohannis de Wuttone, Ricardi de Cosintone, Ricardi de Hethrop, Iohannis Bisshop, Gilberti de Westone, Thome de Croydone, Willelmi Pope, [ ] & Ade de Dentone iuratorum ad inquirendum super venditione bladi in duobus diebus mercati proximo precedentibus venditi in Oxonia, scilicet frumenti, ordei, & auenarum; qui dicunt per sacramentum suum quod duobus diebus mercati predictis quarterium melioris frumenti se vendebatur pro v s. vi d., secundi melioris pro v s., et tercii pro iiii s. vi d.; quarterium uero melioris [ordei pro] & alterius melioris pro xl d.; et quarterium auenarum pro xxxii d.; et secundum istam temptacionem consideratum est quod braciatrices vendant lagenam bone ceruisie in cuuis pro ob. qua. & in doleis pro i d.; et sic proclamatum. [Nov. 30, 1313]

Ponderacio panis facta die Sabbati in crastino sancti Thome apostoli anno r. r. E. septimo per sacramentum Willelmi de Puseye, Iohannis Atteyate, Thome de [, Thome] Somer, Ade de Dentone & Thome le Irmongere iuratorum; qui dicunt per sacramentum suum quod die Mercurii proxima precedente melius quarterium [Dec. 22, 1313] frumenti se vendebatur pro v s. vi d., secundum melius pro v s. & tercium pro iiii s. vi d.

Panis ob. de clermatin Matillidis de Thomele def. vi s. (ii s.)

Panis ob. de tract' Ricardi de Tiwe, de parochia Omnium Sanctorum, def. xiii s. vi d. Postea per sacramentum Roberti le Grynder, Walteri le Marchal, Thome Pouk, Nicholai de Westone, Thome le Irmongere, Thome de [ ] & Iohannis de la More iuratorum, in quos Ricardus de Tiwe del huth posuit se coram custodibus huius assise & magistro Iohanne de [superuisore huius] assise ex parte Uniuersitatis & aliis fidedignis compertum est quod panis predictus qui irrotulatur sub nomine Ricardi de Tiwe fuerat panis [quorundam forin]secorum pistorum & non Ricardi de Tiwe del huthe; ideo ipse Ricardus del huthe inde quietus.

[Jan. 12, 1314] Ponderacio panis facta die Sabbati proxima ante festum sancti Hillarii anno r. r. E. septimo per sacramentum Thome de Mortone, Ricardi de Stratford, [ ], Nicholai de Glettone, Willelmi le Teinturer & Willelmi de la More iuratorum; qui dicunt per sacramentum suum quod die Mercurii prox. precedente quarterium melioris frumenti se vendebatur pro v s. vi d., secundi melioris pro v s., & tercii pro iiii s. vi d.

In ista temptacione nullus inuenitur defectus.

[Apr. 20, 1314] Ponderacio panis facta die Sabbati prox. ante festum sancti Georgii martiris anno r. r. E. septimo per sacramentum Ade de Tilhurst, Iohannis [, le] Grasier, Nicholai de Glettone, Ade de Dentone & Willelmi de Wodestoke, Ade de Dentone, Willelmi de la More, Iohannis Atteyate, [ ]burne, Iohannis de Wintone & Ricardi de Cosintone iuratorum; qui dicunt per sacramentum suum quod die Mercurii proxima precedente melius quarterium frumenti se vendebatur [pro], secundum melius pro v s., & tercium pro iiii s. vi d.

Panis ob. de clermatin Thome de Hasele def. ii s. (vi d.)

[July 13, 1314] Ponderacio panis facta die Sabbati prox. post festum Translacionis sancti Thome martiris anno r. r. E. octauo per sacramentum Roberti de la Bache, [ ], Thome le Irmongere, Iohannis de Odyham, Nicholai de Glettone & Willelmi de la More iuratorum, qui dicunt per sacramentum suum quod die [ ] quarterium melioris frumenti se vendebatur pro dimidia marca, secundi melioris pro vi s. iiii d., & tercii pro vi s.

Nullus fuit defectus in pane in temptacione ista.

Ponderacio panis facta die Sabbati in festo sancti Laurencii martiris [Aug. 10, 1314] anno r. r. E. octauo per sacramentum Iohannis de Perschore, Thome de Mortone, [ ], Nicholai de Glettone, Willelmi de la More & Gilberti de Westone iuratorum; qui dicunt per sacramentum suum quod die Mercurii proxima precedente quarterium melioris frumenti se vendebatur pro vii s. ii d., secundi melioris pro vi s. viii d., & tercii pro vi s.

Panis ob. de coketto Ade de Wareberghe def. ii s. vi d. (Nichil)
Panis ob. de coketto Radulfi de Stockenechirche def. v s. vi d. Fecit finem pro xii d.
Panis denar. de integro Ricardi de Tiwe def. v s. vi d. (xii d.)

Ponderacio panis facta die Veneris in vigilia Exaltacionis sancte [Sept. 13, 1314] Crucis anno r. r. E. octauo per sacramentum Thome Somer, Ricardi de Mortone, Iohannis [, Thome] le Irmongere, Ricardi de Uptone & Nicholai de Glettone iuratorum; qui dicunt per sacramentum suum quod die Mercurii prox. precedente quarterium melioris frumenti se vendebatur [ ], secundi melioris pro v s. vi d., et tercii pro v s.

Panis ob. de integro Iohannis de Westone def. x s. (ii s.)
Panis ob. de omnibus Roberti filii Henrici le Gaoler def. xi s. Adiudicatur pillorie; & habet iudicium [die] sancte Frideswide hoc anno.

Ponderacio panis facta die Sabbati prox. ante festum Translacionis [Oct. 12, 1314] sancti Edwardi regis anno r. r. E. octauo per sacramentum Roberti de la Bache [ ], Radulfi de Hailles, Iohannis Prest, Willelmi le Teinturer & Iohannis de Coumbe iuratorum; qui dicunt per sacramentum suum quod die Mercurii prox. precedente quarterium melioris frumenti se vendebatur pro vi s. viii d., secundi melioris pro vi s., & tercii pro v s. iiii d.

Panis ob. de coketto Henrici de Rollendright def. iii s. vi d. (Nichil)
Panis ob. de consimili Iohannis de Leye def. iii s. (xii d.)
Panis ob. de consimili Walteri de Hereford def. ii s. (vii d.)

Temptacio ceruisie facta die Veneris prox. ante festum sancti [Nov. 8, 1314] Martini anno r. r. E. octauo per sacramentum Ricardi de Hethrop, Ricardi de Uptone, Iohannis de S[taun]dene, Willelmi de la More, Stephani de Adintone, Iohannis de Odyham, Iohannis Bat', Gilberti de Westone, Thome le Irmongere, Thome Somere, Ricardi de

Hedindone & Iohannis de Berkele iuratorum; qui dicunt per sacramentum suum quod die Mercurii prox. precedente quarterium melioris frumenti se vendebatur pro vii s., secundi melioris pro vi s. vi d., & tercii pro vi s.; quarterium melioris ordei pro iiii s. iiii d., secundi melioris pro iiii s.; et quarterium auenarum pro iii s.

[Apr. 5, 1315] Ponderacio panis facta die Sabbati prox. post festum sancti Ambrosii anno r. r. E. octauo per sacramentum Thome Somer, Iohannis de Odyham, Iohannis Atteyate, Thome le Irmongere, Willelmi de Puseye, Ricardi de Uptone, Willelmi de la More & Ade de Dentone; qui dicunt quod die Mercurii prox. precedente quarterium melioris frumenti se vendebatur pro vii s. vi d., secundi melioris pro vii s., et tercii pro vi s. vi d.

Panis qua. de wastello Ricardi Persun de Wodestoke def.	vi d. (nichil)
Panis qua. de eodem Gilberti Lyon de Wodestoke def.	ii s. (xii d.)
Panis qua. de eodem Willelmi Louerich def.	xii d. (vi d.)
Panis qua. de eodem Willelmi de Kent def.	xii d. (vi d.)
Panis qua. de eodem Hugonis de Kent def.	vi d.
Panis qua. de eodem Thome King deficit	vi d.
Panis qua. de eodem Ricardi King def.	vi d.
Panis qua. de eodem Henrici Horn def.	vi d.
Panis qua. de eodem Thome le Sawyer def.	vi d.
Panis ob. de coketto Iohannis Prest def.	v s. (ii s.)
Panis ob. de eodem Willelmi de Wyghthulle def.	iiii s.
Panis ob. de eodem Gilberti de Schipford def.	xii d.
Panis ob. de eodem Henrici de Neubotle def.	xii d.
Panis ob. de clermatin Willelmi de Wyghthulle def.	iii s. vi d.
Panis ob. de integro Iohannis de Weston def.	v s.
Panis denarr' de integro Walteri de Middeleye def.	vi s.
Panis denarr' de eodem Agnetis Attehuthe def.	ii s. vi d.
Panis ob. de omni blado Iohannis de Weston def.	iii s.
Panis denarr' de eodem Stephani de Stoford def.	iii s.

Summa panis forisfacti ii d. qua., unde
I. Wawelok' respond[ebit]

[June 21, 1315] Ponderacio panis facta die Sabbati prox. ante festum Natiuitatis sancti Iohannis Baptiste anno r. r. E. octauo per sacramentum Thome Somer, Thome le Irmongere, Iohannis Atteyate, Nicholai le Mercer, Ricardi de Cosintone, & Roberti de la Bache; qui dicunt per sacramentum suum quod die Mercurii proxima precedente quarterium melioris frumenti se vendebatur pro viii s., secundi melioris pro vii s. vi d., & tercii pro vii s.

Panis ob. de coketto Thome de Southleye	def.	xviii d. (iii d.)
Panis ob. de eodem Nicholai de Westone	def.	xviii d. (iii d.)
Panis ob. de eodem Thome de Stauntone	def.	xviii d. (nichil)
Panis ob. de eodem Gilberti de Schiptone	def.	xii d. (nichil)
Panis ob. de eodem Willelmi de Wighthulle	def.	xii d. (nichil)
Panis ob. de eodem Iohannis de Horspathe	def.	xii d. (nichil)
Panis ob de clermatin Willelmi de Wighthulle	def.	iii s. (xii d.)
Panis ob. de eodem Cecilie de Witteneye	def.	ii s. vi d. (vi d.)
Panis ob de eodem Henrici de Witteneye	def.	iii s. (xii d.)

Temptacio panis facta apud Oxoniam III Idus Aprilis coram domino Henrico Gower, cancellario Uniuersitatis Oxonie, & Roberto de Watlyngtone maiore eiusdem ville anno regni regis Edwardi filii regis Edwardi decimo septimo, custodibus assise panis & ceruisie in villa supradicta & eius suburbiis virtute cuiusdam commissionis domini regis in hec uerba: 'Edwardus dei gracia rex Anglie, dominus Hibernie & dux Aquitanie omnibus ad quos presentes littere peruenerint salutem. Sciatis quod commisimus Cancellario Uniuersitatis Oxonie & maiori ville qui pro tempore fuerint custodiam panis & ceruisie in uilla predicta & suburbiis eiusdem, habendam quamdiu nobis placuerit, reddendo inde nobis per annum ad Scaccarium nostrum centum solidos, unam uidelicet medietatem ad Scaccarium nostrum Pasche & aliam medietatem ad Scaccarium nostrum sancti Michaelis per equales porciones, quamdiu custodiam habuerint supradictam. In cuius rei testimonium has litteras nostras fieri fecimus patentes. T' me ipso apud Westmonasterium XVI die Marcii anno regni nostri decimo septimo', per sacramentum Willelmi Lirmongere, Thome de Curtlyngtone, Iohannis de Odyham, Thome Lirmongere, Roberti le Marchal, Willelmi de la More, Petri de Ew, Thome Somer, Ricardi Ouerhe, Willelmi de Puseye, Ricardi de Wyndesore, Iohannis de Westone iuratorum; qui dicunt per sacramentum suum quod ultimo die mercati quarterium melioris frumenti valebat dimidiam marcam, quarterium vero secundi vi s., quarterium vero tercii v s. vi d. Unde assisa facta est super vi s.

[Apr. 11, 1324]

[Mar. 16, 1324]

Thomas le Kynge habet I wastell' de qua. & deficit in pondere vi d. (iii d.)

Idem Thomas habet I wastell' de qua. & def. in pondere xiii d. (iii d.)

Reginaldus Lodere habet I wastell' de qua. & def. in pond. ii s. (vi d.)

Ioh' de Burcestre habet I wastell' de qua. & def. in pond. iii d.

Robertus le Chepman habet I wastell' de qua. & def. in pond. xv d. (iii d.)

Will. de Gretteworth habet I panem de clermatin de ob. & def. ii s. vi d. (vi d.)

Will. de Hasele habet I panem de frumento[1] de ob. & def. iiii s. (xii d.)

[May 3, 1324] Temptacio panis facta die Iouis tercio die Maii anno predicto per sacramentum Henrici de Bedeford, Willelmi de Ottele, Roberti le Marchal & Thome de Curtlyngton, Alani de Hetone, Willelmi Lirmongere, Thome Chichele, Iohannis de Aumbresbury, Walteri de Miltone, Nigelli de Godwynstone, Walteri le Tauerner & Willelmi de Puseye; qui dicunt per sacramentum eorum quod die Sabbati proximo precedente quarterium melioris frumenti vendebatur pro vi s. viii d., secundum melius pro vi s., tercium pro v s. vi d.

Thomas de Goseford habet I wastell de qua. & def. ii s. vi d. (vi d.)

Idem Thomas habet I wastell de qua. & def. xviii d.

[ ][2] Clok' de Wodestoke habet I wastell de qua. & def. xviii d.
" " " " " " vii d.
" " " " " " xii d.
" " " " " " xv d.
} (vi d.)

Thomas de Goseford habet I wastell de qua. & def. xii d.

Philippus Kyng habet I wastell de qua. & deficit ix d. (ii d.)

Will' Leuerich habet I wastell de qua. & def. iii d.

Simon Wilekyn habet I wastell de qua. & def. vi d.

Alicia Hichecoke habet I wastell de qua. & def. vi d.

Ricardus de Warberghe habet I panem de coket de ob. & def. ix d.

Gilbertus de Shuptone habet I panem de coket de ob. & def. xv d. (iiii d.)

Idem Gilbertus habet I panem de coket de ob. & def. vi d.

Ioh' Coket habet I panem de coket de ob. & def. vi d.

Idem Ioh' habet I panem de coket de ob. & def. xxi d. (vi d.)

[1] In the margin 'panis integer'.
[2] The scribe leaves a space for the Christian name.

Ioh' de Stangrave habet I panem de coket de ob. & def. xviii d. (iii d.)
Gilb' de Shuptone habet I panem de coket de ob. & def. xii d.
Rob' le Chepman habet I panem de wastell de qua. & def. iii d.
Agnes Huchecoke habet I panem de wastell de qua. & def. vi d.
Ric. Leveriche habet I panem de wastell de qua. & def. iii d.
Ioh' Pachet habet I panem de wastell de qua. & def. iii d.
Idem Ioh' habet I panem de wastell de qua. & def. iii d.
Ioh' Coket habet I panem de clermatin de ob. & def. xii d. (ii d.)

Temptacio ceruisie facta apud Oxoniam coram predictis custodibus die Veneris in crastino Inuentionis sancte Crucis anno predicto per sacramentum Thome Somer, Thome de Curtlyntone, Iohannis de Isslep, Ricardi Grasiere, Willelmi Bagard, Willelmi Lirmongere, Willelmi de Suttone, Walteri de Warberghe, Ricardi de Warberghe, Iohannis de Wytteneye, Iohannis Lauendrye & Walteri Tauerner; qui dicunt per sacramentum suum quod quarterium melioris frumenti vendebatur ultimo die mercati pro dimidia marca et quarterium melioris ordei pro iiii s. & quarterium auenarum pro ii s. iiii d. Summa xiii s. Ideo consideratum est quod lagena melioris ceruisie [ ] vendatur pro i den. [**May 4, 1324**]

Temptacio panis facta die Sabbati proxima post festum Inuencionis sancte Crucis anno predicto. [**May 5, 1324**]

Ioh' de Goseford habet I wastell de qua. & def. ii s. iii d. (vi d.)
Agnes la Chapman habet I wastell de qua. & def. xvi d. (iii d.)
Rob' le Chapman habet I wastell de qua. & def. vi d.

Temptacio panis facta coram predictis custodibus die Lune prox. ante [1] festum sancti Iohannis ante portam Latinam anno predicto per sacramentum Roberti le Marchal, Galfridi Scot, Iohannis de Odyham, Ricardi de Wyndesores, Walteri Tauerner, Ricardi Ouerhee, Nigelli de Godwynstone, Ricardi de Suttone, Thome de London, Iohannis de Broghtone, Iohannis Waget & Iohannis de Hadenham; qui dicunt per sacramentum suum quod quarterium melioris frumenti vendebatur ultimo die mercati pro vi s. x d., quarterium vero secundi pro vi s., quarterium vero tercii pro v s. vi d. [**May 7, 1324**]

Ioh' Pache habet I wastell de qua. & def. in pondere ix d.
Ioh' Horn habet I wastell de qua. & def. in pondere ix d.

[1] The scribe means *post*. Sunday, May 6, was the day of St. John 'ante portam Latinam'.

Reginaldus Heite habet I wastell de qua. & def. in pondere xv d. (iii d.)
Hen. le Neuman habet I wastell de qua. & def. in pond. xv d. (iii d.)
Agnes la Chapman habet I wastell de qua. & def. in pond. ii s. (vi d.)
Ioh' de Goseford habet I wastell de qua. & def. in pond. xii d. (iii d.)
Ric' de Warberghe habet I panem de clermatyn de ob. & def. xv d. (differtur)
Adam de Tilhurst habet I panem de coketto de ob. & def. xv d. (iii d.)
Walterus de Middele habet I panem de omni genere bladi & def. ii s. vi d. (vi d.)

[May 12, 1324] Tastatores ceruisie electi die Sabbati prox. post festum sancti Iohannis ante portam Latinam: Will' Lirmonger, Ric' Hoppere, Thomas Curtlyntone, Ric' Warberghe.

[May 26, 1324] Temptacio panis facta coram prefatis custodibus die Sabbati proxima ante festum Petronille anno predicto per sacramentum Iohannis de Ew, Willelmi Attemore, Willelmi Ottele, Alani de Hetone, Ricardi de Edrop mercer, Radulfi de Erdyntone, Willelmi Lirmongere, Iohannis de Odyham, Thome Chichele, Iohannis de Hadenham, Iohannis de Westone & Ricardi de Wyndesore; qui dicunt per sacramentum suum quod quarterium melioris frumenti vendebatur ultimo die mercati pro vi s. viii d.; quarterium vero secundi pro vi s.; quarterium vero tercii pro v s. vi d.

Rob' le Chapman habet I wastell de qua. & def. vi d.
Reginaldus Fisik habet I wastell de qua. & def. vi d.
Will' de Kent habet I wastell de qua. & def. vi d.
Gilbertus de Lyoun habet I wastell de qua. & def. vi d.
Rob' de Newentone habet I clermatyn de ob. & def. xxi d. (iiii d.)

[June 26, 1324] Temptacio panis facta coram prefatis custodibus die Martis prox. ante festum apostolorum Petri & Pauli anno predicto per sacramentum Thome de Curtlyntone, Iohannis de Wytteneye, Alani de Hetone, Iohannis de Staundene, Walteri de Miltone, Willelmi de la More, Ricardi de Wyndesore, Radulfi de Erdyntone, Iohannis de Odyham, Ricardi de Stauntone, Thome Chichele & Iohannis Aumbresbury; qui dicunt per sacramentum suum quod quarterium melioris frumenti vendebatur ultimo die mercati pro vii s. iiii d., quarterium vero secundi vi s. viii d., quarterium vero tercii pro vi s.

Temptacio panis facta die Sabbati proxima post festum Translacionis sancti Thome martiris anno r. r. E. filii regis E. decimo octauo per sacramentum Iohannis de Ew, Iohannis de Aumbresbury, Thome Chicheli, Henrici de Bedeford, Iohannis de Westone, Iohannis de Merstone, Iohannis Waget, Iohannis le Mareschal, Willelmi de Suttone, Roberti Treweloue, Ricardi de Suttone & Iohannis Colesburne; qui dicunt per sacramentum suum quod quarterium melioris frumenti vendebatur ultimo die mercati pro vi s. viii d., secundum melius pro vi s., tercium melius pro v s. vi d. [July 14, 1324]

Reginaldus Hickes habet I wastell de qua. & def. iii s. iii d. (Iudicium)
Philippus Saweie habet I wastell de qua. & def. xviii d. (iii d.)
Ioh' Pacche habet I wastell de qua. & def. ii s. vi d. (vi d.)
Hugo Kyng habet I wastell de qua. & def. ii s. ix d. (Iudicium)
Ioh' de Goseford habet I wastell de qua. & def. ii s. (iiii d.)
Rob' Chepman habet I wastell de qua. & def. xviii d. (iii d.)
Alicia filia Ricardi Kyng habet I wastell de qua. & def. ii s. iii d. (iiii d.)
Hen' Bette habet I panem de coket de ob. & def. ii s. (iiii d.)
Will. de Gretteworth habet I coket de ob. & def. xviii d. (iii d.)
Rob. de Leye habet I coket de ob. & def. xvi d. (ii d.)
Thomas de Leye habet I coket de ob. & def. xii d.
Will' de Emyntone habet I clermatyn de ob. & def. xviii d. (ii d.)
Adam de Tylhurst habet I clermatyn de ob. & def. xviii d. (iii d.)

Temptacio panis facta die Lune prox. sequente per temptacionem predictam & appreciacionem. [July 16, 1324]

Ioh' Pache habet I wastell de qua. & def. ii s. (iiii d.)
Thomas Kyng habet I wastell de qua. & def. ii s. (iiii d.)
Agnes Chapman habet I wastell de qua. & def. xviii d. (iii d.)
Reginaldus Fisyk habet I wastell de qua. & def. ii s. (iiii d.)
Ioh' Broun habet I wastell de qua. & def. ii s. (iiii d.)
Gilbertus Lyon habet I wastell de qua. & def. ii s. vi d. (vi d.)
Isabella Hakes habet I wastell de qua. & def. xii d. (ii d.)
Hen' Neuman habet I wastell de qua. & def. ii s. iii d. (iiii d.)
Alic' Kyng habet I wastell de qua. & def. ii s. (iiii d.)

Affer[atores] Will. de Whatele, Ric. de Edrope, Pet. de Ew, Rad. de Erdynton } iurati — Summa xiiii s.

Memb. 5 [Oct. 11, 1325]

Temptacio assise panis facta die Veneris prox. post festum sancti Dionisii anno regni regis E. filii regis E. decimo nono coram domino Henrico Gouwer cancellario Oxonie & Willelmo de Burncestre maiore per sacramentum Thome Lyrmongere, Willelmi de Ottele, [Ioh'] de Odyham, Ricardi de Wyndesore, Willelmi de Strykelond, Willelmi atte More, Ade le Northerne, [ ], Iohannis de Weston, Roberti le Marchal, Ricardi de Sutton & Iohannis le Marchal; qui dicunt per sacramentum suum quod ultimo die mercati quarterium melioris frumenti vendebatur pro v s. viii d., secundi melioris pro v s. iiii d., & tercii melioris pro v s.

Panis wastell Iohannis Page de qua. def. xxi d. (iiii d.)
Panis wastell Simonis Wilkyns de qua. def. xxi d. (iiii d.)
Panis wastell Roberti Broun de qua. def. xii d. (ii d.)
Panis wastell Gilberti Lyon de qua. def. xii d. (ii d.)
Panis wastell Iohannis Goseword de qua. def. —
Panis wastell Dionisie Kynges de qua. def. ii s. (vi d.)
Panis coket Walteri de Quenyntone de ob. def. ii s. (iiii d.)
Panis integer de frumento minoris precii Agathe Rouland-right de ob. def. vii s. (iudicium)
Panis integer de frumento Simonis Kynt de ob. def. vi s. (iudicium)

[Nov. 9, 1325]

Temptacio assise panis facta die Sabati prox. ante festum sancti Martini coram custodibus supradictis anno supradicto per sacramentum Thome Lirmongere, Willelmi Lirmongere, Gilberti le Furbur, Iohannis de Odyham, Roberti le Marchal, Thome de Curtlyntone, Willelmi le Mercer, Thome Somer, Willelmi Strykelond, Willelmi de Ottele, Ricardi de Wyndesore & Radulfi de Erdyntone qui dicunt super sacramentum suum quod ultimo die mercati quarterium melioris frumenti vendebatur pro vi s., secundi melioris pro v s. vi d., tercii melioris v s.

Panis de coket Willelmi de Gruteworth de ob. def. xiiii d. (finis ii s.)
Panis de coket Ioh' de Hynkele def. xv d.
Panis de coket Henrici Botte def. xviii d. (iiii d.)
Panis de coket Ricardi Leyk' de ob. def. vi d. (ii d.)
Panis tusseyn Iohannis de Hales de ob. def. xviii d. (vi d.)
Panis de omni genere bladi Henrici de Witteneye de ob. def. iiii s. (xii d.)

Temptacio panis facta die Sabati in festo sancti Clementis coram custodibus supradictis anno supradicto per sacramentum Thome Lyrmongere, Iohannis [,] de Erdyntone, Ricardi de Wyndesore, Thome de Curtlyntone, Willelmi de Ottele, Willelmi le Mercer, Alani de Heton, Willelmi de Strykelond, Ricardi de Edrope, Roberti le Marchal & Willelmi de la More ; qui dicunt per sacramentum suum quod ultimo die mercati quarterium melioris frumenti vendebatur pro v s. x d., secundi melioris v s. vi d., tercii melioris v s. [Nov. 23, 1325]

Panis de gastel Gilberti Lyon de qua. def. xxi d. (vi d.)
Panis de coket Iohannis de Leghe de ob. def. vi d. (ii d.)
Panis clermatyn Nicholai le Marchal de ob. def. vi d. (ii d.)
Panis integer de frumento Roberti Droci de ob. def. vi s.
(Passus est iudicium die Sabati in festo sancti Pauli per consideracionem custodum infrascriptorum).

Temptacio panis facta die Martis prox. post festum sancti Andree apostoli anno supradicto coram custodibus supradictis per sacramentum [Gilberti le] Furbur, Iohannis de Westone, Ricardi de Wyndesore, Iohannis de Hodyham, Thome Lyrmongere, [Thome] de Curtlynton, Roberti le Marchal, Walteri le Tauerner; qui dicunt per sacramentum suum quod ultimo die mercati quarterium melioris frumenti vendebatur pro v s. viii d., secundi melioris v s. iiii d., tercii melioris v s. [Dec. 3, 1325]

Panis de coket Thome de Godestre de ob. def [ ] (ii d.)
Panis de coket Willelmi de Westone de ob. def. [ ] (iiii d.)
Panis integer de frumento Rad. de Stokenechirche def. [ ] (viii d.)
Panis de omni genere bladi Thome de [ ] def. [ ] (iudicium)

Temptacio panis facta die Mercurii in festo sancti Vincencii anno r. r. E. fil. regis E. decimo nono per sacramentum Thome Lirmongere, Willelmi Lirmongere, Ricardi de Gloucestria, Radulfi de Erdyntone, Willelmi le Mercer, Thome de Curtlyntone, Roberti le Marchal, Willelmi de Ottele, Willelmi de Strikelond, Ricardi de Churchulle & Ade de Remyntone; qui dicunt per sacramentum suum quod ultimo die mercati quarterium melioris frumenti vendebatur pro v s. iiii d., secundi melioris v s., tercii melioris pro iiii s. viii d. [Jan. 22, 1326]

Panis de omni genere bladi Thome de Horspathe de ob. def. ii s. (vi d.)

Panis de omni genere bladi Willelmi Chapleyn de ob. def. iiii s. (viii d.)
Panis de coket Willelmi de Stanlake de ob. def. xii d. (iiii d.)
Panis de gastel Reginaldi Fisik de qua. def. ii s. viii d. (xii d.)
Panis de gastel Thome le Kyng de qua. def. xii d. (iii d.)
Panis de gastel Iohannis de Goseworde de qua. def. ii s. vi d. (viii d.)
Panis de gastel Thome de Goseuorde de qua. def. xix d. (iiii d.)
Panis de gastel Simonis Wilkyng de qua. def. xxvii d. (viii d.)
Panis de gastel Hugonis de Kent de qua. def. ii s. (vi d.)
Panis de gastel Agnetis Hobekyns de qua. def. xviii d. (iiii d.)
Panis de gastel Gilberti Lyon de qua. def. xviii d. (iiii d.)
Panis de gastel Hugonis Pudding de qua. def. xxi d. (vi d.)
Panis de gastel Reginaldi Hikkes de qua. def. ii s. (vi d.)
Panis de gastel Dionisie Kynges de qua. def. xxiii d. (v d.)
Panis de gastel Philippi Crommes de qua. def. xviii d. (iiii d.)
Simon de Erdynton ponit se in misericordia pro transgressione facta servienti custodum assise panis per plegium Walteri le Marchal ; (xii d.)
Willelmus de Ottele ponit se in misericordia pro transgressione deliberacionis panis attachiati per servientem custodum assise (condonatur)

[Feb. 15, 1326] Temptacio panis facta die Sabbati prox. post festum sancti Valentini anno supradicto per sacramentum Willelmi le Irmongere, Thome Lirmongere, Iohannis Wachet, Radulfi de Erdyntone, Willelmi de Ottele, Willelmi Strikelond, Willelmi Mercer, Thome de Curtlyntone, Ade de Remyntone, Roberti Marchal, Ricardi de Edrop & Walteri Mercer; qui dicunt quod ultimo die mercati quarterium melioris frumenti vendebatur pro v s. iiii d., secundi pro v s., tercii pro iiii s. vi d.

Panis coket Iohannis Coke de ob. def. xii d. (finis xl d.)

[Feb. 20, 1326] Taxacio amerciamentorum suprascriptorum die Iouis prox. ante festum sancti Petri in Cathedra anno supradicto: taxatores Thomas de Curtlintone & Ioh' de Odiham.

[Feb. 28, 1326] Temptacio panis facta die Veneris prox. ante festum sancti Dauid coram custodibus supradictis anno supradicto per sacramentum Iohannis de Odyham, Iohannis de Coryngham, Willelmi Lirmongere, Ricardi de Wyndesore, Iohannis de Westone, Radulfi de Erdyntone,

Willelmi de Strykelond, Willelmi le Mercer, Ade de Remynton, Roberti le Marchall, Walteri le Mercer & Iohannis Wachet; qui dicunt super sacramentum suum quod ultimo die mercati quarterium melioris frumenti vendebatur pro v s., secundi melioris pro iiii s. vi d., tercii melioris iiii s.

Panis de treiyt Thome de Mershe de ob. def. in pondere xxxvii s. & in alio pane xxvii s. vi d.

Panis integer de frumento Willelmi de Hasele de ob. def. vii s.

Panis integer de frumento Isabelle de Shiptone de ob. def. v s.

Panis integer de frumento Margarete atte Huthe de ob. def. ii s.

Temptacio panis facta die Martis prox. ante festum apostolorum Philippi & Iacobi anno r. r. E. decimo nono per sacramentum Thome Lirmongere, Gilberti le Furbur, Iohannis Wachet, Willelmi de Ottele, Iohannis de Coryngham, Willelmi Strikelond, Roberti le Marchal, Ade de Remyntone, Walteri le Mercer, Galfridi Skot & Radulfi de Thornhawe; qui dicunt super sacramentum suum quod ultimo die mercati quarterium melioris frumenti vendebatur pro v s., secundi melioris pro iiii s. viii d., tercii melioris pro iiii s. iiii d. [Apr. 28, 1326]

Nullus erant [*sic*] defectus eodem die. Forisf' vii d. de pane caballino.

Temptacio panis facta die Mercurii prox. post festum sancti Augustini anno r. r. E. fil. regis Edwardi decimo nono per sacramentum Iohannis de Odyham, Willelmi Lirmongere, Ricardi de Wyndesore, Iohannis de Westone, Willelmi Strikelond, Roberti le Marchal, Walteri de Lyuorde, Iohannis de Broghtone, Willelmi de Ottele, & Thome de Curtlyntone; qui dicunt quod ultimo die mercati quarterium melioris frumenti vendebatur pro v s., secundi melioris pro iiii s. viii d., tercii melioris pro iiii s. iiii d. [May 28, 1326]

Panis de coket Hugonis de Godestre de ob. def. xviii d.

Panis de coket Gilberti Lyein de qua. def. ii s. ix d.

Panis de coket Willelmi de Emynton de ob. def. xviii s. (Finis xl d.)

Agnes atte Huthe uxor Willelmi de Bartone habet panem de frumento de integro frumento; deficit [ ]

[Mar. 4, 1327] Tempore Iohannis de Dokelyntone; anno r. r. E. tercii post conquestum primo.

Temptacio panis facta die Mercurii, IIII die Marcii, anno r. r. predicti primo per sacramentum Roberti Marchal, Walteri Mercer, Iohannis Broghtone, Iohannis le Coke, Iohannis de Odiham, Iohannis de Westone, Iohannis Waget, Willelmi de Ottele, Nicholai de Glettone, Ricardi de Eynesham, Rogeri Pyroun, & Iohannis de Whasstone; qui dicunt per sacramentum suum quod ultimo die mercati quarterium melioris frumenti vendebatur pro iiii s. iiii d., secundi melioris pro iiii s., et tercii melioris pro iii s. vi d.

Gilbertus de [ ] habet I wastell de qua. & def. xviii d.
Rad' de Leye habet I panem omnium generum bladi de qua. & def. v s.

[Mar. 12, 1327] Temptacio panis facta die Iouis in festo sancti Gregorii anno supradicto per sacramentum Thome Lirmongere, Willelmi Lirmongere, Iohannis de Westone, Willelmi Strikelond, Thome de Curtlyntone, Roberti le Marchal, Willelmi de Lyfford, Iohannis de Brouchtone, Ade de Rymyntone, Ricardi de Kirketone, Ricardi de Wenge, Iohannis le Coke; qui dicunt per sacramentum suum quod quarterium melioris frumenti secundi & tercii vendebatur ultimo die mercati sicut die temptacionis supradicte.

Rob' le Chepman habet I wastell de qua. & def. xviii d.
Alicia de Leyghtune habet I wastell de qua. & def. xviii d.
Thomas de Goseford habet I wastell de qua. & def. vi d.
Reginaldus Fisik' habet I wastell de qua. & def. ii s.
Will' de Thomele habet I coket de ob. & def. xii d.
Will' de Stanlake habet I coket de ob. & def. ii s.
Rob. de Legh' habet I coket de ob. & def. vi d.

In vino ii d. qua.[1]

[May 16, 1327] Temptacio panis facta die Sabbati prox. ante festum sancti Dunstani anno predicto per sacramentum Willelmi Strikelond, Thome de Curtlyntone, Ade de Rimyntone, Galfridi Scot, Iohannis le Vyneter, Willelmi Cogges, Iohannis le Coke, Thome de Chisilhamptone, Walteri de Lyfford, Iohannis de Broghtone, Radulfi de Thornhaghe & Ricardi de Churchulle; qui dicunt quod quarterium melioris frumenti vende-

[1] This would be a quart, if wine was at *9d.* a gallon, which was a common price.

batur ultimo die mercati pro iii s. vi d., secundi pro iii s. iiii d., tercii pro iii s. ii d.

Walterus de Dunsterre habet I payndemayn Bastard & def. xiiii d.
Ric' Godandfayr habet I coket de ob. & def. ii s. ix d.
Walterus de Densterre (*sic*) habet I panem de trayt de ob. & def. xxxviii s.

Temptacio panis facta die Sabbati prox. post festum sancti Barnabe apostoli anno predicto per sacramentum Walteri de Lyfford, Iohannis de Broghtone, Willelmi Strikelond, Alani de Hetone, Ade de Rimyntone, Iohannis le Vyneter, Willelmi Lirmongere, Radulfi de Erdyntone, Iohannis de Westone, Ricardi de Suttone, Iohannis Waget, Radulfi de Thornhaghe; qui dicunt quod quarterium melioris frumenti vendebatur ultimo die mercati pro xl d., secundi pro iii s., tercii pro ii s. viii d. [June 13, 1327]

Walterus de Warberghe habet I panem de coket de ob. & def. ii s. vi d.
Ric' de Leye habet I panem de coket de ob. & def. iii s.
Will' le White habet I panem de coket de ob. & def. iiii s.
Hugo Tidemershe habet I panem de coket de ob. & def. xii d.
Will' Attehide habet I panem de coket de ob. & def. xii d.
Hen' Botte habet I panem de coket de ob. & def. xii d.
Walt' de Quenyntone habet I panem de coket de ob. & def. v s.
Will' Gutynghe habet I panem de coket de ob. & def. ix d.
Editha de Emyntone habet I panem de coket de ob. & def. ii s.
Rob' de Newentone habet I panem de coket de ob. & def. iii s.
Edithadc Emyntone habet I panem de ob. de clermatin & def. ii s. vi d.
Ric' de Home habet I clermatin de ob. & def. xii d.
Ioh' de Leghe habet I clermatin de ob. & def. xii d.
Will' Gutynge habet I clermatin de ob. & def. xviii d.

Die Lune prox. sequente.

Rob' le Chepman habet I wastell de qua. & def. iii s. vi d.
Agnes Hikkes habet I wastell de qua. & def. xx d.
Ioh' de Goseford habet I wastell de qua. & def. iii s. vi d.
Simon le Chepman habet I wastell de qua. & def. ii s.

Simon Wilekyn habet I wastell de qua. & def. iii s. vi d.
Dionisia Kynges habet I wastell de qua. & def. iii s. iii d.

Memb. 16 [Sept. 19, 1337] Rotulus[1] de assisa panis & ceruisie tempore magistri Roberti de Stretforde cancellarii Uniuersitatis Oxonie & Henrici de Stodeleighe maioris eiusdem ville, custodum assise, a die Veneris prox. ante festum sancti Mathei apostoli anno r. r. E. tercii a conquestu undecimo usque &c.

Temptacio panis facta coram prefatis custodibus die Veneris prox ante festum sancti Mathei apostoli anno predicto.

f' xviii d. Matill' Loud' habet I panem coket de ob. & def. ii s.
f' iiii s. Rob' de Newentone habet I clermatyn de ob. & def. ii s.
f' xviii d. Ioh' de Tademartone habet I coket de ob. & def. xii d.
f' xii d. Ioh' Hales habet I toyseyn de ob. & def. xii d.
mia. iii d. Ioh' Pache habet I panem de qua. & def. iii s.
for' ii d. Item de pane forisfacto hac die

[Oct. 1, 1337] Scrutacio assise predicte facta coram predictis custodibus die Mercurii prox. post festum sancti Michaelis anno supradicto.

mia. xii d. Gilbertus Lyen habet I wastell de qua. & def. iii s.
mia. vi d. Idem Gilb' Lyen habet I wastell de qua. & def. ii s.
mia. viii d. Margareta Lyen habet I wastell de qua. & def. iii s.
mia. xii d.[2] Ioh' Pache habet panem de qua. de omni genere bladi & def. ix s.
mia. xviii d. Idem Ioh' habet I album panem de qua. & def. x s.
for' ii s. De pane forisfacto hac die

[Oct. 7, 1337] Temptacio panis facta coram predictis custodibus die Martis prox. ante festum sancti Dionisii, anno predicto.

f' ii s. Will' Meleward habet I cok' de ob. & def. ii s.
f' desuper. Ioh' Coket habet I coket de ob. & def. ii s.
f' xx d. (pers[olvit] xiiii d., condonatur vi d.) Ric. de Warberghe habet I coket de ob. & def. xii d.

[1] This roll is an indenture.
[2] Altered to 'soluit vii d. ob.'

Pers'. f' viii d.; solv' vi d. Rogerus de Abyndone habet I coket de ob. & def. xx d.
f' desuper. Ioh' de Rodestone habet I coket de ob. & def. ii s.
f. ut prius. Will' le Meleward habet I clermatyn de ob. & def. ii s.

Temptacio panis facta coram prefatis custodibus die Iouis prox. ante festum sancte Frideswide virginis anno predicto. [Oct. 16, 1337]

f' xii d. Walt' de Warberghe habet I coket de qua. & def. ii s.
mia. ii d. Ric' de Leghe habet I coket de qua. & def. xxi d.
mia. i d. Idem Ricardus habet I coket de ob. & def. xii d.
f' desuper. Ioh' Coket habet I coket de ob. & def. xxi d.
f. vi d. Ioh' de Rodestone habet I coket de ob. & def. xii d. (secundo)
f. xx d. Will' de Westone habet I coket de ob. & def. iii s. (secundo)
f. desuper. Thomas de Stanlake habet I coket de ob. & def. iiii s.
f. desuper. Gilb' de Shuptone habet I coket de ob. & def. xii d.
f. vi s. pro tempore precedente. Ioh' Coket habet I clermatin de ob. & def. ii s. ix d. (quinto)
f. iiii s. Gilb' de Shuptone habet I clermatin de ob. & def. ix d. (secundo)
f. xii d. Thomas de Horspathe habet I clermatin de ob. & def. xxi d.
mia. iii d. Ric' de Leghe habet I tons' de ob. & def. ii s. ix d. (tercio)
f. vi d. Ric' Daper (*sic*) habet I tons' de ob. & def. xxii d.
mia. ii d. Matill' de Wolford habet I tons' de ob. & def. xii d.
mia. ii d. Agnes Attehuthe habet I tons' de ob. & def. xii d.
f. ut prius. Ioh' de Hales habet I tons' de ob. & def. iii s. (secundo)
iudicium { Ric' Withemele habet I tons' de ob. & def. iii s.
Ric' Wythemele habet I treyt de ob. & def. xl s. }
f' ut prius. Rob' de Nywentone habet I coket de ob. & def. xii d.

Per scrutinium factum coram predictis custodibus die Veneris in vigilia Omnium Sanctorum anno predicto. [Oct. 31, 1337]

mia. i d. Alicia Lyen habet I wastell de qua. & def. xii d.

mia. i d. Rob' Broun habet I wastell de qua. & def. xii d.
mia. ii d. Rob' le Freman habet I wastell de qua. & def. xviii d.
mia. vi d. Ioh' Tommes habet I coket de qua. & def. iiii s.
mia. iii d. Thomas de Goseford habet I coket de ob. & def. ii s.
f' dim. marca pro tempore peracto. Thomas de Stanlake habet I coket de ob. & def. xviii d. (quarto)
f' ut prius. Gilb' de Shuptone habet I coket de ob. & def. xl d. (tercio)

for. ii s. { De wastell' forisfacto hac die xiiii d.
De clermatyn forisfacto ii d.
De omni genere bladi forisfacto x d. }

[Nov. 26, 1337] Temptacio panis facta coram prefatis custodibus die Mercurii prox. post festum sancte Katerine virginis anno predicto.

mia. iii d. Rob' de Hoggestone habet I coket de ob. & def. ii s. (primo)
mia. i d. Matill' de Leghe habet I panem de omni genere bladi de ob. & def. xii d.

Presentatum est per xii iuratores quod Walterus atte Huthebrigg' & Henricus de Malmesbury vendiderunt post festum sancti Michaelis prox. preteritum ceruisiam contra proclamationem &c. & contra assisam &c. videlicet unam lagenam pro i d. ob.

[Dec. 15, 1337] Per scrutinium factum die Lune prox. post festum sancte Lucie virginis anno predicto.

iudicium. Thom' de Staumford habet I panem de ob. de omni genere bladi & def. vi s.
iudicium. Ioh' de Shuptone habet I coket de ob. & def. v s. ix d.
mia. ii d. Matill' de Leghe habet I panem de ob. de omni genere bladi & def. ii s. (secundo)
mia. ii d. Ioh' de Kyngestone habet I coket de ob. & def. ix d.
mia. iii d. Matill' Loud' habet I coket de ob. & def. xx d. (primo)
f. ii s. Walterus de Quenynton habet I coket de ob. & def. ix d. (tercio)
f. ut prius. Ric' de Warberghe habet I coket de ob. & def. xx d. (tercio)
f. ut prius. Will' Meleward habet I coket de ob. & def. xii d. (tercio)

f. vi s. Rob' de Newentone habet I clermatin de ob. & def. vi s.
f. ut prius. Rob' de Newentone habet I coket de ob. & def. ix d. (sexto)
f. ut prius. Walterus de Warberghe habet I coket de ob. & def. ix d. (secundo)
Summa in toto xlv s. iiii d.; inde sol' per manus pistorum xxii s. vii d. preter ix d. per I. Leghe in rotulo precedente.

Temptacio panis facta die Martis prox. ante festum Natalis domini anno xi. [Dec. 23, 1337]

Perdonantur quia panes de etate octo dierum [1] { Ric' de Leghe habet I coket de ob. & def. xxi d.
Walterus de Quenynton habet I coket de ob. & def. xxi d.

f. ut prius. Rob' de Newentone habet I clermatin de ob. & def. xxi d.

Scrutinium factum die Veneris prox. ante festum Purificationis beate Marie anno r. r. predicti xii. [Jan. 30, 1338]
F. xl d. Ricardus de Leghe habet I tonseyn de ob. & def. xxi d. (quarto)
Simon de Bedone r[espondet] usque huc; comp[utavit] usque huc.
Rem' man' Wolast[one].

Temptacio panis facta coram prefatis custodibus die Martis prox. post festum Purif' beate Marie virginis anno duodecimo. [Feb. 3, 1338]
Hic incip[iunt] novi procuratores.
Ioh' Pache habet I wastell de qua. & def. ix d.

Temptacio panis facta coram prefatis custodibus die Veneris prox. post festum sancti Gregorii pape anno predicto. [Mar. 13, 1338]
F. desuper. Ioh' de Hales habet I tons[eyn] de ob' & def' in pond' ii s.
Thom' Goseford habet I wastell de qua. & def. ii s. vi d.

[1] In the Northampton Custumary it was reckoned that bread would lose 6*d*. in weight every twenty-four hours (*Records of the Borough of Northampton*, vol. i, p. 324). The record forgets to state of what size the loaf must be, if this allowance is to hold true.

Hen' le Neuman habet I wastell de qua. & def. ix d.
F. xii d. pro tempore merc[ati] istius. Ioh' de Kyngestone habet I panem de qua. & def. xii d.
Ioh' Cloke habet I wast' de qua. & def. ii s. vi d.
De pane forisfacto hac die vii d.
Item de pane forisfacto die Sabbati in crastino per scrutinium x d.

[Mar. 21, 1338] Per scrutinium factum die Sabbati prox. ante festum Annunciacionis beate Marie Virginis anno predicto.
Ioh' Pache habet I simenell' de qua. & def. ii s. vi d.
Ric' Goseford habet I simenell' de qua. & def. xviii d.
Thom' de Goseford habet I simenell' de qua. & def. iiii s. vi d.
Rob' le Neuman habet I semenell' de qua. & def. xii d.
Ric' le Chapman habet I simenell' de qua. & def. xii d.
Alic' de Leghtone habet I simenell' de qua. & def. iiii s.
Isolda la Neuman habet I simenell' de qua. & def. xviii d.
Item de pane forisfacto hac die xiiii d.; de quibus I. de Adyntone & R. Warbergh r[espondent].

[May 9, 1338] Scrutinium factum die Sabbati prox. post festum sancti Iohannis ante portam Latinam anno predicto.
Ioh' de Fauelore pistor habet I cok' de ob' & def' iiii s. vi d.
Idem Ioh' habet I clermatyn de ob. & def. v s.
Finis v s. per plegium Gilberti Scriptoris & Willelmi Brehulle solvendo in festo Pentecost' unam medietatem & in festo Nativitatis sancti Iohannis aliam medietatem.

[May 19, 1338] Temptacio panis facta coram prefatis custodibus die Martis in festo sancti Dunstani anno supradicto; unde assisa capta fuit super summam iii s. vi d.
mia. iii d. Philippus de Bathe habet I coket de ob. & def. ii s.
f' xii d. Ioh' de Legh' pistor habet I coket de ob. & def. ii s.
f' pro ii transgressionibus ii s. Ric' de Warbergh' habet I coket de ob. & def. ii s.
mia. vi d. Ioh' de Kyngestone habet I coket de ob. & def. iii s.
mia. vi d. Philippus de Bathe habet I clermatyn de ob. & def. iiii s.

f. xii d. Ric' Daper habet I tonseyn de ob. & def. ii s.
mia. iii d. Agnes atte Huhte habet I tonseyn de ob. & def. ii s.
f' vi d. Will' de Brehulle habet I tonseyn de ob. & def. xii d.
f' pro ii transgressionibus xii d. Ioh' de Hales habet I tonseyn de ob. & def. xii d.
De wastell' foris[facto] de Wodestoke & de aliis pan[ibus] hac die [*blank*].

Per scrutinium factum coram prefatis custodibus die Sabbati prox. post festum Ascensionis domini anno predicto. **[May 23, 1338]**
Walterus de Warberghe habet I cok' de ob. & def. ii s.
f' pro ii transgressionibus xviii d. Rob. de Newentone habet I coket de ob. & def. xii d.
mia. iii d. Walterus de Quenyntone habet I coket de ob. & def. xii d.
Ioh' de Shyptone habet I coket de ob. & def. iiii s. ix d.
(f. iiii s. ix d., solvendo medietatem in festo sancti Petri ad vincula & aliam medietatem in festo Decollationis sancti Iohannis)
De pane foris[facto] [*blank*]
mia. vi d. Phil' de Bathe habet I cok' de ob. & def. iii s. ix d. (tercio)

Scrutinium factum coram prefatis custodibus die Mercurii prox. ante festum sancti Laurencii anno predicto. **[Aug. 5, 1338]**
mia. ix d. Thos' de Horspathe habet I cok' de ob' & def. iii s.
f' viii d. Agn' de Warberghe habet I cok' de ob. & def. ii s.
f' ut prius. Rob' de Newentone habet I cok' de ob. & def. ii s.
mia. ix d. Ioh' de Fauelore habet I tons' de ob. & def. iiii s. ix d. & mutavit signum.

De pane forisfacto hac die [*blank*]
Cancellarius & maior receperunt particulas tottatas.[1]

Per scrutinium factum coram prefatis custodibus die Mercurii prox. post festum sancti Laurencii anno predicto. **[Aug. 12, 1338]**
fin' sol. ix d. Will' de Westone habet I coket de ob' & def. xviii d.
Desuper. Ric' de Leghe habet I coket de ob. & def. ii s.

[1] Some of the entries have a T. against them.

f' ii s. Thomas Godestre habet I coket de ob. & def. iii s. ix d.
fin' vi d. sol'. Rob' de Hoggestone habet I coket de ob. & def. xii d.
fin' sol' vi d. Will' de Brehulle habet I tonseyn de ob. & def. xii d.
De pane forisfacto hac die [*blank*]

[Sept. 15, 1338] Temptacio panis facta coram prefatis custodibus die Martis prox. post festum Exaltacionis sancte Crucis anno r. r. E. III. duodecimo.
f' pro ii transgress. ii s. sol' in festo Frideswide. Ric' de Leghe habet I coket de ob. & def. ii s.
f' desuper. Ric' de Warberghe habet I coket de ob. & def. xii d.
fecit finem iii d. Rob' de Newentone habet I coket de ob. & def. xii d.
f' sol. ii s. Ric' de Warberghe habet I clermatyn de ob. & def. iiii s.
Summa de qua servientes onerantur xi s. vi d. & nichil inde solverunt.
Et debentur de amerciamentis cervisie pro ultimo dimidio anno viii s. v d.
Summa debit' xix s. xi d. De quibus assignantur II servientibus collectoribus dicte assise & clerico pro labore suo per tempus predictum dim. marca; et rem[anent] aretro [*blank*].

THE ASSISE OF ALE

The rolls of the assise of ale differ in many respects from the rolls of the assise of bread. The courts were held but twice a year, about Easter and Michaelmas, and the offenders were presented ward by ward. This was the way at the view of frankpledge, which also was held only twice a year, the presentments being made by each ward separately; and the same was the rule at the court which was held under the Statute of Labourers, each of the four wards being taken separately.

In the records of the court the sellers of ale are divided into two classes represented by the letters B. and R.; the former is sometimes expanded to Bra or Bre, and must represent *Brasiator* or *Brewer*;

the latter is expanded to Regr', and stands for *Regrator* or *Regratarius*. A regrator of beer was one who in modern language 'kept a public house'. The word was used of other occupations as well, but that it meant a publican is proved by one of the Parliamentary Petitions (*Collectanea*, iii, p. 103, O. H. S.). It is not easy to see why it was necessary to state on the roll whether a man was a regrator or a brewer. From notes on our second roll it is evident that a regrator was not always a man who sold another man's ale, but that sometimes he brewed it himself. It is puzzling that in some cases a man is described as a regrator in one ward, but in another ward in the same roll he is described as a brewer.

There can be no doubt that the names on these rolls occur in a geographical order, and in some cases we have sufficient knowledge of the residents of mediaeval Oxford to identify the course which was taken by the man who made the list. For the purpose of reconstructing a directory of Oxford in the fourteenth century these records will be of value. It is true that they do not give us a complete list of the inhabitants of the town; not only are all householders omitted who belonged to the University, but many others as well; but so common was it to brew ale and sell it that our rolls must contain more than half the householders of the town for the years they cover.

What was the exact method of procedure is a little uncertain, but, if we may argue from the court which was held under the Statute of Labourers, we should assume that shortly before the court was held the constable of each ward passed through his ward and noted the names of those who were selling ale or had sold it since the previous court. A copy of this list he would give to the appointed tasters of ale, who soon afterwards would go their rounds to see if the ale was of good quality. Whether they made the circuit of the whole of Oxford in one day is uncertain, but it seems unlikely that even four men would be enough to taste the ale of over 300 brewers in one day. When the court was held, each name was taken in turn; the tasters would say whether the quality of the ale was satisfactory, and apparently public notoriety settled whether the price at which it was sold was that which had been laid down according to the value of grain. It seems that there were not many who had not broken either the standard of price or the standard of quality.

Michaelmas, 1311.

The roll which comes first is dated the fifth year of King Edward, and from the writing it would be uncertain whether it was of Edward II or Edward III. But as it mentions Robert de Wormenhale who died in 1324, Joanna Attemore who died in 1326, and Henry de Hethrop who died in 1329,[1] the date must be 5 Ed. II. The next question to settle is whether it is the Easter or the Michaelmas court, i. e. Michaelmas 1311, or Easter 1312. We know from the rolls of the Assise of Bread that in Nov. 1310 the price of ale was fixed at 1¼*d.*, wheat being at 8*s.* a quarter, and that in Nov. 1311 it was fixed at ¾*d.*, wheat being at 5*s.* 4*d.* a quarter. Between those dates the price must have been at 1*d.* a gallon for a certain time; though we do not know the day on which this price was fixed, we learn from the rolls of the Assise of Bread that wheat was at 6*s.* 4*d.* in June 1311, and at that price for wheat the gallon of ale would be 1*d.* In our roll the proper price is evidently 1*d.*, and we conclude that its date is between June and Nov. 1311. At the Easter court of 5 Ed. II, i. e. Easter 1312, the price of wheat was still as low as 5*s.* 4*d.* a quarter, and the gallon of ale would have remained at ¾*d.* The date therefore is Michaelmas 1311.

[Sept. 1311] Presentacio Walteri de Burcestria, Ricardi le Grasier, Iohannis Prest, & Iohannis de Caumpedene piscatoris tastatorum cervisie anno r. r. E. quinto.

Northwestwarde[2]

Ric' Culverd	xii d.	B.	i d. ob. [*erased*]
Rad' de Hampton	xviii d.	B.	i d. ob.
Will' de Eynesham	vi d.	R.	i d.
Cristina Culverd	vi d.	B.	i d. ob.
Ioh' de Horspath	xviii d.	B.	i d.
Ioh' de Arderne	ii s.	B.	i d. ob.
Hen' de Lenne	xii d.	B.	i d. ob.
Ioh' de Aylesbury		B.	i d. ob.
Gilb. de Wynchecumbe		B.	i d. ob.
Matilda Loud	xii d.	B.	i d. ob.
Will' de Emynton	vi d.	R.	i d. ob.
Hen' le Sclattere	iii d.	R.	i d.
Rob' Eustace	iii d.	R.	i d.

[1] These dates are ascertained from the *Oxford Book of Wills*.

[2] The list starts from Carfax and goes westward along Queen Street, then up New Inn Hall Street, and so to St. Michael's Church; then southward to Carfax.

Thom' le Masoun	xii d.	B.	i d. ob.
Will' de Bartone	iii d.	B.	i d.
Will' Mounfort	iii d.	B.	i d.
Isabella atte Corner	vi d.	B.	i d.
Ioh' de Carpenter	iii d.	R.	i d.
Nich' Crabbe	vi d.	B.	i d.
Will' de Egleshale	iii d.	R.	i d.
Ioh' de Odyham	xii d.	B.	i d. ob.
Thos. de Staunton		R.	i d.
Will' Pouel	vi d.	B.	i d. ob.
Rad' de Stauntone	iii d.	R.	i d.
Iohanna Molend'	iii d.	B.	i d.
Will' de Wodestoke	vi d.	R.	i d. ob.
Thom' de Wortone	iii d.	R.	i d.
Ioh' de Mixebury	iii d.	R.	i d.
Hen. le Marchal	iii d.	B.	i d.
Iohanna de Heyford	xviii d.	B.	i d. ob.
Ric' de Berkele	xviii d.	B.	i d. ob.
And. de Pusye	vi d.	R.	i d. ob.
Ioh' de Couele	ii s.	B.	i d. ob.
Pet' fil' Iohannis	xii d.	R.	i d. ob.
Nic' le Mercer	vi d.	B.	i d. ob.
Margar' de Tewe	vi d.	R.	i d.
Alic' de Rouforde	iii d.	R.	i d.
Adam Haym debil'		R.	i d.
Walt' le Coupere	vi d.	R.	i d.

Summa xxiii s. vi d.

Afferatores, Rad. de Cockeswelle, Iohannes Bisshop, Ricardus de Cosintone, Gilbertus de Ros, Thomas de Croydon, Laurencius le Gaunter, iurati.

North-est Warde [1]

Will' de Leye	iii d.	Regr'	i d. ob.
Ric' le Lythe	vi d.	R.	i d. ob.
Ric' le Grendone	vi d.	R.	i d.
Ioh' le Webbe	vi d.	R.	i d. ob.
Will' de Deueleston	xii d.	Bras.	i d. ob.

[1] The order starts from Carfax, goes eastward, then up and down the Turl; thence to Cat Street; up and down Cat Street; then eastward, and apparently turns north at East Gate; works round to North Gate, and then southward to Carfax.

Nich' Aurifaber	xii d.	B.	i d. ob.
Ioh' de Gonewardeby	xii d.	B.	i d. ob.
Rob. de Watlinton	xviii d.	B.	i d. ob.
Phil. de Wormenhale		B.	i d. ob.
Alic. de Hakeburne	xviii d.	B.	i d. ob.
Ioh' de Hamptone	xviii d.	B.	i d. ob.
Ioh' le Latoner	iii d.	R.	i d.
Rob. de Watlinton stacioner	xii d.	B.	i d. ob.
Margareta de Wormenhale	iii d.	R.	i d.
Ioh' de Brumptone	iii d.	B.	i d. ob.
Ioh' le Leche	iii d.	B.	i d.
Ioh' de Bissopestone	xii d.	B.	i d. ob.
Walt' de Wyck'	vi d.	R.	i d.
Margareta de Mortone		R.	i d.
Rob. le Notur	xviii d.	B.	i d. ob.
Ioh' de Cristeschyrche	xii d.	B.	i d. ob.
Thom' de Graunpount	xviii d.	B.	i d. ob.
Matild' Bocbyndere	xii d.	B.	i d. ob.
Will' le Grasiere	xii d.	B.	i d. ob.
Ioh' de Stafforde	vi d.	R.	i d.
Will' Pyck		R.	i d.
Fulcon' le Manciple		R.	i d.
Steph' de Abindone	iii d.	R.	i d.
Petr' de Milton	xii d.	B.	i d.
Ric' le Manciple	vi d.	B.	i d.
Rob' de Euerton, flexman	vi d.	R.	i d.
Ioh' de Bradenhach	vi d.	B.	i d.
Ric' de Roulesham	iii d.	R.	i d.
Rob' de Wyleby	iii d.	R.	i d.
Rog' le Flexman	iii d.	R.	i d.
Will' de Wythull'	xii d.	B.	i d.
Alic' de Shulderne	iii d.	R.	i d.
Thomas Louel	iii d.	R.	i d.
Cristina de Clanefeud	iii d.	R.	i d.
Iohanna de Watele	vi d.	R.	i d.
Claricia de Wynchestre	iii d.	R.	i d.
Matild' la Glouere	iii d.	R.	i d.
Matild' Scriptor	iii d.	R.	i d.
Ioh' de Campedene	vi d.	R.	i d.
Matild' de Couele	vi d.	R.	i d.

Rad' de Hayle	xviii d.	B.	i d. ob.
Ioh' de Cumbe	xii d.	B.	i d.
Will' le Leche	xii d.	B.	i d.
Walter Cryk'	iii d.	R.	i d.
Alic' de Saunforde	iii d.	R.	i d.
Ric' le Flechere	iii d.	R.	i d.
Hen. le Ros	iii d.	B.	i d.
Gilb' le Acotoner		R.	i d.
Thos. le Waterman		R.	i d.
Dulcia de Tackele	iii d.	R.	i d.
Agn' de Dunham	iii d.	R.	i d.
Ioh' de Worthe	xii d.	B.	i d. ob.
Simon de Worton	xii d.	B.	i d.
Rob. de Bache	ii s.	B.	i d. ob.
Iuliana de Dene		R.	i d.
Sibbilia de Colesburne	xviii d.	B.	i d. ob.
Emma Sewy	xii d.	B.	i d. ob.
Alic' la Hore		B.	i d.
Thomas le Irmongere	ii s.	B.	i d. ob.
Ric' de Gloucestre	vi d.	B.	i d. ob.
Rob. le Coupere	vi d.	B.	i d. ob.
Ric. de Stauntone	xii d.	B.	i d. ob.
Reginaldus de Merchcham	iii d.	R.	i d. ob.
Iohanna de Bedeforde	ii s.	B.	i d. ob.
Ioh' de la Marche	vi d.	B.	i d.
Walterus de Swyneshulle	xii d.	B.	i d.
Illaria de Parys	xviii d.	B.	i d. ob.
Iuliana de Bedeforde	iii d.	B.	i d.
Hugo Kary	xviii d.	B.	i d. ob.
Will' de Sutton	xii d.	R.	i d. ob.

Summa l s. iii d.

Summa huius rotuli & rotuli precedentis lxxiii s. ix d., unde G. de Stoke oneratur; inde soluit I[ohanni] de Dokelintone lx s.; et sic debet xiii s. ix d.

Suth est Warde

[ ]kewan	iii d.	R.	i d.
[ ]ynge	xii d.	B.	i d.
Hen' de Campedene	xii d.	B.	i d. ob.
Thom' le Taylor	vi d.	B.	i d.

Ad' de Houtone	vi d.	B.	i d.
Isolda de Stauntone (pelu' cum lotor')	ii s.	B.	i d. ob.
Ioh' de Coggesgrave	vi d.	R.	i d.
Will' le Plomer	vi d.	B.	i d.
Hen' de Grettone	iii d.	R.	i d.
Gilb' de Grimstede	xviii d.	B.	i d. ob.
Hen' le Lomenur (*sic*)	iii d.	R.	i d.
Nic. de Dryhulle	iii d.	R.	i d.
Rob. de Dryhulle	vi d.	R.	i d.
Ioh' de Harndone	iii d.	R.	i d.
Ph' de Kent	iii d.	R.	i d.
Davy de Cornubia	iii d.	R.	i d.
Agn' la Setoler	iii d.	R.	i d.
Ioh' le Grasiere	vi d.	R.	i d. ob.
Alic' la Barber	iii d.	R.	i d.
Lucia de Shydyerd	xii d.	B.	i d. ob.
Ioh' le Pulter	xviii d.	B.	i d. ob.
Will' le Bocbyndere	xii d.	B.	i d. ob.
Will' Attemore	vi d.	R.	i d. ob.
Ioh' de Wodestoke	iii d.	R.	i d.
Will' de Wynchecumbe	iii d.	R.	i d.
Alic' de Thame	iii d.	R.	i d.
Simon de Bradewey	iii d.	R.	i d.
Will' de Sturtone [1]	xii d.	B.	i d. ob.
Will' de Watele	xii d.	B.	i d.
Matild' la Leche [2]	iii d.	R.	i d.
Iohanna de Ew	xii d.	B.	i d. ob.
Hen' de Hetrop	ii s.	B.	i d.
Ioh' de Frylforde	iii d.	R.	i d.
Ric' de Wpton	iii d.	R.	i d.
Hen' le Barber	xii d.	B.	i d. ob.
Will' de Eynstone	vi d.	B.	i d.
Will' le Messager	iii d.	R.	i d.
Ioh' de Tame	iii d.	R.	i d.
Will. de Pennarth	xii d.	B.	
Ric. le Spicer	xii d.	B.	i d. ob.
Thom' le Marchal	xii d.	B.	i d. ob.
Ioh' Prest			

[1] In the margin *pelu'*.

[2] In the margin *clok'*.

Thom' Aurifaber	ii s.	B.	i d. ob.
Ric' de Hetrop	ii s.	B.	i d. ob.
Will. de Pusye	vi d.	B.	
Rob. de Amondesham	vi d.	R.	
Ioh' le Sauser	xii d.	R.	i d. ob.
Walterus de Bokingham	iii d.	R.	
Gunnilda de Langeforde		R.	i d.
Will' le Peintur	vi d.	R.	i d. ob.
Rad' Stoke	xviii d.	B.	i d. ob.
Ioh' le Tauerner	vi d.	B.	i d. ob.
Iohanna de Wycumbe	xii d.	R.	i d. ob.
Ioh' le [ ]	iii d.	R.	
Will. de [ ] orw		B.	i d. ob.
Thos. de Curtlintone	iii d.	R.	
Ioh' de Wynchestre	iii d.	R.	i d.
Galf' de Hengeseye	vi d.	B.	
Ric' de Hedindone		B.	i d.
Math' de Cornubia	vi d.	R.	i d. ob.
Thos. de Mortone	ii s.	B.	i d. ob.
Ioh' Scot	xii d.	B.	
Gilb' de Ros		R.	i d.
Rad' de Cockeswalle		R.	i d. ob.
Nic' le Brut	iii d.	R.	i d.
Simon Clericus	iii d.	R.	i d.
Rob. de Stoke	vi d.	R.	i d.
Thom. le Dyere	vi d.	R.	i d.
Walt' le Carpenter	iii d.	R.	i d.
Ioh' atte Dyche	iii d.	R.	i d.
Simon de Trillemille		R.	i d.
Will' de Wodeforde	iii d.	R.	i d.
Ric' le Peintur	vi d.	B.	i d.
Isabella de Henx'	iii d.	R.	i d.
Rob. de Bolcryue		R.	i d.

Summa xliii s. vi d.

Summa huius rotuli infra xliii s. vi d.; unde W. de Pyria habet extract', & inde idem W. recepit xxvii s. de nominibus punctuatis ut patet in hoc rotulo, & de illis xxvii s. receptis soluit I. de Dokelintone xxiiii s., & debet adhuc (*the rest is indistinct. In the roll some of the names have a dot against them.*)

Swth-west Warde [1]

Ioh' atte Montes	iii d.	R.	i d.
Rad' le Wal	vi d.	B.	i d.
Isabella la Cha	xii d.	B.	i d.
Ric' le Cha	xii d.	B.	i d.
Walterus le Parmenter	iii d.	R.	i d.
Margareta la Fyssere	vi d.	B.	i d.
Simon de Etone	vi d.	B.	i d.
Dulcia la Rede	xii d.	B.	i d. ob.
Iohanna Attemore	vi d.	B.	i d.
Alic' de Henxs'	vi d.	B.	i d.
Galf' de Grauntpount	vi d.	B.	i d. ob.
Rob' de Bowes	iii d.	R.	
Ric' de Morton	ii s.	B.	i d. ob.
Fille Fayreye	iii d.	R.	i d.
(A.) Ric' de Hordle	iii d.	R.	i d.
Hen' de Hales	iii d.	R.	i d.
Ric' de Stretford	xii d.	B.	i d. ob.
Ioh' de Westone	vi d.	B.	i d.
Ioh' de Staunforde	vi d.	B.	i d.
Emma Buffild	vi d.	B.	i d.
Ad' de Tilhurst	xii d.	B.	i d.
Iohanna la Wilde	vi d.	B.	i d.
Iohanna de Lauendrie	vi d.	B.	i d.
Alic' la Brumstere	iii d.	R.	i d.
Ioh' de Lyndeseye	iii d.	R.	i d.
Ioh' de Yslep, tannere	iii d.	R.	
Hen. de Ocle	iii d.	B.	i d.
Will' le Clerke contra fratres minores	vi d.	R.	
Alic' de Neubury	iii d.	R.	i d.
Rog' Pygas	iii d.	R.	i d.
Ioh' Oliuer	iii d.	B.	i d.
Ric' de Eynesham	vi d.	B.	i d.
Oliuerus le Taylor [2]	vi d.	B.	i d.
Ad' de Remyntone	iii d.	R.	i d.
Sibillia Kypharm	xii d.	B.	i d.
Ioh' de Dokelintone		B.	i d. ob.

[1] Begins at South Bridge, goes north, then along Brewers Street, returns to Fish Street; north to Carfax, then westward.

[2] *uxor* inserted before *Oliuerus*.

Alic' la Mercer	xviii d.	B.	i d. ob.
Galf' le Mercer		R.	i d.
Thos. de Croydone		R.	i d. ob.
Will' Metesarp	vi d.	B.	i d. ob.
(B) Vincenc' de Grimest'	iii d.		
(D) Ioh' Batte	vi d.	R.	i d. ob.
(C) Ioh' de Bernewelle	iii d.		
Hen' Iolif'		B.	i d. ob.
Rob' de Shylle	vi d.	R.	i d. ob.
Will' le Tenturer	xii d.	B.	i d. ob.
Rob' de Quenyntone	iii d.	R.	i d.
Nigillus de Godwynestone		B.	i d. ob.
Thomas Leswys		B.	i d. ob.
Ioh' de Hamstede		B.	i d. ob.
Ioh' de Coleshulle		B.	i d. ob.
Rob' de Wormenhale		B.	i d. ob.
Ioh' le Ferur		B.	i d. ob.
Hen' de Neubotle	vi d.	B.	i d.
Nic' de Emyntone	iii d.	R.	i d.
Emma de Westone	iii d.	B.	i d. ob.
Will' de Puseye	xviii d.	B.	i d. ob.
Simon Louesone	vi d.	B.	i d.
Walterus de Heyham	iii d.		
Ioh' de Liccheborw	vi d.	B.	i d.
Will' Brun sen.	xii d.	B.	i d.
Rob. de Wolgaricote	vi d.	B.	i d.
Isolda de Tenforde	iii d.	R.	i d.
Galf' de Coquina	xii d.	B.	i d. ob.
Hen' le Graunger	vi d.	B.	i d.
Ioh' de Waltham	xii d.	noluit monstrare	
Will' atte Glorie	iii d.	R.	i d.
Will' Deuenes	xii d.	B.	i d.
Rob. le Carpenter	vi d.	B.	i d.
Will' le Quariur	iii d.	B.	i d.
Alic' de Wodestone	vi d.	B.	i d.
Emma la Clodmongere	iii d.	B.	i d.
Will' de Wygentone	iii d.	R.	i d.

Summa xxxiiii s. iii d.

Summa huius rotuli infra xxxiiii s. iii d.; unde P. de Mixeburi habet extract'; inde soluit Iohanni de Dokelintone xxx s., et debet iiii s. iii d.

Summa totalis istorum rotulorum vii li. xiii s. iii d.

[June, 1324] Mense Iunii anno r. r. E. fil. regis E. xvii^o.

INDENTVRA ASISE

Northwest warde[1]

iii d. Rob. le Gryndere regr' communis cogn' vendidisse I quart'[2] ceruisie pro i d. ob. post proclamationem sed nunc ad den'; suff'.

vi d. Will' Maufey brac' cogn' vendidisse I quart' cervisie pro i d. ob. post proc. sed nunc ad den'; non suff'.

xii d. Hen' de Stodlee brac' cogn' vendidisse I quart' cervisie pro i d. ob. post proc. sed nunc ad den'; suff'.

Will' le Melleward regr' communis dicit se vendidisse post proclamationem pro i den', sed nunc non vend'.

Emma de Chucchele brac' non vend' nisi ad den' post proc', et hoc suff'.

xii d. Matilda Loud' brac' dicit se non vendidisse nisi ad den' post proc', sed hoc non suff'.

xii d. Nich' de Langeford brac' vendidit ad iii ob. post proc', sed nunc non habet.

vi d. Rad' Ouerhee brac' vend' ad i d. ob. post proc.

xviii d. Adam Nottherne brac' vend' I quart' ad i d. ob. post proc., sed nunc ad den' non suff'.

iii d. Ric' Ouerhee brac' dicit se vendidisse nisi ad den' post proc', sed hoc suff' (*must mean* non suff').

Thos. le Tawiere regr' dic' se vend' post proc. nisi pro denario, & inde ponit se.

Nic. le Mercer regr' dic' se vend' nisi ad den' post proc.; & hoc suff'.

xii d. Emma de Shulle regr' dic' se vend' nisi ad den' post proc., sed non suff'.

iii d. Iohanna de Heyford brac' vendidit pro i d. ob. post proc., sed nunc non habet.

[1] In this and subsequent rolls the names in the North-west Ward begin at the west end of Queen Street, thence to Carfax, and so to North Gate. This roll is an indenture.

[2] This does not mean *quart*, but *quarter*, a large measure containing many gallons.

iii d. Alicia de Berkele brac' pro i d. ob. ut dicit, sed nunc non habet.

vi d. Will' atte More brac' dicit se vend' nisi ad den' post proc.; sed nunc non habet.

iii d. Will. de Wodestoke regr' dic' se vend' nisi ad den' post proc.; sed non suff'.

xii d. Isabella Brodheye regr' vend' cerv' pro i d. ob. post proc.; nunc facit.[1]

Thomas Stokeman brac' dicit se non vendidisse post proc. [sed braciabit in posterum][2].

vi d. Ioh' de Odyham brac' vendid' cerv' pro i d. ob. post proc., sed nunc habet ad fac[iendum].

Summa ix s. ix d.

Southwestward[3]

Ioh' de Claryndone regr' vend' cerv' contra assis' post proc', sed nunc non habet.

ii s. Thos. le Mason brac' cogn' se vend' cerv' pro i d. ob. post proc.

Elena de Rypoun brac' cogn' se vend' non nisi ad den' post proc., sed nunc non habet.

Thomas Broun brac' dicit se non vendidisse post proc., sed nunc brac' pro den'.

iii d. Will. Quarreour brac' dicit se vendidisse vi lagenas cerv' pro i d. ob. post proc', sed nunc non habet.

iii d. Laur' le Mason brac' dicit se vendidisse nisi ad den' post proc., sed non suff'.

Rob' Clothmongere brac' non vendidit cerv' nisi ad den' post proc., sed nunc non habet.

Will' de Ros regr' vendidit cerv' contra assisam post proc., sed nunc ad den'; non suff'.

Alic' la Granger brac' dicit se vendidisse nichil contra assisam post proc', & suff'.

vi d. Will' de Herdewyke brac' vend' cervisiam contra assisam post proc., sed nunc non habet.

[1] At first was written 'sed nunc non habet'. Where a brewer had none now, it was impossible to judge its quality as sufficient or not.

[2] The words in brackets are dim and doubtful.

[3] Begins at West Gate and ends at South Bridge.

iii d. Galf' ad coquinam brac' vend' cervisiam contra assisam post proc., sed nunc ad den'; suff'.

vi d. Will' Broun brac' vend' cervisiam contra assisam post proc., sed nunc non habet.

vi d. Ioh' de Leye brac' vend' cervisiam contra assisam post proc., sed nunc ad den'; suff'.

vi d. Ioh' le Northerne brac' vend' cervisiam contra assisam post proc., sed nunc ad den'; suff'.

iii d. Adam de Warberghe regr' vend' cervisiam contra assisam post proc., sed nunc ad den'; non suff'.

iii d. Hen. Botte brac' non vendidit nisi ad den' post proc' ut dicit, et nunc non habet.

vi d. Thos' de Leghe brac' vendidit ceruisiam ad i d. ob. post proc', & nunc facit.

iii d. Will' Paternoster brac' dicit se vendidisse nisi ad den' post proc', sed non suff'.

iii d. Will' de Puseye regr' dicit se vendidisse II lag. pro i d. ob.; sed nunc non habet.

vi d. Rob. de Newenton brac' & vendidit cerv' contra assisam post proc', sed nunc non habet.

iii d. Ric' le Peyntur regr' vendidit cerv' contra assisam post proc', sed nunc ad den'; non suff'.

Walterus le Fox brac' dicit se vendidisse nisi ad den' & est suff'.

xviii d. Reg' de Gloucestre regr' vend' cerv' contra assisam post proc., sed nunc ad den' & suff'.

Ric' de Eynesham regr' dicit se non vendidisse nisi ad den' post proc., & suff'.

Walt' de Heyham regr' dicit se vendidisse nisi ad den' post proc., sed nunc non habet.

Iohanna de Pirie regr' dicit se vendidisse nisi ad den' post proc', sed nunc non habet.

vi d. Agnes Battes regr' vendidit ceruisiam ad den' ob. post proc., sed nunc ad den', & suff'.

Andreas de Wormenhale brac' dicit se vendidisse nisi ad den' post proc. & suff'.

iii d. Agnes la Lighte brac' vendidit cerv' ad den' ob' post proc. sed nunc ad den', & suff'.

vi d. Ioh' le Vyneter brac' vendidit cerv' ad den' ob' post proc., & nunc non habet.

Will' le Mercer brac' & non vendidit cerv' nisi ad i den. post proc., & suff'.

Walt' de Lyford non vendidit nisi pro i d.

iii d. Rob' de Marre regr' vendidit cerv' ad i d. post proc', & non suff'.

xii d. Sibilla Kepharm brac. & vendidit cerv' ad i d. ob. post proc. & nunc ad den' & non suff'.

vi d. Rob. le Marchal brac. & vendidit totam cervisiam novam.

iii d. Rob. Trewelove regr' & non vendidit nisi ad i d. post proc., & non suff'.

xviii d. Adam de Tylhurst brac' & vendit ceruisiam pro i d. ob. & nunc facit, & non suff'.

iii d. Hawis la Conuers regr' & non vendit nisi ad i d. post proc. & non suff'.

Galfridus Scot regr' & non vendit nisi ad i d. post proc. et est suff'.

vi d. Hugo de Barton brac' vendit cerv' ad i d. ob. post proc. et nunc non habet.

Thos. de Habindone regr' & non vend' nisi ad i d. post proc., et est suff'.

Rob. de Grendone regr' & vend' ad i d. post proc. et est suff'.

iii d. Will' de Stanlake regr' vendidit cerv' contra ass. post proc., & nunc non habet.

Magota Flexweuman regr' non vend' cerv' nisi ad i d. post proc., sed nunc non habet.

xii d. Elena atte Yate brac' vend' cerv' ad i d. ob. post proc. & nunc ad den', & non suff'.

xii d. Ioh' de Staunden brac' vend' cerv' totam novam in loco [1] isto.

iii d. Hugo le Deyere brac' & vend' cerv' ad i d. & nunc non habet.

Iohanna atte More brac' & vend' cerv' ad i d. post proc., et est suff'.

Ioh' de Hudden brac' & non vend' cerv' nisi ad i d. post proc. & nunc non habet.

Galf' Warmwell brac' & non vend' cerv' nisi ad i d., & communiter novam post proc'.

Isabella la Cha brac' & non vend' nisi totam novam, et non habet.

Summa xvi s. vi d.

[1] Somewhat doubtful.

Suthestwarde [1]

Matill' Shepherde regr. & non vend' nisi ad i d. post proc'; est suff'.

Isabella Spicer regr' & non vend' nisi ad i d. post proc'; est suff'.

Ioh' Bruseboce regr' & non vend' nisi ad i d. post proc'; est suff'.

Edmundus Neel regr' & non vend' nisi ad i d. post proc'; est suff'.

Alanus Scolmayster regr' & non vend' nisi ad i d. post proc'; est suff'.

iii d. Pety Iohan regr' & non vend' nisi ad i d. post proc'; & non est suff'.

vi d. Rob' de Stoke brac', vend' cerv' post proc. ad i d. ob. & modo ad den' ut dicit, & est suff'.

Nichasius Kaskyn regr' & non vend' nisi ad den' post proc', et est suff'.

vi d. Matild' Caveresfeld regr' & non vend' nisi ad den' post proc', et non est suff'.

Alicia de Walyngford regr' & non vend' nisi ad den' post proc', et est suff'.

Ric' de Stratford regr' & non vend' nisi ad den' post proc', et est suff'.

Dionisia Ros regr' & non vend' nisi ad den' post proc', et est suff'.

vi d. Ioh' de Hampstede brac' & vend' cerv' pro i d. ob. post proc', & non suff'.

Iuliana de Mortone brac', non vend' nisi pro i d. post proc', et suff'.

vi d. Iohanna de Bereford [? Boreford] regr' non vend' cerv' nisi pro i d. post proc., & non est suff'.

vi d. Adam de Rimyntone regr' non vend' cerv' nisi pro i d. post proc', & non est suff'.

Rad' de Thornhaghe regr' & non vend' cerv' nisi pro i d. post proc', & est suff'.

vi d. Rob' de Lokyng regr' & vend' cerv' ad i d. & ob. post proc., sed nunc ad den', & non suff'.

[1] Probably starts at South Bridge, northward to Carfax, then eastward.

Ioh' de Persshore regr' & vend' cerv' ad i d. & ob. post proc., sed nunc ad den'; & non suff'.

vi d. Iohanna de Wycumbe regr' vend' cerv' pro i d. ob. post proc. sed modo ad den', sed non suff'.

Lucia de Grenstede brac', non vend' cerv' nisi ad den' post proc. et est suff'.

vi d. Ric' Cary brac' & vend' cerv' pro i d. ob. post proc. & nunc ad den' & suff'.

vi d. Alanus de Hetone brac' & vend' cerv' pro i d. ob. post proc' sed nunc ad den' & suff'.

alibi. Ioh' de Staundene[1] brac' alibi sed vend' cerv' pro i d. ob. post proc' sed nunc ad den' & suff'.

Ioh' de Lyndeseye regr' dicit se vend' nisi IIII lagenas ad i d. ob. post proc. sed modo ad den' & est suff'.

iii d. Ioh' de Milton regr' vend' cerv' ad i d. ob. post proc. sed modo ad den' et est suff'.

iii d. Alic' de Neubury regr' vend' cerv' ad i d. ob. post proc. sed modo ad den' et est suff'.

xii d. Thom' le Goldsmyth brac' vend' cerv' ad i d. ob. post proc. sed modo ad den' et est suff'.

xii d. Ioh' de Whassheburne brac' vend' cerv' ad i d. ob. post proc. sed modo ad den', et non suff'.

Simon de Gloucestre[2] brac. vend' cerv' ad i d. ob. post proc. sed modo ad den', et est suff'.

xviii d. Ioh' de Hamptone brac' vend' cerv' ad i d. ob. post proc' et nunc facit.

xviii d. Rob' de Watlyntone stac' brac' vend' cerv' ad i d. ob. post proc' & modo facit, ut dic[unt] vicini.

Ioh' de Comptone regr' vend' cerv' ad i d. post proc' & est suff'.

xii d. Thomas Chicele brac' vend' cerv' ad i d. ob. post proc' sed nunc ad den', & est suff'.

Hen' de Edrope brac' non vend' nisi pro i d. post proc', et nunc non habet.

xii d. Ioh' de Aumbresbury brac' vend' cerv' ad i d. ob. post proc', sed nunc ad den' & non suff'.

[1] The scribe wrote at first 'Ioh' de Staundene regratarius scribitur superius'.

[2] This entry was at first 'non vendidit nisi ad i d. post proc.'

Iohanna de Ew brac' non vendidit cerv' nisi ad i d. post proc', et est suff'.

vi d. Ioh' de Maydenstone brac' vend' cerv' pro i d. ob. post proc', sed nunc non habet.

iii d. Will' de Whatele brac' vend' cerv' pro i d. ob. post proc., & nunc facit.

Will' de Stourton regr' non vend' cerv' nisi ad i d. post proc', sed [*sic*] suff'.

Ioh' le Horner regr' non vend' cerv' nisi ad i d. post proc'; sed nunc suff'.

Alic' de Hilesdone regr' non vend' cerv' nisi ad i d. post proc'; et suff'.

Rob' Grasiere regr' non vend' cerv' nisi ad i d. post proc'; et suff'.

Thom' Gynendale regr' non vend' cerv' nisi ad i d. post proc'; et suff'.

iii d. Alic' la Barber brac' vend' cerv' ad i d. ob. post proc'; sed nunc ad den' & suff'.

Isabella de Aylesbury regr' non vend' cerv' nisi ad i d. post proc'; sed suff'.

iii d. Cristiana de Toucestre regr' non vend' cerv' nisi ad i d. post proc'; sed non suff'.

Ioh' de Cokesgrave regr' non vend' cerv' nisi ad i d. post proc'; et suff'.

iii d. Alic' de Langebrghe brac' vend' cerv' pro i d. ob. post proc'; et nunc ad den' & suff.

vi d. Adam de Bekenesfeld brac' vend' cerv' pro i d. ob. post proc'; et nunc non habet.

vi d. Ioh' de Whasshtone brac' vend' cerv' pro i d. ob. post proc'; sed nunc ad den', sed suff'.

Ric' de Wenge brac. non vend' cerv' nisi ad den' post proc'; et est suff'.

Ioh' le Marchal regr. non vend' cerv' nisi ad den' post proc'; et est suff'.

Will' Deyere brac' non vend' cerv' nisi ad den' post proc'; et nunc non habet.

Will' Marchaunt regr' non vend' cerv' nisi ad den' post proc'; et est suff'.

Will' atte More regr' non vend' cerv' nisi ad den' post proc'; et est suff'.

Simon Wyth brac' non vend' cerv' nisi ad den' post proc'; et est suff'.

Iohanna de Gareford brac' non vend' cerv' nisi ad den' post proc'; et nunc non habet.

vi d. Thomas Tyeis brac' vend' cerv' ad i d. ob. post proc'; sed nunc non habet.

Summa xv s. iii d.

Northestwarde

xii d. Will' Fourbur brac', vend' cerv' pro i d. ob. post proc. sed nunc ad den', et est suff'.

Ioh' de Ew brac' non vend' cerv' post proc., sed nunc habet de novo & ad den'.

xviii d. Rob. de la Bache brac' vend' cerv' pro i d. ob. post proc., sed nunc ad den', et est suff'.

viii d.[1] Sibilla de Colesburne brac' vend' cerv' pro i d. ob. post proc', sed nunc ad den', et est suff'.

vi d. Rad' de Erdyntone brac' vend' cerv' pro i d. ob. post proc', sed nunc ad den', et est suff'.

Benedictus Cordewaner brac' non vend' cerv' nisi pro i d. post proc. & est suff'.

xviii d. Thomas Lirmongere brac' vend' cerv' pro i d. ob. post proc. sed nunc ad den' & non suff'.

Ric' de Stauntone brac' non vend' cerv' post proc., set uult de novo.

Ric' de Gloucestre brac' non vend' cerv' nisi pro i d. post proc., & est suff'.

vi d. Steph' de Adyntone brac' vend' cerv' pro i d. ob. post proc., sed nunc ad den' & suff'.

xii d. Ioh' de Walton brac' vend' cerv' pro i d. ob. post proc., & extraxit signum contra adventum tastatorum, & sequestraverunt x lagenas.

vi d. Will' de Ottele brac' vend' cerv' pro i d. ob. post proc., sed nunc ad den' et est suff'.

Walterus de Mixebury regr' non vend' cerv' post proc. nisi pro i d., & est suff'.

vi d. Will' de Pirie brac' vend' cerv' pro i d. ob. post proc., sed nunc ad i d. & suff'.

[1] Originally vi d.

iii d. Will' Mustarder regr' non vend' cerv' nisi ad i d. post proc'; sed non suff'.

Ioh' de Denchesworth regr' non vend' cerv' nisi ad i d. post proc'; & suff'.

xii d. Walt' de Milton brac' vend' cerv' pro i d. ob. post proc'; sed nunc ad den' & suff'.

vi d. Pet' de Ew brac' vend' cerv' pro i d. ob. post proc'; sed nunc ad den' & suff'.

Ioh' de Gonewardby brac' non vend' nisi pro i d. post proc'; & suff'.

Rob' de Watlyntone brac' non vend' nisi pro i d. post proc'; & suff'.

vi d. Will' de Burcestre brac' vend' cerv. pro i d. ob. post proc'; sed nunc ad den' & suff'.

Isabella Hattere brac' non vend' cerv' nisi pro i d. post proc'; et suff'.

xi d. Hen' de Bedeford brac' vend' cerv' pro i d. ob. post proc'; et nunc fac' & [ ][1] tast'.

i d. Rob. le Taillur regr' non vend' cerv' nisi pro i d. post proc'; et non suff'.

xii d. Ioh' de Stangrave non vend' cerv' nisi pro i d. post proc'; et non suff'.

Steph' Molendinarius brac' non vend' cerv' nisi pro i d. post proc'; & suff'.

Beatrix la Stacioner brac' non vend' cerv' nisi pro i d. post proc'; & suff'.

iii d. Will' Lodelowe regr' non vend' cerv' nisi pro i d. post proc'; & non suff'.

Steph' de Abyndone brac' non vend' cerv' nisi pro i d. post proc'; & est suff'.

vi d. Ioh' Poul brac' non vend' cerv' nisi pro i d. post proc.; & non suff'.

Ioh' de Halghtone brac' non vend' cerv' nisi pro i d. post proc.; & nunc non habet.

Ioh' de Lokyntone brac' non vend' cerv' nisi pro i d. post proc'; et suff'.

Walterus de Arderne regr' non vend' cerv' nisi pro i d. post proc'; et suff'.

[1] Possibly 'reprob[avit] tast[atores]'.

Hen' le Sclattere brac' non vend' cerv' nisi pro i d. post proc'; et non habet.

xii d. Ioh' de Bysshopestone brac' vend' cerv' pro i d. ob. post proc., sed nunc ad den'; suff'.

xii d. Ioh' de Cristechurche brac' vend' cerv' pro i d. ob. post proc., sed nunc ad den'; suff'.

xii d. Thos. de Grauntpont brac' vend' cerv' pro i d. ob. post proc., sed nunc ad den'; suff'.

xii d. Matill' la Bocbyndere brac' vend' cerv' pro i d. ob. post proc., sed nunc ad den'; suff'.

vi d. Ioh' de Cambestone brac' vend' cerv' pro i d. ob. post proc., sed nunc ad den'; suff'.

Walt' Aylmer brac' non vend' cerv' nisi pro i d. post proc.; et suff'.

iii d. Ioh' de Stafford regr' non vend' cerv' nisi pro i d. post proc.; et non est suff'.

Pet' de Milton regr' non vend' cerv' nisi pro i d. post proc.; sed nunc non habet.

iii d.[1] Ioh' de Cokesgrave sutor regr' non vend' cerv' nisi pro i d. post proc.; sed non suff'.

xii d. Nic' de Glattone brac' vend' cerv' pro i d. ob. post proc., sed nunc ad den' & suff'.

xii d. Isabella de Couele brac' vend' cerv' pro i d. ob. post proc., sed nunc ad den' & suff'.

Edmundus Maunciple regr' non vend' cerv' nisi pro i d. post proc'; sed nunc non habet.

iii d. Will' Elmeshale regr' non vend' cerv' nisi pro i d. post proc'; et non suff'.

xii d. Rob' de Louthe brac' vend' cerv' ad i d. ob. post proc'; sed nunc ad den' & non suff'.

Rob' de Lyncolne regr' non vend' cerv' nisi pro i d. post proc'; & nunc non habet.

iii d. Iohanna de Ascote regr' vend' cerv' ad i d. ob. post proc'; sed nunc ad den' & suff'.

vi d. Ioh' Bradenhache brac' vend' cerv' ad i d. ob. post proc'; sed nunc ad den' & suff'.

[1] Possibly this amercement and also Rob. le Taillur above have been erased. This will make the total at the end correct.

Barth' le Corour brac' non vend' cerv' post proc., sed nunc habet ad den' de novo.

Rob' de Forderyngeye regr' non vend' cerv' nisi ad i d. post proc. & suff'.

Rogerus Pyroun brac' non vend' cerv' nisi ad i d. post proc. & nunc non habet.

Ioh' Iuerye brac' & non vend' cerv' post proc.; nec habet.

Galf' Coke brac' non vend' cerv' nisi pro i d. post proc.; & suff'.

Adam de Radenache regr' [*sic*].

Summa xxiii s. ix d.

Summa lxv s. iii d.

Tastatores cervisie, Thomas de Curtlyntone, Ric' le Hoppere, Ioh' de Wytteneye, Ric' de Wareberge.

Taxatores amerciamentorum, Thomas Somer, Hugo Tidemershe, Ric' le Grasiere, Ioh' de Isslepe, Ioh' le Marchal.

April, 1335 Assisa seruisie de termino Pasche anno r. r. E. tercii post conq. nono.

Northwestwarde

Walterus de Wareburghe	R.	iiii d.
Will' de Wormenhale	R.	ii d.
Matill' Battes	R.	iii d.
Ric' le Taillour	R.	iii d.
Ric' de Seukeworth	R.	iii d.
Ric' de Wyndesore	B.	vi d.
Matill' Lond'	B.	xii d.
Nich' de Langeford	B.	vi d.
Ioh' Mymcan	B.	xii d.
Ad' de Tershawe	B.	viii d.
Iohanna Ouerhee	B.	iiii d.
Ioh' Sowy	R.	iii d.
Thos. de Leghtone	B.	viii d.
Felicia de Herdewyke	R.	vi d.
Will' de Chilleham	R.	iiii d.
Alic' de Garsyndone	R.	iii d.
Rogerus le Taillour	R.	iii d.

Thos. de Berkele	B.	vi d.
Ioh' de Bamptone	B.	iiii d.
Steph' de Adyntone	B.	x d.
Ric. de Hamptone	R.	iiii d.
Benedictus le Skynnere	R.	iii d.
Emma de Lutlemor	R.	iii d.
Alicia de Adewelle	R.	iii d.
Walterus de Cudlyntone	R.	iii d.
Thomas Stokeman	B.	vi d.
Ioh' de Odyham	B.	vi d.
Walterus de Honycote	R.	iii d.
Ad' de Malteby	R.	iii d.

Northestwarde[1]

Ric' de Sutton	B.	vi d.
Hugo le Fourbour	R.	iii d.
Ioh' le Smyth	B.	vi d.
Phil' de Oo	B.	iiii d.
Walterus de Watteford	B.	vi d.
Rob' de la Mare	B.	iiii d.
Rad' de Seteryntone	B.	viii d.
Ioh' de Sutton	R.	iii d.
Ric' de Gloucestre	B.	vi d.
Iuliana de Walton	B.	iiii d.
Ioh' de Mustertone	B.	vi d.
Thos. de Wotton	B.	iiii d.
Nich' atte Bere	B.	viii d.
Will' de Chilham	B.	xii d.
Walt' de Muxebury	R.	iii d.
Ioh' de Hoggenortone	B.	vi d.
Ioh' de Pershore	R.	iii d.
Barth' de Cornubia	B.	xii d.
Ric' le Chaundeler	R.	iii d.
Ioh' le Sawyer	R.	iii d.
Will' de Shirebourne	R.	iii d.
Walt' de Milton	B.	viii d.
Iuliana de Strikelond	B.	vi d.
Ioh' de Wantyng	R.	iii d.

[1] Begins at North Gate; ends at East Gate.

Will' le Peyntur	R.	iii d.
Ioh' de Gunwardeby	B.	vi d.
Iohanna de Watlyntone	B.	viii d.
Alicia de Burcestre	R.	iiii d.
Phil' de Bathe	B.	iiii d.
Ioh' de Stangrave	B.	vi d.
Edwardus le Goldsmyth	B.	vi d.
Ioh' le Bowyer	R.	iii d.
Ioh' le Latoner	R.	iii d.
Ric' de Sibford	B.	vi d.
Steph' de Abyndon		viii d.
Ioh' Powel	B.	vi d.
Gilb' de Lynham	B.	vi d.
Ioh' de Lokyntone	B.	vi d.
Will' Turteys	R.	iii d.
Will' de Driffeld	R.	iii d.
Margeria de Mortone	R.	iii d.
Petronilla de Stafford	R.	iii d.
Will' de Levertone	R.	iii d.
Ric' le Taillour	R.	iii d.
Will' de Rolondright	B.	vi d.
Alanus de Killyngworth	B.	xii d.
Beatrix de Cristchirche	B.	vi d.
Ric' le Skynnere R.	B. [*sic*]	vi d.
Matill' la Bokebynder	B.	x d.
Ioh' de Coutone	B.	vi d.
Ioh' de Kent	B.	vi d.
Alicia de Merstone	R.	iii d.
Ioh' de Malteby	B.	iiii d.
Ric' de Eynesham	B.	vi d.
Rad' le Deuenysshe	R.	iii d.
Nic' de Glettone	B.	vi d.
Thos. de Haltone	B.	iii d.
[ ] de Henxey	R.	ii d.
[ ] de Abyndone	R.	iii d.
W[ ] le Barebour	R.	iii d.
Ioh' de Shipton	R.	iii d.
Ioh' de Melbourn	R.	ii d.
Ioh' le Flexman	R.	iii d.
Rog' Pyroun	B.	vi d.

Edmundus de Bermyngham	B.	vi d.
Ioh' de Baldyndon	B.	iiii d.
Galf' de Clay	R.	iii d.
Hen' de Skyptone	B.	vi d.
[ ] de [ ]alis	R.	iii d.
Ioh' de Mercham	R.	iii d.
Ioh' le Mareschal	B.	iii d.
Beatrix la Webbe	R.	iii d.

Southestwarde[1]

Reginaldus le Shereman	B.	vi d.
Will' le Dighere	B.	vi d.
Felicea Wenge	R.	iii d.
Ioh' de Brailles	R.	iii d.
Will' Blaunkpayn		iii d.
Will' Russel	R.	iii d.
Ric' le Coke	R.	iiii d.
Steph' le Mareschal	R.	iiii d.
Nic' de Brailles	B.	viii d.
Ioh' de Waisshetone	B.	iiii d.
Adam de Bekenysfeld	B.	vi d.
Ioh' de Coggesgrave	R.	iii d.
Ioh' de Aukland	B.	iiii d.
Nic' le Clerk de Mertonehalle	B.	iiii d.
Walterus atte Wyke	R.	iii d.
Gilb' le Soutere	R.	iii d.
Will' Marchaunt	R.	iii d.
Will' le Maunsiple	R.	iii d.
Nic' de Drihulle	R.	iii d.
Will' de Mertonehalle	R.	iii d.
Matild' la Tapstere	R.	iii d.
Hen. le Grasiere	R.	iii d.
Nic' le Grasiere	R.	iii d.
Ioh' de Shareshulle	R.	iii d.
Rob. Clyne	B.	iiii d.
Iohanna la Tapstere	R.	iii d.
Rob. Marre	R.	iii d.
Thos. Stanes	R.	iii d.

[1] Begins at East Gate; ends at South Bridge.

Rob. de York	R.	iii d.
Ioh' de Brampton	R.	iiii d.
Agnes Kelme	R.	iii d.
Ioh' le Barebour	R.	iii d.
Agnes la Newecok'	R.	iii d.
Isolda la Stacioner	B.	iiii d.
Adam de Welyntone	R.	iii d.
Will' de Whatele	B.	vi d.
Emma de Hanebourn (*sic*)	R.	iii d.
Ioh' de Kent	R.	iii d.
Alic' de Maydenstone	B.	vi d.
Agnes la Tapstere	R.	iii d.
Will' le Tapermaker	B.	iiii d.
Ioh' de Warewyk'	B.	iiii d.
Agnes de Edrope	B.	vi d.
Ioh' le Cok'	R.	iii d.
Cecilia Chuchely	R.	iii d.
Ioh' de Swanebourne	B.	viii d.
Ioh' de Strettone	R.	iii d.
Ioh' de Comptone	R.	ii d.
Ric' de Kirketone	B.	viii d.
Symon de Gloucestre	B.	xii d.
Ric' de Selewode	B.	iiii d.
Will' de Abyndone	B.	iiii d.
Galf' de Orton	R.	iii d.
Alic' de Neubury	R.	iii d.
Ioh' de Milton	R.	iii d.
Matill' de Amundesham	R.	iii d.
Adam de Tershawe	R.	iii d.
Ioh' Bost	B.	vi d.
Ric' Cary	B.	xii d.
Iohanna de Wycombe	R.	iii d.
Alanus de Hetone	B.	viii d.
Thos. de Curtlyntone	B.	vi d.
Ric. le Barebour	R.	iii d.
Thos. le Waterman	B.	iiii d.
Galf. Scot	R.	iiii d.
Rog. de Whitewelle	B.	iiii d.
Ioh' de Elsefeld	R.	iii d.
Andreas Ros	R.	iii d.

Iohanna de Benham	B.	iiii d.
Adam de Warmestone	[*blank*]	iii d.
Ric. Flax	R.	iii d.
Hen. le Plomer	R.	iii d.
Cristina Stoke	B.	vi d.
Adam le Northerne	R.	iii d.
Margreta (*sic*) Skolmaystres	R.	ii d.
Ric. de Wymbourne	R.	iii d.
Ioh' de Hatton	B.	iiii d.
Rob. de Yeftele	R.	ii d.

Southwestwarde [1]

Hen. le Glouere	B.	iiii d.
Hen. de Yiſtelere (*sic*)	B.	iiii d.
Galf. de Warmwell	B.	vi d.
Matill' la Hocstere	R.	iii d.
Hugo le Dighere	R.	iii d.
Petrus de Ew	B.	iii d.
Elena atte Yate	B.	vi d.
Agnes de Norhamptone	R.	iii d.
Adam le Northerne	B.	iiii d.
Will' le Peyntour	R.	
Ioh' Wildelond	B.	vi d.
Matill' de Hereford	B.	iiii d.
Thos. atte Pole	B.	vi d.
Margareta Wylde	B.	iii d.
Ioh' de Alestone	B.	vi d.
Will' de Leye	R.	iii d.
Ric' de Leye	B.	iiii d.
Will' le White	B.	iiii d.
Matill' de Redyng	R.	iii d.
Margeria la Marischal	B.	iiii d.
Galſ' de Mer'	R.	iii d.
Thos. Helmeden	R.	iii d.
Ioh' de Adyntone	B.	iiii d.
Sibilla Kepharm	B.	x d.
Will' filius Willelmi le Mercer	B.	vi d.
Ioh' de Stillyntone	B.	vi d.

[1] Begins at South Bridge; ends at St. Thomas's.

Ric' de Edrope	R.	iii d.
And. de Wormenhale	B.	viii d.
Domus Batte	R.	iii d.
Ioh' de Whaisshebourne	B.	vi d.
Hugo Tichemerch	R.	iii d.
Will' Muleward	R.	iii d.
Ioh' de Nortone	B.	vi d.
Ioh' Cosyn	B.	vi d.
Iulyana Puseye	R.	iii d.
Ioh' de Whitele	B.	iiii d.
Ric' de Wareburghe	B.	iiii d.
Walterus de Quenyntone	R.	iii d.
Ioh' de Lughteburghe	B.	xii d.
Ioh' de Leye	B.	viii d.
Rob' le Gryndere	R.	iii d.
Ric. de Lacheforde	B.	iii d.

Sancti Thome

Will' le Dighere	B.	iiii d.
Galf' le Bailfesmauerraunt	B.	iii d.
Alic' Graunger	B.	iii d.
Laur' le Masun	B.	iiii d.
Emma de Boteleye	R.	iii d.
Hugo Whitecoke	B.	iii d.
Emma le Fisshere	R.	iii d.
Agnes de Tubbeneye	R.	iii d.
Will' de Bartone	B.	iiii d.
Agnes la Masun	B.	xii d.
Ioh' Clyne	R.	iii d.
Will' Gylmyn	R.	iii d.
Iohanna Basse	B.	iii d.
Agnes Barettes	R.	iii d.
Maria de Botele	R.	iii d.
Isolda la Lauender	R.	iii d.

The membrane is indented but has no lettering.

De amerciamentis assise cervisie a festo sancti Michaelis anno r. r. E. tercii post conquestum undecimo usque festum Pasche proximo sequens per dimidium annum tempore Roberti de Stretford episcopi Cicestren' & cancellarii Universitatis Oxon' & Henrici de Stodeleghe tunc maioris Oxonie in quatuor wardis eiusdem ville.[1] **[March, 1338]**

Northwestwarde

De Waltero de Warberghe	R.	iii d.
De Will. le Gryndere	B.	vi d.
De Matill' Battes	R.	iii d.
De Ric. le Taillour	R.	iii d.
De Rogero Kirketone	R.	iii d.
De Durant le Taillur	R.	iii d. nichil
De Ric. de Wyndesore	B.	x d.
De Rob. de Hoggestone	B.	vi d.
De Nich. de Langeford	B.	x d.
De Ioh' Mimmecan	B.	x d.
De Adam le Longe	B.	xii d.
De Iohanna Ouerhe	B.	viii d.
De Ioh' Sowy	R.	iiii d.
De Barth' de Cornubia	B.	xvi d.
De Iohanna Grene	B.	x d.
De Will. de Chilham	B.	xii d. o[nerat]ur
De Iohanne de Watforde		[*blank*]
De Thoma de Berkele	B.	iiii d. nichil
De Ric. Chaundeler	B.	x d.
De Steph. de Adyntone	B.	xii d. nichil
De Benedicto Skynnere	R.	iii d.
De Galf. de Odyham	R.	ii d.
De Will. de London	R.	iii d.
De Hen. de Hamptone	R.	iii d.
De Thoma Stokeman	B.	vi d.
De Ioh' de Odyham	B.	xii d.
De Nic' de Redyng	B.	viii d.
De Adam Cotiller	R.	iii d.
De Waltero de Honycote	R.	iii d.
De Roberto le Barber	R.	iii d.

Summa clara xiii s. iiii d. recept' xv s. xi d.

[1] This assise is on two rolls; they are both indented on the right-hand side; along the one is written CANCELLARIVS : MAIOR and along the other CANCELLARIVS : MAIOR : OXON.

Northestwarde[1]

De Rob. Druery	R.	ii d.
De Ric. de Suttone	B.	vi d. Pars iii d.
De Ioh' le Smyth	B.	x d.
De Waltero de Watford	B.	iiii d.
De Ioh' Carreu	R.	iii d.
De Rob. de Dernynton	B.	vi d.
De Rad. de Seteryntone	B.	xviii d.
De Rob. de Bolwyk	R.	iii d.
De Ioh' de Cadesby	R.	iii d.
De Ioh' de Eynesham	B.	vi d.
De Ioh' de Mustertone	B.	viii d.
De Ioh' atte Marche	R.	iiii d.
De Waltero de Mixebury	R.	iii d.
De Galf. le Saucer	R.	iii d.
De Ioh' de Persshore	R.	iii d.
De Ioh' le Somenour	B.	viii d.
De Ric. de Adyntone	B.	iii d.
De Ioh' de Strattone	R.	ii d. nichil
De Will. Chaundeler	R.	iiii d.
De Agnete de Adyntone	R.	iii d. nichil
De Ioh' Terry	R.	iii d.
De Will' de Shirebourne	R.	iii d.
De Waltero de Miltone sen.	B.	xii d.
De Ioh' de Spene	R.	iii d.
De Iuliana Strikelonde	B.	viii d.
De Ioh' de Wanetyng	B.	xii d.
De Edwardo Goldsmyth	R.	iii d.
De Ioh' Bost	B.	vi d. nichil quia car-
De Ric. le Tauerner	B.	vi d. cer[arius]
De Ioh' de Gunwardby	B.	vi d.
De Iohanna de Watlyntone	B.	x d.
De Alicia de Burcestre	B.	vi d.
De Philippo de Bathe	B.	viii d.
De Iuliana de Waltone	R.	iii d.
De Rob. le Hattere	R.	iii d.
De Ioh' de Stangrave	B.	xii d.
De Alic' de Sheldon	B.	iii d.

[1] Begins at North Gate; ends at East Gate.

De Ric. de Sybforde	R.	vi d.	
De Steph' de Abyndone	B.	xvi d.	
De Ioh' Poul	B.	xii d.	
De Thoma le Lumynour	R.	iii d.	
De Ioh' Hedde	R.	iii d.	
De Agn' la Lighte	R.	iii d.	
De Will. de Lynham	B.	viii d.	
De Ioh' de Lokyntone	B.	xii d.	
De Will. Torteys	R.	iii d.	
De Walt. de Arderne	R.	iii d.	
De Alano atte gate	R.	iii d.	
De Hen. le Sclattere	B.	iii d.	
De Egidio de Cornubia	R.	iii d.	
De Will. de Leuertone	R.	iii d.	
De Petronilla de Stafford	R.	iii d.	
De Willelmo de Rollendrighte	B.	viii d.	
De Alano de Killeworthe	B.	xvi d.	
De Beatrice de Cristechurche	B.	vi d.	
De Ric. le Skynnere	B.	viii d.	
De Matild' Bocbyndere	B.	xii d.	
De Ioh' de Kent	R.	vi d.	
De Will' de Chilmeleghe	R.	ii d.	
De Alic' de Mersshetone	R.	iii d.	
De Iuliana de Maltebv	R.	iii d.	
De Ric' atte Wyndmulle	B.	xii d.	
De Galf. de Cley	R.	iii d.	
De Agn' la Coke	R.	iii d.	nulla tal*is*
De Ric. le Cok	B.	viii d.	
De Ioh' Alenstone	B.	iii d.	
De Nich' de Glettone	B.	vi d.	
De Sibilla de Skyptone	R.	iii d.	
De Alicia de Walyngford	R.	iii d.	
De Ioh' de Shuptone	R.	iii d.	
De Hen. de Chelmeleghe	R.	iii d.	
De Agn. de Couele	R.	iii d.	
De Ioh' de Milbourne	R.	iii d.	
De Iohanna de Colump	R.	ii d.	
De Rog. Pyroun	B.	viii d.	
De Edmundo de Bernyngham	B.	viii d.	
De Ioh' de Baldyndone	R.	iiii d.	

De Ioh' de Brayles	R.	iii d.
De Hen. de Skyptone	B.	vi d.
De Will. le Hunte	R.	iii d.
De Ioh' de Bradenhache	R.	iii d.
De Ioh' le Mareschal	B.	vi d.
Summa clara xxxvi s. iii d. recept'		xxxvii s. viii d.

Suthestwarde [1]

De Reginaldo le Sherman	B.	viii d.
De Will' le Deghere	B.	viii d.
De Felicia Ioye	R.	iii d.
De Will. Blankpayn	R.	iii d.
De Will. Russel	R.	iii d.
De Ioh' atte Wode	R.	iii d.
De Nich' de Brayles	B.	x d.
De Ioh' de Whaysstone	B.	viii d.
De Iohanna de Berkhampstede	B.	xii d.
De Ric. de Fyndene	R.	iii d. nichil quia pauper
De Will' Marchaund	R.	iii d.
De Will' Prat	R.	iii d.
De Agnete de Drihulle	R.	iii d. ignota
De Will. atte More	R.	ii d.
De Nich' le Clerke	B.	viii d.
De Nich' de Drihulle	R.	iii d.
De Hen. de Malmesbury	B.	xviii d.
De Ioh' de Cokesgrave	R.	iii d.
De Ioh' de Aucloude	R.	iii d.
De Simone le Manciple	R.	ii d.
De Sibilla de Bedeforde	R.	iii d. nichil quia uxor Simonis
De Agnete de Hodescoumbe	R.	iii d.
De Thoma le Carpenter	R.	iii d.
De Nich' le Grasiere	R.	iiii d.
De Ioh' de Shareshulle	R.	ii d.
De Rog' de Nywentone	B.	iiii d.
De Rog' de Swyneford	R.	iii d.
De Rob. de Marre	R.	iii d.
De Thoma de Stanes	R.	iii d.
De Ioh' de Bramptone	R.	iii d.

[1] Begins at East Gate; ends at South Bridge.

De Rob. de York	R.	iii d.	
De Eua la Barber	R.	iii d.	
De Ioh' de Croke	R.	iii d.	
De Ioh' de Brehulle	R.	vi d.	
De Adam de Wylyntone	R.	iii d.	
De Iohanna de Dunyntone	[*blank*]	iii d.	
De Will. de Whatele	B.	vi d.	
De Alic' de Carsyntone	R.	iiii d.	
De Math' le [ ]		iii d.	
De Alic' de Maidenstone	B.	vi d.	
De Waltero le Flecchere	R.	iii d.	
De Ric. de Grynstede	R.	iii d.	
De Ioh' de Etone	R.	iii d.	
De Will. Tapermaker	B.	xii d.	Canc[ellarius]
De Agn' atte Redcokke	B.	viii d.	r[espondit]
De Ioh' de Swanebourne	B.	xii d.	
De Waltero Gautron	R.	iii d.	
De Ioh' de Comptone	R.	iii d.	
De Ric' de Kirketone	B.	xii d.	
De Margareta Shippestere	R.	iii d.	nichil quia pauper
De Matill' Lond'	B.	xvi d.	
De Simone de Gloucestre	B.	xvi d.	nichil quia alder-
De Katerina de Miltone	B.	viii d.	mannus
De Will' de Abyndone	B.	viii d.	
De Galf' de Ouertone	R.	iii d.	
De Ioh' de Bedeford	R.	iii d.	
De Ioh' de Watlyntone	R.	iii d.	
De Alic' de Neubury	R.	iii d.	
De Ioh' de Stauntone	R.	iii d.	
De Waltero de Miltone Minore	R.	iiii d.	
De Adam le Long	B.	iiii d.	
De Ric. de Seukworth	R.	vi d.	
De Ric. Cary	B.	xii d.	nichil quia alder-
De Iohanna de Wycoumbe	R.	iiii d.	mannus
De Alano de Hetone	B.	xvi d.	
De Thoma de Curtlyntone	B.	xii d.	
De Cristina de sancta Frideswida	R.	iii d.	
De Ric. le Barber	R.	iii d.	
De Ioh' de Wytteneye	R.	iii d.	nichil quia non ven-
De Ioh' de Lokyng	R.	vi d.	d[idit] ceruisiam

De Galf. Scot	B.	iiii d.	
De Rog. de Whitewelle	B.	xii d.	
De Will. Cloudesdale	R.	iii d.	
De Elizabetha de Clyftone	R.	iii d.	
De Ioh' de Thame	R.	iii d.	
De Will' le Peyntour	R.	iii d.	
De Nich. atte Bere	B.	xii d.	
De Thoma le Carpenter	R.	ii d.	
De Ioh' de Sutton	R.	iii d.	
De Matill' la Plomer	R.	iii d.	
De Margareta Nel	R.	iii d.	
De Steph. de Cornubia	R.	iii d.	
De Rob. de Yeftele	R.	iii d.	
Summa clara recept' xxxi s. ii d.		xxv s. iiii d.	

Southwestwarde [1]

De Rob. de Tersshagh	B.	x d.	nichil quia non in
De Hen. de Yeftele	B.	x d.	extract'
De Will. Bruyn	R.	iii d.	
De Thoma de Boclonde	R.	ii d.	
De Galf. le Cha	B.	xii d.	
De Ioh' de Langrysshe	B.	vi d.	Pars iiii d.
De Ric. de Wymbourne	R.	iii d.	
De Pet. de Ew	R.	iii d.	
De Rosa de Spaldyng	R.	iii d.	
De Elena atteyate	R.	viii d.	
De Petronilla de Adyntone	R.	iii d.	
De Ioh' de Ryngedale	R.	ii d.	nichil quia me-
De Will' le Peyntour	R.	iii d.	nestre
De Alic' Brid	R.	iii d.	
De Ioh' de Alestone	B.	xii d.	
De Hen. de Goseford	R.	vi d.	
De Ioh. de Hales	B.	viii d.	
De Matill' Hereford	B.	vi d.	
De Ioh' Wildelond	B.	vi d.	
De Will' le Tannere	R.	iii d.	
De Galf' de Mere	B.	viii d.	
De Sibilla Kepharm	B.	xvi d.	

[1] Begins at South Bridge; ends at West Gate.

De Ioh' Metessharp	R.	iii d.	nichil quia non
De Will. Gylot	B.	viii d.	vend' cervisiam
De Ioh' de Stylyntone	B.	viii d.	
De Rob. de Cauntebrugg'	R.	iii d.	
De And. de Wormenhale	B.	vi d.	nichil quia alder-
De Rob. de Beaumond	R.	iii d.	mannus
De Alic' la Tappestere	R.	iii d.	
De Ioh' de Whaysshebume	B.	xii d.	
De Ioh' de Tademartone	B.	vi d.	
De Will' le Muleward	R.	iii d.	
De Ioh' Soth	R.	iii d.	
De Ioh' de Nortone	B.	viii d.	
De Rog. de Abyndone	R.	iii d.	
De Margeria la Mareschal	R.	iii d.	
De Matill' de Redyng	R.	iii d.	
De Will' le White	B.	vi d.	
De Waltero le Fox	R.	iiii d.	
De Will' de Leghe	R.	ii d.	
De Ioh' Cosyn	B.	x d.	
De Ioh' de Whitele	B.	x d.	
De Alic' de Puseye	R.	iii d.	
De Rob. de Fenne	R.	vi d.	
De Ioh' le Latoner	R.	iii d.	
De Waltero de Quenyntone	B.	iii d.	
De Ioh' le Northerne	B.	xvi d.	
De Ioh' de Leghe	B.	xii d.	
De Ric. de Pirye	B.	iii d.	nichil quia com-
De Rob. le Gryndere	R.	iii d.	munis serviens
De Rob. Clyue	B.	viii d.	
De Ric. de Lacheford	R.	ii d.	
De Ric. de Cressale	R.	iii d.	
De Will. le Deghere	B.	vi d.	
De Felicia Herdwyk	R.	iii d.	
De Laur' le Masoun	R.	iii d.	
De Alic' de Chyvele	R.	iii d.	nichil quia pauper
De Agn' de Tobbeneye	R.	iii d.	
De Nich' le Coureur	R.	iii d.	
De Ioh' de Staunton	R.	iii d.	
De Ioh' le Taillur	R.	iii d.	
De Walt' Vaureal	B.	xvi d.	

De Iohanna Basse	R.	iii d.	
De Agnete Baret	R.	iii d.	nichil quia extra libertatem
De Iohanne de Londone	R.	iii d.	nichil quia pauper
Summa clara recept' xxv s. ix d.		xviii s. iiii d.	

Summa totalis clar' recept' & onerata cvi s. vi d. De quibus solu' maiori per W. de Wolastone l s. et Cancellario l s. et in expensis temptacionis cervisie hac vice ii s., in expensis factis circa affor' & alios super comp' exist' ii s. xi d. Et sic deb' xix d.

[Sept. 1338] De amerciamentis assise cervisie a festo Pasche anno r. r. Ed. III a conquestu xii° usque festum sancti Michaelis proximo sequens per dimidium annum tempore magistri Roberti de Stretford episcopi Cicestrensis & Cancellarii domini regis & Universitatis Oxonie & Henrici de Stodeleghe tunc maioris Oxonie in villa Oxonie & eius suburb' per quatuor wardas.

Cancellar'

Northwestwarde

De Waltero de Warberghe	R.	iii d.	
De Will. le Gryndere	B.	vi d.	
De Matill. Battes	R.	ii d.	
De Ric. le Taillour	R.	iii d.	
De Rog. de Kirkeby	R.	ii d.	
De Durant le Taillour	R.	iii d.	
De Ric. de Wyndesore	B.	x d.	
De Rob. de Hoggestone	B.	vi d.	
De Nich' de Langeford	B.	x d.	
De Ioh' Mimecan	B.	x d.	
De Adam le Longe	B.	xii d.	
De Iohanna de Ouerhe	B.	vi d.	
De Ioh' Sowy	R.	iiii d.	
De Barth' de Cornubia	B.	xii d.	
De Ioh' Grene	B.	x d.	
De Ric. de Hamptone	B.	x d.	
De Steph. de Adyntone	B.	xii d.	nichil quia aldermannus [1]
De Roesia de Pidyntone	R.	ii d.	
De Agnete de Halghtone	R.	ii d.	nichil

[1] On Sept. 29, 1338, he was made mayor.

De Adam le Cotiller	R.	iii d.	
De Thom. le Barber	R.	ii d.	
De Hen. de Hamptone	B.	iii d.	
De Thom. Stokeman	B.	iiii d.	
De Ioh' de Odyham	B.	x d.	
De Alic' la Longebr'	[*blank*]	iiii d.	
De Ioh' de Walyngforde	R.	iii d.	
De Walt' de Honycote	R.	iii d.	
De Rob. le Barber	R.	ii d.	
De Will' de Chilham	B.	xii d.	
De Ioh' de Bamptone	[*blank*]	x d.	nichil quia subballivus

Summa xv s. i d. Summa clara xiii s. i d.

Northestwarde

De Cristina Bathes	B.	iiii d.	nichil quia non braciavit
De Rob. Druery	R.	ii d.	
De Ric. de Suttone	B.	iiii d.	
De Ioh' Smyth, skinnere	B.	x d.	
De Waltero de Watford	B.	vi d.	
De Ioh' Carew	B.	iiii d.	
De Rob. de Derlintone	R.	iii d.	nichil quia non pot[est] le[uari]
De Rad. de Seteryntone	B.	xii d.	
De Rob. Bolewyk	R.	ii d.	
De Ioh' de Eynesham	B.	x d.	
De Ioh' de Mustertone	B.	viii d.	
De Thoma de Wortone	B.	iiii d.	
De Steph' de Brampton	B.	iiii d.	
De Waltero de Mixebury	R.	iii d.	
De Galf. le Saucer	R.	ii d.	
De Ioh' de Persshore	R.	iii d.	
De Ioh' de Adyntone	B.	x d.	
De Cok' le Chaundeler	R.	iii d.	
De Ioh' Terry	R.	iii d.	
De Will' de Shireburne	B.	iii d.	
De Walt' de Miltone	B.	viii d.	
De Ioh' Spence	R.	ii d.	
De Iuliana Strikelond	B.	viii d.	
De Ioh' de Wanetyng	B.	x d.	

De Ioh' Bost	B.	x d.	nichil quia minister communis
De Ric. le Taberner	B.	vi d.	
De Ioh' de Gonewardby	[*blank*]	iiii d.	
De Iohanna de Watlyntone	B.	viii d.	
De Alic' de Burcestre	B.	vi d.	
De Phil' de Bathe	B.	vii d.	
De Iuliana de Waltone	B.	vi d.	
De Ioh' de Stangrave	B.	x d.	
De Dionisia de Westone	R.	ii d.	
De Alicia de Sheldone	R.	ii d.	
De Thoma del Unicornhalle	B.	vi d.	
De Ioh' le Latoner	R.	iii d.	
De Ric. de Sibford	B.	viii d.	
De Steph. de Abyndone	B.	x d.	
De Ioh' Poul	B.	viii d.	
De Matill' Lumynour	R.	iii d.	
De Agnete la Lighte	R.	iiii d.	
De Ioh' Hedde	B.	vi d.	
De Gilb. de Lynham	B.	viii d.	
De Ioh' de Lokyntone	B.	x d.	
De Cecilia Torteys	R.	iii d.	solvit ii d.
De Margeria de Mortone	R.	iiii d.	
De Alano de Padebury	R.	iii d.	
De Matilda atte Naysshe	R.	ii d.	
De Egidio de Cornubia	R.	ii d.	
De Willelmo de Leuertone	R.	iii d.	
De Willelmo de Rollendright	B.	vi d.	
De Alano de Kilworth	B.	xiiii d.	
De Beatrice de Cristechurche	B.	iiii d.	
De Ricardo le Skynnere	B.	x d.	
De Matill' Bocbyndere	B.	viii d.	
De Ioh' de Kent	B.	vi d.	
De Willelmo de Chilmeleye	R.	ii d.	
De Iuliana Smyth	R.	ii d.	
De Ric. de Eynesham	B.	x d.	
De Galf. Cley	R.	iii d.	
De Ric. le Coke	B.	vi d.	
De Ioh' de Halghtone	R.	ii d.	
De Nic. de Glettone	B.	vi d.	
De Iohanna Castel	R.	iii d.	

De Alicia Walyngford	R.	iii d.	
De Ioh' de Shuptone	R.	iii d.	
De Rad' le Deuenysh	R.	ii d.	
De Iohanna de Milbourne	R.	ii d.	
De Iohanna de Culne	R.	ii d.	
De Rogero Pyroun	B.	vi d.	
De Edmundo de Bernyngham	B.	vi d.	
De Ioh' de Baldyndone	R.	iii d.	
De Ioh' de Brayles	R.	iii d.	
De Hen. de Skypton	B.	vi d.	
De Iuliana Hales	B.	iii d.	
De Iohanna de Cadesby	R.	ii d.	
De Ioh' le Smyth	B.	vi d.	

Summa clara xxxi s. xi d. xxxiii s. v d.

Southestwarde

De Reginaldo le Sherman	B.	viii d.	
De Will. le Deghere	B.	viii d.	
De Felicia Ioye	R.	iii d.	
De Ioh' Blankpayn	R.	ii d.	
De Will' Russel	R.	iii d.	
De Nic. de Brayles	B.	viii d.	
De Ioh' de Whaisshtone	B.	viii d.	
De Will' le Barbour	R.	ii d.	
De Hen. de Malmesburi	B.	xv d.	
De Isabella de Skyptone	R.	ii d.	
De Ioh' de Cokesgrave	R.	ii d.	
De Nich. le Clerke	B.	vi d.	
De Will. Marchand	R.	ii d.	
De Nich. de Forsthulle	R.	ii d.	
De Isabella de Mussendene	R.	ii d.	
De Nich. de Drihulle	R.	ii d.	
De Cecilia la Latoner	R.	ii d.	nichil quia non
De Cecilia de Waltham	R.	ii d.	pot[est] le[vari]
De Agnete de Hodescombe	R.	iii d.	
De Nic. le Grasiere	R.	iii d.	
De Rog. de Newentone	B.	vi d.	
De Rob. Marre	R.	iii d.	
De Rog. Swyneford	R.	iii d.	

De Thoma Stanes	R.	iii d.
De Ioh' de Bramptone	R.	iii d.
De Rob. de Yorke	R.	iii d.
De Eua le Barber	R.	ii d.
De Ioh' Croke	R.	iii d.
De Ioh' de Brehulle	B.	vi d.
De Adam de Welyntone	R.	iii d.
De Will. de Whatele	B.	viii d.
De Alic' de Gersyndone	R.	ii d.
De Alic' Maydenstone	B.	vi d.
De Waltero le Flecchere	R.	iii d.
De Ric. de Grymstede	R.	iii d.
De Will. Tapermakere	B.	x d.
De Agnete atte Redecokke	B.	viii d.
De Ioh' de Swaneburne	B.	viii d.
De Waltero Gautron	R.	iii d.
De Ioh' de Comptone	R.	iii d.
De Ric. de Kirketone	B.	xii d.
De Margeria la Shupestere	R.	iii d. nichil quia non potest le[vari]

respice in rotulo incipiente 'De Matill' Lond'[1]

[Sept. 1340] Amerciamenta assise ceruisie in villa Oxon' & eius suburb' a festo Pasche anno r. r. Ed. III post conquestum xiiii usque festum Michaelis proximo sequens tempore magistri W. de Skeltone cancellarii & W. de Burcestria maioris Oxonie, custodum dicte assise.

Northwestward

De Walt' de Warberghe	R.	iii d.
De Will. le Gryndere	R.	iiii d.
De Adam de Tersshaghe	B.	xii d.
De Matill' Battes	R.	iii d.
De Ric. le Taillur	R.	iii d.
De Alic. de Gonewardby	R.	ii d.
De Ric. de Adyntone	B.	iiii d.
De Ric. de Wyndesore	B.	viii d.
De Rob. de Hoggestone	B.	viii d.

[1] The roll, in which would have been the conclusion of this ward and the whole of the South-west Ward, is missing.

De Alic. de Eynesham	B.	viii d.
De Ioh' Mimmekan	B.	viii d.
De Iohanna Ouerhe	B.	viii d.
De Ioh' Sowy	R.	iiii d.
De Barth' de Cornubia	B.	xii d.
De Alic' de Burcestria	R.	iiii d.
De Will' de Chilham	B.	viii d.
De Hugone de Mussewyke	R.	iiii d.
De Ric. de Hamptone	B.	viii d.
De Ioh' de Bamptone	B.	xii d.
De Steph' de Adytone	B.	x d.
De Ioh' le Peyntour	R.	ii d.
De Adam le Cotiller	B.	vi d.
De Will. de Londone	R.	ii d.
De Thom. le Barbur	R.	ii d.
De Ioh' de Odyham	B.	x d.
De Nich' de Redyng	B.	vi d.
De Walt' de Honycote	R.	iii d.
De Rob. le Barbour	R.	iii d.

xiii s. xi d.

Northestwarde

De Ric. de Suttone	viii d.
De Ioh' Smyth, skynnere	x d.
De Phil. de Ew	iiii d.
De Walt. de Watforde	vi d.
De Will. Attemore	viii d.
De Ioh' Carreu	viii d.
De Rad. de Setertone	xii d.
De Rob. de Bolwyk	ii d.
De Ioh. de Wynerdby	viii d.
De Ioh. de Eynesham	viii d.
De Will. de Norton	ii d.
De Ioh. de Mustertone	viii d.
De Thom. de Worton	viii d.
De Thom. de Bourn	iii d.
De Ioh. de Lilleburne	x d.
De Gilb. de Bristowe	ii d.
De Ioh. de Stylyntone	vi d.

De Ioh. Kepharm	xii d.
De Ioh. de Adyntone	x d.
De Ric. Chaundeler	iiii d.
De Ioh. Terry	iiii d.
De Will. de Shirebourne	iiii d.
De Walt. de Miltone	x d.
De Ioh. de Bereford	x d.
De Ioh. Bost	viii d.
De Ric. Tauerner	x d.
De Iohanna de Watlyntone	viii d.
De Iohanna de Hedesham	ii d.
De Agnete de Bekkeford	iii d.
De Ric. de Norton	vi d.
De Rob. le Hattere	ii d.
De Ioh. Torald	vi d.
De Ioh. de Hulle	ii d.
De Ioh. de Stangrave	viii d.
De Ric. de Sibford	viii d.
De Ioh. de Sheldone	ii d.
De Thom. del Unicornhalle	viii d.
De Thom. le Latoner	ii d.
De Steph. de Abyndone	x d.
De Ioh' Poule	viii d.
De Rob. Manciple	iii d.
De Ioh' Hedde	vi d.
De Gilb. de Lynham	vi d.
De Ioh. de Lokyntone	x d.
De Agn. de Rollendright	vi d.
De Alano de Kilworth	xii d.
De Ric. de Walyngford	viii d.
De Ric. de Hamme	ii d.
De Ioh. de Kent	vi d.
De Ioh. Cole	ii d.
De Iuliana Smythes	iiii d.
De Ric. de Eynesham	x d.
De Ric. le Coke	viii d.
De Ioh. de Halghtone	ii d.
De Nich. de Glettone	vi d.
De Thom. de Wermenhale	ii d.
De Iohanna de Kent	vi d.

De Alicia de Walyngford	iii d.
De Ioh. de Shuptone	iii d.
De Agn. de Coueleye	iii d.
De Rog. Pyroun	vi d.
De Edmundo de Bernyngham	vi d.
De Ioh. de Baldyndone	iiii d.
De Hen. de Skyptone	vi d.
De Iuliana la Hunte	iii d.
De Iohanna de Gatesby	iii d.
De Ioh. le Marshal	vi d.
De Ioh. de Brayles	ii d.
De Margareta de Shuptone	ii d.
xxxiii s. x d.	

Southestwarde

De Reginaldo le Deghere	x d.
De Walt. le Deghere	viii d.
De Felicia Ioye	ii d.
De Walt. Coupere	ii d.
De Will. Blancpayn	iii d.
De Will. Russel	iii d.
De Rog. Nortwode	vi d.
De Nic. de Brayles	viii d.
De Ioh' de Whaisstone	viii d.
De Agn' la Barber	ii d.
De Agn' de Horspath	ii d.
De Will' Marchaund	ii d.
De Sibilla de Mussendene	ii d.
De Alic' de Bourton	ii d.
De Nic. le Clerk	vi d.
De Sibilla de Neubury	ii d.
De Hen. de Malmesbury	xii d.
De Ioh' de Cokesgrave	iii d.
De Alic' la Tappistere	vi d.
De Rob. de Lyndes'	iii d.
De Leonardo Bedel	vi d.
De Nich. Grasiere	iii d.
De Rog. de Nywenton	vi d.
De Rob. de Marre	iii d.

De Will. de Wyke	vi d.
De Ioh' de Bramptone	ii d.
De Simone le Mauncíple	iii d.
De Ioh. Croke	vi d.
De Adam de Welyntone	iii d.
De Will. de Whatele	vi d.
De Alic. de Carsyntone	iii d.
De Alic. de Maidenstone	vi d.
De Ioh' de Dentone	iii d.
De Iohanna de Aylesbury	iii d.
De Ric. de Grymstede	iii d.
De Isolda la Stacioner	ii d.
De Thom. le Webbe	ii d.
De Alianora de Huntyngfeld	ii d.
De Will. le Tapermakere	xii d.
De Agn' de Edrope	viii d.
De Cecilia Chicchele	ii d.
De Ioh. de Swanbourne	viii d.
De Walt. Gautron	ii d.
De Ioh. de Comptone	ii d.
De Ric. de Kirketone	x d.
De Marg. la Shipstere	ii d.
De Matill' Lond'	x d.
De Simone de Gloucestre	x d.
De Ioh. de Melton	x d.
De Will. de Abyndone	vi d.
De Galf. de Worton	iii d.
De Ioh. de Watlyntone	iii d.
De Alic. de Neubury	iii d.
De Walt. de Milton	iii d.
De Adam le Longe	iiii d.
De Will. de Aldewyncle	ii d.
De Ric. Cary	viii d.
De Iohanna de Wycombe	iii d.
De Alano de Hetone	x d.
De Thom. de Curtlyntone	viii d.
De Rob. de Lokyng	iii d.
De Agn. Spayne	iii d.
De Ric. le Barber	ii d.
De Ioh' de Lokyng	iiii d.

De Ioh' de Hales	viii d.
De Rog. de Whitewelle	viii d.
De Will. de Cloudesdale	iii d.
De Cecilia de Clyfton	ii d.
De Ioh. de Tame	ii d.
De Roesia Paynes	vi d.
De Ioh. le Boltere	iii d.
De Ioh. de Henxeye	iii d.
De Nich. atte Bere	vi d.
De Ioh. le Peyntour	ii d.
De Ioh. de Suttone	ii d.

xxviii s. x d.

Southwestwarde

De Will. Broun	vi d.
De Hen. de Yeftele	viii d.
De Galf. le Cha	viii d.
De Ioh. Langrysshe	iiii d.
De Pet. de Ew	iiii d.
De Ioh. de Alestone	viii d.
De Hen. de Goseford	vi d.
De Iohanna atte Yate	iiii d.
De Waltero de Cudelyntone	ii d.
De Agn' la Tapstere	iii d.
De Roesia de Spaldyng	vi d.
De Thom. de Halmedone	ii d.
De Will. le Tannere	ii d.
De Cristina de sancta Frideswida	vi d.
De Ioh' de Persshore	iiii d.
De Ioh' le Fysshere	ii d.
De Iohanna de Rimyntone	ii d.
De Will. Gylot	vi d.
De Adam de Shrovesbury	ii d.
De Agn. la Lighte	iii d.
De Andrea de Wormenhale	vi d.
De Hospicio Battes	iiii d.
De Will. de Nortone	ii d.
De Ioh' Whaisssheburne	x d.
De Durant le Taillour	iii d.

De Will. le Meleward	ii d.
De Ioh. de Nortone	vi d.
De Rob. Maunciple	iii d.
De Will. le White	vi d.
De Ioh. Cosyn	viii d.
De Ioh. de Whiteleye	viii d.
De Alic. de Puseye	ii d.
De Rob. atte Fenne	vi d.
De Ioh' Wildelond	vi d.
De Walt. de Quenyntone	ii d.
De Matill' Northerne	viii d.
De Ioh' de Leghe	viii d.
De Ric. de Pirie	iiii d.
De Rob. Gryndere	iii d.
De Rob. Clyue	iiii d.
De Ric. de Lachford	ii d.
De Alic. atte Kichene	ii d.
De Will. le Deghere	iiii d.
De Galf. le Criour	ii d.
De Laur. le Mason	iiii d.
De Thoma Borstall	ii d.
De Ioh' le Taillour	ii d.
De Walt. Vaureal	xii d.
De Ioh' Basse	ii d.
De Cristina Haukyns	ii d.

xviii s. vii d.

Summa totalis iiii li. xv s. ii d.

Aff' Ioh' de Falle,
Will. le Sporiere,
Ioh' Ouremaister,
Will. le Peyntour.

[The roll is indented but has no writing along the indentation.]

[April, 1344] Assaia ceruisie termino Pasche anno r. r. Ed. III post conquestum Anglie xviii° coram W. de Bergeueny cancellario & R. Cary maiore.

Northwestwarde

Walterus de Warburghe	R.	iiii d.
Ioh' Lillebourne	R.	ii d.
Iohanna de Fencote	R.	ii d.

Thomas Dedewythe	R.	ii d.
Ric. de Wyndesore	B.	vi d.
Matill' Lond	B.	xii d.
Ioh' Dokelyntone	B.	vi d.
Ioh' Mymecan	B.	vi d.
Rob. Manyfeld	B.	iiii d.
Iohanna Ouerhe	B.	vi d.
Iuliana Helle	R.	iiii d.
Barth' de Cornubia	B.	viii d.
Ioh' Bost	B.	vi d.
Will. de Chilham	B.	xii d.
Hugo Musselwyke	R.	vi d.
Ric. de Hamptone	B.	viii d.
Ioh. de Bamptone	B.	viii d.
Steph. de Adyntone	B.	viii d.
Phil' Hauuille	R.	iii d.
Iohanna de Watford	B.	iii d.
Thom. le Barbour	R.	iii d.
Walt. Honycote	R.	iii d.
Rob. le Correour	R.	iii d.
Nich. le Couke	R.	ii d.
Will. le Correour	R.	iii d.

Summa x s. v d.[1]

Northestward

Rob. Drewery	R.	ii d.
Ric. de Sutton	B.	viii d.
Ioh' Ouremaister	B.	x d.
Ioh' le Smyth, skynnere	B.	x d.
Ioh' Hulle	R.	iii d.
Ioh' Caru	B.	iiii d.
Rob. le Irmongere	B.	x d.
Rad. de Setertone	B.	ii s.
Nich. le Brewere	B.	iiii d.
Ioh' Wynordeby	B.	xii d.
Thomas Dawes	R.	ii d.
Ioh' de Eynesham	B.	x d.

[1] The total should be 10*s.* 10*d.*, but the last two entries seem to have been added after the total had been made up.

Ioh' de Mustertone	B.	viii d.
Thomas de Wortone	B.	xx d.
Elena Hernys	B.	vi d.
Rad. de Adyntone	B.	iiii d.
Ioh' Kepharm	B.	viii d.
Ioh' de Adyntone	B.	[*blank*]
Cristina Sowys	R.	ii d.
Ioh' de Bury	R.	iiii d.
Ioh' de Redynge	B.	xii d.
Will. de Shirebourne	R.	iii d.
Walt. de Miltone	B.	viii d.
Hen. Goseford	B.	vi d.
Ioh' de Bereford	B.	viii d.
Rob. Seynt Iohan	B.	vi d.
Rog. de Whitewell	B.	xii d.
Rob. le Goldsmyth	R.	ii d.
Rob. le Hattere	R.	ii d.
Aubr' Hendy	R.	iii d.
Simon le Barbour	R.	iii d.
Ioh' de Stangraue	B.	viii d.
Rob. Havehunte	B.	x d.
Ioh' le Bower	R.	iii d.
Ioh' Olneye	R.	iii d.
Thom. de Unycornhalle	B.	vi d.
Thom. le Latoner	R.	iii d.
Ioh. le Latoner	R.	iii d.
Iuliana de Abyndone	B.	xii d.
Will. de Ebor'	B.	iiii d.
Will. de Leuertone	B.	vi d.
Ioh' de Lokyntone	B.	x d.
Ioh' Wadenore	R.	iiii d.
Agn. la Tappestere	R.	iii d.
Ioh' Auklond	R.	ii d.
Gilb. Pottowe	B.	viii d.
Ioh' Brailes	R.	ii d.
Hen. le Taillour	R.	ii d.
Ric. le Maunciple	R.	ii d.
Ioh' de Cornubia	B.	viii d.
Galf' de Gloucestria	R.	ii d.
Alanus de Kelyngworth	B.	xii d.

Ric. de Sibford	B.	vi d.
Ioh' Poul	B.	vi d.
Ioh' Drenfeld	B.	viii d.
Nich. Gerland	B.	xvi d.
Ioh. de Kent	B.	iiii d.
Alic' de Mersshtone	R.	ii d.
Ric. de Eynesham	B.	xii d.
Ric. de Nortone	B.	viii d.
Ioh' de Haltone	R.	iii d.
Nich. de Glettone	B.	vi d.
Ioh' Astel	B.	iiii d.
Alic' de Walyngford	R.	ii d.
Ioh' de Shiptone	R.	iii d.
Thom. de Wormenhale	R.	ii d.
Agn' de Couele	R.	iii d.
Ioh' le Flexman	R.	ii d.
Rog. Piroun	B.	vi d.
Edmundus Bernyngham	B.	vi d.
Ric. le Couke	B.	viii d.
Hen. de Skyptone	R.	iii d.
Ric. de Coutone	R.	iii d.
Iuliana Hunte	R.	iiii d.
Will. Twyford	R.	iii d.
Ioh' le Mareschal	R.	iii d.
Thom. le Webbe	R.	[ ]

Summa xxxviii s. [ ]

Suthestwarde

Reg. le Deghere	B.	xii d.
Walt. le Deghere	B.	xii d.
Ioh' Brailes	R.	iii d.
Felicia Ioye	R.	iiii d.
Will' le Felichere	R.	iii d.
Ioh' de Wantyng	R.	iiii d.
Adam Gow	R.	ii d.
Will. de Blancpayn	R.	ii d.
Will. le Smyth	R.	iii d.
Will. Russel	R.	ii d.
Ioh' de Burcestre	R.	ii d.

Eliz. Goreway	R.	ii d.
Nich. de Brailes	B.	viii d.
Alic' de Whaishtone	B.	iii d.
Nich. de Kebnesham	B.	xii d.
Alic' Puseye	R.	ii d.
Eliz. Bannebury	R.	ii d.
Ric. Fyndene	R.	ii d.
Will. Marchaund	R.	ii d.
Elena la Clerke	R.	ii d.
Tibot' de Mussendene	R.	ii d.
Ioh' Semere	R.	ii d.
Nich. le Clerk	B.	iiii d.
Thom. le Spenser	R.	iii d.
Hen. Malmesbury	B.	xii d.
Tibot' de Skyptone	R.	iii d.
Rob. de Lyndeseye	R.	iii d.
Rog. Norwode	B.	iii d.
Ioh' de Suttone	R.	iii d.
Will. Coltone	R.	iii d.
Nich. le Grasyere	R.	[ ]
Emma de Newentone	B.	[ ]
Agn. de Garsyntone	R.	iii d.
Iohanna Cornys	R.	ii d.
Emma de Newentone[1]	B.	iiii d.
Agn' de Brehull	R.	ii d.
Emma la Shuppestere	R.	ii d.
Rog. de Swyneford	R.	ii d.
Rob. Marre	B.	vi d.
Will. Wyke	B.	vi d.
Ioh' Torald	R.	ii d.
Ioh' de Bramptone	R.	iii d.
Rob. de York	R.	ii d.
Purnell' atte Corner	R.	iii d.
Simon le Manciple	R.	iii d.
Ioh' Croke	B.	vi d.
Will' Horn	R.	ii d.
Adam de Welyntone	R.	iii d.
Ioh' Donyntone	R.	ii d.

[1] We have already had this name.

Will. Whatele	B.	viii d.
Alic' Heyttebury	R.	iii d.
Alic' Maidestone	B.	vi d.
W[ ] de Henxeye	R.	ii d.
Ric. Grymstede	R.	iii d.
Rob. Carsyntone	R.	iii d.
Cusse Cokes	R.	iii d.
Phil' le Clerke	B.	iiii d.
Agn' Cockes	B.	vi d.
Iohanna Cokes	R.	iii d.
Thom' Chichely	R.	iii d.
Ioh'. Swanebourn	B.	viii d.
Walt' Gautrone	R.	ii d.
Will' Rolf'	R.	ii d.
Iohanna la Lauender	R.	ii d.
Hug' Mey	R.	ii d.
Ioh' Cade	R.	ii d.
Iuliana de Comptone	R.	iii d.
Matill' Kyrketone	B.	viii d.
Ioh' Peggy	B.	viii d.
Isabella Orltone	R.	iii d.
Simon de Gloucestria	B.	x d.
Agn' Bareyns	R.	iii d.
Ioh' de Milton	B.	xii d.
Alic' Orltone	B.	vi d.
Ioh' Russel	R.	iii d.
Phil' le Dissere	R.	iiii d.
Alic' de Neubury	R.	iii d.
Ioh' de Watlyntone	R.	iii d.
Katerina de Milton	R.	iii d.
Galf. de Ouertone	R.	ii d.
Adam le Longe	B.	xii d.
Ric' Tademartone	R.	iii d.
Ric' Cary	B.	[*blank*]
Iohanna de Wycombe	R.	iii d.
Alanus de Hetone	B.	xii d.
Will. de Saunford	B.	vi d.
Rob. Lokynge	R.	iii d.
Matill' la Potager	R.	iid
Ioh' de Lokynge	B.	vi d.

Hen. de Mersshtone	R.	iii d.
[Will' de Burcestre	R.	*erased*]
Will. Cloudesdale	R.	iii d.
Cella [1] de Clyftone	R.	iii d.
Ioh' de Thame	R.	ii d.
Roesia Paynes	R.	iii d.
Ioh' Benham	R.	ii d.
Ioh' le Boltere	R.	iii d.
Rob' Clyue	R.	ii d.
Agn' atte Bere	B.	viii d.
Ioh' le Peyntour	R.	ii d.
Nich' Isak'	R.	ii d.
Baudewynus Scriptor	R.	ii d.
Steph' Lagge	R.	ii d.

Summa xxxiii s. iii d.

Suthwestwarde

Will' Broun	B.	vi d.
Matill' de Yeftele	B.	iiii d.
Iohanna de Leghe	R.	vi d.
Nich. de Forsthulle	B.	iiii d.
Ioh' de Langrisshe	B.	vi d.
Hen. le Coupere	R.	iii d.
[Pet. de Ew	B.	*erased*]
[Ioh. de Shrouesbury		*erased*]
Adam Scriptor	R.	ii d.
Adam le Coke	B.	iiii d.
Ioh' de Alestone	B.	xii d.
Iohanna Benham	B.	iiii d.
Thom. de Curtlyntone	B.	vi d.
[Galf' Scot	R.	*erased*]
Agn. la Tappestere	R.	iii d.
Matill' Herford sen.	B.	vi d.
Ioh' Aysshewell	R.	iii d.
Ric' Whitchurche	R.	ii d.
Ioh' de Redynges	R.	ii d.
Matill' Phelpot	R.	ii d.
Thom. Helmedene	R.	ii d.

[1] Short for Cecilia.

Ioh' atte Marche	R.	ii d.
Iohanna Pershore	R.	ii d.
Hen. le Coke	R.	ii d.
Iohanna atte Kechene	R.	iiii d.
Will. Gylot	R.	ii d.
Galf. Mere	R.	iii d.
Will. Aldewyncle	R.	ii d.
Isolda de Wormenhale	B.	viii d.
Will. de Nortone	R.	ii d.
Ioh' de Waysshebourne	B.	viii d.
Ioh' South	R.	iii d.
Ric' de Warburghe	R.	ii d.
Ioh' de Nortone	B.	vi d.
Thom. de la More	R.	ii d.
Will. le White	B.	iii d.
Rob. de Hoggestone	B.	vi d.
Marg. de Stanlake	B.	xii d.
Will' Kyrkeby	R.	ii d.
Ric' Lacheforde	R.	ii d.
Phil' de Bathe	R.	ii d.
Rob. atte Fenne	B.	vi d.
Ioh' Wyldelonde	B.	vi d.
Hen. Roulondrithe	R.	ii d.
Walt. de Quenyntone	R.	iii d.
Matill' la Northerne	B.	xii d.
Ioh' de Bedeforde	B.	vi d.
Ric' de Walyngforde	B.	x d.
Matill' la Gryndere	R.	iii d.
Ioh' le Coupere, Deghere	R.	ii d.
Will' le Deghere	B.	viii d.
Will' Rokaille	R.	iiii d.
Mich' Pille	R.	iii d.
Elena Rye	R.	ii d.
Ioh' de Lutelmor	R.	ii d.
Thom. de Borstall	B.	iiii d.
Nich. le Carpenter	R.	iii d.
Will. de Bartone	R.	iii d.
Ioh' Brochole	R.	ii d.
Ioh' le Taillour	R.	ii d.
Walt' le Vaureal	B.	ii s.

Nich' le Courreour	R.	ii d.
Katerina de Loughteburghe	R.	ii d.
Ioh' Bokenhulle	R.	ii d.
Magg' Haukyns	R.	ii d.
Isabella Ragamuffyn	R.	ii d.

xxii s. iiii d.

Summa totalis ciiii s. iiii d.

Aff' Ioh' de Walyngford
Hen. Torald
Hen. de Culne
Ioh' le Hostiller

[The two rolls are not indented.]

Northwode; Cary [1]

[Oct. 1345] Assaia ceruisie in Oxonia et eius suburbio: de termino Michaelis anno XIX.

Northwestward

Walt' de Warborghe	R.	iii d.
Thos. de Leghe	R.	ii d.
Thos. Dedewyth	R.	ii d.
Will. de Saunford	B.	vi d.
[Durancius le Taillur	B.	*erased*]
Ric. de Wyndesore	B.	viii d.
Matilda Lond	B.	xii d.
Will. Brunne	B.	vi d.
Iohanna Ouerhe	B.	iiii d.
Barth' de Cornubia	B.	viii d.
Ioh' Bost	B.	vi d.
Will' Chilham	B.	vi d.
Hugo Mussewyk	R.	vi d.
Thos. Bugworth	R.	iii d.
Ric. de Hamptone	B.	viii d.
Ioh' de Bamptone	B.	viii d.
Iohanna de Adyngtone	B.	xii d.
Iohanna Watford	R.	ii d.

[1] Richard Cary did not become mayor until Sept. 29, 1345; John de Northwode was appointed Chancellor in May 1345.

Ric. le Clerk	R.	iii d.
Thos. le Barber	R.	iii d.
Will. Felawe	R.	iii d.
Ric. le Barber	R.	iii d.
Ioh' Ouremaister	B.	vi d.
Rob. le Coriour	R.	ii d.
Rob. le Cutiler	R.	ii d.
Walt' Honicote	R.	iii d.
Rob. le Barber	R.	iii d.

Summa x s. x d.

Northestwarde

Agnes de Meltone	R.	ii d.
Will' Coreour	R.	ii d.
Hen. Rolondryght	R.	ii d.
Rob. le Irmongere	B.	viii d.
Ric. de Sutton	B.	vi d.
Ioh' Fitz-perys	B.	viii d.
Walt. de Watford	B.	iii d.
Ioh' Hulle	R.	ii d.
Ioh' Astel	B.	iiii d.
Ioh' Carru	B.	iiii d.
Rad. de Setertone	B.	xii d.
Nich. le Bruer	B.	vi d.
Ioh' Wynardby	B.	vi d.
Rob. le Hattere	R.	ii d.
Agn' de London	R.	ii d.
Ioh' Dauyntre	B.	viii d.
Ioh' de Mustertone	B.	viii d.
Ioh' Rothewelle	B.	iiii d.
Elena Hernys	B.	vi d.
Ric. Hauuyle	R.	iii d.
Ioh' Kepeharm	B.	vi d.
Ric. Tademartone	B.	vi d.
Ioh' de Bury	R.	iiii d.
Ric. Lond	R.	iii d.
Ioh' de Couentre	R.	iii d.
Walt. de Milton	B.	vi d.

Hen. Goseford	B.	vi d.	
Ioh. de Bereford	B.	viii d.	
Rob. Leche	B.	vi d.	
Ioh. de Milton	B.	vi d.	
Phil' le Clerk	B.	vi d.	
Rob. le Goldsmyth	R.	iii d.	
Ioh. de Stangraue	B.	viii d.	
Rob. Hauehunte	B.	viii d.	
Ioh' Sheldone	R.	iii d.	
Thom. del Unicornhalle	B.	vi d.	
Thom. le Latoner	R.	iii d.	
Ioh' le Latoner	R.	iii d.	
Hugo Scriptor	R.	iii d.	
Iuliana de Abyndone	B.	viii d.	
Will. de York	B.	iiii d.	
Will. de Leuertone	B.	vi d.	
Ioh' de Lokyntone	B.	viii d.	
Ioh' Wadener	R.	iiii d.	
Rob. Broun	R.	iii d.	
Gilb. Potto	B.	vi d.	
Hen. le Taillour	R.	ii d.	
Isabella Silebys	R.	ii d.	
Ioh' de Cornubia	B.	vi d.	
Galf. de Gloucestria	R.	iii d.	
Alanus de Kylyngworth	B.	xii d.	
Ric. de Sibford	B.	viii d.	
Ioh' Poul	B.	vi d.	
Nich' de Kelmesham	B.	vi d.	
Ioh' Dranefeld	B.	viii d.	
Nich. Gerlaund	B.	viii d.	
Ioh' de Kent	B.	vi d.	
Ric. de Eynesham	B.	x d.	
Ric. Coutone	R.	ii d.	
Ioh' de Halghtone	R.	ii d.	
Nich. de Glattone	R.	iiii d.	
[Will. de London	R.	ii d.	*erased*]
Ioh' de Burcestre	R.	ii d.	
Alic' de Walyngford	R.	iii d.	
Ioh' de Shiptone	R.	iii d.	
Petronilla le [*sic*] Coke	R.	iii d.	

Agnes Couele	R.	iii d.
Ioh' le Spicer	R.	ii d.
Thom. le Skynnere	R.	ii d.
Rog. Pyroun	B.	vi d.
Eadmundus Mancipium	B.	vi d.
Ric. le Cooke	B.	viii d.
Ioh' Baldyndone	R.	ii d.
Hen. de Skiptone	B.	iiii d.
Will. le Hunte	R.	iii d.
Will. Twyford	R.	iii d.
Ric. Nortone	B.	iii d.
Ioh' le Mareschall	R.	iii d.
Thos. le Webbe	R.	iii d.

xxxi s. vi d

Southestward

Will. Skryueyn	R.	iii d.
Reg. le Deghere	B.	vi d.
Walt' de Faryndone	B.	vi d.
Ioh. de Brailles	R.	ii d.
Felicia Ioye	R.	iiii d.
Rosya Gow	R.	iii d.
Will' Blancpayn	R.	ii d.
Will' le Smyth	R.	iii d.
Will' Russel	R.	iii d.
Alic' de Wasshtone	B.	vi d.
Symon de Saunford	B.	vi d.
Hen. de Malmesbury	B.	xii d.
Ioh' Anye	R.	iii d.
Leonardus Bedellus	B.	vi d.
Will' Bergeueny	R.	iii d.
Nich' le Clerke	B.	vi d.
Will' Marchaunt	R.	ii d.
[Alic' Aylesbury	R.	*erased*]
Elizabetha Bannebury	R.	ii d.
Will' atte More	R.	iii d.
Tibot' Mussyndene	R.	ii d.
Thom. Mancipium	R.	iii d.
Rob. de Lyndeseye	R.	iii d.

Rog. Northwode	B.	iiii d.
Ioh. de Sutton	R.	iii d.
Agnes Thacham	R.	ii d.
Agnes de Lambourne	R.	iii d.
Nich' le Grasier	R.	iii d.
Emmota de Newentun	R.	vi d.
Adam Perschore	R.	iii d.
Emmota Schepster	R.	iii d.
Rog. Swynneford	R.	iii d.
Rob. Marre	B.	vi d.
Bele[1] Neubyry	R.	iii d.
Ioh' de Brampton	R.	iii d.
Rob. de Ebor'	R.	iii d.
Petronilla de Stafford	R.	iii d.
Simon le Chaundeler	R.	iiii d.
Ioh' Croke	B.	vi d.
Adam de Welygtone	R.	iii d.
Ioh' le Taylour	R.	iii d.
Will' Wathle	B.	vi d.
Alic' Garsyngtone	R.	iii d.
Alic' Maydenstone	B.	vi d.
Alic' Henxay	R.	ii d.
Lucia Leche	R.	iii d.
Will' Takle	R.	ii d.
Rad. le Barber	R.	ii d.
Ioh' de Selwode	B.	vi d.
Will. de Coltone	R.	iii d.
Cusse Cokes	R.	iii d.
Ioh' de Eynssham	B.	vi d.
Agn' atte Kokke	B.	vi d.
Thomas Chycchely	R.	iii d.
Ioh' Swanbourn	B.	vi d.
Walt' Gautron	R.	iiii d.
Reginaldus le Taylour	R.	ii d.
Agn' Wattes	R.	ii d.
Iohanna Lauender	R.	ii d.
Ioh' Cade	R.	ii d.
Iuliana Comptone	R.	ii d.

[1] i. e. Sibilla, as in the previous roll.

Ric. Crysshale	B.	viii d.
Ioh' Peggy	B.	viii d.
Bele Orletone	R.	iii d.
Simon de Gloucestria	B.	viii d.
Will. de Tekene	B.	vi d.
Alic' Abindone	B.	vi d.
Ioh' Dros'	R.	iii d.
Ioh' Dischers	R.	iii d.
Alic' Neubyry		ii d.
Ioh' de Watlygtonc		iii d.
Thos. de Milton		iii d.
Galf. de Ouertone		ii d.
Adam Longe		vi d.
Will. de Norton		iii d.
Ioh' de Lenne	R.	iiii d.
Katerina Wycombe	R.	iii d.
Alanus de Etone	B.	viii d.
Ioh' Dokelygtone	B.	vi d.
Rob. Lokynge	R.	iii d.
Iohanna Derlygg	R.	ii d.
Ioh' Lokynge	B.	vi d.
Alic' Erraunt		ii d.
Cloudesdale		ii d.
Cell' Clyfton		ii d.
Ioh' de Tame		ii d.
Ric' le Mazon		ii d.
Rosa Payne		iiii d.
Ioh' Bolter		iii d.
Agn' at Bere	B.	vi d.
Adam Scryueyn		ii d.
Ioh' Tanner		ii d.
Nich' Ysak		ii d.
Baudwynus Scriptor		ii d.
Rob. Yiftele		ii d.
Ioh' Russell		iii d.

xxix s. vi d.

Sowtwestwarde

Will. Broun	R.	iii d.
Matild' Yeftele	B.	iiii d.

Iohanna de Lye	B.	iiii d.
Alic' Pusey	R.	ii d.
Nich' Forsthulle	B.	iiii d.
Hen. Coupere	R.	iii d.
Pet. de Ewe	R.	ii d.
Adam Coke	B.	vi d.
Ioh' de Bensey	R.	ii d.
Agn' Aschewelle	R.	ii d.
Rob. Oliue	B.	iiii d.
Ioh' Bloxhale	R.	iii d.
Ioh' Houlonde	B.	iiii d.
Iohanna Benham	B.	iiii d.
Thos. de Kyrtlygtone	B.	vi d.
[Ryngedale		*erased*]
Agn' atte Cornere	R.	iii d.
Leticia Cokes	R.	ii d.
Will' Burcestre	R.	ii d.
Thos. Elmedene		ii d.
Magot' March'		ii d.
Rog' de Wytewelle	B.	vi d.
Iohanna Perschore	R.	iiii d.
Nich' Trewelof'		ii d.
Ioh' Stanes	R.	iii d.
Galf' Mere	R.	vi d.
Ioh' Oxenford	R.	iiii d.
Ioh' Chilley	R.	iii d.
Isoud' Wormenhale	B.	viii d.
Elena Schepster		iii d.
Ioh' Waschebourne	B.	vi d.
Ric' de Warburg'	R.	iii d.
Ioh' de Nortone	B.	viii d.
Ioh' Hales	R.	iii d.
Will. Wythte	B.	iiii d.
Rob. Hogston	B.	vi d.
Magot' Stanlake	B.	x d.
Roger de Kyrkeby	R.	ii d.
Ric. Bat[h]	R.	ii d.
Ioh' de Ebor'	R.	ii d.
Rob. Fenne	B.	vi d.
I. Wildelond	B.	vi d.

Thos. Henxy	R.	ii d.
Matild' North[ern]	B.	xii d.
Agnes de Lye	B.	viii d.
Will. Bettes	R.	iii d.
Ric. Bracle	R.	ii d.
Ioh' Couper	R.	ii d.
Alic' at Kychen	R.	ii d.
Will' Rokayle	R.	iii d.
Michael Pille	R.	ii d.
Thos. Borstall	R.	ii d.
Nich' Carpenter	B.	vi d.
Margareta Taylour		ii d.
Agnes Mazon	B.	xii d.
Elena Correours	R.	ii d.
Thomas Loughtebourg		ii d.

xviii s. vi d.

Summa iiii li. x s. iiii d.

Expense facte eodem die in vino et speciebus xxiii d. q.
Afferr'

Ioh' de Eynesham sadeler }
Ric' Gerewey } iurati
Ioh' de Walyngford }
Rob' le Sporiere }

Summa totalis iiii li. x s. iiii d. De quibus alloc[atum est] pro non leuab[ilibus] viii s. vi d.; [et sic remanet] iiii li. xxii d.; [unde] clerico x s. [et remanet iii li.] xi s. x d.

[*The roll is not indented.*]

Assisa ceruisie de termino Pasche anno xxii^o tempore I. de Nortwode C. & R. Selewode M[aioris]. [April, 1348]

Northwestward

Walt' de Warbourghe	R.	iiii d.
Will' de Saumford	B.	vi d.
Ric' de Wyndesore	R.	iiii d.
Matill' Lond'	B.	xii d.
Galf' Mountsorel	B.	vi d.

Ioh' Mymecan	R.	iii d.
Will' de Colton	B.	xii d.
Iohanna Ouerhe	R.	ii d.
Barth' de Cornubia	R.	iii d.
Alanus de Hetone	B.	xii d.
Hugo Musselwyke	R.	vi d.
Ric. le Smyth	R.	ii d.
Ric. de Hamptone	B.	xii d.
Ioh' de Bamptone	B.	vi d.
Will' Chilham	B.	xii d.
Ric' de Sutton	B.	iiii d.
Ioh' le Maister	B.	xii d.

ix s. x d.

Northestward

Rob. le Irmongere	B.	xii d.
Ioh' le Smyth, skynnere	B.	xii d.
Iohanna Watford	B.	iii d.
Katerina de Walyngford	R.	iii d.
Ioh' Astel	B.	iii d.
Ioh' Carreu	B.	vi d.
Rad' de Seteryntone	B.	xii d.
Iohanna de York	R.	iii d.
Ioh' de Wynordby	B.	viii d.
Ioh' de Mustertone	B.	vi d.
Nich' le Brewester	B.	vi d.
Agn' de Bere	B.	xvi d.
Ric' de Whatele	R.	[*erased*]
Ric' Hauuyle	R.	[*erased*]
Ioh' Kepharm	B.	iii d.
Ric' de Tademartone	B.	vi d.
Ioh' de Bury	R.	iii d.
Ioh' de Couyntre	R.	iii d.
Hen. de Goseford	B.	vi d.
Thos. de Gonewardby	R.	iii d.
Rob. le Goldsmyth	B.	iiii d.
Cristina de Welles	R.	iii d.
Rob. le Hattere	R.	ii d.
Ioh' le Taillour	R.	ii d.

Ioh' de Dauentre	B.	vi d.
Ioh' de Stangrave	B.	viii d.
Ioh' de Sheldone	R.	iii d.
Thos. le Latoner	R.	iii d.
Ioh' Fothot	R.	iii d.
Thos. Caue	R.	iii d.
Rob. Dalderby	R.	iii d.
Will. de Leverton	B.	xii d.
Ioh' de Lokyntone	B.	viii d.
Gilb. Pottow	B.	vi d.
Ioh' Auklond	R.	ii d.
Isabella Silby	R.	iii d.
Hen. le Taillour	R.	iii d.
Ioh' de Cornubia	B.	vi d.
Alanus de Kylyngworth	B.	xii d.
Ric. de Sibford	B.	xii d.
Ioh' Dranfeld	B.	xii d.
Nich. Gerland	B.	xii d.
Alic' Erion'	B.	vi d.
Will. Stenyng	B.	vi d.
Alic' de Stratton	R.	iii d.
Ric. de Eynesham	B.	xii d.
Ric. de Coutone	R.	ii d.
Ioh' de Haulghtone	R.	iii d.
Nic. de Glettone	B.	vi d.
Nic. le Maunciple	R.	iii d.
Agn' de Strattone	R.	iii d.
Ioh' de Shyptone	R.	iii d.
Agn' de Couele	R.	iii d.
Ioh' le Spicer	R.	iii d.
Rog' Piroun	R.	iii d.
Edmundus Bermyngham	B.	vi d.
Ric' le Couke	B.	viii d.
Iohanna Cley	R.	iii d.
Hen. de Skyptone	R.	iii d.
Will. Hunte	R.	iii d.
Ioh' le Carpenter	R.	iii d.
Ric' de Nortone	R.	ii d.

xxvii s. ii d.

Suthestwarde

Reg' le Deyghere	R.	iii d.
Alic' de Brailles	R.	iii d.
Felic' Ioye	R.	iii d.
Walt' de Lyndeseye	R.	iii d.
Ioh' Boderham	R.	iii d.
Will' Blampayn	R.	ii d.
Will' Russel	R.	ii d.
Rob' Olyue	B.	iiii d.
Alic' de Whaisshtone	B.	vi d.
Ric' Estryche	R.	iii d.
Will' Mourdon'	R.	iii d.
Will' Marchaunt	R.	iii d.
Ric' de Cornewaill'	R.	iii d.
Ioh' Pache	R.	iii d.
Nich' le Clerke	B.	viii d.
Simon de Saumford	B.	vi d.
Hen. de Malmesbury	B.	xii d.
Ioh' Nany	R.	iii d.
Rob. de Lyndeseye	R.	iii d.
Rog. Nortwode	R.	iii d.
Steph' le Lyndraper	R.	iii d.
Nich' le Grasier	R.	iii d.
Ioh' atte Brouke	R.	iii d.
Emma la Shuppestere	R.	iii d.
Rob. Marre	B.	vi d.
Ioh' de Bramptone	R.	iii d.
Purnell' Stafford	R.	iii d.
Simon le Warner	R.	iii d.
Ioh' Crouke	B.	viii d.
Nich' le Taillour	R.	iii d.
Will' Whatele	B.	vi d.
Will' Brikelesworthe	R.	iii d.
Alic' Maidestone	B.	vi d.
Ioh' de Selewode	B.	vi d.
Rob. Hafhunte	B.	viii d.
Thos. de Couele	R.	iii d.
Adam le Couk'	R.	iii d.
Ioh' de Eynesham	B.	viii d.

Agn' atte Coke	B.	vi d.
[Ric' Chichele	R.	*erased*]
Will' Munt'	R.	iii d.
Ioh' de Swanebourne	B.	vi d.
Walt' Gautrone	R.	ii d.
Rad. Wylot	R.	ii d.
Will' atte Chaumbre	R.	iii d.
Iohanna la Lauendre	R.	ii d.
Iuliana de Comptone	R.	iii d.
Ric' Cressale	B.	xii d.
Isabella Orletone	R.	iii d.
Will' le Clerk	R.	iii d.
Alic' de Abyndone	B.	vi d.
Rob. le Tabletter	R.	iii d.
Ioh' le Dysshere	R.	iiii d.
Alic' de Neubury	R.	ii d.
Adam le Longe	B.	xii d.
Ioh' le Peyntour, fysshere	R.	iii d.
Katerina de Wycombe	R.	iii d.
Ioh' le Ostiller	R.	iii d.
Ioh' de Dokelyntone	R.	iii d.
Rob' Lokyng'	R.	iii d.
Ioh' Lokyng'	R.	iiii d.
Will' Sulby	B.	iiii d.
Rob. de Seltone	B.	vi d.
Iohanna Sprot	R.	ii d.
Ioh' de Thame	R.	iii d.
Ioh' de Elsefeld	R.	ii d.
Ioh' de Pirie	B.	vi d.
Ioh' le Boltere	R.	ii d.
Mag' Peblesbury	R.	ii d.
Ioh' Cade	R.	[*erased*]
Walt' Cosyn	B.	vi d.
Rog. le Goldsmyth	R.	ii d.
Thos. Trillemulle	R.	ii d.
Will. Tekene	R.	ii d.
Alic. Puseye	R.	iii d.
Ioh' Baudewyne	R.	ii d.
Rob. de Yiftele	R.	[*erased*]

xxiiii s. vii d.

Suthwestwarde

Will. Broun	B.	iiii d.
Iohanna de Leyghe	B.	vi d.
Cristina Forsthulle	R.	[*erased*]
Nich' de Forsthulle	B.	iiii d.
Adam le Couke	B.	vi d.
Iohanna Benham	B.	iiii d.
Isabella Curtlyntone	B.	vi d.
Galf. Drynkewater	R.	ii d.
Iohanna de Abyndone	R.	ii d.
Agnes atte Corner	R.	iii d.
Matill' Herford	R.	iii d.
Elena de Circestre	R.	ii d.
Ioh' le Couke	R.	iii d.
Thos. Elmedone	R.	ii d.
Rog. Whitewelle	B.	vi d.
Ioh' Benham	R.	iii d.
Galf' Mere	B.	viii d.
Ric. Ierewy	R.	iii d.
Isolda Wormenhale	B.	viii d.
Steph' de Bedeford	R.	iii d.
Ioh' Wassebourne	B.	vi d.
Ioh' South	B.	vi d.
Iohanna la Longe	R.	iii d.
Katerina la Coupere	R.	iii d.
Rob. de Hoggestone	B.	vi d.
Mag' Stanlake	B.	xii d.
Will' de Kirkeby	R.	iii d.
Galf' de Ouertone	R.	ii d.
Ioh' Wyldelonde	B.	viii d.
Matill' la Northerne	B.	xii d.
Ric' de Walyngford	B.	xii d.
Will' le White	B.	vi d.
Eliz' la Hukkestere		iii d.
Ioh' le Coupere	R.	iii d.
Alic' atte Kechene	R.	iii d.
Will' Rokaille	R.	iii d.
Ioh' de Rodestone	R.	ii d.
Mich' Pille	R.	ii d.

Godefridus le Deyghere	R.	iii d.
Nich' le Carpenter	R.	iii d.
Walt' Vaurial		xii d.

xv s. xi d.

Summa iii li. xvii s. vi d.

Affer'

Thomas Burnham
Ioh' de Eynesham, sadeler
Gilb' Comeneye
Rob' le Sporiere
} iurati

In expens' affer' predictorum omnibus computatis ii s. vi d. ob.

De assisa ceruisie in uilla Oxon' & suburb' eiusdem tempore Iohannis [Oct. 1348] Northwode Cancellarii et Ricardi de Selewode maioris de termino sancti Michaelis anno r. r. E. tercii post conquestum Anglie XXII.[1]

Northwestwarde

De Matill' de Warburghe	iiii d.	R.	i d. ob.
De Iohanna Hocke	iii d.	R.	
De Will. Saumford	vi d.	B.	
De Ric. de Wyndesore	vi d.	R.	
De Matill' Lond	xii d.	B.	i d. ob.
De Galf' Mountsorel	viii d.	B.	i d. ob.
De Ioh' Mymecan	iiii d.	R.	i d. ob.
De Will' de Coltone	xii d.	B.	i d. ob.
De Iohanna Ouerhe	iii d.	R.	i d. ob.
De Barth' de Cornubia	iii d.	R.	i d. ob.
De Isabella atte Knaphalle	xvi d.	B.	i d. ob.
De Cristina Helle	iii d.	R.	i d. ob.
De Hugone Mussewyke	vi d.	R.	i d. ob.
De Ric. de Hamptone	xii d.	B.	i d. ob.
De Ioh' de Bamptone	viii d.	B.	i d. ob.
De Will' Chilham	xviii d.	B.	i d. ob.
De Alic' de Cherteseye	iii d.	R.	
De Ric. de Sutton		B.	[*erased*]
De Thom' le Barber	iii d.	R.	
De Ioh' Ouremaister	ii s.	B.	i d. ob.

Summa xii s. x d.

[1] There are two records of this assise, rot. 27 and also rot. 28; the former is apparently the 'extract' made for the officer who collected the amercements. It omits B. & R.

Northestwarde

De Rob. le Irmongere	xviii d.	B.	i d. ob.
De Will' Pouke	iii d.	R.	
De Ioh' le Smyth, skynnere	xviii d.	B.	i d. ob.
De Iohanna Colbourne		B.	i d. ob. [*erased*]
De Iohanna de Yorke	iii d.	R.	i d. ob.
De Ioh' Astel	iiii d.	R.	i d. ob.
De Ioh' Carreu	viii d.	B.	i d. ob.
De Rad' de Setertone	xviii d.	B.	i d. ob.
De Iohanna Wynordby	x d.	B.	i d. ob.
De Ioh' de Warmestone	iii d.	R.	i d. ob.
De Ioh' de Mustertone	x d.	B.	i d. ob.
De Nich' le Brewere	viii d.	B.	i d. ob.
De Agn' atte Bere	ii s.	B.	i d. ob.
De Ric' de Whatele	iii d.	R.	
De Ioh' Kepharm	vi d.	B.	i d. ob.
De Ric' Tademartone	viii d.	B.	i d. ob.
De Ioh' de Bury	iii d.	R.	i d. ob.
De Ioh' de Couyntre	iii d.	R.	
De Hen. de Goseford	viii d.	B.	
De Ioh' Stodlegh'	xvi d.	B.	i d. ob.
De Rob' Seint Iohn	iii d.	R.	i d. ob.
De Rob. de Milkesham	vi d.	B.	
De Cristina Welles	iii d.	R.	
De Rob. le Hattere	ii d.	R.	
De Ioh' de Dauyntre	vi d.	B.	
De Ioh' de Stangraue	x d.	B.	i d. ob.
De Ioh' Sheldone	iii d.	R.	i d. ob.
De Thoma le Latoner	iii d.	R.	i d. ob.
De Ioh' Fothot		R.	[*erased*]
De Thoma Caue	iii d.	R.	
De Rob. Dalderby	ii d.	R.	
De Will. de Leuertone	x d.	B.	i d. ob.
De Ioh' de Lokyntone	viii d.	B.	i d. ob.
De Ioh' le Innour	ii d.	R.	
De Gilb' Pottow	vi d.	B.	
De Thom' Hedyngtone	ii d.	R.	
De Ioh' de Cornubia	viii d.	B.	
De Galf' de Gloucestria	iii d.	R.	i d. ob.

De Alano de Kylyngworth	xviii d.	B.	i d. ob.
De Ric. de Sibbeford	xii d.	B.	i d. ob.
De Hug' le Taillour	iii d.	R.	
De Ioh' Poul		B.	[*blank*]
De Ioh' Dranfeld	xii d.	B.	i d. ob.
De Nich' Gerland	xviii d.	B.	i d. ob.
De Alic' Erione	vi d.	B.	
De Cristina Cole		R.	ii d.
De Will. Steneiyng		B.	
De Amicia Swanebourne		R.	
De Ric' de Eynesham	xii d.	B.	i d. ob.
De Will' le Barber	iii d.	R.	
De Hen. Berd		R.	
De Ric. Couton		R.	
De Will. Throxford		R.	
De Ioh. Haulghtone		R.	ii d.
De Nich' de Glettone	vi d.	B.	i d. ob.
De Alic' de Heyterbury	iii d.	R.	i d. ob.
De Agn' de Strattone	ii d.	R.	
De Alic' de Strattone	ii d.	R.	
De Agn' de Couele	iiii d.	R.	i d. ob.
De Ioh' le Spicer	iii d.	R.	i d. ob.
De Rog' Piroun	iiii d.	B.	i d. ob.
De Edm' de Bermyngham	vi d.	B.	i d. ob.
De Ric' le Couke	xvi d.	B.	i d. ob.
De Alic' de Walyngford	ii d.	R.	
De Hen' de Skyptone	iii d.	R.	
De Will' Hunte	iii d.	R.	i d. ob
De Ioh' le Carpenter		R.	
De Ric. de Norton		R.	
De Ioh' le Smythe	iiii d.	B.	

Summa xxxiii s. iiii d.

Suthestwarde

De Reg' le Deighere	viii d.	B.	
De Walt' le Deighere	viii d.	B.	i d. ob.
De Ioh. Brailles		R.	[*erased*]
De Felicia Ioye	iiii d.	R.	i d. ob.
De Walt' de Lyndeseye	vi d.	B.	i d. ob.

De Ioh' Blauncpayn	iii d.	R.	
De Will' le Smyth	iii d.	R.	
De Will' Russel	iii d.	R.	
De Rob. Olyue	vi d.	Br.	i d. ob.
De Ioh' de Suttone	vi d.	Br.	i d. ob
De Simone de Saumford	x d.	Br.	i d. ob.
De Ioh' le Maunciple	iii d.	R.	
De Cristina Estriche		R.	
De Eliz. de Bannebury		R.	
De Ioh. de Beuerle		R.	
De Ric. Fyndone		R.	
De Will. Morden		R.	
De Will' Marchaunt	ii d.	R.	
De Ric' de Cornewaille	ii d.	R.	
De Nich. le Clerk	x d.	B.	i d. ob
De Leonardo le Bedel			
De Phil' le Maunciple	iii d.	R.	
De Hen. de Malmesbury	xviii d.	Br.	i d. ob.
De Rob. de Lyndeseye	iiii d.	R.	
De Ioh' Pate	iii d.	R.	
De Agn' de Salesbury	ii d.	R.	
De Isabella Plomer	ii d.	R.	
De Agn' la Drapere	ii d.	R.	
De Nich' le Grasiere	iii d.	R.	
De Ibet' de Shareshulle		R.	[*erased*]
De Rog' de Newentone	vi d.	Br.	
De Emma la Shuppestere	ii d.	R.	
De Will. Aldewyncle	ii d.	R.	
De Rob. Marre	viii d.	Br.	i d. ob.
De Will. Wyke		Br.	
De Thoma de Pirie	ii d.	R.	
De Alic' de Somertone	ii d.	R.	
De Ioh' de Bramptone	iiii d.	R.	i d. ob.
De Rob. de York	[*erased*]	R.	
De Marg' de Salesbury	[*erased*]	R.	
De Tibot'[1] le Chaundeler	iiii d.	R.	i d. ob.
De Ioh' Crouke	xii d.	Br.	
De Nich' le Taillour	iiii d.	R.	

[1] Originally *Simon*.

De Will' Whatele	iiii d.	Br.		
De Tibot' Suttone	iii d.	R.		
De Cusse Cankes	iii d.	R.		
De Ioh' Selewode	viii d.	Br.		
De Rob' Hafunte	xii d.	Br.	i d. ob.	
De Will' Brikelesworth	iii d.	R.		
De Adam Couke	iiii d.			
De Ioh' de Eynesham	viii d.	Br.	i d. ob.	
De Agnete atte Cokke	viii d.	Br.		
De Will' Munt	iiii d.	R.		
De Iohanna de Walyngford	[*erased*]	R.	i d. ob.	
De Ioh' Swanebourne	viii d.	B.	i d. ob.	
De Walt' Gautron	ii d.	R.	[*erased*]	
De Will' atte Chaumbre	ii d.	R.		
De Rog. Steremouthe		R.	[*erased*]	
De Iuliana Comptone	iii d.	R.		
De Matill'[1] Cressale	xii d.	Br.	i d. ob.	
De Ioh' Peggi	xvi d.	Br.	i d. ob.	
De Isab' Orletone	iiii d.	R.		
De Will' le Clerk	iii d.	R.	i d. ob.	
De Alic' de Abyndone		Br.	i d. ob.	[*erased*]
De Rob. le Tableter	iiii d.	R.		
De Ioh' le Dysshere	iii d.	R.		
De Alic' Neubury	ii d.	R.		
De Steph' Bedeford	iiii d.	R.		
De Adam le Longe	ii 3.	R.		
De Ioh' le Peyntour, fysshere	iii d.	R.		
De Katerina Wycombe	iii d.	R.		
De Ioh' le Hostiller	viii d.	R.		
De Ioh' de Dokelyntone	vi d.	R.		
De Rob. Lokyng	iiii d.	R.		
De Ioh' Lokyng	viii d.	Br.		
De Will' Sulby	vi d.	Br.		
De Rob. de Selton	x d.	Br.		
De Iohanna Sprot'	iii d.	R.		
De Ioh' Elsefeld	ii d.	R.		
De Ioh' de Tame		R. }	[*erased*]	
De Ric' Mason		R. }		

[1] Originally *Ric'*.

De Ioh' de Pirie	iii d.	Br.	
De Matill' Bolter		R.	[*erased; only in rot.* 28]
De Marg' atte Cornere	iii d.	R.	
De Walt' Cosyn	xii d.	Br.	
De Rog' le Goldsmyth		R.	[*erased*]
De Will' Tekene		R.	[*erased*]
De Ioh' Baudewyne	ii d.	R.	
De Iohanna de Yeftele	ii d.	R.	

Summa xxxi s. ii d.

Suthwestward

De Agnete[1] Broun	iiii d.	R.		
De Hug' de Yeftele		Br.	[*erased*]	
De Iohanna Leygh		Br.	[*erased*]	
De Alic' Puseye		R.	[*erased*]	
De Nich' Forsthill	vi d.	Br.		
De Adam le Couke	viii d.	Br.		
De Ioh' de Alestone	x d.	Br.		
De Iohanna Benham	vi d.	Br.		
De Is' Curtyntone	x d.	Br.		
De Ryngedale		R.	[*erased*]	
De Agnete atte Cornere	iiii d.	R.		
De Matill' Herford	iii d.	R.		
De Ioh' Blaxhale		R.	[*erased*]	
De Agn' Whitheleye	ii d.	R.		
De Letic' atte Cornere	iii d.	R.		
De Nich' Treweloue	ii d.	R.	i d. ob.	
De Rog' Whitewelle	xii d.	Br.	i d. ob.	
De Iohanna Wycombe		R.	i d. ob.	[*erased*]
De Ioh' Benham	iii d.	R.		
De Galf' Mere	viii d.	Br.	i d. ob.	
De Rob. Caumpedene	iii d.			
De Ric. Ierewey[2]	iii d.	R.		
De Isold' Wormenhale	viii d.	Br.		
De Walt' le Taillour	iii d.	R.		
De Ioh' Waisshebourne	vi d.	Br.		
De Ioh' Southe	viii d.	Br.		

[1] Originally *Will'*.

[2] In rot. 27 *Gerewy*.

De Dicon' le Maunciple		R.	[*erased*]
De Iohanna la Longe	iii d.	R.	
De Galf' de Ortune		R.	[*erased*]
De Ioh' Hales	ii d.	R.	
De Katerina Coupere	iii d.	R.	
De Agn' de Newentone	iii d.	R.	
De Rob. Hoggestone	viii d.	Br.	
De Mag' Stanlake	xviii d.	Br.	
De Will' Kirkeby		R.	[*erased*]
De Th' Dedewyth	ii d.	R.	
De Ioh' Wyldelond	vi d.	Br.	
De Matill' la Northerne	xviii d.	Br.	
De Ric' de Walyngford	x d.	Br.	
De Will' le White	vi d.	Br.	
De Isabella la Hockestere	ii d.	R.	
De Ioh' le Coupere, deighere	iii d.	R.	
De Walt' Vauriole	xii d.		

Summa xvii s. iiii d.

Summa iiii li. xiiii s. viii d.

In expensis circa affer' istius rotuli ii s. vi d. ob.

[*Rolls not indented.*]

Assisa ceruisie tempore Iohannis Wyliot cancellarii & I. Bereford maioris de termino Michaelis anno XXIII. [Oct. 1349]

Northwestward

De Ric. Wiccheford	R.	vi d.
De Will. Bottesdene	R.	iiii d.
De Ric. Sibforde	R.	iiii d.
De Ioh' le Correour	R.	vi d.
De Ioh' Wyndesore	Bre.	xii d.
De Hen. le Porter	R.	vi d.
De Ric. Wacman	Bre.	viii d.
De Isabella Cnappehalle	Bre.	ii s.
De Alic' atte Brodeyates	Bre.	vi d.
De Hugone Moslewike	Re.	vi d.
De Ric. de Hamptone	Re.	vi d.
De Iohanna Chilham	Bre.	xii d.

De Waltero Peutrer	Re.	iiii d.
De Hen. de Barstaple	Re.	iii d.
De Dauid Workman	Re.	iii d.
De Agn' Tappestere	Re.	iii d.
De Ric. de Sottone	Bre.	vi d.
De Ioh' le Barbour	Re.	iii d.
De Ioh' de Oxenforde	Bre.	xviii d.

Summa xi s. viii d.

Northestwarde

De Ioh' Þrapstone	Bre.	viii d.
De Ioh' de Bury	Re.	vi d.
De Hen' Cole	Bre.	vi d.
De Thom' Croke	Bre.	xii d.
De Ioh' Bloxale	Bre.	xii d.
De Ric' Hauuile	Re.	iii d.
De Ioh' Kempherme (*sic*)	Re.	vi d.
De Ric. de Tadmertone	Bre.	xviii d.
De Mich. de Cornwaille	Re.	iiii d.
De Agn' uxor Atyngdone	Re.	iii d.
De Will' Sanforde	Re.	vi d.
De Ioh' Couentre	Re.	iii d.
De Ioh' Southe	Bre.	vi d.
De Will' Combe	Bre.	ii s.
De Rob. Mauncel	Bre.	vi d.
De Ioh' de Pirye	Bre.	vi d.
De Ioh' Lolly	Re.	vi d.
De Rob. Golsmith	Bre.	x d.
De Thoma Cnaphall baker	Bre.	vi d.
De Ioh' Ware	Re.	iiii d.
De Iuliana Eucornhalle	Bre.	xii d.
De Adam Taillour	Re.	vi d.
De Hugone le Taillour	Re.	iiii d.
De Iohanna Lokyngtone	Bre.	xii d.
De Pet' Kyllyngworth	Re.	iii d.
De Ioh' Beuerleghe	Re.	iii d.
De Matild' Pikwille	Re.	iiii d.
De Agn' Steuenes	Re.	iii d.
De Rob. Mershstone	R.	viii d.

De Ioh' Paul	Bre.	[*blank*]
De Nich' Garlond	Bre.	xii d.
De Ioh' Mertonhalle (*at first* Ioh' Davyngtre)	Re.	iiii d.
De Isabella de Couele (*at first* Is' Windmille)	Bre.	xviii d.
De Ric' Coutone	Re.	iiii d.
De Isabella Haltone	Re.	iii d.
De Ioh' Killingworth	R.	iii d.
De Nich' Hettisbyry	Bre.	viii d.
De Isabella Haltone	Re.	iii d.
De Thoma Coke	Re.	iii d.
De Iohanna Spicer	Re.	iiii d.
De Hen. Cornwaille	Bre.	viii d.
De Ric. Clerke	Re.	vi d.
De Ric. Coke	Bre.	xviii d.
De Alic' Rolesham	Re.	iii d.
De Iuliana Nortone	Bre.	iiii d.
De Ioh' le Marchall	Bre.	viii d.
De Hen. Carpenter	Bre.	xii d.
De Alic' Wodecoke	Re.	iii d.

xxvii s. ix d.

Southestwarde

De Symone le Deghere	Bre.	viii d.
De Thoma Hosbond	R.	iii d.
De Alic' Rossel	R.	iii d.
De Iohanna Codingtone	Re.	iii d.
De Matild' Sottone	Bre.	x d.
De Hen' Malmisbury	Bre.	xii d.
De Eliz. Bannebury	Re.	iiii d.
De Will. Bate	Re.	ii d.
De Ioh' Pate	Re.	ii d.
De Katerine (*sic*) Wallingforde	Re.	iii d.
De Matild' Spenser	Re.	iii d.
De Alic' Schepster	Re.	iii d.
De Ioh' Bokingham	Re.	vi d.
De Iohanna Marrys	Bre.	viii d.
De Alic' Wyke	Bre.	xii d.

De Emmote (*sic*) Neutone	Bre.	vi d.
De Iohanna . . . ond	Re.	iii d.
De Pernel Stafford	R.	?
De Isabella Chaundeler	Re.	iiii d.
De Ioh' Croke	Bre.	xii d.
De Marg' Marris'	Re.	iii d.
De Will' Clerico	R.	iii d.
De Iohanna Taillour	Re.	vi d.
De Rog' Nortworde	Bre.	xviii d.
De Rob. Halfonte	Bre.	xii d.
De Iohanna Briccisworth	R.	iii d.
De Ioh' Lond'	Re.	iii d.
De Ioh' Stodle	Bre.	xii d.
De Ioh' le Lord		ii d.
De Amicia Swanbourne	Re.	iii d.
De Thom' Cook	Re.	iii d.
De Will' le Northirne	Br.	viii d.
De Thom' Appeltone	Re.	vi d.
De Ric. Bramptone	Re.	iiii d.
De Ioh' Mostertone	Re.	iii d.
De Ioh' Longe	Re.	viii d.
De Hen. de Bathe	Re.	vi d.
De Iuliana Bestelowe	R.	ii d.
De Will. Marche	Re.	iii d.
De Marg. Wycombe	Re.	iii d.
De Ioh' Fredeswide	Bre.	x d.
De Ioh' Langriche	R.	[*erased*]
De Ric' Wayte	R.	iii d.
De Will' Odingdone	Re.	iii d.
De Thom' Swinushulle	B.	viii d.
De Rob. Selton	Br.	x d.
De Ioh' Beuerleghe	Re.	iii d.
De Ric. Cornwall	Re.	iii d.
De Walt' Correour	Bre.	viii d.
De Ric. Sompnour	Re.	ii d.
De Walt' Cliue	R.	[*erased*]
De Morice Cacchecute	Re.	iii d.
De Walt' Fox	Re.	ii d.

Summa xxiii s. iiii d.

Southwestwarde

De Hugone de Yiefteleghe	Bre.	viii d.
De Nic. Forsthulle	Re.	iii d.
De Ioh. Benham	Bre.	viii d.
De Nic. Treweloue	Bre.	viii d.
De Agn' atte Corner	Re.	iiii d.
De Cecelia Eton	Re.	iii d.
De Ric. Barbour	Re.	iii d.
De Iohanna Sottone, tappest'	Re.	iiii d.
De Leticia atte Corner	Re.	iii d.
De Will' Alstone	Bre.	viii d.
De Ric. Forster	Bre.	viii d.
De Ioh' Nortone	Bre.	xii d.
De Rob. Caumpedene	Re.	iiii d.
De Petr' Coke	Re.	iii d.
De Hen. de Walton	Bre.	xii d.
De Ioh' Cary	Bre.	xviii d.
De Alic' Polter	Re.	iii d.
De Ioh' Marschal	Re.	iii d.
De Will' Fenne	Re.	iiii d.
De Matild' Gibbes	Bre.	[*erased*]
De Ioh' Bedeford	Bre.	
De Petr' Panter	Bre.	
De Leticia Bedeforde	R.	iii d.
De Rog. Madoke	Re.	iii d.
De Ioh' Slattere	Re.	iii d.
De Iohanna Wildelonde	Bre.	x d.
De Nich' Hoggestone	Bre.	x d.
De Katerina Couper	Re.	iii d.
De Mages Stanlake	Bre.	xviii d.
De Ioh' le Northerne	Bre.	xii d.
De Will' le Wite	Re.	iii d.
De Ioh' Leghe	Re.	iii d.
De Alic' atte Kichene	Re.	iii d.
De Iohanna Ascheby	Re.	iii d.
De Agn' Rokale	Re.	iii d.
De Isabella Stanlake	Re.	iii d.
De Iohanna Tan'	Re.	iii d.
De Alic' Herward	Re.	iii d.

De Ioh' Stantone	Br.	vi d.
De Will. Loder		iii d.
De Ioh' le Sclattere		iii d.

Summa xviii s.

Summa totalis iiii li. ix s.

[May, 1350] Assisa ceruisie tempore magistri Willelmi Pelmerua cancellarii & Iohannis de Bereford maioris de termino Pasche anno XXIIII.

Northwestwarde

Ric. Sibford	R.	vi d.
Will. Patenmaker	R.	iii d.
Ioh' Wyndesore	Br.	xii d.
Ric. Sompnour	R.	iiii d.
Hen. le Porter	R.	vi d.
Rog. Cary	Br.	viii d.
Ric. Wackman	Bre.	x d.
Isabella Cnappehelle	Br.	ii s.
Rob. Cornwaille	Re.	iii d.
Ioh' Kepharme	Bre.	xii d.
Hugone Muslewike	Re.	vi d.
Ioh' le Hore	Re.	iii d.
Iohanna Chilham	Bre.	xviii d.
Walt' Peutrer	Re.	iiii d.
Hen. Barstaple	Re.	iii d.
Ric. Suttone	Re.	xii d.
Ioh' Barbour	Re.	iiii d.
Steph' Lyndraper	Re.	iiii d.
Ioh' Oxon' mercer	Bre.	vi d. [*erased*]

xii s. iii d.

Northestwarde

Ioh' Thrapstone	Bre.	xviii d.
Ioh' de Bury	Bre.	xii d.
Ric. Hamptone	Re.	xii d.
Hen. Colbourne	Bre.	x d.
Thom. Crocke	Bre.	xviii d.
Ric. Hauuyle	Re.	viii d.

Ric. Tormertone	Bre.	xviii d.
Will. Saunforde	Re.	x d.
Ioh' de Couyntre	R.	vi d.
Ioh' Soth	Bre.	xii d.
Will' Dene	Re.	[*erased*]
Thomas serviens Iohannis Herteuill	Re.	vi d.
Will' Coumbe	Br.	iii s.
Rob. Mauncel	Bre.	vi d.
Ioh' Lolly	Re.	vi d.
Rob. Golsmith	Bre.	xii d.
Nic. Garland	Bre.	[*erased*]
Adam le Taillour	Re.	ii d.
Ioh' Lokingtone	Bre.	xiiii d.
Agn' Steuenys	Re.	iiii d.
Matilda Pikwelle	Re.	iiii d.
Ioh' Beuerlee	Re.	iiii d.
Rob. de Merschtone	Re.	viii d.
Ioh' de Mertonhalle	[*erased*]	
Ioh' Olneye	Br.	xii d.
Ioh' le Flecchere	Re.	iiii d.
Ric' Coutone	Re.	iiii d.
Ric' Logteburghe	Re.	vi d.
Ioh' Kyllingworthe	Re.	vi d.
Nich' Hettesbury	Bre.	xii d.
Will' le Coke	Re.	iiii d.
Petronilla Coke	Re.	iiii d.
Will' Chopindone	Re.	iii d.
Hen. Piroun	Re.	vi d.
Ric. Clerk	Re.	vi d.
Ric. Coke	Bre.	ii s.
Iuliana de Walton	Bre.	vi d.
Ioh' de Abindone	Re.	iiii d.
Ioh' Marchal	Re.	vi d.
Hen. Carpounter	Bre.	xii d.

xxix s. vii d.

Southestwarde

Agn' Tappestere	Re.	iii d.
Sim' le Deghere	Re.	x d.
Thom' Hosebonde	Re.	iiii d.

Rob. atte Chaumbre	Re.	iiii d.
Matilda Suttone	Bre.	xii d.
Elizabetha Bannebury	Re.	iiii d.
Alicia Shuppester	R.	vi d.
Ioh' Pate	Re.	viii d.
Iohanna Bryan	Re.	iiii d.
Ioh' Well'	Re.	iiii d.
Ioh' Spenser	Re.	iiii d.
Ioh' Bokingham	Re.	vi d.
Pernelle (*sic*) Coke	Re.	iii d.
Iohanna Marre	Bre.	viii d.
Emmota Newintone	Bre.	iiii d.
Ioh' Croke	Bre.	ii s.
Tibot' Chaundelere	Re.	vi d.
Iohanna Taillour	Re.	vi d.
Rog' Northwode	Bre.	ii s.
Rob. Haffonte	Bre.	xii d.
Ioh' Lond	Re.	vi d.
Mich' Cornwaill	Re.	iiii d.
Ioh' Pirye	Re.	iiii d.
Will' le Northirne		xii d.
Alic' Bleroke	Re.	iii d.
Thom' Appeltone	Re.	viii d.
Ric' Bremptone	Re.	vi d.
Ioh' Herteuill		xviii d.
Iuliana Bestelau	Re.	iiii d.
Rob. Dibil	Re.	iiii d.
Ioh' Cary	Bre.	ii s.
Marg' Wycombe	Re.	vi d.
Ioh' Seint Fredesuide		xviii d.
Ioh' Langrisshe	Re.	[ ]
Will' Otindone	Re.	iiii d.
Leticia atte Corner	R.	vi d.
Adam le Smith	Re.	vi d.
Rob. Selton	Bre.	xviii d.
Ioh' Beuerlegh	Re.	iii d.
Ric' Cornwaille	Re.	iii d.
Katerina Lenne	Re.	iii d.
Rob. le Fuller		iiii d.
Agn' Eyton	Re.	ii d.

Rog. Cobelere	Re.	iii d.
Mauric' Cachecute	Re.	vi d.

xxvii s. [ ] d.

Sutwestwarde

Hug' Yefteleghe	Bre.	xii d.
Ioh' Bloxale	Bre.	xviii d.
Ioh' Benham	Bre.	viii d.
Nic' Treweloue	Bre.	xii d.
Agn' atte Corner	Re.	vi d.
Iohanna Sutton	Re.	iii d.
Cecilia Etone	Re.	iiii d.
Will' Loder	Re.	iii d.
Hen' Sclatter	Re.	iii d.
Ric. le Barbour	Re.	iii d.
Alex. Coupere	Re.	iii d.
Will' Alstone	Bre.	xii d.
Ric' le Forester	Bre.	viii d.
Walt' Correour	Bre.	viii d.
Rob. Caumpeden	Re.	vi d.
Pet' Coke	Re.	iiii d.
Hen. de Walton	Bre.	xviii d.
Iohanna Marschal	Re.	iiii d.
Will' Fenne	Re.	vi d.
Ioh' Eton	Re.	iiii d.
Rog' Maddock	Re.	iiii d.
Katerina Couper	Re.	iii d.
Ioh' Slattere	Re.	iii d.
Nic. Hoggestone	Bre.	xii d.
Thom. Kingestone	Bre.	xii d.
Magot' Stanlake	Bre.	ii s.
Ioh' le Northirne	Bre.	xviii d.
Ioh' Legh'	Re.	iiii d.
Will' Wite	Bre.	vi d.
Alic' atte Cuchene	Re.	iii d.
Matild' Rocail	Re.	iiii d.
Alicia Hereward	Re.	vi d.
Agn' Milward	Re.	iii d.

Alicia Barton	Re.	iii d.

xxi s. [ ] d.

Summa iiii li. x s.

Affer' Walt' Purfyl
Adam Cobham
Ioh' le Glasier
Will [ ]

Expense eorundem iii s. x d.

[Oct. 1351] Assisa ceruisie de tempore magistri Will' Palmerua cancellarii & I. Ber' maioris termino sancti Michaelis anno xxv.

Northwestward

Will' Fentone (*at first,* Alic' Fentone)	R.	vi d.
Ioh' Gygour	R.	viii d.
Ric. Sibforde	R.	vi d.
Ioh' Beuerlee	R.	iiii d.
Ioh' Windesore	Br.	xii d.
Ioh' Northerne	Br.	ii s.
Hen' Porter	R.	vi d.
Ioh' Sibforde	Br.	viii d.
Will' Sanforde	Br.	ii s.
Ioh' Kepherme	R.	xii d.
Augustinus Sherman	R.	iii d.
Ric. Cornwaille	R.	iiii d.
Hug' Muslewike	R.	viii d.
Ric' Hamptone	R.	vi d.
Iohanna Chilham	Br.	xviii d.
Agn' Skynner	R.	iii d.
Isabella Auntoneye	R.	iii d. [*erased*]
Ric. Sottone	R.	iii d.
Dauid Heuet	R.	iii d.

xiii s. i d.

Northestward

Dauid Meritone	R.	viii d.
Phil' de Ew	R.	iii d.
Rog. le Taillour	R.	iii d.
Ric. le Hay	R.	iii d.

Thom. Croke	Br.	xviii d.
Ric' Hauuyle	R.	vi d.
Ric' More, cordwaner	R.	iii d.
Ric' Tormertone	Br.	xviii d.
Ioh' South	Br.	viii d.
Will' le Northerne	Br.	xii d.
Ioh' Ware	R.	iii d.
Nich' Garlond	Br.	xviii d.
Ioh' Lokyngtone	Br.	xii d.
Ioh' Horspathe	R.	iii d.
Ioh' Crok	Br.	xii d.
Simon Witthe	R.	iii d.
Ioh' Olney	Br.	xii d.
Ric' Lynne	Br.	xii d.
Rob' Cornwaille	R.	iii d.
Ioh' Kyllingworthe	R.	vi d.
Will' Wite	R.	iii d.
Thom' Coke	R.	iii d.
Hen. Pyroun	Br.	vi d.
Nic' Hutesbury	Br.	xii d.
Alic' Wallyngforde	R.	iiii d.
Ioh' Marchall	Br.	x d.
Hen. Litlemor	Br.	xii d.

Summa xviii s.

Southestwarde

Simon Dyeger	R.	x d.
Ioh' Wodecokhalle	R.	vi d.
Rob. atte Chaumbre	R.	iii d.
Alic' Rossel	R.	ii d.
Matilda Burg'	R.	iiii d.
Hen. Malmesbury	Br.	xviii d.
Ioh' Pate	R.	viii d.
Iohanna Bryan	R.	iiii d.
Ioh' Welles	R.	iiii d.
Ioh' Bokyngham	R.	viii d.
Emme Newentone	Br.	vi d.
Iohanna Marre	R.	vi d.
Tibot' Chaundelere	R.	iiii d.

Petronilla Stafford	R.	iiii d.
Iohanna Taillour	R.	vi d.
Ioh' Spenser	R.	iiii d.
Magota le Northerne	R.	iii d.
Mich' Cornwaille	R.	vi d.
Marioun Cokes	R.	iiii d.
Rog' Northwode	Br.	ii s.
Rog' Mauncipie	R.	vi d.
Ioh' Mostertone	R.	iii d.
Ioh' Thrapstone	Br.	xii d.
Walt' Peutrer	R.	iiii d.
Ioh' le Peintour	R.	iiii d.
Will' Elstowe	R.	iiii d.
Ioh' Hertewelle	Br.	ii s.
Iuliana Bestelawe	R.	iiii d.
Ioh' Cary	Br.	xviii d.
Ric' le Barbour	R.	iiii d.
Will' Otindone	R.	iii d.
Ioh' Chaumbre	R.	iii d.
Leticia atte Corner	R.	vi d.
Adam Smith	R.	iiii d.
Will' Bedeman	R.	iii d.
Moric' Cachecute	R.	iii d.

Summa xix s. xi d.

Southwestwarde

Hug' Yeftleghe	Br.	viii d.
Nic' Treweloue	Br.	vi d.
Agn' atte Corner	R.	vi d.
Iohanna Suttone	R.	iii d.
Matilda Faryndone	Br.	vi d.
Hen. ? Fischere	R.	iiii d.
Ioh' Goundy	R.	iii d.
Ioh' Benham	R.	iiii d.
Ioh' Broune	R.	iii d.
Hen. Brewere	Br.	viii d.
Iohanna Wyllelonde	Br.	xviii d.
Nic' Hoggestone	Br.	viii d.
Katerine (*sic*) Coupere	R.	iiii d.

Marget' Stanlake	Br.	ii s.
Ric' Penkriche	R.	vi d.
Ioh' Salesbury	R.	vi d.
[ ]encius Mason	R.	iiii d.
T[ ] Hereward	R.	vi d.
Rob. Wakman	Br.	xii d.
Ioh' de Eton	R.	iiii d.
Ric. Dugwell	Br.	xii d.

xii s. xi d.

Summa lxiii s. xi d.

Affer'

Walterus Purfyl
Will. de Dene
Adam Cobham
Rog' [Fel]awe

THE ASSAY OF WEIGHTS AND MEASURES, 1340–6

The next roll contains a court for the assay of weights and measures, the only record of this kind that survives in Oxford. It is undated, but the statement that John de Selewode was an alderman at that time shows that the date must be between Michaelmas 1340 and Michaelmas 1346; until the former date Selewode was bailiff and therefore could not have been an alderman; at the latter date he became mayor, and held the office until his death. He was an alderman for the year beginning Michaelmas 1344, but for the other five years in question the aldermen are unknown; and we have no means of fixing the date of our record more closely than Michaelmas 1340–6.

The assay of weights and measures was closely connected with the assise of bread and ale; for purchasers might be cheated not only in the price and quality of the bread and ale, but also by defect in the weights and measures that were used. But though the assay and the assise were closely connected, they could be, and sometimes were, in different hands; and the assay dealt not only with the weights and measures used in the sale of bread and ale, but also with measures of length, such as the ell, and with weights of avoirdupois scale which were used in the sale of wax and candles; in the sale of bread the troy scale was used.

At this time the assay was conducted by the aldermen of Oxford and the Chancellor together. On February 18, 1327, the King issued a writ [1] that the Chancellor and the Mayor should have 'the assise of weights and measures'; but it seems that some difficulty was made, probably by the aldermen; and Twyne (xxii. 273) quotes a record [2] which he saw in the Town Archives in which the representatives of the Town in October 1328 state before Parliament at New Sarum that the assay of measures had never been part of the assise of bread and ale, but that they agreed that in future the Chancellor and the

[1] *Univ. Archives*, i. 108 (O. H. S.).

[2] Compare the petition printed in *Munim. Civitatis Oxonie*, p. 72 (O. H. S.).

Mayor should hold the assay, provided that the profits were taken by the Town. On October 25 the King decreed[1] that the Mayor and the Chancellor should conduct 'the assise of ale and bread', and the Aldermen and the Chancellor 'the assise of weights and measures'. On July 12, 1348, it was agreed between the Town and the University that the Mayor and the Chancellor should conduct both the assise and the assay, but that the University should receive none of the profits of the assay; one-tenth was to be given to St. John's Hospital and the rest to the Town.[2] After the riot of St. Scolastica the Chancellor alone conducted the assay, but the profits were still to be divided as by the agreement of 1348.

The term used was indifferently 'the assise of weights &c.' or 'the assay of weights &c.', but in process of time it was found more convenient to use the word assay when dealing with weights and measures, and assise when dealing with bread and ale.

Assaia mensurarum de Aldermanria Iohannis de Selewode del Suthwestwarde.

Agn' la Tappestere habet I potellum & I quartam fals'
Ioh' Whitele habet I quartam fals'
Nich' de Forsthulle habet I quartam fals'
Iohanna de Leghe habet I quartam fals'
Alic' Puseye habet I quartam fals'

Northwestward

Ioh' Mymecan habet I galonem fals'
Walterus de Warburghe habet I galonem fals' & I quartam
Thomas de Leghe habet I bussellum minorem standardo
Matill' Lond' habet I bussellum minorem standardo
Adam le Longe habet I bussellum minorem standardo

Suthestward

Ioh' de Warmestone habet I quartam fals'
Ioh' le Couk habet I quartam fals'

[1] *Univ. Archives*, i. 111.   [2] Ib. i. 144.

A POLL TAX

The next document is a roll of payments in the South-east Ward; it is undated, but from the handwriting it must be of the fifteenth century. We should conclude that it is between 1426 and 1452, because Henry Lolly and Edmund Kyppyng appear in the rental of the Hospital of St. John as dwellers in the South-east Ward in 1426, while in the rental of 1452 they are not mentioned. On the other hand, John Asschebury is in the rental of 1452 in All Saints Parish, while in 1426 the house was occupied by Thomas Withyg, who is known to have been his stepfather. Wood has dated the roll as *circa 1429*, and that is probably not far wrong.

The payments have the appearance of a poll tax of *2d.* a head, i. e. half a groat; but there was no poll tax, as far as is known, between 1426 and 1452. If it gives payments for breaches of the assise of ale, all that can be said is that it was a strange system to amerce all offenders at the same sum. For the same reason, it can hardly be the payments for breaches of the statutes of labourers.

Whether the names are in a strictly geographical order is at present uncertain.

Sowthestward

Mich' Hawterfeld	ii d.
Walt' Sklatter	ii d.
Ioh' Yonge	ii d.
Ioh' Bodeman	ii d.
Hen' Lollye	ii d.
Thom' Martyn	ii d.
Ioh' Burlegg'	ii d.
Ioh' Dyer	ii d.
Galf' Dobber	ii d.
Ioh' Hurne, cobler	ii d.
Thom. Dobber	ii d.

Thom. Shawe	ii d.
Iohanna Harpere	ii d.
Ioh' Vynsent	ii d.
Will' Hosyer	ii d.
Will' Portar de sancta Fryd'	ii d.
Ioh' Whyngg'	ii d.
Ioh' Lownde	ii d.
Ioh' Lowthys	ii d.
Will' Offord, fyssher	ii d.
Ioh' Collys, tayleour	ii d.
Pers	
Rawlyn, mason	ii d.
Will' Sturmy	ii d.
Ioh' Stomylle	ii d.
Nic' George	ii d.
Hen' Hamptone	ii d.
Ioh' Tylney	ii d.
Ioh' Wylmot	ii d.
Walt' Okeborne	ii d.
Ioh' Bolde	ii d.
Ioh' Dobbys	ii d.
Ioh' Buntynge	ii d.
Ioh' Morton	ii d.
Ioh' Wareyn	ii d.
Will' Swanborne	ii d.
Ric' Weste	ii d.
Ioh' Asschebur'	ii d.
Ioh' Lodelowe	ii d.
Gybbyn' Mason	ii d.
Ioh' Chaperleyn	ii d.
Shurborne	
Ioh' Fyrsden	ii d.
Ioh' Baylye	ii d.
Ioh' Bawdewayn	ii d.
Ioh' Braddele	ii d.
Thom' Wymond	ii d.
Ioh' Merssfeld	ii d.
Ioh' Hasseley	ii d.
Ioh' Carre	ii d.

Ioh' Telme	ii d.
Ric. Wyke	ii d.
Ioh' Pecer, tanner	ii d.
Ioh' Ballard	ii d.
Ioh' Hertale	ii d.
Ioh' Berford jun.	ii d.
Ioh' Lambard	ii d.
Ioh' Lawrence, steyner	ii d.
Will' Groue	ii d.
Rob. Maunceple	ii d.
Will. Skynner	ii d.
Thom. atte þe Were	ii d.
Will. Langeley	ii d.
Ioh' Barbor	ii d.
Daniel Tayler	ii d.
Ioh' Clerke, manciple	ii d.
Ioh' Dounyng	ii d.
Ioh' Westone	ii d.
Steph' Gosselyn	ii d.
Will' Barbur	ii d.
Ioh' Rede	ii d.
Will' Wybram	ii d.
Ioh' Gambrey	ii d.
Ioh' Coke	ii d.
Hankyn Barow	ii d.
Ioh' Perchemaner	ii d.
Martyn Fuller	ii d.
Will' Burgatt	ii d.
Edmundus Cerpyng[1]	ii d.
Nic' Perchemaner	ii d.
Thom' Porter	ii d.
Thom' Faukener	ii d.
Will' Clerke	ii d.
Ioh' White	ii d.
Ioh' Laurence	ii d.
Denys Manc'	ii d.

[1] Perhaps *Ceppyng*. In the Rental of the Hospital of St. John for 1426 the name is *Kyppyng*.

Ioh' Coke	ii d.
Ioh' Barbour'	ii d.
Ioh' Leche	ii d.
Math' Fuller	ii d.
Ioh' Barfot	ii d.
Nic' Fuller	ii d.
Will' Manc'	ii d.
Ioh' Stowe	ii d.
Thom' Spenser	ii d.

PROCTORS' ACCOUNTS

THE mediaeval Proctors' accounts which survive are no more than fifteen in number, ranging from 1464 to 1496; then there is a blank until the year 1562. At Cambridge the Proctors' accounts, which begin with the year 1455, are almost complete from that date, and are now available for students in Grace Books A and B, edited by Mr. Stanley Leathes and Miss Bateson respectively. There is this difference between what survives at Oxford and Cambridge; at Cambridge the Proctors' books survive, but not the final accounts as audited by the University; at Oxford the audited accounts survive, but not the Proctors' books. One consequence is that in the Cambridge accounts there is more detail but less arrangement than in the Oxford accounts. The reason why the arithmetic of the Oxford accounts is often at fault may be that the addition was done in the Proctors' books, and when the entries and the balance were transcribed on the final accounts some figures were slightly incorrect.

At Cambridge it was the custom to carry forward the balance from year to year, very much in the modern way; but at Oxford if there was money in hand it was deposited in a chest, and might never reappear in the Proctors' accounts. It might be thought at the first glance that Oxford had no balance, but a study of the rolls makes it appear that the average income of the University in these fifteen years was about £58, and the average expenditure less than £45; the difference was placed in various chests, and was, no doubt, used towards the expensive buildings which were being erected in the latter half of the fifteenth century. Not only was the Divinity School a continual drain, but the School of Canon Law was rebuilt, and finally St. Mary's Church. A portion of the expenditure on the Divinity School and the School of Canon Law appears in these rolls, but there were other accounts for both these buildings; and no doubt, if they survived, we should find that the sums transferred by the Proctors to the University chests reappeared in these accounts. The average income at Cambridge at this time seems to have been under £30, and the average expenditure less than £20, although the two Universities were much alike in numbers.

The following is the income of the University of Oxford, grouped under different headings.

	From Doctors.	Graces.	Bachelors and Masters.	Rents.	Oseney and Eynsham.	Breaches of the peace.	Grammar Masters.	Miscellaneous.	Total.
1464	50 0 0	9 11 8	1 17 2	4 6 0½	4 14 8	9 0	2 0 0	nil	72 18 6½
1469	40 0 0	35 16 8	2 17 5	1 19 8¾	4 14 8	4 15 0	4 0 0	8 8	94 12 1¾
1471	nil	10 13 4	1 16 10	6 1 7	4 14 8	13 8	3 0 0	4 0	27 3 10
1472	20 0 0	11 5 0	2 8 2	5 5 4	4 14 8	18 0	2 13 4	3 0	47 7 6
1473	20 0 0	17 18 4	3 1 6	5 6 5½	4 14 8	19 4	1 0 0	3 4	53 3 7½
1474	10 0 0	19 2 0	2 3 4	5 9 5½	4 14 8	18 0	1 0 0	5 4	43 10 9½
1477	nil	16 9 8	2 11 5	4 12 10	4 14 8	7 8	2 0 0	3 4	30 19 7
1478	42 0 0	35 9 7	3 9 10	5 5 1	4 14 8	2 4 8		3 4	93 7 2
1479	60 0 0	10 11 5	5 4 10	4 16 5	4 14 8	17 9		3 10 0	89 15 1
1481	33 6 8	21 1 8	2 13 3	5 2 8	4 14 8	1 17 4		6 8	69 7 11
1482	37 1 8	20 0 0	4 6 9	4 2 10	4 14 8	15 5		3 4	71 4 8
1488	11 6 8	8 10 8	3 0 11	2 5 8	4 14 8	1 19 10		2 3 4	34 1 9
1492	8 13 4	7 15 4	2 0 7	4 12 1½	4 14 8	1 0 5		6 8	29 3 1½
1494	51 6 8	12 6 4	3 6 10	7 5 6	4 14 8	1 11 1		3 4	80 14 5
1496	6 13 4	13 5 0	4 6 3	4 14 4	4 14 8	1 2 8		8 10	35 5 1

Of the various sources from which the income of the University was derived the most profitable was the payments for the degrees of Doctor; the average receipts were £26 a year, nearly half the average income of the University. The fees for this degree were, to our ideas, very high; even Friars had to pay £10, and Benedictine monks paid £20. In 1447 John Gudwyn, Austin friar, paid £10 'vice convivii sui',[1] while in 1451 William Seton, a Benedictine monk, paid £20.[2] In the accounts of 1472 and 1474 we find Friars paying £10. In 1460 the Friars complained that this fee of £10 was higher than the fee demanded at Cambridge; but the University answered that though the fee at Cambridge was only five or six marks, yet in addition there was the expense of providing a feast for the regents.[3] This does not seem to be the truth. In 1455 a Friar paid only £2 at Cambridge, and the words are added *pro non convivando*[4]; in one case a Friar[5] pays £8 'quia non convivavit'; but in no case is the figure as high as £10. In 1465 Oxford complained that some of the Benedictines had changed their place of study, i.e. deserted Oxford for Cambridge[6]; this may have been because of the high fees. In the year 1478, perhaps as a result of the complaint of the Friars or because Cambridge was 'cutting the rates', Oxford lowered her fees; Friars were to pay in future £6 13*s.* 4*d.* 'loco convivii', monks were to pay £13 6*s.* 8*d.* or more in certain cases.[7] Our Accounts agree with this Statute, and show that Friars paid only ten marks from 1478 onwards.

Each year the University received a considerable sum from graces; in 1469 and 1478 it was as much as £35, and the average for fifteen years was nearly £17. A grace was a permission given by the University to abridge or omit some of the conditions which were attached by statute to the taking of degrees. Some graces were granted without conditions (*simpliciter* is the word used); others had one or more conditions attached, and frequently a payment of money was one of the conditions. Whether a payment was made for a grace or not depended, no doubt, on the value of the grace; if it was merely the permission to shorten the period of study by a term or two, the grace was given *simpliciter*, and most graces were of this kind; but there were also many graces to which a payment of a mark or a noble was annexed.[8] At Cambridge it seems that very few graces were

[1] *Mun. Ac.*, p. 564.
[2] Ibid. p. 732.
[3] *Ep. Ac.*, p. 353.
[4] *Grace Book A*, pp. 4, 9, 18.
[5] Ibid. p. 5.
[6] *Ep. Ac.*, p. 375.
[7] *Mun. Ac.*, p. 353.
[8] Ibid. p. 732.

granted for money; there are instances,[1] but less than one a year. On the other hand, there was a source of income at Cambridge of which we hear nothing at Oxford, namely the forfeited pledges (*cautiones*) when a man on taking a degree did not carry out the tasks that were due from him. On this point the statutes of the two Universities must have been radically different. At Oxford a man was bound to carry out the duties of his degree by his oath; and he would be guilty of perjury if he omitted these duties; his only course would be to ask from the Congregation of Regents for a grace to omit the duties in question. But at Cambridge it seems that a man could omit the duties if he was willing to forfeit his caution.

The fees for taking the degrees of Bachelor and Master of Arts were small. No doubt there were payments to beadles and presents to Regent Masters, of which little is known at present, but to the University the only payment was one week's commons for the M.A. degree and half a commons for the degree of Bachelor.[2] At Cambridge the Statute was that a full commons should be paid for each degree, and the Cambridge accounts mention each person by name who paid a commons. The general rule at Cambridge was that a *questionist*, i.e. candidate for B.A., paid 12*d*., an inceptor 20*d*.; but at Oxford the commons seems to have been slightly less. Thus in 1550 the half commons, though usually sixpence,[3] was fivepence in one case,[4] and in another case fourpence[5]; the full commons is not specified except that it was to be 'secundum usum loci in quo inhabitat',[6] and few Colleges and Halls had a commons as high as twenty pence. As the average receipts at Oxford from this source were about £3, we may estimate that about thirty would take the degree of M.A. each year, and perhaps forty the degree of Bachelor. This rough estimate is corroborated by a statement in Registrum Aa, fol. 122, that in 1462 a full congregation of regents numbered sixty, and as a man was a regent for two years after taking his degree, it means that about thirty incepted each year. A study of the Cambridge *Grace Book A* suggests that the degrees at Cambridge were slightly fewer, if the lists are complete in that book. It is obvious from these figures how small were the numbers at both Universities. If no more than forty took the degree of Bachelor each year, the undergraduates can hardly have been more than three hundred, if we allow that more than half of

1 *Grace Book A*, p. 39.
2 *Mun. Ac.*, pp. 156, 457.
3 *Ancient Kalendar of the Univ. of Oxf.* (O. H. S.), pp. 64, 65.
4 Hearne, *Diary*, vi. 273.
5 Ibid. p. 272.
6 Ibid. p. 274.

them left Oxford without taking a degree; to these we may add about one hundred bachelors, seventy regents, and about one hundred and fifty non-regents. This, of course, omits manciples, cooks, choir-boys, and servants, who all were reckoned as of the University. In a letter of 1438 the University asserts that its numbers did not reach a thousand.[1]

Little need be said about the receipts from house property. The previous volume (pp. 275–323) shows what properties the University had, and when they were obtained, and these accounts show what they were worth at the end of the fifteenth century. Both Cat Hall and William Hall had ceased to be halls, and were rented at only 4*s.*; William Hall is described in 1490 as 'aula sive tenementum'[2], and as the rent was to be 2*s.* the tenement can have been but small; it was probably a stable, which it certainly was in the seventeenth century; Tingwick Inn and Black Hall were rented at 13*s.* 4*d.* and 16*s.*, and as the annual rent of a chamber was 10*s.* we may guess what the size of these halls was. A rent of 2*s.* paid yearly by Balliol College for Sparrow Hall is explained by the deed printed in *Balliol Deeds* (O. H. S.), p. 30. In addition to the tenements mentioned in vol. i, the accounts show that 6*s.* 8*d.* was paid from the New Inn, or as it is in one place 'the New Inn by the church of St. Mary Magdalen'. This was the inn known later as the Cardinal's Hat[3]; it was a property of Oseney, and the Oseney rentals record the quitrent paid from it annually to the University. The amount which was received from the house property of the University varied according to the amount of repairs that was necessary, and of the rooms that were vacant. The gross rental was rather over £7, the net receipts were on an average under £5, and would have been less if the buildings had been kept in first-rate repair; for our accounts show that Beef Hall and the School of Canon Law required heavy expenses, apart from the annual repairs.

There is no difficulty in tracing the history of the payments from Eynsham and Oseney Abbeys. In 1214 Nicholas, Bishop of Tusculum,[4] decreed that the Town of Oxford should pay to the University 52*s.* a year 'for the use of poor scholars', and also 16*s.* 8*d.* to provide a feast on the day of St. Nicholas to 100 poor 'clerks'. These duties were undertaken by the Abbey of Eynsham,[5] though it is not

[1] *Ep. Ac.*, p. 156.
[2] Ibid. p. 60.
[3] For its situation see *Balliol Deeds* (O. H. S.), frontispiece.
[4] *Univ. Archives*, i. 2.
[5] *Cart. of Eynsham* (O. H. S.), ii. 163.

known for what reason; and in our accounts we find that each year 16 shillings[1] is paid for a feast of 100 undergraduates, and the 52 shillings are distributed among the Regent Masters, who would be correctly described as *scolares*. This was according to the University Statutes.[2] The payment from Oseney Abbey dates from the time of Robert Grosteste. When he was Bishop of Lincoln, Oseney obtained from him the appropriation of the church of Fulwell, a church which has long disappeared, but stood in what is now part of the parish of Mixbury. In return for this concession, the bishop bargained that Oseney Abbey should pay 26*s.* 8*d.* a year to the University of Oxford. Not long after the dissolution of the monasteries, when Christ Church had inherited the rights and duties of Oseney, the payment was extinguished, as part of the arrangement by which the University acquired the Schools of Arts which had been the property of Oseney

The accounts show that the University obtained yearly a small amount from those who had caused breaches of the peace. In 1469 this reached the exceptional figure of £4 15*s.*; we do not know what the reason may have been, but Warwick and Clarence raised disturbances in many parts of England in the early months of 1470, and they may have been at work at Oxford as elsewhere. The average receipts were about twenty shillings a year, and the accounts show that the figure was rising slightly at the end of the century. The Statute beginning 'Cum effrenata' passed in 1432 laid down a schedule of fines for breaches of the peace according to the enormity of the offence,[3] and decreed that one-third of the proceeds should be received by the University, one-third by the Chancellor, one-eighth by each of the Proctors, and one-twelfth by the beadle.[4] When the Chancellor's Register (Reg. Aaa) is printed, it will be seen that, in addition to the fines, there were small sums received from the sale of confiscated weapons. In the year 1488 our accounts show receipts from the sale of weapons, but probably in other years the receipts from both sources are merged in one total. At Cambridge the Proctors' Accounts show receipts from those who 'had been convicted',[5] and in one place the entry is in full 'convicted of disturbing the peace'[6]; but at Cambridge the fine seems to be always 20*d.* or 40*d.*, and the cases are much fewer than at Oxford, the receipts being only a few shillings in the course of a year.

[1] The odd eightpence is dropped.
[2] *Mun. Ac.*, p. 501.
[3] Ibid. p. 314.
[4] Ibid. p. 318.
[5] *Grace Book A*, p. 58.
[6] Ibid. p. 61.

Another source of the income of the University was a payment made by those who kept grammar schools in Oxford. In the list of the moneys that were received by the Proctors in 1411[1] we find *pecunia sex marcarum grammaticis recipi consuetae* (read *consueta*), 'a sum of six marks received from the grammar masters'. In 1447, when there were three grammar masters, Richard Bulkley, John Cobbow, and John Russell, an attempt was made to evade this payment of six marks, but it was enforced.[2] In our accounts a sum sometimes of £4, sometimes less, is paid until the year 1477, but not afterwards; but in some years a portion of the sum was returned to the payers, as though the profits of the grammar schools were dwindling. That such was the case, we should gather from a letter which the University wrote in 1466 to the Bishop of Lincoln[3] that 'grammar, the base of all education, has gone into exile and deserted this realm'. Although no payment was received by the University after 1477, yet the old statute was not revoked, and in 1478 it was decreed that although any free grammar school, should such be founded, was to be exempt from payment to the University, yet the others who teach grammar shall pay 'the sum which of old was recovered from them'.[4] From the University Statutes it is not clear when the payment was begun, why it was exacted, or how much it was to be; but they show that from early times the University legislated about the grammar schools, although the students at the schools were not members of the University[5]; and appointed two regent masters to supervise the teaching in grammar schools.[6] As early as 1322 Nicholas de Tingewick granted two messuages, Beef Hall and Tingwick Inn, to the University to provide a salary of four marks for these two superintendents,[7] and a statute which is assigned by Mr. Anstey to 1344 gives the salary as six marks, of which four marks were to come from the rents of the University, and two marks apparently from the masters who had grammar schools.[8] But these statutes must have been altered in the next century, when, as we have seen, the grammar masters had to pay six marks, while at the same time our rolls show that the salary of the superintendents was reduced to one mark. An undated statute[9] informs us that the sum of £4 received from the grammar masters was to be distributed annually,

[1] *Mun. Ac.*, p. 259.
[2] Ibid. p. 563.
[3] *Ep. Ac.* (O. H. S.), p. 381.
[4] *Mun. Ac.*, p. 354.
[5] Ibid. pp. 85–7.
[6] Ibid. p. 440.
[7] *Univ. Arch.* (O. H. S.), i. 285.
[8] *Mun. Ac.*, p. 440.
[9] Ibid. p. 501.

together with other money, among the Regents in Arts, and such was the custom at the time of our Proctors' Accounts. At Cambridge the supervision of the grammar schools seems to have been the work of the Master of Glomery, the word Glomery being a form of the word Grammary, and no doubt he received a salary from the grammar school masters; and this may be the reason why the accounts of the Cambridge Proctors show no receipts from the grammar masters. At both Universities the grammar schools died out towards the end of the fifteenth century; at Cambridge they omitted sometimes to appoint a Master of Glomery,[1] while at Oxford it was decided in 1492 that as the superintendents of the grammar schools had now no work, but still received a salary, they should be made superintendents of the disputations at the Austin Friars.[2]

In 1464 there was only one grammar master, named Cobbaw, and in 1477 also only one, but in the intervening years there was more than one. Something is known of Cobbaw, *alias* Cobbow, *alias* Gobbo. In 1435 Oseney granted to John Cobbow, clerk, a lease of Lyon Hall in St. Mary's parish, on the east side of Grove Street, to be held by him for life at a rent of fifty shillings; and each year the Abbot of Oseney was entitled to send a boy to his school to be instructed in grammar free of charge, unless he was a boarder, in which case the abbot was to pay one shilling a quarter.[3] In the Oseney rental of 1453 Mag. Ioh. Gobowe rents Lyon Hall. Possibly he was in some way connected with Leyland, one of the most famous of schoolmasters; for in a charter at the Bodleian John Leyland and Margaret his wife in 1422 acquire certain lands in Cowley, and about 1460 they are held by John Gobow, of the gift of John Leyland.[4] They were both buried at St. Frideswide's, Leyland dying April 30, 1428, and Cobbow October 15, 1472.[5] In Rous's list of Halls,[6] which is apparently of about 1450, we learn that Leyland's school had been at Peckwater Inn, and that about 1450 there were five grammar schools in Oxford, namely Ing Hall in St. Mary's, Boster Hall and White [7] Hall in St. Peter's in the East, Lyon Hall and Tackley's Inn both in St. Mary's. It is noteworthy that of the three grammar masters of whom there is mention in 1447, Bulkley was of Tackley's

1 *Grace Book A* (ed. Leathes), p. xxxvii.

2 *Mun. Ac.*, p. 363.

3 Deed at Ch. Ch.

4 *Bodl. Charters*, pp. 278, 324.

5 Wood, *City of Oxf.* (O.H.S.), ii. 175.

6 Ibid. i. 639.

7 For these three halls see *Cart. of the Hosp. of St. John.*

Inn, Cobbow of Lyon Hall, and Russell was of Ing Hall. Young Eglesfield attended Leyland's school[1] between 1419 and 1420, and young Edmund Stonor about 1380 was at a boarding school in Oxford,[2] which was kept by a married man.

We are left to guess why the grammar schools at Oxford and Cambridge suffered eclipse at the end of the fifteenth century. It was evidently not owing to any decrease in the number of educated persons, for there is no decrease in the degrees that were taken at the two Universities. Perhaps the solution is provided by the clause of the Oxford statute about free grammar schools; it shows that some free grammar schools had been recently founded, and this may have emptied the old grammar schools.

Among the smaller receipts four deserve some mention. In 1492 and 1496 the accounts record 3*s.* 4*d.* received from the guild of tailors, and in 1494, if the payment was omitted, it must have been by oversight. This payment was made by the tailors in return for a regulation made by the Chancellor and Congregation of Regents in 1491, to restrain tailors who were not of the guild.[3] In the year 1473 and all subsequent years there is a record that 3*s.* 4*d.* was paid annually by the representatives of the town on St. Scholastica's day and that the money was distributed on the same day to poor scholars. After the riot of St. Scholastica's day it was decreed that sixty representatives of the town, the Mayor, and the two bailiffs should attend Mass on St. Scholastica's day and each offer one penny. It would be natural that this offering, like all the other oblations, should be received by the incumbent, which in the case of St. Mary's was Oriel College; and, in accordance with this, we find in the earlier Oriel accounts that the College received 5*s.* 3*d.* on St. Scholastica's day. But the accounts also record that in 1453 the Proctors of the University claimed 3*s.* 4*d.* of the amount, and after long disputes the Vice-Chancellor in February 1462 decided that Oriel ought to receive only 23*d.*, and was to pay to the Proctors the sum of £4 16*s.* 8*d.*, being 3*s.* 4*d.* for the previous twenty-nine years. If the accounts of 1464, 1469, 1471, and 1472 omit this sum of 3*s.* 4*d.*, it must be for the reason that it was paid away on the spot, as soon as it was received, and did not need to be entered on the accounts. In the year 1469 there is a receipt of 6*s.* 8*d.* for issuing letters testimonial.

[1] *Hist. of Queen's Coll.*, i. 321.
[2] *Stonor Letters* (Camden Soc.), i, p. 21.
[3] *Ep. Ac.*, p. 595.

This entry is hard to explain, for the volumes of *Epistole Academice* show that letters testimonial were issued in many years of which we have the accounts, yet no payment was received for them. Lastly, in some years there is an entry of 2*s*. or 3*s*. 4*d*. forfeited, after an appeal had been made. An early statute about such forfeits is contained in *Munimenta Academica*[1]; even if it was not in force in the time of these accounts, something like it was in force. The appeals in question were not appeals to the Court of Arches, an appeal which the University never allowed, but appeals from the Chancellor's decision to the congregation of regents, or from the congregation of regents to the congregation of regents and non-regents. There were similar fines at Cambridge for unsuccessful appeals, as may be seen in the accounts in *Grace Book A*.[2]

Turning to the expenditure, first comes a large sum that was spent each year on the vigils of St. John the Baptist and St. Peter; it ranged from £5 7*s*. 6½*d*. in 1488 to over £7. We are not told how this money was spent until we reach the accounts of 1492, where we are told that it was for a 'recreatio omnium graduatorum'. In 1496 not only were all graduates (i. e. inceptors) entertained, but also bachelors in law; and the cost rose to £8 19*s*. 3½*d*. Perhaps we may assume that this was spread over two days, because it would be difficult to entertain all the graduates at once. In 1492 there is the expense of 4*s*. 6*d*. for lights (*luminibus*) on the two days, and in other years there is often money for wax torches (*cereis*), and for rushes, no doubt to strew the floor. In 1494 repairs were needed 'in locis ubi tenebantur dicte recreaciones'. In 1469 the entertainment seems to have been held at Queen's College, and 12*d*. was paid for carrying of benches (*scabellorum*)[3] to the College. In 1471 the spot was Durham College, whither the clerk of St. Mary's carried the benches at a charge of 12*d*., and there was a payment of 2*s*. 6*d*. for napkins soiled on the vigil of St. Peter. In 1473 there is the usual payment for carrying the benches, but we are not told whither. Only in one year is this payment omitted, namely in 1478; and in that year we have the unique entry that the Proctors were paid £3 6*s*. 8*d*. because of their dangers in the time of the plague. The two facts, no doubt, are connected; the plague was so severe that the University had been dispersed before June 23. In the accounts of 1464 this expenditure

[1] p. 75.
[2] pp. 18, 21, 41, &c.
[3] *formularum* is the word used in 1464. The words are evidently synonymous.

on June 23 and 28 is stated to have occurred *in circuitibus Cancelarii*; and in a letter of the King in 1444 it is stated[1] that there were two 'circuits' at Oxford on June 23 and 28; but we are not told what the word means.

Another heavy expense was the annual distribution of money to the regents. A man was a regent for two years after taking his degree of Doctor or Master, and during that time had to give twenty-four lectures each term, unless he obtained exemption by means of a grace. Not only was he bound to give these gratuitous lectures, but he was bound by oath to attend all University processions, and to be present in the Congregation of Regents, whenever he was summoned. During these two years his life must have been a burden, and if there was any class that deserved a distribution, it was the regents. From 1478 onwards the sum distributed was always £3 18*s.* 8*d.*, which represents the 52*s.* paid by Eynsham for distribution among *scolares*, and the sum of £1 6*s.* 8*d.* paid annually by Oseney. Before 1478 the sum was larger, being as high as £7 5*s.* 4*d.* in 1464 and 1469. A statute of the University lays down[2] that the amount to be distributed among the regents was 52*s.* received from Eynsham, two marks received from Oseney, and six marks received from the grammar school masters, or £7 18*s.* 8*d.* in all; but it was the custom by the year 1464 to deduct the one mark that was paid to those who inspected the grammar schools, leaving £7 5*s.* 4*d.* As the payment received from the grammar schools diminished, so the sum to be distributed diminished: and after 1477, when the last payment was made by the grammar schools, the total was no more than £3 18*s.* 8*d.*

Each year there was a feast to the auditors of the account, costing usually £2. The amount is always a round sum, and perhaps the Proctors provided the feast, and were allowed to keep the balance. A similar, but smaller, expense was the refreshment provided for the Chancellor, the Proctors, and the Beadles on the day on which they visited the 'rents' of the University, i.e. the houses which belonged to the University. In 1494 the phrase is 'in visitacione aularum', i.e. visiting the halls owned by the University, to see in what repair they were. The cost was usually two or three shillings.

Next we take three payments which seem to have been used as a means to give the Proctors a salary. Each year sums are paid to the Proctors for their night watch (*nocturnis vigiliis*), for the hire and

[1] *Mun. Ac.*, p. 540. [2] Ibid. p. 501.

repair of armour, and for their small expenses. It is to be noticed that these are always round sums, and cannot be the reimbursement of what was actually spent. It is also to be noticed that each entry ends *ut placet iudicibus*, 'as the auditors please'; the Proctors did not fix the sum, but left it to the auditors, and it is easy to detect by the writing that the sums for these three entries were added at the end. No doubt the amount allowed by the auditors depended to some extent on the balance; but it is probable that it also depended on the amount that the Proctors had received from other sources. The Statutes make no mention of a salary for the Proctors beyond stating that each Proctor was to receive one-eighth of the fines inflicted for carrying arms and breaking the peace; but in the most turbulent years this would mean no more than £1 for each of the Proctors. Now we have good evidence that the profits of the Proctor were much more than this; for Richard Bradley of Exeter College, who was Proctor in 1474, paid tithes to Lincoln College, as rectors of the church of St. Michael, for the profits of his Proctorship; as he paid 11*s.* 8½*d.*,[1] his profits must have been £5 17*s.* 1*d.* Part of this would be from his fees from those who took their degrees; in most cases seven shillings was paid to the Chancellor and Proctors, and from those who could expend £40 the Proctors each received two marks.[2] But part of it may have been from the payments by the University for the night watch, for the hire of arms, and for small expenses, the University in each case granting a sum that was well above the disbursements. Occasionally we have other sums granted to the Proctors as though to provide them a salary; in 1481 the Southern Proctor is allowed 20*s.* for supervising the builders at Beef Hall, and each Proctor has 10*s.* for his diligence. Next year the Proctors are granted £2 6*s.* 9*d.* for their labours and diligence; and when a servant is wounded or slain, the Proctor receives recompense on a liberal scale.

There were four rents which the University paid every year. From Beef Hall there was a quitrent of 3*s.* which belonged to Eynsham Abbey from the earliest times.[3] For the site of the Divinity School there was a fixed rent of 7*s.* to Balliol College.[4] In the year 1472 and in subsequent years there was a payment of 3*s.* 4*d.* to St. Frideswide's; and if it does not appear in the accounts of 1464, 1469, and 1471 it may be merely an accident. It was due for the part of Patrick

[1] From the MS. College accounts at Lincoln College.

[2] Hearne's *Diary*, vi. 273, 274.

[3] *Cart. of Eynsham*, ii. 248.

[4] *Balliol Deeds*, p. 151.

Hall which was required for the site of the Divinity School.[1] Lastly there was the payment of one penny a year for the possession of the assise of bread and ale.[2] The money was due to the Exchequer, but it was sometimes paid to the bailiffs of the Town, who conveyed it to the Exchequer when they paid the fee farm. In 1472 this penny is mentioned; in 1479 it is included in the 3*s.* 5*d.* paid to the bailiffs, of which 3*s.* 4*d.* was the customary fee to the bailiffs, when seisin of a freehold was given, and the other penny would be for the assise of bread and ale.

Among the annual salaries paid by the University, the first is that of the Registrar, who was also known as *scriba* or *tabellio Universitatis*, with a salary of four marks a year. It is curious that in the University Statutes as printed in *Munimenta Academica*, there is no mention of this official; but the Statute by which this office was instituted has been found by Mr. Strickland Gibson in a Cambridge MS., and will be printed in his forthcoming edition of the Statutes. It was decreed that the Registrar should be a Master of Arts and a public notary; he was to be appointed by the smaller congregation, the congregation of regents; his salary was to be four marks a year, and he was to receive a fee for each degree that he registered; his work was to draw up leases, acquittances, and letters of the University, and enrol all Acts of the University whether done before the Chancellor or before Congregation and also all University letters. The date of the decree is unknown, and as the earliest letter book of the University begins at the year 1421 it might be thought that the Registrar existed at that date or earlier. But there is some reason for thinking that the first portion of that book is in the handwriting of the various Chancellors, and all that can be definitely stated is that in 1446, when Registrum Aa begins, there was a Registrar in office named Manyngham. At Cambridge we find a Registrar in 1454, when their accounts begin. The Registrar not only kept the University Letter Book and the Acts of Congregation, but once a year his hand appears in the Chancellor's register, when on the morrow of the Nativity of St. Mary a list of halls and principals was drawn up.

The Registrar whose name appears in the first accounts, John Farley, is a man of whom we should like to know more. He entered Winchester College in 1444,[3] and New College in 1448.[4] Being of

[1] *Cart. St. Frid.* i. 485.
[2] *Univ. Arch.* i. 230.
[3] *Winchester Scholars* (ed. Kirby), p. 64.
[4] *Regist. Univ. Oxon.* (O. H. S.), p. 32.

New College he did not apply for a grace,[1] and we have no means of tracing his degrees, but he was Registrar as early as October 1458.[2] Our accounts show that he ceased to hold office at Christmas 1464, and the records at New College give the reason; he died in December 1464. In New College Library, MS. 281 is the Almagest of Ptolemy with the inscription 'Liber Collegii beate Marie Winton ex dono magistri Ioannis Farley, quondam socii huius collegii, cuius anime propicietur deus'. The interesting point about Farley is that he has left his name written in Greek characters in several places. It is found in Registrum Aa, fol. 106, and twice in the letter book of the University.[3] The editor of this latter volume says that Farley 'was not a little proud, perhaps, of being able' to write Greek characters; but the writing is so neat and firm that he must have known much more than the Greek characters. He has also written his name in Greek in a Greek Psalter now in the Library of C. C. C. Cambridge,[4] and we may assume that Farley had studied that manuscript. Part of it is said to be transliterated in an Italian hand, which may prove to be Farley's; for Registrum Aa shows that, when he liked, Farley could write a beautiful Italian hand. Farley's name, though not in Greek, occurs in another manuscript in that Library.[5] It is possible that he is the writer of one, or even both, of the Chaundler manuscripts recently printed by the Roxburgh Society. Internal evidence suggests that both are before 1465, and probably by a Wykehamist. They seem to be in two different hands, one using an upright *d*, the other using a *d* with a rounded head; but in Registrum Aa Farley uses both forms, and it is evident that an Italian hand was not an ordinary handwriting which did not vary, but what we should call a printing hand, and varied from day to day or week to week according to the taste of the writer. It is noticeable that Farley will often begin a line in the Italian hand, and drift into his ordinary, somewhat untidy, English hand. New College and Thomas Chaundler are known to have been connected with the introduction of Greek to Oxford, and if we could discover more about Farley, it might prove that he had a hand in the same movement; but there is little space in Farley's life for any long visit to Italy to study Greek. He cannot have been M.A. before 1455; he would not have finished his years of regency

[1] Statutes of New College, p. 50, in *Statutes of the Colleges of Oxford* (1853).

[2] *Regist. Univ. Oxon.* p. 32.

[3] *Ep. Ac.*, pp. 367, 371.

[4] *Catalogue of MSS. at C. C. C.* (ed. James), ii. 422.

[5] Ibid. ii. 325.

until 1457; and he was Registrar in 1458. At the time of his death he cannot have been more than thirty-four.

Next we come to the salary of the chaplain of the University; from the Proctors' Accounts he receives only 6*s.* 8*d.* a year, but in addition he obtained £5 from the profits of the assise of bread and ale. In 1401 King Henry IV granted to the University the assise of bread and ale at a rent of one penny a year, which had hitherto been held for a payment of £5; and in 1412 the University decreed[1] that the chaplain of the University, who in future was to be the University Librarian as well, should receive that sum of £5 in addition to the 6*s.* 8*d.* which the chaplain had hitherto received for celebrating the masses of the University. It was not his duty to say mass daily, but only on the dates appointed by the University. In the Calendar printed in *Munim. Ac.*, pp. cxxxix–cl, there are thirteen masses with deacon and subdeacon, and seventeen other masses; and by the time of our accounts two or three may have been added. The accounts from 1481 onwards show that the chaplain received an extra payment of ninepence a year 'by statute'. This may have been in connexion with the mass in commemoration of John and Thomas Kempe which was instituted by statute in 1478.[2]

There are various payments to the parish clerk of St. Mary's, which increased in number year by year and by 1496 amounted to nearly thirty shillings. First comes the regular payment of 4*d.* for ringing the bell on the morrow of the Nativity of St. Mary. On that day all who wished to secure an Academic Hall came to St. Mary's to give cautions for the rent of the Halls that they desired, and as long as the bell was ringing no house that had been an Academic Hall could be refused.[3] Besides this he received 18*d.* a year for ringing the curfew; this does not mean that he rang the curfew every day, but, as stated in the accounts of 1471, at the exequies of Walter de Grey and Reginald the Beadle. For Walter de Gray there were two days (May 1 and November 12) and for Reginald the Beadle one (May 10)[4]; and that the payment was sixpence each time is proved by a document printed in Hearne's *Diary*.[5] The curfew was rung at the exequies, i. e. not on the evening of the day when mass was said, but on the previous evening, the exequies being the service of the eve. In the later accounts the clerk is paid two shillings for the curfew;

[1] *Mun. Ac.*, p. 262.
[2] Ibid. p. 352.
[3] Ibid. p. 14.
[4] Ibid. pp. cxxxix–cl.
[5] Hearne's *Diary*, vi. 271.

probably the commemoration of the Kempes which commenced about 1480 supplied one more day when the curfew was rung. No doubt these payments for ringing are high, but a parish clerk, like many mediaeval officials, was expected to do much work without pay on the condition that he should be overpaid when any payment could be secured. He had no salary from the churchwardens, like a modern parish clerk. From 1469 onwards he was paid for the care of the clock in St. Mary's; it is not mentioned in 1464, and probably it had not been acquired by that time. He was paid 4*s.* a year for this work, and in the last two accounts it seems to be six shillings. He was also paid 4*d.* for carrying the cross whenever there was a procession. In 1481 there were twelve processions, four of them being in Long Vacation at the King's desire. In 1488, besides eight processions, there was a meeting of the King, for which the clerk received a shilling. In 1496 there were nine processions, for which he received three shillings, and two meetings of the 'Prince', each at a fee of two shillings. He was also paid for the custody and cleaning of the house of congregation; and after 1490, about which time the books were moved from the old University Library to the upper room of the School of Divinity, the clerk had also the custody of the 'upper house of congregation'. He was also paid, as has been mentioned, for carrying the forms to the place where the 'recreacions' took place on June 23 and 28; he was also paid for carrying the forms to the place where 'the vesperies of artists' were held; in one year the vesperies took place five times. Lastly he was paid for reading the Epistle at those masses which were celebrated with a deacon and subdeacon; they varied from year to year, sometimes being twelve, sometimes more; he was paid twopence each time.

There was a payment, also, to the clerk of St. Peter's in the East. On the six Sundays in Lent and Easter Day there were special sermons by the University in that church, and in the Chancellor's Register in certain years can be found the names of those who were appointed to preach. For ringing for these sermons the clerk received 4*d.* each time.

Each year there was a payment to the man who filled the post of deacon by reading the Gospel at the masses of the University; he was paid at the same rate as the reader of the Epistle. There was also an extra payment at the masses of Walter de Grey and Reginald the Beadle; for by statute every regent should attend these masses and offer a penny, which was to be supplied from the University funds.[1] It is evident that this statute was not strictly observed; for if all the regents had attended, the oblations would have been more than five shillings at each of the three masses.

In the later accounts there are payments each year to *Collegium Regale* or the rectors of St. Mary's. The debt was incurred in connexion with the commemorations of the Duke of Gloucester and the Kempes. It seems that there was an unusual use of candles on these days, some of them being the candles of the University and some the candles of the church. For the latter the University had to pay Oriel, which was rector of St. Mary's.

In the accounts year by year there are a few entries which help towards the history of the University. In 1464 there is mention of straw at the New Schools as covering, probably to cover some unfinished walls as a protection against frost. It is difficult to discover what was the state of this New School of Theology. In a letter of 1470 the University laments that it is unfinished,[2] yet in 1466 it ordered some expensive fittings showing that the School was roofed over and in use.[3] Probably the 500 marks paid in 1452 by Cardinal Beaufort's executors was enough to complete the walls and roof, but the two towers at the west end, which were to contain staircases to reach the library, may have been incomplete in 1464 and in 1470.

In 1469 more than £16 was spent on the New Schools, partly in carving the seats which were ordered in 1466 and partly in glazing (*clausura*) of windows, probably the windows of the upper room which was not yet in use. The Chancellor was met at Thame and consulted. As he was at this time the King's Chancellor, he would move with the King; and probably the Court passed through Thame.

In 1471 there is a reference to the battle of Tewkesbury and the expenses of keeping the peace for the next week. The University had much expense this year in the King's Exchequer, and the sum of £6 13*s*. 4*d*. was drawn from the Chest of Five Keys to meet it; of this £4 was spent on journeys to the King by John Boswell, one of the beadles, and magister Veysey on matters concerning the University; Thomas Woode received 13*s*. 4*d*. for acting as proctor (i. e. barrister) in the Court of the Exchequer; three visits were paid to the King at Beckley, when wine was given to the King's chaplains and there were other expenses amounting to £4 10*s*. in all. It was a troublesome year for the University. It had written a letter to

[1] Hearne's *Diary*, vi. 270, 271.
[2] *Ep. Ac.*, p. 391.
[3] *Mun. Ac.*, p. 716.

Henry VI on December 22, 1470, expressing delight that he had recovered his throne[1]; and on June 28, 1471, it wrote a similar letter to Edward IV, expressing equal delight at his success. It does not seem that Edward IV bore malice towards Oxford; and he must have perceived that as George Nevyle was Chancellor of the University not much emphasis was to be laid on the letter to Henry VI; the University could hardly do otherwise. But if Edward was placable, it may have been necessary to buy the favour of his officials. One royal messenger was given 3*s.* 4*d.*, another 20*d.*, his secretary a pair of gloves, his minstrels 3*s.* 4*d.* The whole expense was nearly £10. In building there was an outlay of £13 6*s.* 8*d.* on the School of Canon Law, although within twenty years the whole school had to be rebuilt. At the Divinity School there was 29*s.* spent on walls, apparently boundary walls, and as the supervisors were paid £1 for their trouble there was probably more money spent from some other source.

Next year there were heavy expenses about the privileges of the University, and £17 was borrowed for this purpose from the Chest of Five Keys. Of this sum £5 9*s.* 4*d.* was spent 'on the confirmation of privileges by Parliament', and £3 13*s.* 4*d.* for having them enrolled in the King's Exchequer, perhaps on the Remembrancer's roll; William Fowler, who seems to have been a member of Parliament, received gloves for his support of the privileges; Henry Bathe, the Oxford carrier, had 2*s.* 8*d.* for conveying to Oxford the confirmation by Parliament; John Boswell and Doctor Rowce received nearly £4 for their work. The matter will be found in *Rotuli Parliamentorum*, vi. 33; the grant of 1461 by which the King allowed the University to have the assise of bread and ale at a payment of one penny a year had 'been resumed and voide for lak of certeyn provisions upon certain acts of Resumption'. The University petitioned that the grant might be declared good and effectual by the authority of Parliament. There was an expense of 16*s.* in keeping order about the feast of Epiphany, but the reason is not given; also 3*s.* for cleaning the Divinity School and for the *clausura* of the upper windows; as *clausura* seems to mean 'glazing' in the accounts of 1469, it probably has this meaning here.

In 1473 the accounts are normal, but in 1474 there is an entry that wine and gloves were given to the Bastard of Burgundy and

[1] *Ep. Ac.*, p. 392.

other gentlemen. The Bastard of Burgundy must have been in England in connexion with the King's preparations for the invasion of France. It is possible that he came to Oxford on April 5, 1475, which would be within the year of the accounts; for a commission of the peace was issued at Oxford on that date.[1] This would imply that the Lord Chancellor was in Oxford, though not necessarily the King, and we might guess that the Bastard of Burgundy, the Chancellor, and others might have come over from Woodstock. On the Divinity School there was spent £14 13*s.* 4*d.* in repairs, and the supervisor, no doubt a Master of Arts, received 26*s.* 8*d.*, and the Chancellor had expenses in London, amounting to £6 10*s.*, apparently in connexion with the University privileges.

In 1477 there were further expenses at the Exchequer; £2 was borrowed for this purpose, and the Chancellor's expenses amounted to four marks. The matter may have been that the officials of the Exchequer laid upon the Chancellor the collection of a tenth. The University appealed to the King saying that it was a burden never imposed on the Chancellor before.[2] There was also a dispute about the assise of bread and ale.[3] In this year a new copy of the Statutes was made, and there is payment for the binding of it, the illumination, and the clasps. There seems to have been special disturbance when the judges and other strangers came to Oxford; a sum of 24*s.* was spent in keeping order, and a friar was killed. Life was not safe at this time. The accounts tell us that two Bachelors were wounded in 1478, a servant of the Proctors killed in 1479, a priest injured in 1488. The Oriel accounts tell us that a clerk of Brasenose Hall was killed in 1474, and a deed at Bridgwater mentions the murder of Thomas Ludlow, sub-bailiff of Oxford, in 1491.

The accounts for 1478 are the most interesting of the series. In January the University wrote to the Bishop of London saying that the School of Theology, though begun long ago was maimed (*mancus*) and almost neglected, entreating his aid.[4] In the accounts we find that Thomas Karver was paid twenty shillings for his expenses in soliciting the Bishop of London to complete the work, so that we may assume that he carried the letter. On February 12 a letter was written to Oxford by Thomas Chaundeler, who was Chancellor of the University, declaring the good intentions of the Bishop of London.[5] On

[1] *Cal. of Patent Rolls*, p. 626.
[2] *Ep. Ac.*, p. 424.
[3] Ibid. p. 427.
[4] Ibid. p. 430.
[5] Ibid. p. 432.

May 6 the University sent to the bishop a statute that had been passed, ordaining the observance of the commemoration of the Kempes[1]; no doubt this was the substance of the letters patent which was written out at a cost of 8*d.* We read of a journey to Hinksey where the Chancellor, the Commissary, and many others treated about the intention of the Bishop of London to complete the School of Theology. If it is asked why the meeting was at Hinksey, the answer may be that the itinerant judges had to be consulted. There is an entry that the Proctors journeyed to Hinksey to obtain the good-will of the judges, probably the itinerant judges for Berkshire, who usually held their court in that part of Grampound which was in Berkshire, in the parish of Hinksey. Two horses were hired at a cost of 12*d.* to visit the Chancellor about the oath of William Orchard; evidently the Chancellor was not far away, and as there is evidence that this was a year of severe plague he may have been in a neighbouring village. William Orchard is known to have been the architect and builder of much of Magdalen College, and the evidence is increasing which shows that he was the architect of all the chief buildings of Oxford that were erected between 1460 and 1504, the date of his death. There can be little doubt that the initials W. O., which occur more than once on the roof of the Divinity School, stand for William Orchard. We do not know why an oath was required from him; perhaps the Bishop of London desired that he should take an oath to complete the work within a certain date. There is also a payment to Boswell, the beadle, for a journey that he made to the King about masons. This must have been when he carried to the King a letter written by the University on February 24, 1479, asking that he should not summon to Windsor the masons who had finished their work at Magdalen College, but should allow the University to engage them.[2]

The accounts of 1479 twice record that there was a crowd of visitors at Oxford when 'magister Leonellus' (i. e. Wydeville) took his degree. In March or April the University had sent him a letter, announcing that a grace had been passed in his favour that he should be 'licenced in decrees', but not obliged to incept.[3] Among those who came to see the sight was his nephew, Richard Grey. In this year Doctor Robert Halle gave Wolstan Hall to the University,[4] and our accounts show

[1] *Ep. Ac.*, p. 433.
[2] Ibid. p. 446.
[3] Ibid. p. 448.
[4] *Univ. Arch.* i. 323.

the legal expenses and the consumption of wine when possession was obtained.

In 1481 there was much building at Beef Hall amounting to £23, and the Southern Proctor was paid £1 for supervising the work. Apparently the hall was improved, for the rent was raised slightly. For the School of Canon Law twenty-one cart-loads of stone were bought, but no building was begun. The King visited the University and stayed at Magdalen on Sunday, September 23; his mother also came and his sister, the Duchess of Suffolk. Another visitor was *dominus Stanley*, no doubt Thomas Stanley, first Earl of Derby. In this year wine was given to *dominus Edwardus* and *magister Iacobus Stanley*; the latter is James Stanley, sixth son of Thomas Stanley, born about 1465, who was Bishop of Ely from 1506 to 1515, having been Archdeacon of Richmond from 1500 to 1506 [1]; the former is Edward Pole, son of John de la Pole, Duke of Suffolk, who married the sister of Edward IV; Suffolk was at this time Steward of the University. Both in the Proctors' Accounts and in the letter in which the University thanks the King for sending Pole and Stanley to Oxford [2] we find that Stanley is called *magister*, while Pole who was of royal blood is merely *dominus*. It is obvious that Stanley, if born in 1465, cannot have been Master of Arts in 1481, and in the letter of the University he is definitely described as a youth. Perhaps Stanley had already begun his course of Arts and is therefore given the title *magister*, whereas Pole was still studying grammar. There is some uncertainty about the subsequent career of Edward Pole. In the *Dictionary of National Biography* he is in one place identified with Edmund Pole who was executed in 1513; in another place he is identified with Edward Pole who was made Archdeacon of Richmond in 1485 and died soon after. As he was a younger brother of Edmund, he cannot have been more than eight at this time. On June 24, 1481, Magdalen gave a feast 'to the sons of Suffolk and Stanley'.[3] There were meetings with the Chancellor, Lionel Wydeville, at Abingdon and at Cumnor; it has yet to be discovered what his connexion was with Abingdon.

In 1482 there is the purchase of 107 loads of stone for the School of Canon Law; they were bought from mag. Will. Horcherd, in other words, William Orchard the builder and architect, who tells us

[1] *D.N.B.*
[2] *Ep. Ac.*, p. 478.
[3] *Reg. of Magd. Coll.*, p. 7 (ed. Macray).

in his will in the Chancellor's Register that he owned a quarry at Headington. He is generally styled *magister* as a mark of respect. The Chancellor, though now Bishop of Salisbury, still seems to be living at Cumnor, and was given wine there on three occasions. William Orchard rides to the Bishop of London probably to consult him about the vaulting of the Divinity School. The coats of arms show that it was set up about 1482,[1] and as the Bishop of London was supplying the money he may have been consulted about the plan. The entry about 'removing books in the library' cannot mean the transference of books from the old library to the new, for a letter which seems to be of October 1488 states[2] that even then the new library was not ready for books.

In the accounts of 1488 there is mention of a visit to Oxford paid by Henry VII. The same visit is mentioned in the accounts at Magdalen[3] between Michaelmas 1487 and Michaelmas 1488. We can, therefore, now assert that the visit was between April 16 and September 29, 1488. It was in this year that the School of Canon Law was rebuilt,[4] but it has left no trace in the Proctors' Accounts.

In the accounts of 1496 there is mention that Prince Arthur paid two visits to Oxford. They are also mentioned in the accounts of Magdalen College between Michaelmas 1495 and Michaelmas 1496.[5] The Bishops of Lincoln and Lichfield paid three visits to Oxford, and there was an outlay of £2 13*s.* 4*d.* over 'abbots, priors and gentlemen'. Perhaps this was when St. Mary's church was opened again, after rebuilding.

[1] See a paper on 'The vault of the Divinity School' by W. H. St. John Hope in the *Archaeological Journal* for 1914, pp. 217–260.

[2] *Ep. Ac.*, p. 533.

[3] *Reg. of Magd. Coll.*, p. 15 (ed. Macray).

[4] See *Ep. Ac.*, pp. 510, 516, 556.

[5] *Reg. of Magd. Coll.*, p. 22 (ed. Macray).

I.

[April 11, 1464—April 24, 1465.]

Compotus magistrorum Thome Pawntone & Iohannis Payntour procuratorum alme Uniuersitatis Oxonie de per eosdem receptis et administratis ex officio ab xi die mensis Aprilis anno domini millesimo CCCCLXIIII ad vicesimum quartum diem anno reuoluto.

In primis receperunt de magistris Iohanne Farmer et Willelmo Appylby collectoribus reddituum Uniuersitatis iii lib. viii s. viii d. ob.

Et de suscipientibus gradus hoc anno pro communis et dim' xxxvii s. ii d.

Et de abbate et conuentu de Eneshame pro distribucione facienda inter magistros regentes lii s.

Et de abbate et conuentu de Eneshame ad pascendum centum pauperes scolares in festo sancti Nicholai xvi s.

Et de abbate et conuentu de Oseney pro consimili distribucione xxvi s. viii d.

Et de magistro Cobbawe xl s.

Et de pecuniis leuatis de diuersis personis propter transgressionem pacis ix s.

Et de doctoribus componentibus cum Uniuersitate hoc anno l lib.

Et de condicionibus graciarum hoc anno ix lib. xi s. viii d.

Et [1] de collegio Animarum pro annua pensione xvii s. iiii d.

Summa receptorum lxxii lib. xviii s. vi d. ob.

Et in primis solutum est pro refeccione centum pauperum in die sancti Nicholai xvi s.

Et solutum diacono et subdiacono seruientibus in missis pro benefactoribus Uniuersitatis iiii s. ii d.

Et sol' magistris offerentibus in duabus missis Walteri le Grey [2] et missis [3] Reginaldi Bedelli xii s. iii d.

[1] This is entered in another hand. It is the rent of Tingwick Inn and Cat Hall. With £3 8*s.* 8½*d.* it makes the total of £4 6*s.* 0½*d.*, as on the dorse of the roll.

[2] Brey, MS.

[3] *missa* should be the word. There was only one mass for Reginald the Beadle.

Et sol' pro delacione crucis et cereorum in xi processionibus generalibus hoc anno iii s. viii d.
Et sol' preconi proclamanti ad Quadrivium ad mandatum Cancellarii ad vices hoc anno ii s. viii d.
Et sol' tabellioni Farley xl s.
Et sol' tabellioni Sultone xiii s. iiii d.
Et sol' capellano Uniuersitatis vi s. viii d.
Et sol' magistris Phylyppys et Belle superuisoribus scolarum grammaticalium xiii s. iiii d.
Et sol' magistro Belle collectori reddituum collegii Balleoli pro quodam annuali redditu de nouis scolis sacre theologie vii s.
Et sol' abbati de Enesham pro quodam annuali redditu Aule Bouine iii s.
Et sol' pro candelis cereis, posicione formularum et preconi mortis et aliis necessariis in obitu domini Humfridi, ducis Glocestrie iiii s. iiii d.
Et sol' Willelmo Perys pro custodia domus congregacionis ii s. viii d.
Et sol' pro stramine transeunte ad cooperturam nouarum scolarum [1] xvi d.
Et sol' operariis laborantibus circa predictam cooperturam iii s. vi d.
Et sol' pro expensis factis ad custodiam pacis in nocturnis vigiliis iii lib.
Et sol' pro reparacione ciste de Dauvarse et pro bursa in qua reponuntur pecunie eiusdem ciste ii s.
Et in predicta cista de Dauvarse imposuimus xxx lib.
Et sol' pro expensis factis ad mandatum domini Cancellarii et aulsamentum doctorum et magistrorum venerabilium pro custodia pacis in nocturnis vigiliis tribus noctibus succedentibus quando domini le Barnesse et le Wenloke & Harcowrt [2] & multi alii venerabiles ibidem aderant iii lib. xii s.
Et sol' pro uno collato dominis predictis, scilicet le Bernesse, Wenloke & Harcowrt vii s. vi d.

[1] This cannot mean that the Divinity School had a thatched roof. If such an idea was possible, the sums here mentioned are much too small for such a work, and four or five years later the walls were still in building. Probably it means that, as the University had no funds, the walls were thatched to keep them dry. It will be noticed that no other money was spent on the New Schools in this year.

[2] On May 3, 1464, John Bourchier of Berners, knight, John Wenlok of Wenlok, knight, and Robert Harecourt, knight, were appointed on a commission to array the king's subjects in Oxfordshire and the four neighbouring counties (*Cal. of Pat. Rolls*, p. 391).

Et sol' pro uno collato et cirotecis aliis venerabilibus de domo regia et domini Cancellarii — iiii s.

Et sol' Willelmo Perys pulsanti in crastino Natiuitatis Marie ad exposiciones caucionum pro aulis et pro portatu formularum in vigiliis sanctorum Iohannis et Petri — xvi d.

Et sol' pro quatuor clausuris librorum communis librarie et pro reparacione unius fenestre eiusdem — iiii s. ii d.

Et sol' pro le sowdrynge eiusdem — xii d.

Et sol' pro distribucione facta inter regentes — vii lib. v s. iiii d.

Et sol' pro conduccione et reparacione armorum — xxxiii s. iiii d.

Et sol' pro papiro et pergameno et rubea cera ad vices hoc anno — xiii d.

Et sol' pro expensis factis in circuitibus Cancellarii in vigiliis sanctorum Iohannis et Petri[1] — vi lib. xvii s. viii d

Et sol' pro redempcione cuiusdam caucionis Uniuersitatis quondam exposite in cista Wynton', scilicet duorum candelabrorum argenteorum — iiii lib.

Et sol' pro renouacione aliarum caucionum ad vices — iiii s.

Et sol' pulsanti ad sermones in ecclesia sancti Petri in oriente — ii s. iiii d.

Et sol' collectoribus reddituum Uniuersitatis — [*blank*]

Et sol' pro refeccione facta auditoribus huius compoti una cum scriptura eiusdem — xxxii s.[2]

Et sol' magistro Waltero Hylle,[3] summa indebitata sibi ex parte Uniuersitatis — xix s. iiii d. ob.[4]

Et petunt dicti procuratores pro expensis diminutis — xl s.

Summa expensarum et solucionum una cum xxx libris repositis in cista de Danvers lxix lib. viii d. ob.; et sic computatis computandis et allocatis allocandis debent dicti procuratores Uniuersitati iii lib. xvii s. x d., quam summam soluerunt super compoto procuratoribus anni sequentis, magistris Gane et Whitwey et sic quiete dimissi sunt.

On the dorse.

Compotus magistri Iohannis Fermere et Willelmi Appulby collectorum reddituum Uniuersitatis anno supradicto.

De Aula Nigra — viii s.

[1] A note in the margin, 'Non trahatur posteris in exemplum'.

[2] In the margin, 'Non trahatur posteris in exemplum'.

[3] He was of New College and became Warden in 1475; he was Proctor in 1463.

[4] The amount written at first was 19*s.* 0½*d.*; the addition of 4*d.* makes the total at the end incorrect.

Et de magna scola iuris canonici liii s. iiii d.
Et de orto annexo eidem scole xvi d.
Et de Aula Bouina xxx s.
Et de Aula Willelmi in Kybbalstrete iii s. iiii d.
Et de Aula Mureligorum iiii s.
Et de orto iuxta ecclesiam sancti Egidii xvi d.
Et de collegio Balleoli ii s.
Et de gardino in Hospicio Novo vi s. viii d.
Et de Tewchewyke Halle xiii s. iiii d.

Summa receptorum vi lib. iii s. iiii d.

Allocaciones facte in reparacionibus diversorum locorum predictorum.

In primis in Aula Bouina xi s. v d.
Item pro Aula Nigra in manibus magistri Summaster remanent iiii s. viii d.
Et pro orto annexo scole iuris canonici nichil recipitur quia vacat et sic existunt aretro xvi d.
Item pro orto vacante iuxta ecclesiam sancti Egidii ii s.
Et pro pensione collectorum dictorum reddituum xiii s. iiii d
Item respectuantur pro Aula Willelmi xvi d.
Item procuratores Uniuersitatis receperunt de collectoribus iiii lib. vi s. ob.

Summa cum xvi d. respectuatis super Aula Willelmi vi lib. i d. ob.

Et sic computatis computandis et allocatis allocandis debent predicti collectores iii s. ii d. ob. quas tradiderunt procuratoribus Uniuersitatis coram iudicibus deputatis.

Mem. de sedecim denariis respectuatis super collectoribus pro Aula Willelmi.

2.

[April 13, 1469—May 5, 1470.]

Compotus magistrorum Ricardi Mayhow & Georgii Strangwysche procuratorum Alme Uniuersitatis, de per eosdem receptis ac administratis ex officio, a terciodecimo die Aprilis anno domini millesimo CCCCLXIX usque ad quintum diem mensis Maii anno reuoluto.

Recepta per procuratores de magistris I. Harrow et Nicholao Langtone procuratoribus anni precedentis cxvi s. x d.

Et de suscipientibus gradus hoc anno pro communis et dimidiis lvii s. v d.
Et de abbate et conuentu de Eynysham ad pascendum C scolares in die sancti Nicholai xvi s.
Et de abbate et conuentu de Eynysham pro distribucione facienda inter regentes lii s.
Et de abbate de Oseney & pro consimili distribucione fienda xxvi s. viii d.
Et de magistris docentibus gramaticam iiii lib.
Et de duobus doctoribus in sacra theologia pro suis compositionibus, scilicet magistro Iohanne Borow & magistro I. Marchal xl. lib.
Et de condicionibus graciarum de suscipientibus gradus hoc anno xxxv lib. xvi s. viii d.
Et de diuersis propter transgressiones factas in perturbacione pacis iiii lib. xv s.
Et de collegio Ballioli pro quadam pensione annua pro aula Passerina ii s.
Et pro sigillacione cuiusdam littere testimonialis sigillo Uniuersitatis[1] vi s. viii d.

Summa totalis receptorum iiii^{xx}xviii lib. ix s. iii d.

Soluta pro Uniuersitate:—
Primo, capellano Uniuersitatis pro stipendio suo hoc anno vi s. viii d.
Et pro stipendio scribe Uniuersitatis liii s. iiii d.
Et pro expensis factis in vigiliis sanctorum Iohannis Baptiste & apostolorum Petri & Pauli cxvii s. vii d.
Et pro oblacionibus & aliis in binis exequiis Grey & Reginaldi Bidelli ix s. x d.
Et in delatione crucis & cereorum in nouem processionibus generalibus hoc anno iii s. ii d.
Et proclamatori apud Quadrivium ad mandatum Cancellarii pro bannitionibus & aliis xiiii d.
Et diacono & subdiacono seruientibus in missis pro benefactoribus Uniuersitatis vi s. viii d.
Et in deliberat' custodibus ciste de Danvers xx li.
Et in deliberat' custodibus ciste quinque clavium x li.

[1] A letter testimonial for William Wykwyk was granted on Oct. 24, 1469 (*Ep. Ac.*, p. 305, O. H. S.).

Et magistris superuisoribus nouarum scolarum, pro completione edificacionis muri ex deliberacione congregacionis x li.
Et eisdem magistris pro clausura fenistrarum & pro quodam hostio ordinando in nouis scolis ex condicione gracie iii lib.
Et solut' pro inscisione capitum ambonum in nouis scolis iii lib. vi s. viii d.
Et magistris Willelmo Maior [*blank*] superuisoribus scolarum grammaticalium xiii s. iiii d.
Et magistro Willelmo Cleuelonde & Ricardo Payne collectoribus reddituum Uniuersitatis xiii s. iiii d.
Et pro custodia pacis in nocturnis vigiliis li s. iiii d.
Et pro reparacione & conduccione armorum x s. vi d.
Et clerico Uniuersitatis pro custodia domus congregationis & mundacione ii s.
Et proclamatori in obitu ducis Glocestrie & pro cereis ii s. vi d.
Et solut' clerico laboranti circa eundem obitum xii d.
Et pro expensis factis versus Enysham pro acquisitione pensionis iiii d.
Et alloc' abbati de Enysham pro aula Bovina iii s.
Et pro custodia horilegii [*sic*] iii s.
Et pro reparacione fenestrarum librarie & mundacione tecti eiusdem xvi d.
Et in vino dato Chocke [1] iudici bis et alteri venienti secum ii s.
Et in vino dato domino Stortone [2] & aliis militibus secum venientibus xvi d.
Et pro refeccione pauperum die sancti Nicholai xvi s.
Et pro delacione scabellorum ad collegium Regine vigiliis sanctorum Iohannis Baptiste & apostolorum Petri & Pauli xii d.
Et in renovacione caucionis Uniuersitatis in cista de Robery xii s.
Et clerico parochiali beate Marie pro pulsatione ignitegii [3] xviii d.
Et pro pulsatione compane in crastino Nativitatis beate Marie iiii d.
Et clerico parochiali sancti Petri in oriente pro pulsatione ad sermones in Quadragesima ii s. iiii d.

[1] Richard Chokke was on the Commissions of the Peace for Oxfordshire in 1469 and 1470 (*Cal. of Pat. Rolls*, p. 625). He was a judge and was appointed on many commissions throughout England.

[2] Probably William Stourton of Dorsetshire, a man much employed by Edward IV (see *Cal. of Pat. Rolls*).

[3] i. e. on the commemorations of Walter de Grey and Reginald the Beadle.

Et in vino dato episcopo Eliensi xvi d.
Et in expensis unius procuratoris usque Londoniam in negociis Uniuersitatis una cum conduccione equorum per vi dies xv s.
Item pro distributione facta inter regentes vii lib. v s. iiii d.
Et in expensis unius procuratoris in obviando domino Cancellario apud Thame pro certis negociis ex voluntate Commissarii ii s. viii d.
Et in vino dato Cancellario & aliis post visitacionem parochiarum & aularum xiii d.
Et pro regardo dato ducenti litteras regis Uniuersitati una cum cerotecis & vino xxi s. ix d.
Et pro papiro & reparacione librorum Commissarii et procuratoris Australis viii d.
Et in pecuniis ex graciis condicionatis ad edificacionem scolarum canonistarum applicandis x lib.
Et solut' pro pixide in qua imponuntur predicte decem libre una cum claue & serura xii d.
Et magistris superuisoribus nouarum scolarum pro suis laboribus ut placet auditoribus xx s.
Et collectori reddituum collegii Ballioli pro quodam fundo nouarum scolarum theologie vii s.
Et pro expensis diminutis secundum discretionem auditorum l s.
Et de allocatis magistris docentibus grammaticam ut asserunt ex consuetudine xii d.[1]
Et pro refeccione facta auditoribus xxvi s. viii d.
Et in scriptura huius compoti & pergameno, ut placet xiii d.

Summa omnium solucionum iiii^{xx}vii lib. xviii s. iii d.[2]; et sic remanent x lib. xi s. quas procuratores soluerunt & sic quieti recesserunt.

Item predicti iudices receperunt de collectoribus reddituum istius anni, allocatis allocandis & disallocatis disallocandis ut patet in dorso istius rotule [*sic*] xxxix s. viii d. ob. qua.

Summa totalis omnium receptorum per prefatos iudices xii lib. x s. viii d. ob. qua., de qua summa v lib. reposite sunt in cista v clavium & summa residua remanens in manibus procuratorum anni sequentis summa vii lib. x s. viii d. ob. qua.

[1] A note in the margin, 'Caue; quia non ex consuetudine'.

[2] The total should be £87 17*s.* 11*d.*

On the dorse.

Compotus magistrorum Willelmi Cleuelond & Ricardi Payn collectorum reddituum Uniuersitatis Oxonie, anno domini MCCCC [*sic*] anno supradicto.

Et primo de Aula Nigra	xv s.
Et de magna scola iuris canonici	liii s. iiii d.
Et de orto annexo eidem scole	xvi d.
Et de Aula Bouina	xxx s.
Et de Aula Willelmi in Kybalstrete	xx d.
Et de Aula Mureligorum	iiii s.
Et de Tynchewykehalle	xiii s. iiii d.
Et de orto iuxta ecclesiam sancti Egidii	xx d.
Et de collegio Ballioli	ii s., computat' in alia parte
Et de gardino in Hospicio Novo	vi s. viii d.

Summa vi lib. vii s.

Et petunt allocari

Pro Aula Bouina	xvi s. viii d.
Et pro Aula Nigra	xv s. qua.
Et pro scola iuris canonici	liii s. iiii d.
Et pro orto annexo scole canonistarum	iiii d.
Et pro orto in parochia sancti Egidii	xx d.

Summa iiii lib. vii s. iii d. qua.[1] et sic remanent xxxix s. viii d. ob. qua. soluend', quas iudicibus soluerunt & quieti recesserunt.

3.

[April 29, 1471—April 13, 1472.]

Compotus magistrorum Nicholai Good et Ricardi Dauys procuratorum Uniuersitatis Oxonie, anno domini millesimo quadringentesimo septuagesimo primo, a uicesimo nono die Aprilis usque ad tercium decimum diem Aprilis anno domini MCCCCLXXII.

Arreragia nulla.

Sed respondent de receptis :—

In primis de magistris Willelmo Brew & Thoma Biston predecessoribus suis	viii lib. xi s. ix d.
Item de cista quinque clauium pro expensis in vigiliis sanctorum Iohannis et Petri	v lib.

[1] The total should be £4 7*s*. 0¼*d*.

Item de abbate de Eynsham ad pascendum C pauperes in festo sancti Nicholai — xvi s.
Item de abbate de Osney — xxvi s. viii d.
Item de magistris docentibus grammaticam[1] — iiii lib.
Item de magistro Willelmo Brew pro quibusdam graciis in anno precedente — viii lib.
Item de suscipientibus gradus hoc anno pro communis et semicommunis — xxxvi s. x d.
Item de cista quinque clauium pro acquietacione Uniuersitatis in Scaccario regis — vi lib. xiii s. iiii d.
Item pro condicionibus gratiarum hoc anno — iiii marc.
Item de collegio Ballioli pro Aula Passerina — ii s.
Item de cista quinque clauium pro redemptione caucionum Uniuersitatis in cista de Gilforde — x lib.
Item de collectoribus reddituum Uniuersitatis — vi lib. xix d.
Item de forisfacturis in perturbatione pacis — xiii s. v d.
Item de cista quinque clauium pro reparacione scolarum canonistarum — x lib.
Item de domino Humfrido Hawerden pro caucione amissa in quadam appellatione cui cessit[2] — ii s.
Item de abbate de Eynsham — lii s.

Summa totalis receptorum lxviii lib. viii s. xi d.

Et computant liberata :—

In primis capellano Uniuersitatis pro stipendio suo — vi s. viii d.
Item scribe Uniuersitatis pro stipendio suo — liii s. iiii d.
Item pro expensis factis in vigiliis sanctorum Iohannis et Petri — vi lib. xvi s. ix d.
Item clerico beate Marie pro portatione scabellorum ad collegium Dunolmie utraque nocte — xii d.
Item pro oblationibus & aliis in binis missis Grey et Reginaldi Bedelli — ix s. iiii d.
Item proclamatori apud Quadriuium in bannitionibus et aliis — ii s.
Item pro delatione crucis in septem processionibus generalibus — ii s. iiii d.

[1] The note at the end of the account shows that £1 was remitted to the grammar masters.

[2] Hawardyn deposited a caution on March 13, 1472, that he would prosecute an appeal (*Ep. Ac.*, p. 393), but as he did not proceed the caution was forfeited. Probably it was an appeal to the Congregation from the sentence of the Chancellor.

Item magistris superuidentibus grammaticam xiii s. iiii d.
Item magistris collectoribus reddituum Uniuersitatis xiii s. iiii d.
Item pro custodia pacis post bellum de Teuxbury[1] continue per septimanam integram ad mandatum Cancellarii xliiii s.
Item diacono & subdiacono in diuersis missis pro benefactoribus Uniuersitatis v s. viii d.
Item clerico Uniuersitatis pro custodia & mundacione domus congregationis v s. iiii d.
Item pro cereis in exequiis ducis Gloucestrie et proclamatori vi s. vi d.
Item clerico laboranti circa easdem exequias xii d.
Item abbati de Eynsham pro allocatione pro Aula Bouina iii s.
Item pro refeccione pauperum in die sancti Nicholai xvi s.
Item pro reparatione horilogii vi s. viii d.
Item clerico sancti Petri pro pulsatione ad sermones in Quadragesima ii s. iiii d.
Item bursario collegii Ballioli pro quieto redditu nouarum scolarum theologie vii s.
Item clerico sancte Marie pro pulsatione ad ignitegium in exequiis Grey & Reginaldi xviii d.
Item superuisoribus operis nouarum scolarum iuxta decretum congregationis xx s.
Item pro custodia pacis in nocturnis vigiliis secundum discretionem iudicum l s.
Item pro expensis magistri Veysy & Iohannis Boswell equitancium ad regem in negociis Uniuersitatis ad diuersas vices[2] iiii lib.
Item clerico Uniuersitatis pro custodia horilogii iii s.
Item in vino dato doctori Smyth per Cancellarium et nos diuersis vicibus ii s. iiii d.
Item pro reparacione facta circa muros nouarum scolarum et tectura eorundem xxix s. viii d.
Item Thome Woode ad procurandum pro nobis in Scaccario regis diuersis vicibus xiii s. iiii d.
Item clerico pro ordinatione scabellorum in vesperiis artistarum xvi d.
Item Thome Philipp nuncio regis iii s. iiii d.

[1] May 4, 1471.
[2] In *Ep. Ac.* (p. 395) it will be seen that the University sent one or more letters to the king to recover his favour.

Item pro expensis in visitacione regis apud Bekley et in reuentu vi s. iiii d.
Item in vino dato capellanis regis et aliis generosis eadem nocte v s. vi d.
Item pro expensis factis in bis visitando regem apud Bekley iiii lib. v s. ii d.
Item pro custodia pacis eodem tempore cum multitudine xxiiii s.
Item pro sera nova et clavi ad cistam de Robrey xiii d.
Item pro inchatenatione cuiusdam libri in libraria xii d.
Item pro vino dato Cristofero Harcourt xvi d.
Item pro reparatione vitri nouarum scolarum viii s.
Item pro conduccione & reparatione armorum xxxiii s. iiii d.
Item clerico beate Marie pro pulsatione in crastino Nativitatis beate Marie iiii d.
Item pro lotura manitergiorum tinctorum vino & manitergio perdito in vigilia sancti Petri ii s. vi d.
Item pro expensis diminutis secundum disposicionem iudicum liii s.
Item pro reparacione bursarum ciste de Robrey ii d.
Item pro distributione facta inter magistros regentes vi lib. xviii s. viii d.
Item pro cirotecis datis domino Mountjoy & secretario regis xx d.
Item in vino dato iudicibus regis x d.
Item pro noua corda ad magnam companam xvi d.
Item pro reparatione sere et claui noua ad cistam de Gylford viii d.
Item pro potatione facta maiori et villanis in cedatione [*sic*] litis inter nos & villanos iii s. vii d.
Item pro vino & cirotecis datis doctori Danell nuncio regis xx d.
Item pro cirotecis missis per eum ad Iohannem Par militem ii s.
Item pro cereis in vigiliis Iohannis Baptiste & Petri iii s.
Item pro sera ad ostium congregationis viii d.
Item pro refeccione facta doctoribus et magistris auditoribus huius compoti, ut uidetur iudicibus xxvi s. viii d.
Item pro redempcione caucionum Uniuersitatis in cista de Gylford viii lib.
Item pro vino dato Cancellario & Bidellis post visitacionem aularum & parochiarum & reddituum et recreatione iiii s. ii d.
Item tibicinibus regis pro regarda iii s. iiii d.
Item pro reparatione scolarum canonistarum xiii lib. vi s. viii d.
Item pro cera rubea et pargameno hoc anno xii d.

Item pro vino dato fratri Regine per Cancellarium & procuratores ii s. ii d.
Item computantibus superuisoribus operis scolarum canonistarum ut placet iudicibus x s.[1]
Item pro scriptura huius compoti et pergameno, ut placet iudicibus xiiii d.
Item pro scriptura trium warantarum apud Wodstok ii s.
Item pro expensis doctoris Brent laborantis cum una waranta ad Stowode per duos dies xv d.
Item pro expensis unius procuratoris visitantis dominum Cancellarium ex certis causis xiii s. iiii d.

Summa omnium solutorum lxx lib. vi s. vi d.[2] Et sic in pleus[agio] xxxvii s. vii d. Item allocantur eis per iudices pro magistris grammaticalibus xx s. et sic clare in pleus' lvii s. vii d.

On the dorse.

Compotus magistrorum Ricardi Bradeleyghe & Simonis Bakster collectorum reddituum Uniuersitatis Oxonie, anno domini MCCCCLXXII.
Et primo de Aula Nigra xv s.
Item de Magna Scola iuris canonici liii s. iiii d.
Item de orto annexo eidem scole xvi d.
Item de Aula Bouina xxx s.
Item de Aula Willelmi in Kybalstrete xx d.
Item de Aula Mureligorum iiii s.
Item de Tenchwykehalle xiii s. iiii d.
Item de orto iuxta ecclesiam sancti Egidii xvi d.
Item de orto in Hospicio Novo vi s. viii d.

Summa receptorum vi lib. vi s. viii d.

Et petunt allocari pro reparacione Aule Bouine ii s. vi d. ob.
Petunt eciam allocari pro reparacione dixtorum [3] in scola iuris canonici x d. ob.
Item petunt sibi allocari pro orto annexo scole iuris canonici xvi d.[4]
Et petunt pro reparatione orti in parochia sancti Egidii iiii d.

[1] A note in the margin, 'Pro factis et faciendis circa opus inceptum ab eisdem'.
[2] The total should be £70 7*s.* 8*d.*
[3] Not in Ducange; probably for 'descorum', desks.
[4] In the margin, 'quos adhuc debet Nicholaus Croke cum qua summa onerati sunt collectores futuri'.

Summa allocatorum v s. i d. Et sic remanent vi lib. xix d. quam summam collectores soluerunt procuratoribus & sic quieti recesserunt.

4.

[April 8, 1472—April 30, 1473.]

Compotus magistrorum Willelmi Maior et Iohannis Acherle procuratorum Uniuersitatis Oxonie, anno domini millesimo quadringentesimo septuagesimo secundo ab octauo die Aprilis usque ad ultimum diem Aprilis anno domini MCCCCLXXIII.

Reddunt compotum de receptis

In primis de duobus doctoribus theologie, videlicet Payne et Isaak fratribus	xx lib.
Item de condicionibus graciarum in isto anno	xi lib. v s.
Item de suscipientibus gradus hoc anno pro communis et dimidiis	xlviii s. ii d.
Item de abbate et conuentu de Eynsham ad pascendum C scolares in die sancti Nicholai	xvi s.
Item de abbate et conuentu de Eynsham pro distribucione facienda inter regentes	lii s.
Item de abbate et conuentu de Osney pro consimili distribucione fienda	xxvi s. viii d.
Item a magistris docentibus grammaticam [1]	iiii lib.
Item a diuersis propter transgressiones factas in perturbacione pacis	xviii s.
Item de Collegio Ballioli pro quadam pensione annua pro Aula Pascerina	ii s.
Item pro lamine quodam meremii vendito a nouis scolis	xii d.
Item de cista quinque clauium pro expensis factis in vigiliis sanctorum Iohannis et Petri	vi lib.
Item de collectoribus reddituum Uniuersitatis	v lib. v s. iiii d.
Item de cista quinque clauium pro diuersis negociis factis circa priuilegia	xvii lib. iii s. iiii d.
Item de eadem cista pro reparatione facta circa tectum nouarum scolarum & pro aliis necessariis Uniuersitatis	xl s.

Summa totalis receptorum lxxiii lib. xvii s. vi d.

[1] The note at the end of the expenses shows that two marks were remitted to the grammar masters this year.

Soluta pro Uniuersitate:—

Primo, magistris Nicholao Good & Ricardo Davys procuratoribus anni precedentis pro pede compoti precedentis anni — lvii s. vii d.

Item capellano Uniuersitatis pro stipendio suo — vi s. viii d.

Item pro cera rubia ad sigillandum literas Uniuersitatis — ii d.

Item proclamatori ville apud Quadriuium pro clamationibus & bannitionibus — ii s. x d.

Item pro uino & cirotecis datis magistro Courteney — iii s. iiii d.

Item pro delatione crucis et ceriorum in sex processionibus — ii s.

Item clerico parochiali sancti Petri in oriente pro pulsatione ad sermones in Quadragesima — ii s. iiii d.

Item pro oblationibus et aliis expensis debite factis in exequiis Grey et Reginaldi Bidelli — viii s. xi d.

Item diacono & subdiacono in sedecim missis — v s. iiii d.

Item pro duobus pixidibus in quibus deferebantur litere ad dominum regem — i d.

Item scribe Uniuersitatis pro stipendio suo hoc anno — iiii marc'

Item Iohanni Boswelle pro adquisitione priuilegiorum — xxiii s. iiii d.

Item Doctori Rowce pro negociis factis ad regiam magestatem — li s. viii d.

Item pro expensis factis in uigiliis sanctorum Iohannis et Petri — vi lib. iiii s. viii d.

Item pro cereis et sirpis in eisdem vigiliis — iii s. iiii d.

Item magistris superuisoribus scolarum grammaticalium — xiii s. iiii d.

Item magistris Ley et Luptone collectoribus reddituum Uniuersitatis — xiii s. iiii d.

Item pro delatione scabellorum in uesperiis artistarum — ii s.

Item pro custodia horilogii — iiii s.

Item clerico Uniuersitatis pro custodia et mundacione domus congregacionis — iii s. ii d.

Item pro mundacione nouarum scolarum theologie, pro clausura fenestrarum superiorum et obstruccione foraminum — iii s.

Item pro pulsatione in crastino Natiuitatis beate Marie — iiii d.

Item pro emendacione sere cuiusdam ciste — i d.

Item pro expensis factis circa confirmationem priuilegiorum per parleamentum — v lib. ix s. iiii d.

Item magistro Sowthworthe et Henrico Bathe pro vectura priuilegiorum — ii s. viii d.

Item pro scriptura cuiusdam scedule ostense in parleamento continentis tenorem quorundam priuilegiorum iiii d.
Item pro expensis factis per magistrum Broke et cirothecis datis Willelmo Fowler pro defencione priuilegiorum iii s. ii d.
Item pro cereis in exequiis ducis Glowcestrie iiii s. xi d.
Item pro conduccione caparum et candelabrorum in eisdem exequiis iiii d.
Item clerico pulsanti et pro aliis laboribus circa obitum eiusdem ducis xii d.
Item pro duodecim cathenis pro libris cathenandis vi s. viii d.
Item pro distribucione facta inter regentes v lib. xviii s. viii d.
Item collegio Regali[1] pro briga sedanda in exequiis ducis Glowcestrie xiiii d.
Item uectura librorum quos Uniuersitati dedit magister Grawnte[2] xiiii d.
Item pro tectura nouarum scolarum theologie et pro renouatione plumbi eiusdem tecture xxvi s. viii d.
Item pro expensis diminutis, ut placet iudicibus liii s. iiii d.
Item pro pergameno et scriptura huius compoti, ut placet iudicibus xiiii d.
Item pro emendatione fenestrarum communis librarie Uniuersitatis iiii s. viii d.
Item in deliberat' custodibus ciste quinque clauium xvii lib. vii s.
Item pro custodia pacis in nocturnis uigiliis, ut placet iudicibus iii lib. vi s. viii d.
Item pro equo conducto et aliis expensis factis in negociis necessariis in festo sancti Michaelis ii s. viii d.
Item pro refeccione facta auditoribus compoti, ut placet iudicibus xxx s.
Item pro ordinacione scabellorum in uigiliis sanctorum Iohannis et Petri xii d.
Item recreacione facta Cancellario, Procuratoribus et Bidellis in uisitacionibus iiii s.
Item collegio Ballioli pro quieto redditu nouarum scolarum theologie vii s.
Item abbati de Eynsham pro quadam pensione annua Aule Bouine iii s.

[1] Oriel.

[2] Thomas Graunt, precentor of St. Paul's, gave books to the University Library on more than one occasion (see *Ep. Ac.*, pp. 382, 397).

Item pro expensis factis circa adquisitionem pecuniarum ab abbate de Eynsham x d. ob.
Item pro rotulacione priuilegiorum in Scaccario domini regis iii lib. xiii s. iiii d.
Item cuidam famulo ducis Southefolchie senescalli Uniuersitatis pro delatione ferinarum distribuendarum inter magistros Uniuersitatis iiii s.
Item pro expensis procuratoris borialis factis Londonie pro inquisitione cuiusdam implaciti pretensi contra ipsum et eius seruientem [1] vi s. viii d.
Item pro conduccione et renouatione armorum iii lib.
Item pro custodia pacis duabus noctibus ad mandatum Cancellarii circa festum Epiphanie xvi s.
Item priori sancte Frideswide pro quadam pensione annua trium solidorum et iiii denariorum et pro arreragiis eiusdem vi s. viii d.

Summa totalis omnium solutorum lxvii lib. viii s. ix d. ob., unde petunt allocari pro magistris grammaticalibus xxvi s. viii d., que summa allocatur eis per iudices & clare debent v lib. ii s. ob., quam summam soluerunt iudicibus & sic quieti recesserunt.

On the dorse.

Compotus magistrorum Lee et Luptone, collectorum reddituum Uniuersitatis Oxonie, anno domini MCCCCLXXII.

Primo, de Aula Nigra xvi s.
Item, de magna scola iuris canonici liii s. iiii d.
Item, de orto annexo eidem scole xvi d.
Item, ex arreragiis anni precedentis xvi d.
Item, de Aula Bouina xxx s.
Item, de Aula Willelmi in Kybalstrete xx d.
Item, de Aula Mureligorum iiii s.
Item, de Tenchewikehalle xiii s. iiii d.
Item, de orto iuxta ecclesiam sancti Egidii xvi d.
Item, de orto adiacente nouo hospitio vi s. viii d.

Summa receptorum vi lib. viii s.

Unde petunt allocari pro Aula Bouina x s.
Item pro reparacionibus factis circa scolas canonistarum ix s. iiii d.

[1] Acheley was accused of the death of Gabriel Holme (*Ep. Ac.*, p. 406).

Item pro pecuniis quas debet Nicholaus Croke ii s. viii d.
Item pro decasu cuiusdam orti in parochia sancti Egidii viii d.

Summa allocatorum xxii s. viii d.; et sic remanent v lib. v s. iiii d., quam summam soluerunt procuratoribus et sic quieti recesserunt.

5.

[April 30, 1473—April 20, 1474.]

Compotus magistrorum Ricardi Fytziames & Iohannis Netyltone procuratorum Uniuersitatis Oxonie anno domini MCCCCLXXIII ab ultimo die Aprilis usque ad vicesimum diem Aprilis anno domini MCCCCLXXIIII.

Reddunt compotum de receptis

In primis de duobus doctoribus theologie, uidelicet Akyrtune et Standyshe xx lib.
Item de condicionibus graciarum isto anno xvii lib. xviii s. iiii d.
Item de suscipientibus gradum hoc anno pro communis et dimidiis iii lib. xviii d.
Item de abbate et conuentu de Eynsham ad pascendum C pauperes scolares in festo sancti Nicholai xvi s.
Item de abbate et conuentu de Eynsham pro distribucione facienda inter regentes lii s.
Item de abbate et conuentu de Osney pro consimili distribucione fienda xxvi s. viii d.
Item a magistris docentibus grammaticam [1] iiii lib.
Item a diuersis propter transgressiones factas in perturbacione pacis xix s. iiii d.
Item de cista quinque clauium pro expensis factis in vigiliis sanctorum Iohannis et Petri vi lib.
Item de collectoribus reddituum Uniuersitatis v lib. vi s. v d. ob.
Item de pede compoti procuratorum anni precedentis v lib. ii s. ob.
Item de oblacione burgencium ville in die sancte Scolastice [2] iii s. iiii d.

Summa totalis receptorum lxvii lib. v s. viii d.

[1] The note at the end of the expenses shows that £3 of this payment was remitted to the grammar masters.

[2] Though this does not occur on earlier rolls, the payment might have been made and distributed on the spot.

Soluta pro Uniuersitate :—

Primo proclamatori ville apud Quadriuium pro proclamationibus et bannitionibus — ii s. vi d.

Item pro oblacionibus et aliis expensis debite factis in exequiis Grey et Reginaldi Bedelli — ix s. viii d.

Item pro pergameno ad scribendum bullam Bonifacii pape et pro scriptura eiusdem ad mandatum Cancellarii — v d.

Item diacono et subdiacono in undecim missis pro benefactoribus Uniuersitatis — iii s. viii d.

Item pro delacione crucis et cereorum in septem processionibus — ii s. iiii d.

Item capellano Uniuersitatis pro stipendio suo — vi s. viii d.

Item scribe Uniuersitatis pro stipendio suo — liii s. iiii d.

Item in vino et cirotecis datis magistro Mortone clerico rotulorum — ii s.

Item custodibus ciste quinque clauium — xx lib.

Item pro expensis factis in vigiliis sanctorum Iohannis et Petri — vi lib. xix d.

Item delacione scabellorum in eisdem vigiliis — xii d.

Item pro delacione scabellorum in vesperiis artistarum ad diuersas vices — ii s.

Item pro custodia & mundacione domus congregacionis — ii s. viii d.

Item pro custodia horilegii — iiii s.

Item pro nocturna vagacione ad mandatum Cancellarii per unam noctem — xi s.

Item in vino dato iusticiariis domini regis — xvi d.

Item in cirotecis datis domino Episcopo Winton' — ii s. x d.

Item balliuis ville pro assisa panis et ceruisie — i d.

Item in cirotecis datis magistro Gunthorpe, clerico Parliamenti — ii s.

Item magistro Veysey equitanti ad ciuitatem[1] pro prouisione fienda pro Uniuersitate — xxxvi s. vii d.

Item in refeccione centum pauperum scolarium in festo sancti Nicholai — xvi s.

Item pro nouo collistrigio facto ad mandatum Cancellarii — v s. ii d.

Item in vino dato vicecomiti — xvi d.

Item pro pecuniis receptis de oblacionibus burgencium et distributis inter pauperes — iii s. iiii d.

[1] *civitas* by itself means *town*, i. e. London.

Item pro cereis et aliis necessariis in exequiis domini ducis Glowcestrie iii s. ix d.
Item preposito collegii Regalis pro briga sedanda in eisdem xiiii d.
Item pro expensis diminutis, ut placet iudicibus liii s. iiii d.
Item Cancellario et nobis in visitacione reddituum Uniuersitatis iiii s. ob.
Item in expensis Cancellarii et procuratorum equitancium ad dominum ducem Sowthfolchie iii s. ix d.
Item circa adquisitionem pecunie de Eynsham viii d.
Item pro reparacione circa cistam de Danuers ii d.
Item pro cera rubia ad sigillandum acquietancias et alias litteras Uniuersitatis i d.
Item pro conduccione et reparacione armorum, ut placet iudicibus liii s.
Item pro pergameno et scriptura huius compoti, ut placet iudicibus xiiii d.
Item pro distribucione facta inter magistros regentes iiii lib. v s. iiii d.
Item clerico parochiali sancti Petri in oriente pro pulsatione ad sermones in Quadragesima ii s. iiii d.
Item magistris superuisoribus scolarum grammaticalium xiii s. iiii d.
Item magistris collectoribus reddituum Uniuersitatis xiii s. iiii d.
Item pro pulsatione in crastino Natiuitatis beate Marie iiii d.
Item pro custida (*sic*) pacis et nocturnis vagacionibus, ut placet iudicibus iii lib. vi s. viii d.
Item collegio Ballioli pro quieto redditu nouarum scolarum theologie vii s.
Item abbati de Eynsham pro quadam annua pensione Aule Bouine iii s.
Item pro refeccione facta auditoribus huius compoti, ut placet iudicibus xxx s. iii s. iiii d.[1]
Item priori sancte Friddeswyde pro quadam annua pensione iii s. iiii d.
Item pro corda ad magnam companam in ecclesia beate Marie xvi d.

Summa omnium solutorum li lib. xix s. xi d. ob.; et sic debent xv lib. v s. viii d. ob., unde petunt allocari iii lib. pro magistris grammaticalibus, ut deliberatum est ab Uniuersitate. Et sic clare debent xii lib. v s. viii d. ob., quam summam soluerunt iudicibus & sic clare recesserunt quieti.

[1] This must mean xxxi s. iiii d., if the total is correct.

Item petunt dicti procuratores allocari de certa summa cum qua oneratur procurator borialis per certos iudices ab Uniuersitate deputatos, quam scilicet allocationem detulerunt iudices deliberationi congregationis.[1]

Compotus magistrorum Bradeley et Exam collectorum reddituum Uniuersitatis Oxonie anno domini 1473.

Primo de Aula Bouia (*sic*)	xl s.
Item de Magna Scola iuris canonici	liii s. iiii d.
Item de orto annexo eidem scole	xvi d.
Item de Aula Nigra	xvi s.
Item de Aula Willelmi in Kybalstrete	xx d.
Item de Aula Mureligorum	iiii s.
Item de Tenchwykehalle	xiii s. iiii d.
Item de orto iuxta ecclesiam sancti Egidii	xvi d.
Item de orto adiacente Novo Hospicio	vi s. viii d.
Item de Collegio Ballioli pro quadam pensione annua pro Aula Passerina	ii s.

Summa receptorum vi lib. xix s. viii d.

Item petunt allocari pro Aula Bouina pro decasu unius camere non occupate	x s.
Item in reparacionibus factis circa eandem Aulam	viii s. vi d. ob.
Item in reparacionibus factis circa Aulam Nigram	xiii s. iiii d.
Item in reparacionibus factis circa ortum in parochia sancti Egidii	xvi d.

Summa allocatorum xxxiii s. ii d. ob.; et sic remanent v lib. vi s. v d. ob., quam summam soluerunt procuratoribus et sic quieti recesserunt.

6.

[April 20, 1474—April 8, 1475.]

Compotus magistrorum Ricardi Bradeleghe et Ricardi Estmonde procuratorum Uniuersitatis Oxonie anno domini millesimo quadringentesimo septuagesimo quarto a uicesimo die Aprilis usque ad octauum diem Aprilis anno domini MCCCCLXXV.

[1] The accounts for next year show what happened. It was decided that the proctors should pay to their successors £6 2*s*. 10*d*. only, exactly half of the total of £12 5*s*. 8½*d*., which is here said to be owing.

Reddunt compotum de receptis

In primis de uno doctore theologie, uidelicet Newland fratre x lib.

Item a iudicibus audientibus compotum procuratorum anni precedentis vi lib. ii s. x d.

Item de suscipientibus gradus hoc anno pro communis et dimidiis xliii s. iiii d.

Item a diuersis propter transgressiones factas in perturbacione pacis xviii s.

Item a magistro docente grammaticam xx s.

Item a cista quinque clauium pro expensis factis in uigiliis sanctorum Iohannis et Petri vi lib.

Item de collectoribus reddituum Uniuersitatis v lib. ix s. v d. ob.

Item de condicionibus graciarum isto anno xix lib. ii s.

Item de abbate & conuentu de Eynsham ad pascendum C scolares in die sancti Nicholai xvi s.

Item de abbate & conuentu de Eynsham pro distributione facienda inter regentes lii s.

Item de abbate & conuentu de Osney pro consimili distribucione fienda xxvi s. viii d.

Item de collegio Ballioli pro quadam pensione annua pro Aula Pascerina ii s.

Item de oblacionibus maioris & burgencium ville in die sancte Scolastice iii s. iiii d.

Item de cista quinque clauium vi lib. x s.

Summa totalis receptorum lxii lib. v s. vii d. ob.

Soluta pro Uniuersitate:—

Primo, capellano Uniuersitatis pro stipendio suo vi s. viii d.

Item pro cera rubia ad sigillandum litteras Uniuersitatis ii d.

Item proclamatori ville pro clamationibus apud Quadriuium xx d.

Item pro vino et cirotecis datis Bastardo de Burgundia et aliis generosis et pro pace eadem nocte conseruanda ad mandatum Cancellarii viii s. vii d.

Item alias pro vino dato ac cirotecis datis domino episcopo Lincolniensi ad mandatum Cancellarii vii s. viii d.

Item pro delatione crucis et cereorum ac aliorum necessariorum in receptione episcopi Lincolniensis in eius primo aduentu xii d.

Item pro delatione crucis et cereorum in sex processionibus ii s.

Item clerico parochiali sancti Petri in oriente pro pulsatione ad sermones in Quadragesima ii s. iiii d.
Item pro oblacionibus et aliis expensis debite factis in exequiis et missis Grey et Reginaldi Bidelli vii s. iiii d.
Item diacono & subdiacono in quindecim missis v s.
Item pro expensis ſactis in vigiliis sanctorum Iohannis et Petri v lib. xv s. ii d.
Item pro cereis et sirpis in eisdem vigiliis et aliis laboribus iiii s.
Item pro ordinatione scabellorum in eiisdem (*sic*) vigiliis xii d.
Item pro delatione scabellorum in vesperiis artistarum ii s.
Item pro custodia horilogii iiii s.
Item clerico Uniuersitatis pro custodia & mundatione domus congregationis iii s. ii d.
Item Cancellario pro expensis factis circa priuilegia Londoniis xiii s. iiii d.
Item pro cereis in exequiis ducis Glowcestrie ii s. i d.
Item clerico pulsanti & pro aliis laboribus in missa & in exequiis eiusdem ducis xii d.
Item pro conductione caparum & candelabrorum in eisdem exequiis iiii d.
Item Collegio Regali pro briga sedanda in prefatis exequiis xii d.
Item pro reparatione facta et fienda circa nouas scolas xiiii lib. xiii s. iiii d.
Item superuisori operum earundem scolarum xxvi s. viii d.
Item in deliberatis, custodibus ciste quinque clauium x lib.
Item pro custodia pacis in nocturnis vigiliis, ut placet iudicibus iii lib. vi s. viii d.
Item pro recreacione facta Cancellario, Procuratoribus et Bidellis in visitacionibus ii s. viii d.
Item pro delacione ferinarum distribuendarum inter scolares collegiatos et aulares Uniuersitatis iiii s. viii d.
Item pro ligacione unius libri xiiii d.
Item pro pulsacione in crastino Natiuitatis beate Marie iiii d.
Item pro fune magne campane xvi d.
Item fabro pro duabus clauibus et reparationibus serarum et cathenatione librorum in libraria Uniuersitatis xiii d.
Item uni lathamo pro reparacione pauimenti & pro lapidibus coctis[1] pro eodem pauimento librarie xvi d.

[1] *bricks*; see Ducange, s.v. *lapis coctus*.

Item pro lamine quodam meremii in usum & reparacionem nouarum scolarum — vi d.
Item pro vectura priuilegiorum Uniuersitatis London*iam* — xii d.
Item clerico Uniuersitatis pro mundacione ruderis supra domum congregationis in circuitu — iiii d.
Item pro factura unius muri cum tectura eiusdem — xx s. viii d.
Item pro conuiuacione pauperum scolarium in die sancti Nicholai — xvi s.
Item pro pergameno et scriptura huius compoti, ut placet iudicibus — xiiii d.
Item pro distribucione facta inter regentes — iiii lib. xviii s. viii d.
Item scribe Uniuersitatis pro stipendio suo hoc anno — iiii marc'
Item magistris superuisoribus scolarum grammaticalium — xiii s. iiii d.
Item pro expensis diminutis, ut placet iudicibus — liii s. iiii d.
Item pro pecuniis distributis inter pauperes scolares de oblationibus in die sancte Scolastice — iii s. iiii d.
Item pro refectione facta auditoribus compoti, ut placet iudicibus — xxx s.
Item magistris collectoribus reddituum Uniuersitatis — xiii s. iiii d.
Item Collegio Ballioli pro quieto redditu nouarum scolarum theologie — vii s.
Item abbati de Eynsham pro quadam pensione annua Aule Bouine — iii s.
Item pro expensis factis in adquisitione pecuniarum ab abbate de Eynsham — viii d.
Item pro conduccione et renouatione armorum, ut placet iudicibus — xxx s.
Item priori sancte Frideswide pro pensione annua — iii s. iiii d.
Item Cancellario et aliis magistris pro expensis factis Londoniis — vi lib. x s.

Summa totalis omnium solutorum lxiii lib. vii s. ix d., et sic debet Uniuersitas antiquis procuratoribus xxii s. i d. ob. prouiso tamen quod predicti computantes onerent se ad satisfaciendum carpintariis predictis in reparacionibus predictarum scolarum theologie.

Compotus magistrorum More & Barteram collectorum reddituum Uniuersitatis Oxonie anno domini MCCCCLXXIIII.

Primo de Aula Nigra — xv s.

Item de Magna Scola iuris canonici liii s. iiii d.
Item de orto annexo eidem scole xvi d.
Item de Aula Bouina xl s.
Item de Aula Willelmi in Kybalstrete xx d.
Item de Aula Mureligorum iiii s.
Item de Aula Tenchewyke xiii s. iiii d.
Item de orto iuxta ecclesiam sancti Egidii xvi d.
Item de orto adiacente Nouo Hospicio vi s. viii d.

Summa receptorum vi lib. xvi s. viii d.

Unde petunt allocari pro Aula Bouina viii s. ii d. ob.
Item in reparacionibus factis in scolis canonistarum iii s. vi d.
Item in reparacionibus factis in Aula Nigra ii s. viii d.
Item in reparacionibus factis in Aula Mureligorum ii s. x d.
Item pro decasu unius camere non occupate in Aula Bouina x s.

Summa allocatorum xxvii s. ii d. ob.; et sic clare remanent v lib. ix s. v d. ob.

7.

[April 17, 1477—April 30, 1478.]

Compotus magistrorum Rogeri Hanley & Thome Permenter procuratorum Uniuersitatis Oxonie anno domini millesimo ccc septuagesimo septimo a decimo septimo die mensis Aprilis usque ad tricesimum diem eiusdem mensis anno domini MCCCC septuagesimo octauo.

In primis reddunt compotum pro condicionibus graciarum xvi lib. ix s. viii d.
Item de suscipientibus gradus hoc anno pro communis & dim' li s. v d.
Item de abbate & conuentu de Eynsham ad pascendum centum pauperes scolares xvi s.
Item de abbate & conuentu de Eynsham pro distribucione facienda inter regentes lii s.
Item de abbate & conuentu de Osney pro consimili distribucione fienda xxvi s. viii d.
Item de docentibus grammaticam hoc anno xl s.
Item pro diuersis transgressionibus factis hoc anno vii s. viii d.

Item de cista quinque clauium pro expensis in vigiliis sanctorum Iohannis & Petri v lib.
Item de cista quinque clauium pro solucione facta antiquis procuratoribus, scilicet magistris Bettis & Sowthworth v lib.
Item de cista quinque clauium pro novo libro fiendo xl s.
Item de cista quinque clauium pro expensis factis in Scaccario domini regis xl s.
Item de oblacionibus burgencium in die sancte Scolastice iii s. iiii d.
Item de collectoribus reddituum Uniuersitatis iiii lib. xii s. x d.

Summa totalis receptorum xliiii lib. xix s. vii d.

In primis soluta pro Uniuersitate pro oblacionibus magistrorum et aliis expensis in exequiis Reginaldi Bedelli & Walteri Grey ix s.
Item capellano Uniuersitatis pro stipendio suo hoc anno vi s. viii d.
Item proclamatori ville pro quinque proclamationibus xx d.
Item pro delacione crucis & cereorum in septem processionibus hoc anno ii s. iiii d.
Item pro cera rubra & papiro v d.
Item diacono & subdiacono seruientibus in missis Uniuersitatis vi s.
Item scribe Uniuersitatis pro stipendio suo iiii marc'
Item iudicibus domini regis in vino & cerotecis tempore estiuali ii s. viii d.
Item iudicibus domini regis in vino & cirotecis tempore quadragesimali ii s. viii d.
Item in expensis factis pro Uniuersitate in Scaccario domini Regis per Henricum Michegood xl s.
Item in expensis factis in vigiliis sanctorum Iohannis & Petri v lib. xvi s.
Item pro cirpis et cereis in eisdem vigiliis iii s. iiii d.
Item clerico parochiali sancti Petri in oriente pro pulsacione ad sermones in Quadragesima ii s. iiii d.
Item pro custodia pacis in nocturnis vigiliis, ut placet iudicibus iii lib.
Item in expensis factis in acquisicione pensionis de Eynsham viii d.
Item pro scriptura & materia libri procuratoris iii lib. xvii s. iiii d.
Item pro liminacione eiusdem libri xxv s. viii d.
Item pro ligatura eiusdem libri vii s. ii d.
Item pro pare plusculorum [1] eiusdem libri xii s.

[1] Clasps.

Item procuratoribus & aliis magistris pro copia superuidenda eiusdem libri, ut placet iudicibus xxiii s. iiii d.
Item pro laboribus scriptoris pro perquisicione copie eiusdem libri, ut placet iudicibus xl d.
Item pro delacione scabellorum artistarum in vesperiis ii s. viii d.
Item pro reparacione horilogii iiii s. viii d.
Item clerico pro custodia horilogii iiii s.
Item plumbario pro reparacionibus factis circa tectum librarie Uniuersitatis ii s. viii d.
Item pro custodia & mundacione domus congregacionis ii s. viii d.
Item pro conduccione & renouacione armorum, ut placet iudicibus iii lib.
Item pro pulsatione in crastino Natiuitatis beate Marie iiii d.
Item superuisoribus status ciste de Gyldforde per deliberacionem congregacionis x s.
Item pro cereis in exequiis ducis Gloucestrie iii s. viii d.
Item pro delacione caparum & candelabrorum in eisdem exequiis iiii d.
Item clerico pro pulsacione & pro aliis suis laboribus in eisdem xii d.
Item collegio Regali & parochie pro composicione luminis in eisdem exequiis ii s.
Item procuratoribus antiquis magistris Bettis & Southworth vi lib. vii s. ix d.
Item pro distributione fienda inter regentes v lib. xviii s. viii d.[1]
Item abbati de Eynsham pro quadam pensione annua Aule Bouine iii s.
Item collegio Ballioli pro quieto redditu nouarum scolarum vii s.
Item pro diminutis expensis ut placet iudicibus liii s. iiii d.
Item pro conuiuacione scolarium in die sancti Nicholai xvi s.
Item pro emendacione baculi inferioris bedelli iuris x s.
Item pro expensis factis commissario & aliis in visitando redditus Uniuersitatis iiii s. vi d. ob.
Item magistris superuisoribus scolarum grammaticalium xiii s. iiii d.
Item in expensis factis nocturnis vigiliis, iudicibus domini regis presentibus & aliis extraneis, ad mandatum domini Cancellarii quando unus frater erat occisus xxiiii s. iiii d.

[1] This sum was written at first £3 18*s*. 8*d*., which is the usual amount; when it was raised by £2 the total at the end was raised also.

Item priori sancte Frideswide pro quadam annua pensione iii s. iiii d.
Item in expensis factis ad brigam sedandam[1] inter duas aulas xiiii s. vi d.
Item pro corda magne campane in ecclesia beate Marie xx d.
Item pro pecuniis distributis in die sancte Scolastice inter pauperes scolares iii s. iiii d.
Item pro ly bawdryk pro magna compana viii d.
Item pro refeccione facta auditoribus huius compoti, ut placet iudicibus xxxiii s. iiii d.
Item pro scriptura & pergameno huius compoti, ut placet iudicibus xiiii d.
Item pro diuersis expensis factis per Cancellarium Londoniis pro diuersis negociis Uniuersitatis liii s. iiii d.

Summa totalis omnium solutorum li lib. xix s. ii d. ob.

Mem. quod summa solutorum excedit summam receptorum vii lib. xix s. vii d. ob., quam summam dicti magistri habent recipere a procuratoribus[2] & quiete recesserunt.

On the dorse.

Compotus magistrorum Haukyns & Park collectorum reddituum Uniuersitatis anno domini MCCCCLXXVII.

Primo de Aula Bouina xl s.
Item de Nicholao Croke pro orto a dorso scolarum canonistarum xvi d.
Item a doctore Salter pro scolis canonistarum iiii marc.
Item de Aula Nigra xv s.
Item pro Aula sancti Willelmi in Kyballestrete xx d.
Item de Aula Mureligorum iiii s.
Item pro Aula Tenchewyk xiii s. iiii d.
Item de orto adiacente in Novo Hospicio vi s. viii d.
Item de collegio Ballioli pro Aula Passerina ii s.
Item de Iohanne Rede sclatter pro quodam orto iuxta ecclesiam sancti Egidii xvi d.

Summa totalis vi lib. xviii s. viii d.

Summa receptorum reddituum iiii lib. xii s. x d.

[1] Spelt 'cedandam'. Wood amplifies this entry in an amusing way. He assumes that the visit of the judges was occasioned by the dispute between the halls, but there is no proof that it was so (Gutch, i. 631).

[2] i. e. the new proctors.

Unde petunt allocari pro salariis suis xiii s. iiii d.
Item petunt allocari pro reparacione Aule Bouine xi s. ix d.
Et pro camra [*sic*] eiusdem Aule x s.
Item pro reparacione facta per magistrum Sawlter[1] ii s. i d.
Item pro Catte Halle v s. viii d.
Item pro Aula Nigra iii s.

quas reparaciones reseruamus domino Cancellario doctori Wrangwys et magistro Colman ut finiant et terminent ante festum Pentecostes.

8.

[April 7, 1478—April 22, 1479.]

IHESVS

Compotus magistrorum Galfridi Simeon et David Ireland procuratorum Uniuersitatis Oxonie anno domini millesimo quadringentesimo septuagesimo octauo a septimo die mensis Aprilis usque ad vicesimum secundum diem eiusdem mensis in anno domini millesimo quadringentesimo septuagesimo nono.

In primis reddunt compotum de compositionibus quinque doctorum viz. Archebolde, Lawe, Rotstoke, Bauarde, Iopi Portugalensis xxxviii li. xiii s. iiii d.
Item a magistro Egcombe in decretis licenciato in parte compositionis sue iii lib. vi s. viii d.
Item de condicionibus graciarum hoc anno xxxv lib. ix s. vii d.
Item suscipientibus gradus hoc anno pro communis et dimidiis iii lib. ix s. x d.
Item de abbate et conuentu de Eynsham ad pascendum pauperes scolares xvi s.
Item de abbate et conuentu de Eynsham pro distributione facienda inter regentes lii s.
Item de abbate et conuentu de Oseney pro consimili distribucione fienda xxvi s. viii d.
Item pro diuersis transgressionibus et perturbacionibus pacis hoc anno xliiii s. viii d.
Item a cista quinque clauium ad satisfaciendum antiquis procuratoribus scilicet magistris Hanley & Parmenter iiii lib.

[1] Doctor Gilbert Salter who held Canon School; see the accounts for the year 1488.

Item de oblacionibus burgensium in die sancte Scolastice iii s. iiii d.
Item de collectoribus reddituum Uniuersitatis v lib. v s. i d.

Summa totalis receptorum lxxxxvii lib. vii s. ii d.

Solutiones:—

In primis imposite sunt in cistam quinque clauium xxxii lib.
Item solutum est procuratoribus superioris anni magistris Hanley et Permenter vi lib. xix s. vii d. ob.
Item capellano Uniuersitatis ad complementum stipendii sui hoc anno vi s. viii d.
Item scribe Uniuersitatis pro stipendio suo liii s. iiii d.
Item pro delacione Crucis in quinque processionibus xx d.
Item diacono et subdiacono legentibus euangelia et epistolas in missis vii s. iiii d.
Item proclamatori ville pro quinque proclamationibus hoc anno xx d.
Item clerico parochiali ecclesie sancti Petri in oriente pro pulsatione ad sermones in Quadragesima ii s. iiii d.
Item pro delacione scabellorum in tribus vesperiis artistarum ii s.
Item clerico pro custodia horilogii ii s. viii d.
Item solutum clerico pro custodia et mundacione domus congregationis ii s. viii d.
Item eidem pro laboribus in exequiis ducis Glowcestrie xii d.
Item eidem pro pulsatione in crastino Natiuitatis iiii d.
Item in oblationibus magistrorum in missis Reginaldi et Grey et aliis expensis in eisdem viii s.
Item solutum Gare pro membrana et scriptura litterarum patentium domino episcopo Londoniensi viii d.
Item solutum Henrico Mychegoud pro expensis factis superiori anno in Scaccario domini regis pro assisa panis et ceruisie per deliberationem Congregationis xlvi s. iii d.
Item pro conduccione et renouatione armorum ut placet iudicibus iii lib.
Item in expensis factis Comissario, Procuratoribus et Bidellis visitando Aulas et redditus Uniuersitatis iiii s. vi d.
Item solutum magistro Thome Keruer per deliberationem Congregationis pro expensis in solicitando dominum Londoniensem episcopum pro perfeccione operis scholarum theologie xx s.

Item solutum Iohanni Boswell per deliberationem congregationis equitanti ad dominum regem in negociis Uniuersitatis pro lathomis — xx s.

Item pro factura descorum et formularum in domo capitulari Augustinensium pro doctoribus sacre theologie — vi s. viii d.

Item solutum Priori eiusdem domus pro conduccione domus capitularis — ii s.

Item pro reparacione sere et ostii domus congregationis et pro nova clavi — xii d.

Item pro custodia pacis in nocturnis vigiliis, ut placet iudicibus — iii lib.

Item solutum pro cereis in obitu domini Londoniensis episcopi — ii s. ii d.

Item pro compositione inter rectores ecclesie beate Marie et Uniuersitatem pro eisdem cereis — ii s.

Item solutum clericis Animarum [*sic*] pro delatione caparum et candelabrorum in eisdem exequiis — iiii d.

Item solutum pro cereis in obitu ducis Glowcestrie — ii s. ii d.

Item pro compositione rectoribus ecclesie, ut supra — ii s.

Item solutum clericis Collegii Animarum pro delatione caparum etc. — iiii d.

Item solutum proclamatori pro proclamatione exequiarum — iiii d.

Item pro reparacione baculi inferioris bidelli facultatis Artium per decretum Congregationis — xxiii s. i d.

Item pro reparacione horilogii — xiiii d.

Item pro reparacione pillorie — xii d.

Item in vino dato assistentibus procuratori Australi transeundo ad hospitale sancti Bartholomei pro caucionibus a cista Warwici furatis — xii d.

Item pro reparacione eiusdem ciste et factura serarum et clavium — viii d.

Item in expensis apud Henksey quando dominus Cancellarius, Comissarius, doctor Licheffeld, magister Battis, magister Knygtley, procuratores cum aliis magistris conuenerunt ibidem, tractaturi de certis negociis Uniuersitatis et de voluntate domini Londoniensis episcopi circa perfeccionem operis nouarum scolarum — vi s. iiii d.

Item in cera pro litteris et indenturis sigillandis domino episcopo Londoniensi — iii d.

Item pro scriptura litterarum et pro abortiuo — viii d.

Item pro cirotecis datis domino Londoniensi episcopo et magistris Licheffeld et Knygtley iii s. viii d.

Item in vino dato scolaribus assistentibus procuratoribus visitando iudices domini regis apud Henksey ad mandatum domini Cancellarii pro concilianda eorum benevolentia xviii d.

Item pro minutis expensis, ut placet iudicibus liii s. iiii d.

Item solutum pro pixide pro litteris deferendis domino episcopo London' ii d.

Item pro scriptura statutorum de nouo editorum in nouo libro procuratoris Australis xii d.

Item pro conductione duorum equorum et aliis expensis visitando dominum Cancellarium pro iuramento Wlielmi Orchard xii d.

Item pro claui et reparacione unius cere ciste munimentorum vii d.

Item pro exemplificacione certarum bullarum et pro pergameno xii d.

Item priori sancte Frideswide pro annua pensione iii s. iiii d.

Item in refectione facta pauperibus scolaribus in festo sancti Nicholai xvi s.

Item pro pecuniis distributis pauperibus scolaribus in die sancte Scolastice iii s. iiii d.

Item magistris superuisoribus scolarum grammaticalium xiii s. iiii d.

Item pro distributione fienda inter regentes iii lib. xviii s. viii d.

Item abbati de Eynsham pro quadam pensione annua Aule Bouine iii s.

Item pro cera et papiro vii d.

Item solutum collegio Ballioli pro annua pensione vii s.

Item pro refeccione facta auditoribus huius compoti ut placet eisdem xl s.

Item pro pergameno et scriptura huius compoti, ut placet iudicibus xiiii d.

Item alocatum est magistro Galfrido pro curacione duorum[1] assistencium bachelariorum grauiter vulneratorum in custodia pacis liii s. iiii d

Item allocatum est predictis procuratoribus propter certa pericula emergencia eisdem tempore pestis omnibus

[1] Wood expands this into 'several'.

iudicibus eorum visa racionabilia & allocatione digna
iii lib. vi s. viii d.

Summa omnium solutorum lxxiiii lib. ii s. vi d. ob.; et sic remanent soluend' Uniuersitati preter soluciones superius positas xxiii lib. iiii s. vii d. ob.

Et sic de claro remanent ex procuracione predictorum computancium lv lib. iiii s. vii d. ob., et sic quieti dimissi recesserunt in pace.

Compotus magistrorum Willielmi Lynche et Walteri Aston collectorum reddituum Uniuersitatis anno domini millesimo cccc septuagesimo octavo.

Primo de Aula Bouina xl s.
Item de Nicholao Croke pro orto a dorso scolarum Canonistarum xvi d.
Item a Doctore Salter pro scolis Canonistarum iiii marcas
Item de Aula Nigra xv s.
Item de Aula sancti Wlielmi alias dict' Kibalstret iiii s.
Item de Aula Murilegorum iiii s.
Item de Aula Tenchwike xiii s. iiii d.
Item de orto adiacente Nouo Hospicio vi s. viii d.
Item de Collegio Ballioli pro Aula Pascerina ii s.
Item de Iohanne Rede sclater pro quodam orto iuxta ecclesiam sancti Egidii xvi d.

Summa reddituum vii lib. xii d.

Unde petunt allocari pro camera in Aula Bouina x s.
Item pro reparacionibus factis in eadem Aula ut patent in cedula v s. iiii d.
Item pro sedilibus et clauis et labore carpentarii in scola Canonistarum xv d.
Item pro Aula Vulielmi in Kibalstret iiii s.
unde ii s. debentur per magistrum Fulconem Salysbury & residui duo solidi in decasu fiunt.
Item pro salariis suis xiii s. iiii d.

Summa allocatorum xxxv s. xi d.; et sic remanent v libre v solidi et i d.; quam summam soluerunt iudicibus et quieti recesserunt computantes.

9.

[April 22, 1479—April 13, 1480.]

Compotus magistrorum Roberti Gosebourne et Iohannis Foster procuratorum Uniuersitatis Oxonie anno domini MCCCC septuagesimo nono a vicesimo secundo die mensis Aprilis usque ad xiii diem eiusdem mensis in anno domini MCCCC octogesimo.

Reddunt compotum de receptis

In primis de composicionibus septem componentium videlicet Egcombe, Sapcot, Preston, Kenyngale, Bokyngham, Wendouer et Haley[1]	lx lib.
Item de condicionibus graciarum hoc anno	x lib. xi s. v d.
Item de suscipientibus gradus hoc anno pro communis et dimidiis	v lib. iiii s. x d.
Item de magistro Luke vicario sancti Laurentii London'[2] ex dono Uniuersitati	iii lib. vi s. viii d.
Item de abbate et conuentu de Eynsham pro distribucione fienda inter regentes	lii s.
Item de abbate et conuentu de Oseney pro eadem distribucione	xxvi s. viii d.
Item pro diuersis transgressionibus et perturbacionibus pacis hoc anno	xvii s. ix d.
Item de cista quinque clauium	v lib.
Item de oblacionibus burgensium in die sancte Scolastice	iii s. iiii d.
Item de collectoribus reddituum Uniuersitatis	iiii lib. xvi s. v d.
Item de abbate et conuentu de Eynsham ad pascendum pauperes scolares	xvi s.

Summa totalis receptorum lxxxxiiii lib. xv s. i d.

Unde computant soluta :—

In primis inposite sunt in cistam quinque clauium	xxxvi lib.
Item capellano Uniuersitatis pro stipendio suo	vi s. viii d.
Item scribe Uniuersitatis pro stipendio suo	liii s. iiii d.
Item pro delacione Crucis in septem processionibus	ii s. iiii d.
Item pro diacono et subdiacono legentibus ewangelia et epistolas in missis pro benefactoribus Uniuersitatis	vii s. viii d.

[1] The name seems to be altered to Hall; it is probably the Dr. Hall who gave to the University in this year a tenement next to Beef Hall.

[2] Richard Luke, vicar of St. Lawrence Jewry 1458–84, presented by Balliol.

Item proclamatori ville pro quinque proclamationibus xx d.
Item in oblacionibus magistrorum in missis Reginaldi et Grey et aliis expensis in eisdem viii s. vii d.
Item pro duobus paribus cerothecarum domino episcopo Londoniensi ex mandato Cancellarii ii s.
Item doctori Lechefyld et magistro Knyȝley et suis seruientibus pro vectura ducentarum marcarum, in cerothecis ex mandato domini Cancellarii [1] iii s. ii d.
Item in vino dato eisdem xx d.
Item pro claue noua ad cistam quatuor clauium iiii d.
Item pro pulsacione in crastino Natiuitatis sancte Marie iiii d.
Item pro cereis in exequiis et missa domini Kempe archiepiscopi ii s. ii d.
Item pro compositione inter rectores ecclesie beate Marie et Uniuersitatem pro eisdem cereis ii s.
Item clericis collegii Animarum pro delacione caparum et candelabrorum in eisdem exequiis iiii d.
Item in cerotecis datis iudicibus Urswyke & aliis xx d.
Item in vino dato eisdem xvi d.
Item pro expensis factis in vigiliis sanctorum Iohannis et Petri et Pauli [2] vi lib. xvii s. xi d. ob.
Item pro cirpis & cereis in eisdem vigiliis iii s. iiii d.
Item pro custodia pacis in nocturnis vigiliis, ut placet iudicibus iiii lib.[3]
Item clerico parochiali sancti Petri in oriente pro pulsacione ad sermones in Quadragesima ii s. iiii d.
Item in vino dato domino Ricardo filio Regine ex mandato domini Cancellarii [4] xx d.
Item in cerotecis eidem datis xvi d.
Item in expensis factis in citando magistros Cartmale & Kele [5] per deliberationem congregationis; ad istam summam soluendam tenentur predicti duo magistri citati ad instanciam Uniuersitatis xvi s. xi d.
Item solutum clerico Iohanni pro custodia horelogii iiii s.

[1] See the receipt for the money, dated Sept. 3, 1479 (*Ep. Ac.*, p. 451).

[2] A note in another hand: 'Causa excessus huius stili fuit concursus dominorum ad tunc intuencium et venientium ad Uniuersitatem'.

[3] A marginal note: 'Et causa huius excessus fuit propter presenciam dominorum tunc presencium tempore gradus suscepti magistri Leonelli'.

[4] Lord Richard Grey, son of the Queen by her first marriage; he was knighted in 1473 and beheaded in 1483.

[5] Cp. *Ep. Ac.*, p. 450.

Item eidem pro delacione scabellorum in vesperiis artistarum xvi d.
Item eidem pro mundacione & custodia domus congregacionis ii s. viii d.
Item eidem pro laboribus suis in exequiis ducis Glowcestrie xii d.
Item in expensis factis commissario, procuratoribus, & bedellis in visitando redditus Uniuersitatis iiii s. x d.
Item priori fratrum Augustinencium pro domo sua capitulari hoc anno iii s. iiii d.
Item pro minutis expensis, ut placet iudicibus iii lib. vi s. viii d.
(ex simili causa, ut supra)
Item pro scriptura feoffamentorum cuiusdam domus date Uniuersitati per doctorem Halle xii d.
Item in vino dato Maiori, Aldermannis & balliuis quando data erat possessio xx d.
Item pro feodo balliuorum pro possessione iii s. v d.
Item pro vino dato doctori Halle viii d.
Item in exequiis & missa domini ducis Glowcestrie pro cereis ii s.
Item pro composicione inter rectores ecclesie, ut supra ii s.
Item clericis collegii Animarum pro delacione caparum &c. iiii d.
Item preconi pro proclamatione exequiarum iiii d.
Item in pecuniis distributis pauperibus scolaribus in die sancte Scolastice iii s. iiii d.
Item pro una corda ad magnam campanam xxi d.
Item in refeccione facta pauperibus scolaribus in die sancti Nicholai xvi s.
Item pro duobus pixidibus pro citacionibus ii d.
Item pro cera, papiro et pergameno viii d.
Item in expensis factis in adquirendo pensionem de Eynsham iiii d.
Item pro reparacione bawdryke ad magnam campanam ii d.
Item pro reparacione le claper eiusdem campane viii s.
Item alias Urswyke iudici, duobus assergenticiis, domino Ricardo Harcort & domino Mouford, in cerotecis ii s.
Item pro conduccione & renouacione armorum, ut placet iudicibus lvi s. viii d.
Item priori sancte Frideswyde pro annua pensione iii s. iiii d.
Item magistris superuisoribus scolarum grammaticalium xiii s. iiii d.
Item pro distributione fienda inter regentes iii lib. xviii s. viii d.
Item abbati de Eynsham pro annua pensione Aule Bouine iii s.

Item Doctori Bokyngham per graciam sibi ab Uniuersitate concessam de compositione sua — xxvi s. viii d.

Item Doctori Egcombe de composicione soluta magistris Galfrido Symeon & Dauyd Yrland[1] — iii lib. vi s. viii d.

Item pro refeccione facta auditoribus huius compoti, ut placet eisdem — xxxix s.

Item pro pargameno & scriptura huius compoti, ut placet iudicibus — xiii d.

Item collegio Ballioli pro annua pensione — vii s.

Item in expensis procuratoris borialis missi episcopo London' per decretum congregationis — xl s.

Item eidem alia vice visitando predictum dominum episcopum & procurando a magistro Luke[2] Universitati quinque mercas [*sic*] — x s.

Item procuratori australi allocatum est pro expensis & medicinis factis circa seruum quemdam vulneratum & postea mortuum — l s.

Summa omnium solutorum lxxix lib. xx d. ob., et sic remanent soluend' Uniuersitati preter soluciones predictas xv lib. xiii s. iiii d. ob., quam quidem summam predicti computantes soluerunt; et remanent de claro ex procuratione predictorum procuratorum li lib. xiii s. iiii d. ob., & sic eos quietos dimisimus in pace.

Mem. quod magistri Robertus Gosborne & Iohannes Foster honerati sunt in vi lib. xiii s. iiii d. solvendis Uniuersitati ultra omnem summam receptam in tempore compoti.

Compotus magistrorum Thome Wodward et Nicholai Minskype collectorum reddituum Uniuersitatis anno domini millesimo cccc septuagesimo nono

In primis de Aula Bouina — xl s.

Item de Nicholao Croke — xvi d.

Item de Doctore Salter pro scola Canonistarum — iiii marc'

Item de Aula Nigra — xv s.

Item de Aula sancti Willelmi alias dict' Kybalstrete — iiii s.

Item de Aula Mureligorum — iiii s.

Item de Aula Tenchwyke — xiii s. iiii d.

Item de orto adiacente Novo Hospicio iuxta ecclesiam sancte Marie Magdalene — vi s. viii d.

[1] The proctors of the previous year.
[2] i.e. Richard Luke, vicar of St. Lawrence Jewry, London.

Item de collegio Ballioli pro Aula Pascerina ii s.
Item de Iohanne Rede pro orto iuxta ecclesiam sancti Egidii xvi d.

Summa vii lib. xii d.

Unde petunt allocari pro camera in Aula Bouina x s.
Item pro reparacionibus in eadem, ut patet per billam x s. ii d.
Item pro reparacionibus Aula Nigre, ut patet per billam vi s. i d.
Item pro Aula sancti Willelmi iiii s.
Item pro reparacionibus scole Canonistarum xii d.
Item pro salariis suis xiii s. iiii d.

Summa allocatorum xliiii s. vii d., et sic remanent iiii lib. xvi s. v d., quam summam soluerunt iudicibus tunc debutatis [*sic*] & sic quieti dimissi sunt.

10.

[May 10, 1481—April 17, 1482.]

Compotus magistrorum Willelmi Porter et Radulphi Hampsterley procuratorum Uniuersitatis Oxonie anno domini millesimo cccc octogesimo primo a decimo die mensis Maii usque ad septimum decimum diem mensis Aprilis anno domini millesimo quadringentesimo octogesimo secundo.

In primis reddunt compotum de composicionibus quatuor doctorum theologie, uidelicet Morgan, Browne et Richeforde fratrum ordinis Predicatorum, et Wyȝth ordinis Minorum xxvi lib. xiii s. iiii d.
Item de magistro Foster de arreragiis sui et magistri Gosborne pro compositione doctoris Kenyngale, ordinis Carmelitarum vi lib. xiii s. iiii d.
Item de condicionibus graciarum hoc anno xxi lib. xx d.
Item de suscipientibus gradus hoc anno pro integris communis & dimidiis lviii s. iii d.
Item de abbate & conuentu de Eynsham ad pascendum pauperes scolares xvi s.
Item de abbate & conuentu de Eynsham pro distributione facienda inter regentes lii s.
Item de abbate & conuentu de Oseney pro consimili distributione fienda xxvi s. viii d.

Item pro diuersis transgressionibus et perturbacionibus pacis hoc anno xxxvii s. iiii d.
Item a cista quinque clauium pro noua edificacione cuiusdam magne camere in Aula Bouina per decretum congregationis xx lib.
Item a cista quinque clauium pro expensis factis in vigiliis sanctorum Iohannis et Petri & Pauli vi lib.
Item a collectoribus reddituum Uniuersitatis v lib. ii s. viii d.
Item pro duobus falsis regalibus repertis in cista quinque clauium iii s. iiii d.
Item de oblationibus burgensium in die sancte Scolastice iii s. iiii d.
Item a cista quinque clauium ad edificium scolarum Canonistarum per decretum congregationis liii s. iiii d.

Summa totalis receptorum lxxxxviii lib. xv d.

Soluciones:—

In primis imposite sunt in cistam quinque clauium quinto die Iulii in presencia doctoris Suttone, tunc Comissarii Uniuersitatis, & doctorum Tayler & Fyziamys xiii li. vi s. viii d.
Item eodem die reposite sunt in una bursa cum xx lib. datis a venerabili viro magistro Iohanne Bowser ad edificium scolarum Canonistarum per decretum congregationis de composicionibus huius anni xiii li. vi s. viii d.
Item in expensis factis circa edificium magne camere in Aula Bouina una cum edificio camere & reparacionibus unius muri in parte occidentali aule, ut patet per billam compoti facti coram doctoribus & magistris ad hoc deputatis per congregationem xxiii lib. iiii s. ii d. ob.
Item solutum est pro viginti una bigatis lapidum pro edificio scolarum iuris canonici & quelibet bigata continet quatuor decem[1] pedes, minus in toto quatuor pedibus xliii s. iiii d.
Item pro cariagio eorundem lapidum x s. vi d.
Item est solutum capellano Uniuersitatis pro complemento stipendii sui vi s. viii d.
Item eidem pro diuersis missis ex statutis ix d.

[1] A cart-load is now 27 cubic feet or more, according to the state of the road; with two horses as much as 50 feet.

Cartage 6d a load

Item est solutum tabellioni Uniuersitatis pro stipendio suo liii s. iiii d.
Item est solutum pro delatione crucis hoc anno in duodecem processionibus quarum quatuor habite sunt in tempore magne vacacionis ad optatum regis iiii s.
Item diacono & subdiacono legentibus evangelia & epistolas in missis pro benefactoribus Uniuersitatis vi s. iiii d.
Item proclamatori ville pro vi proclamationibus habitis hoc anno ii s.
Item est solutum clerico parochiali ecclesie sancti Petri in oriente pro pulsatione ad sermones in Quadragesima ii s. iiii d.
Item pro delatione scabellorum in tribus vesperiis artistarum ii s.
Item est solutum clerico ecclesie beate Marie pro custodia horrilogii iiii s.
Item solutum est clerico pro custodia & mundacione domus congregacionis ii s. viii d.
Item eidem pro laboribus in exequiis ducis Glocestrie xii d.
Item eidem pro pulsatione in crastino Natiuitatis beate Marie iiii d.
Item in expensis factis in oblacionibus & aliis in missis Reginaldi & Grey una cum aliis expensis contingentibus vii s. viii d.
Item in expensis factis in vigiliis sanctorum Iohannis & apostolorum Petri & Pauli vi lib. xiii s. iiii d.
Item est solutum pro cirpis et cereis in eisdem iii s. iiii d.
Item pro custodia pacis, ut placet iudicibus iii lib.
Item pro cereis in exequiis & missa domini Kempe quondam episcopi Cantuariensis ii s.
Item in compositione inter rectores ecclesie beate Marie & Uniuersitatem pro eisdem exequiis ii s.
Item clerico collegii Animarum pro delacione caparum et candelabrarum iiii d.
Item est solutum pro preconizacione obitus ducis Glocestrie iiii d.
Item pro cereis in obitu ducis Glowcestrie ii s.
Item solutum est rectoribus ecclesie pro compositione luminis in eisdem ii s.
Item cleric' collegii Animarum pro delacione caparum & candelabrarum iiii d.
Item in vino dato & cerotecis datis domino Stanley in aduentu suo ad villam hoc anno xii s. viii d.
Item in vino & cerotecis datis matri regis & comitisse de Sowtfold & aliis secum venientibus in aduentu suo ad Uniuersitatem hoc anno xvii s. viii d.

Item pro conductione et renouacione armorum, ut placet iudicibus iii lib.

Item pro conductione equorum una cum expensis procuratorum & unius bidelli equitancium Habindoniam ad intimandum Cancellario suam electionem,[1] prout decretum erat per congregationem ii s. viii d.

Item in vino dato domino Edwardo & magistro Iacobo Stanley in primo aduentu eorum ad villam xii s. xi d.

Item solutum est pro tribus unciis argenti emptis ad reparacionem baculi bidelli inferioris in sacra theologia ix s.

Item solutum est Dydycke[2] pro factura et deauracione eiusdem baculi xxiii s. iiii d.

Item est solutum pro reparacione baculi bidelli superioris in facultate artium xviii s.

Item solutum procuratori boriali pro citacione magistri Bryreton, custodis ciste de Danuers, ad reddendum compotum ciste sue vi s. viii d.

Item est solutum pro reparacionibus ciste de Checheley ad manus magistri Haukyns xxii d.

Item solutum est pro cena magistrorum supervidencium statum ciste de Gilforde ii s. iiii d.

Item & in rewardo dato magistris Stevvyns, Ben & Nele pro laboribus in supervisione eiusdem ciste per decretum congregationis v s.

Item pro minutis expensis, ut placet iudicibus iii lib. vi s. viii d.

Item in refectione facta Commissario & aliis magistris audientibus compotum expensarum factarum circa cameram in Aula Bouina vi s. ix d.

Item in vino dato Commissario, procuratoribus & bidellis visitantibus redditus Uniuersitatis ii s. iiii d.

[1] No doubt the re-election of Lionel Woodville to the post of Chancellor, which would normally have taken place about May 1481. Woodville, who became Bishop of Salisbury in 1482, was in charge of the temporalities from Nov. 1481, and had held canonries in the Cathedral for more than ten years. He seems to have resided much at Abingdon, which at that time was in the diocese of Salisbury.

[2] Probably this is identical with Theodoric Rote, one of the first printers at Oxford. He is called Dedych Teutonicus in a register at Magdalen (*Reg. of Magd. Coll.*, p. 10, ed. Macray), while in a rental of 1480 he is Dyryke Dowcheman (*Cart. of Hosp. St. John*, iii. 272). It may seem strange that a printer should be a goldsmith; but to cut seals was part of the work of a goldsmith, and to cut the founts for type was part of the work of a printer. Many of the early printers worked in partnership with goldsmiths or silversmiths.

Item pro expensis Commisarior' [*sic*] & procuratorum visitancium Cancellarium apud Cumnere pro negotiis Uniuersitatis ii s. iiii d.

Item est solutum pro aqua rosarum benedicta in aduentu regis[1] iiii d.

Item est solutum pro tortis conductis in aduentu regis xx d.

Item est solutum clerico pro delacione crucis & aliis laboribus in aduentu regis xii d.

Item eidem pro delacione crucis & aliis laboribus in aduentu matris regis xii d.

Item eidem pro delacione collistrigii ad quadriuium pro punitione unius mulieris bannite iiii d.

Item est solutum tabellioni pro papiro empto pro nouo registro[2] & pro ligatura eiusdem v s. iiii d.

Item est solutum pro laboribus & expensis Thome Fry ad Eynsham pro pecuniis distribuendis in die sancti Nicholai viii d.

Item solutum est Woodman vicecomiti alterius anni pro asisa panis, seruisie & vini pro duobus annis ii d.

Item pro claue & sera ad ipothecam litterarum patencium regis vi d.

Item solutum est priori sancte Frideswyde pro annua pensione iii s. iiii d.

Item in refectione facta pauperibus scolaribus in festo sancti Nicholai xvi s.

Item in pecuniis distributis pauperibus scolaribus in die sancte Scholastice iii s. iiii d.

Item magistris supervisoribus scolarum grammaticalium xiii s. iiii d.

Item pro distributione fienda inter regentes iii lib. xviii s. viii d.

Item abbati de Eynsham pro redditu exeunte de Aula Bouina iii s.

Item collegio Ballioli pro annua pensione vii s.

Item pro pargameno ad registrandum sermones x d.

Item pro pergameno pro indenturis & aquietanciis & aliis hoc anno xvi d.

[1] On Sept. 22, 1481, the King came to Oxford from Woodstock; there was a procession next day, being Sunday (*Reg. of Magd. Coll.*, p. 9, ed. Macray).

[2] As this is a paper register, it cannot be a copy of the Statutes. Perhaps it should be connected with the entry about parchment below, and both paper and parchment were for the *sermones examinatorii* which the Registrar had to record.

Item pro cera & pixidibus ad deferendum litteras & aquietancias hoc anno viii d.
Item pro exemplificacione statutorum diuersarum cistarum episcopo Cantuariensi pro fundacione alterius ciste[1] xii d.
Item pro reparacione facta supra tectum librarie Uniuersitatis iiii d.
Item pro refectione facta auditoribus huius compoti, ut placet eisdem xl s.
Item pro pargameno & scriptura huius compoti, ut placet iudicibus xv d.
Item solutum est pro expensis factis in adquisitione & exactione pecuniarum pro scolis theologie vi s. viii d.
Item solutum est pro una parua cista ponenda in cista quinque clauium ad securiorem custodiam pecuniarum Uniuersitatis xx d.
Item alocatum est procuratori australi pro supervisione edificii circa Aulam Bouinam & alia diuersa xx s.
Item alocatum est procuratoribus pro eorum diligenciis circa melioracionem & promocionem cistarum & reparacionem reddituum & alias causas iudices in hac parte mouentes xx s.

Summa omnium solutorum lxxxxi lib. ix s. viii d. ob. Et sic summa receptorum excedit summam solutorum vi lib. x s. vi d. ob., quam summam predicti computantes soluerunt, et citra istam allocacionem factam receperunt eciam pro graciis concessis illo anno xi s. viii d.; et sic summa de claro remanet vii lib. ii s. ii d. ob., & sic quietos eos dimisimus.

Compotus magistrorum Willelmi Halle et Iohannis Rawe collectorum reddituum Uniuersitatis anno domini millesimo cccc octogesimo primo.

Primo de Aula Bouina xliii s. iiii d.
Item de Nicholao Croke pro orto a dorso scolarum Canonistarum xvi d.
Item a doctore Salter pro scolis Canonistarum liii s. iiii d.
Item de Aula Nigra xv s.
Item pro Aula sancti Willelmi in Kibalstrete iiii s.

[1] This explains the letter of the University to the Archbishop on Feb. 15, 1482; they had heard that he had 'good intentions' to Oxford and hoped that he would carry them out (*Ep. Ac.*, p. 476).

Item de Aula Mureligorum iiii s.
Item de Aula Tenchewyke xiii s. iiii d.
Item de orto adiacente in Nouo Hospicio vi s. viii d.
Item de collegio Ballioli pro Aula Pascerina ii s.
Item de Iohanne Rede, sclatter, pro quodam orto iuxta ecclesiam sancti Egidii xvi d.

Summa reddituum vii lib. iiii s. iiii d.

Unde petunt allocari
In primis pro camera in Aula Bouina que tunc erat in fieri reparacionis x s.
Item pro reparacionibus in eadem Aula xvi d.
Item pro reparacionibus in Aula Nigra xv s.
Item pro vacancia Aule sancti Willelmi per dimidiam partem anni ii s.
Item pro salariis suis xiii s. iiii d.

Summa allocatorum xli s. viii d.; et sic remanent v lib. ii s. viii d., quam summam soluerunt iudicibus tunc deputatis & sic quieti dimissi sunt.

II.

[April 17, 1482—April 9, 1483.]

Compotus magistrorum Thome Karuer & Radulphi Stanhope procuratorum Uniuersitatis Oxonie anno domini MCCCC octogesimo secundo a septimo decimo die mensis Aprilis usque ad nonum diem mensis Aprilis anno domini millesimo quadragintesimo (*sic*) octagesimo tercio.

In primis procuratores reddunt compotum de compositionibus quatuor doctorum in theologia, scilicet doctoris Halstede xiii li. vi s. viii d.
Item ex doctore Auklond pro composicione sua xii li. vi s. viii d.
Item ex doctore Percevalle pro composicione sua vi li. xiii s. iiii d.
Item ex doctore Mores pro composicione sua iiii li. xv s.
Item ex condicionibus graciarum hoc anno & ex magistro Whytney pro graciis concessis in diebus suis xx li.
Item ex suscipientibus gradus hoc anno in integris communis & dimidiis iiii li. vi s. ix d.

Item ex abbate de Eynsame ad pascendum pauperes scolares in die sancti Nicholai xvi s.
Item ex oblacione burgensium in die sancte Scholastice iii s. iiii d.
Item ex convictis hoc anno & perturbantibus pacem xv s. v d.
Item ex collectoribus reddituum Uniuersitatis hoc anno iiii li. ii s. x d.
Item ex abbate de Eynsam pro distributione fienda inter regentes lii s.
Item ex abbate de Oseney pro distribucione simili facienda xxvi s. viii d.

Summa totalis receptorum lxxi li. iiii s. viii d.

Soluciones; in primis in proclamationibus factis hoc anno apud Quadrivium & in Aula Gyldarum ii s. iiii d.
Item clerico Uniuersitatis pro processionibus & domo congregacionis et vesperiis xxi s. xi d.
Item clerico sancti Petri pro pulsacione ad sermones in Quadragesima ii s. iiii d.
Item in itinere ad abbatem Abendone pro privelegiis Universitatis iii s. viii d.
Item in cerothecis eidem iii s.
Item diaconis missarum in oblacionibus[1] magistrorum regencium hoc anno ix s. ii d.
Item tabellioni Universitatis pro stipendio hoc anno liii s. iiii d.
Item capellano Universitatis pro complemento stipendii vi s. viii d.
Item clerico beate Marie virginis pro horrilogio & ministerio in missis iii s. viii d.
Item in expensis ducis Glowcestrie iiii s.
Item in expensis exequiarum domini Kempe iiii s.
Item in pargameno, cera & pixidibus xviii d.
Item pro conduccione & renovacione armorum, ut placet iudicibus iii li.
Item ad missale emptum pro capellano Universitatis xlvi s. viii d.
Item in expensis magistro Whytney in vino x d.
Item in festo sancti Iohannis & Petri vi li. xiii s. x d.

[1] This cannot mean the oblations of the Masters which were made on the days of Walter de Grey and Reginald the Beadle, for they are mentioned subsequently. Possibly there was some solemn opening of the Divinity School this year. As there are no emblems of Edward V and Richard III on the roof, it must have been finished before April 1483.

Item ad unum indumentum pro falsario litterarum	xvi d.
Item in expensis factis in die sancti Nicholai pauperibus	xvi s.
Item uni portanti regias litteras Londonias	xii d.
Item Thome stacionario pro cathenis	vi s. iiii d.
Item pro custodia pacis & nocturnis vigiliis, ut placet iudicibus	iii li.
Item in expensis factis commissario & procuratoribus in visitando aulas & redditus Universitatis	v s. ix d.
Item in preconizacione obitus ducis Glowcestrie	iiii d.
Item priori sancte Frideswide pro annua pensione	iii s. iiii d.
Item in pecunia distribuenda in festo sancte Scholastice	iii s. iiii d.
Item Commissario, doctori Sutton, ducenti a domino Londoniensi centum libras, pro suis expensis	xx s.
Item pro minutis expensis hoc anno, ut placet iudicibus	liii s. iiii d.
Item magistris gramatic' pro stipendio eorum	xiii s. iiii d.
Item pro distributione fienda inter regentes	iii li. xviii s. viii d.
Item in exequiis Reginaldi Grey[1]	vii s. viii d.
Item in cerothecis datis domino Cancellario	ii s. viii d.
Item magistris removentibus libros in libraria & cathenantibus alios	xii d.
Item cuidam transeunti ad Eynsam in festo sancti Nicholai pro pecuniis Uniuersitatis	viii d.
Item in cerothecis datis domino Londoniensi & capellanis suis	iii s. viii d.
Item pro refeccione facta auditoribus compoti, ut placet iudicibus	xl s.
Item collegio Balleoli pro annua pensione	vii s.
Item magistro Willelmo Horcherd equitanti ad dominum Londoniensem pro Universitate	xiii s. iiii d.
Item in expensis in vino dato domino Cancellario ter in vacacione apud Cumnor	xvii s. ix d.
Item in expensis domino Lincolniensi in vino & cerothecis	xvi s. xi d.
Item in cerothecis datis famulis suis	iiii s.
Item in vino dato decano Lincolniensi	v s. ii d.
Item in expensis factis circa magistrum rotulorum	vi s. v d.
Item in expensis factis circa secretarium regis	v s. xi d.
Item iudicibus in vino in diversis temporibus	vii s. x d.
Item in vino magistro Hercorte apud Rewley	v s. vii d.

[1] For 'Reginaldi et Grey'.

Item pro annua pensione Abbatis de Eynsam pro Aula Bovina iii s. iiii d.
Item in cereis in festis sanctorum Iohannis & Petri iiii s.
Item cuidam transeunti ad Eynsam pro pecunia Universitatis distribuenda inter regentes xii d.
Item scribenti hanc rotulam xvi d.
Item in vino dato magistro Hulse & in cerothecis iii s.
Item allocatum est procuratoribus pro eorum laboribus & diligenciis in procurando comoda Universitatis, ut placet iudicibus xlvi s. ix d.

Summa omnium solutorum xli li. iiii s. viii d.; et sic remanent solvend' Universitati, facto sufficienti calculo xxx li. de claro, quam quidem summam receperunt iudices et sic computantes predicti procuratores quieti recesserunt.

On the dorse.

Expense facte circa scolas Canonistarum

In primis a cista quinque clavium per decretum congregacionis iii li.
Item pridie Idus Augusti v li.
Idem Idibus Septembris iiii li.
Item alio tempore ut patet in omnibus hiis summis in registro in cista predicta xx s.

Summa receptorum xiii li.

Soluciones; in primis quarto die Augusti pro vectura 30 bigatarum xv s.
Item quibusdam mensurantibus lapides, ut videretur quod quelibet bigata contineret quatuordecem pedes iiii d.
Item pridie Idus Augusti pro vectura 20 bigatarum x s.
Item eodem die pro lapidibus mag. W. Horchord v li. iii s. iiii d.
Item mensurantibus lapides vi d.
Item pro vectura 10 bigatarum v s.
Item Prytur pro vectura sex bigatarum iii s.
Item famulo magistri W. Horcherd pro vectura 10 bigatarum v s.
Item eidem pro vectura 10 bigatarum v s.
Item pro vectura unius bigate vi d.
Item pro vectura 20 bigatarum x s.
Item pro lapidibus mag. W. Horcherd v li. ii s. iiii d.

Summa solutorum xiii li., et sic facto compoto recesserunt quieti procuratores computantes.

Compotus magistrorum Georgii Burton et Iohannis Rede collectorum reddituum Uniuersitatis anno domini MCCCC octogesimo secundo.

Primo de Aula Bovina	xliii s. iiii d.
Item a Nicholao Croke pro orto a dorso scolarum Canonistarum	xvi d.
Item pro scolis Canonistarum	liii s. iiii d.
Item de Aula Nigra	xv s.
Item pro Aula sancti Willelmi in Kybalstrete	iiii s.
Item de Aula Mureligorum	iiii s.
Item de Aula Tenchewek	xiii s. iiii d.
Item de orto adiacente Novo Hospicio	vi s. viii d.
Item de collegio Balleoli pro Aula Passerina	ii s.
Item de Iohanne Rede sclatter pro quodam orto iuxta ecclesiam sancti Egidii	xvi d.

Summa reddituum vii li. iiii s. iiii d.

Unde petunt allocari

In primis pro reparationibus factis in Aula Bovina	ix s. vi d. ob.
Item pro reparationibus factis in Aula Nigra	xxiii d.
Item allocatum est doctori Gylbard[1] de annua pensione sua pro medietate unius anni	x s.
Item debetur nobis pro dimidia pensione unius anni a doctore Salter	xxvi s. viii d.
Item pro salariis collectorum	xiii s. iiii d.

Summa allocatorum iii li. xvii d. ob.

12.

[April 16, 1488—April 29, 1489.]

Compotus magistrorum Iohannis Hosey & Petri Caseley procuratorum Uniuersitatis Oxonie anno domini millesimo cccc octuagesimo octauo a sexto decimo die mensis Aprilis usque ad uicesimum nonum diem mensis Aprilis anno domini millesimo cccc octuagesimo nono.

In primis reddunt compotum de composicionibus duorum doctorum theologie viz. Maundefelde ordinis predicatorum et Mereke ordinis sancti Augustini	xi lib. vi s. viii d.
Item de condicionibus graciarum hoc anno	viii lib. x s. viii d.

[1] Gilbert Salter, see accounts for 1488.

Item de suscipientibus gradus hoc anno pro integris communis et dimidiis iii lib. xi d.
Item de abbate & conuentu de Eynsham ad pascendum pauperes scolares xvi s. viii d.
Item de abbate & conuentu de Enysham pro distribucione facienda inter regentes lii s.
Item de abbate & conuentu de Oseney pro simili distribucione fienda xxvi s. viii d.
Item de diuersis transgressionibus & perturbacionibus pacis hoc anno xxvi s. viii d.
Item a collectoribus reddituum Uniuersitatis xlv s. viii d.
Item de oblacionibus burgensium in die sancte Scolastice iii s. iiii d.
Item ex donacione doctoris Yue Uniuersitati xl s.
Item pro zona Uniuersitatis inpignorata in cista de Robori ex decreto congregationis vii lib.
Item pro calice inpignorato in cista Wynton' ex eodem decreto iii lib. vi s. viii d.
Item pro armis[1] venditis per procuratorem australem iii s. ii d.
Item pro armis venditis per procuratorem borealem x s.

Summa totalis receptorum xliiii lib. ix s. i d.

Soluciones: inprimis capellano Uniuersitatis pro complemento stipendii sui vi s. viii d.
Item eidem pro diuersis missis ex statutis x d.[2]
Item est solutum tabellioni Uniuersitatis pro complemento stipendii sui liii s. iiii d.
Item diacono & subdiacono legentibus euangelia & epistolas in diuersis missis pro benefactoribus Uniuersitatis vii s. iiii d.
Item proclamatori ville pro quatuor clamacionibus habitis hoc anno apud Quadrivium cum duabus apud Guylhalle ii s.
Item est solutum clerico parochiali ecclesie sancti Petri in oriente in Quadragesima ii s. iiii d.
Item pro delacione scabellorum in quinque vesperiis artistarum iii s. iiii d.

[1] i. e. the forfeited arms of disturbers of the peace.

[2] The total at the end and similar entries in following years show that ix d. is meant.

Item est solutum clerico beate Marie pro custodia horologii iiii s.
Item est solutum eidem pro delacione Crucis in octo processionibus & in aduentu Regis[1] iii s. viii d.
Item eidem pro pulsatione ignitegii ii s.
Item solutum est clerico pro custodia & mundacione domus congregacionis ii s. viii d.
Item eidem pro laboribus in exequiis ducis Glowcestrie & duabus exequiis Kempe hoc anno habitis eo quod mortuus est iii s.
Item eidem pro pulsatione in crastino Natiuitatis beate Marie iiii d.
Item in expensis factis in oblacionibus et aliis in missis Regnoldi Grey[2] una cum aliis expensis contingentibus vi s. vii d.
Item pro expensis factis in vigiliis sancti Iohannis & apostolorum Petri & Pauli v lib. vii s. vi d. ob.
Item est solutum pro cereis in eisdem iii s.
Item pro custodia pacis, ut placet iudicibus xl s.
Item pro cereis in exequiis ducis Glowcestrie, Thome Kempe & Iohannis Kempe vi s.
Item pro composicione inter rectores ecclesie beate Marie & Uniuersitatem pro eisdem exequiis vi s.
Item solutum est pro preconizatione ducis Glowcestrie & Thome Kempe nunc defuncti viii d.
Item in vino dato episcopo Lincoln' in adventu suo iiii s. ii d.
Item in vino dato episcopis Wygornie, Meth & suffraganneo alii v s.
Item in cirothecis datis Regi et ceteris hic cum eo presentibus x s.
Item in vino & cirothecis datis iusticiariis domini Regis duabus vicibus v s. iiii d.
Item pro labore cuiusdam equitantis Lundonias cum litteris regeis [*sic*] ii s. iiii d.
Item in cirothecis & vino datis seruientibus episcopi London' afferentibus Uniuersitati 90 volumina ii s.
Item in cirothecis & vino datis magistro Foster promittenti Uniuersitati viginti nobilia, que soluit doctori Fizthiamus xviii d.
Item pro conductione & renouatione armorum, ut placet iudicibus xl s.

[1] Wood renders this 'The University made eight processions with the King'. The figure shows there were eight processions without the King; and one with the King at a fee of one shilling.

[2] He means 'Regnoldi et Grey'.

Item pro conductione equorum una cum expensis procuratorum & unius Bedelli equitancium ad Oborne ad intimandum Cancellario suam electionem prout decretum erat per congregationem [1] xi s. iiii d. ob.
Item pro conductione equorum procuratoribus & ceteris intendentibus Abyndon Regi etiam ad Wodestoke [2] xi s. vii d.
Item pro expensis unius bedelli equitantis Regi pro excusatione Uniuersitatis, eo quod stipendiarii eius suaserant se perturbatos in Uniuersitate xv s. iiii d.
Item in regardo dato deferentibus ferinam Uniuersitati a rege xxi s. viii d.
Item pro minutis expensis, ut placet iudicibus l s.
Item est solutum priori sancte Frideswide pro annua pensione iii s. iiii d.
Item in refectione facta pauperibus scolaribus in festo sancti Nicholai xvi s. viii d.
Item magistris superuisoribus scolarum grammaticalium xiii s. iiii d.
Item pro distributione fienda inter regentes iii lib. xviii s. viii d.
Item abbati de Eynsham pro redditu exeunti de Aula Bouina iii s.
Item collegio Balioli pro annua pensione vii s.
Item pro pargameno pro indenturis & acquietanciis hoc anno iiii d.
Item pro cera & pixidibus ad deferendum litteras Uniuersitatis xi d.
Item in vino dato magistro Iacobo Stanley xvi d.
Item solutum est Doctori Estmonde in partem arreragiorum Uniuersitatis alterius anni xii lib. vi s. viii d.
Item solutum est diacono & subdiacono in exequiis Kempe, eo quod mortuus est iiii d.
Item in pecuniis distributis pauperibus scolaribus in festo sancte Scolastice iii s. iiii d.
Item pro delatione caparum ad exequias ducis Glowcestrie & Kempe & pro locione vestimentorum xii d.
Item pro isto rotulo & eiusdem scriptura, ut placet iudicibus xx d.
Item pro refectione iudicibus, ut placet eisdem xxxiii s. iiii d.
Item allocatum est procuratori australi pro sanacione cuiusdam presbiteri negligenter lesi ex decreto commissarii xiii s. iiii d.

Summa solutorum xliii lib. v s. ix d. [3]; et sic summa receptorum

[1] The Bishop of Lincoln resigned the post of Chancellor, but was re-elected in June 1488 (see *Ep. Ac.*, p. 530, where however the dates are incorrect).

[2] Originally written 'pro conductione equorum Cancellario, Procuratoribus &c. intendentibus Abyngdon Regi; etiam ad Wodestoke procuratoribus'.

[3] This seems to be ten shillings too much.

excedit summam solutorum xxiii s. iiii d.; quam summam soluerunt in manus iudicum & sic recesserunt quiete ad hunc compotum.

On the dorse.

Compotus magistrorum Iohannis Thomson & Roberti Wekys collectorum reddituum Uniuersitatis, anno domini MCCCC octuagesimo nono.

Primo de Aula Bouina	xliii s. iiii d.
Item de magistro Croke pro orto a dorso scolarum Canonistarum	xx d.
Item a doctore Gylbert Salter pro scolis Canonistarum	liii s. iiii d.
Item de Aula Nigra	xv s.
Item pro Aula sancti Willelmi in Kybbalstrete	iiii s.
Item de Aula Mureligorum	iiii s.
Item de Aula Tenchewyke	xiii s. iiii d.
Item de orto adiacente in Novo Hospicio	vi s. viii d.
Item de Collegio Balioli pro Aula Pascerina	ii s.
Item de Iohanne Rede sclatter pro orto quodam iuxta ecclesiam sancti Egidii	xvi d.

Summa reddituum vii lib. iiii s. viii d.

Unde petunt allocari

Pro reparacionibus in Aula Bouina	xii s. vi d.
Item pro reparacionibus in Aula Nigra	ix s. vi d.
Item pro orto quem tenet Iohannes Rede in parochia sancti Egidii	xvi d.
Item pro reparacionibus cepis in orto quem tenet Croke	xii d.
Item pro scolis Canonistarum, quia vacant	liii s. iiii d.
Item pro Aula sancti Willelmi, quia vacat	iiii s.
Item pro Aula Mureligorum, quia vacat	iiii s.
Item pro stipendiis collectorum	xiii s. iiii d.

Summa allocatorum iiii lib. xix s.; et sic remanent xlv s. viii d., quam summam soluerunt iudicibus, & sic quiete dimissi sunt.

Compotus dictorum procuratorum de datis et receptis Uniuersitati ad usum edificacionis ecclesie beate Marie virginis, anno supradicto

In primis idem reddunt compotum de XL quercubus[1] ex dono

[1] The King is thanked for this timber in a letter of May 1488 (*Ep. Ac.*, p. 526).

Illustrissimi Regis Henrici septimi datis Uniuersitati ad dictum usum habendis in Shotouer cum ramis, frondibus, putaminibusque omnibus aliis, anglice cum toppes & loppes, ex concensu domini Edmundi Rede militis, ibidem locumtenentis, que quidem quercus in Shotouer abcisi [*sic*] adhuc remanent.

Item pro ramis, frondibus, putaminibusque omnibus aliis venditis Alano Rede per dictos procuratores xxvi s. viii d.

Item ex dono venerabilis viri magistri Thome Coper bacallarii in sacra pagina xl s.

Summa receptorum iii lib. vi s. viii d.; unde petunt allocari pro regardis, abcisione quercuum una cum aliis circa dictum meremium expensis factis xxvii s. i d. ob.

Et sic remanent Uniuersitati ad dictum usum xxxix s. vi d. ob., de qua summa soluerunt iudicibus xii s. x d. ob. & remanent in manibus eorum, scilicet Hosey & Caseleghe xxvi s. viii d., ad dictum usum, de quibus habent compotare procuratoribus anni presentis.

Nos doctores et magistri, iudices auctoritate venerabilis congregationis deputati & super stricta examinatione iurati &c., audito & intellecto compoto procuratorum dictorum, percepimus & nouimus ex relacione & testimonio non solum dictorum procuratorum verum etiam & aliorum fidedignorum, quod commissarius detinet seu detinere presumit arma quedam inuasiua & defensiua ad valorem magni precii viz. bryganders &c. Universitati pertinencia & nobis iudicibus tempore compoti presentanda; preterea, iuxta tenorem statutorum dicta concernencium, inquisitione strictaque examinatione per nos facta in hiis que personam Commissarii circa pacem conservandam concernunt, reperimus & probabiliter nouimus quod dictus Commissarius non erat diligens in rebellium punitione & pacis obseruacione; ideoque proprias consciencias disonerando auctoritate statutorum nobis commissa in hac parte decernimus & ipsum condempnamus ad dictorum restitutionem armorum Uniuersitati infra 10 dies a tempore congricionis[1] sub pena periurii quam nos decernimus eum incurrere eo facto. Insuper priuamus premissa auctoritate dictum Commissarium omni parte armorum sibi aliquo iure statutorum competent' cum minus diligens repertus fuerit & ei perpetuum silencium circa peticionem dictorum armorum vel aliqua parte [*sic*] eorum imponimus sub pena premissa &c.

[1] The word is so written. I cannot suggest a meaning.

Quia vero postea dictus Commissarius in plena congregatione magistrorum regencium sacramento prestito ac nullo testium contradicente, innocentiam suam in premissis sufficienter declarauit, propterea nos prefati iudices ex maioris partis nostrum consensu eundem Commissarium dictorum criminum immunem, insuper a sententia necnon condempnatione suprascriptis absolui debere ac absolutum fore iusticia suadente pronunciamus, supradictis sentencia et condempnatione in aliquo non obstantibus.[1]

13.

[May 4, 1492—April 17, 1493.]

Compotus magistrorum Iohannis Dauys et Willelmi Lambtone procuratorum Universitatis Oxonie de omnibus bonis per eosdem receptis et expositis a quarto die mensis Maii anno domini MCCCC nonagesimo secundo usque in decimum septimum diem mensis Aprilis anni sequentis.

In primis dicti procuratores reddunt compotum de compositione unius doctoris ordinis Carmelit'	vi li. xiii s. iiii d.
Item de medietate compositionis cuiusdam doctoris ordinis Predicatorum	[*blank*]
Item de integris & dimidiis communis procedentium hoc anno	xl s. vii d.
Item de condicionibus graciarum hoc anno	vii li. xv s. iiii d.
Item de abbate & conuentu de Eynesham pro scholasticis pascendis in die sancti Nicholai	xvi s. viii d.
Item de abbate & conuentu de Osney pro regentibus	xxvi s. viii d.
Item de abbate & conuentu Eynesham pro regentibus	lii s.
Et de cista quinque clavium ex decreto Congregationis	vi li. iiii d. ob.
Item de collectoribus reddituum Uniuersitatis	iiii li. xii s. i d. ob.
Item de oblationibus burgensium in festo sancte Scholastice	iii s. iiii d.
Et de arte Scissoria pro annuali pensione	iii s. iiii d.
Et de convictis de perturbatione pacis hoc anno	xx s. v d.
Et de parte compositionis domini Thome Castell, monachi ordinis sancti Benedicti	xl s.

Summa totalis omnium receptorum xxxv li. x d.

[1] This paragraph is in another hand.

Soluciones & onera ordinaria una cum extraordinariis edificiis, reparacionibus & aliis hoc anno :—

Inprimis solutum tabellioni Universitatis pro stipendio suo liii s. iiii d.
Solutum capellano Universitatis ad complementum stipendii sui vii s. v d.
Solutum eidem pro diversis missis ex statuto ix d.
Solutum clerico Universitatis pro custodia domus congregationis, pro delacione crucis, pro laboribus in actibus & vesperiis & aliis & in solitis processionibus xviii s. i d.
Solutum clerico ecclesie beate Marie pro custodia orilogii & lectura epistolarum [1] viii s.
Solutum clerico de ecclesia sancti Petri pro pulsatione ad sermones in Quadragesima ii s. viii d.
Solutum legentibus evangelia [2] ii s.
Item pro oblationibus in missis Reginaldi Grey [*sic*] & in aliis & ad bidellos & clerico Universitatis iii s. ii d.
Solutum in vigiliis sanctorum Iohannis & Petri in recreatione omnium graduatorum, ut placet iudicibus vii li.
Solutum pro luminibus in eisdem vigiliis iiii s. vi d.
Solutum pro custodia pacis & nocturnis vigiliis, ut placet iudicibus lvi s. viii d.
Solutum pro conductione & renovatione armorum, ut placet iudicibus lviii s.
Solutum priori sancte Frideswide pro quadam annua pensione iii s. iiii d.
Solutum collegio Ballioli pro annuali pensione vii s.
Solutum abbati de Eynesham pro redditu exeunte de Aula Bovina iii s.
Solutum magistris supervisoribus scolarum grammaticalium xiii s. iiii d.
Solutum pro distributione fienda inter regentes iii lib. xviii s. viii d.
Solutum in minutis expensis super diversis ad decorem & honestatem Universitatis, ut placet iudicibus iii lib.
Solutum pro pergameno & pro scriptura huius compoti, ut placet iudicibus ii s. viii d.
Solutum pro prandio dato iudicibus [3] iuxta laudabilem consuetudinem xl s.
Solutum pro luminibus in exequiis ducis Glocestrie & domi-

1 '& lectura epistolarum' is an addition.

2 At first 'evangelia & epistolas', the last two words underlined for deletion.

3 i. e. the auditors.

norum Kempe & London' episcoporum & ecclesiis ubi celebrate erant exequie viii s.
Solutum pro preconizacione obitus ducis Glocestrie iiii d.
Solutum communi proclamatori ville Oxonie xx d.
Solutum in die sancti Nicholai pro pauperibus scholaribus pascendis xvi s. viii d.
Solutum in distributione pauperum in die sancte Scholastice iii s. iiii d.
Solutum pro cirotecis datis iusticiariis domini regis & pro vino dato eisdem v s. iiii d.
Solutum uni plumbario pro labore suo & pro ly sowder & pro plumbo super novam scholam iiii s.
Solutum uni reparanti domum congregationis vi s. viii d.
Solutum pro uno baculo pro cruce Universitatis iii d.
Solutum tabellioni Uniuersitatis pro papiro, pergameno & rubea cera xii d.
Solutum pro vino & servicia dat' doctoribus & magistris determinatis a congregatione ad supervidendum cauciones in domo stacionarii xvi d. ob.
Solutum pro scriptura statutorum cuiusdam nove ciste per manus Commissarii ii s. iiii d.
Solutum pro remuneracione officialis domini pape[1] xxxviii s. viii d.
Solutum pro cirotecis & vino eidem xxii d.
Solutum pro remuneratione famuli eiusdem & cirotecis iii s. viii d.
Solutum pro potu magistris supervidentibus deliberationem librorum in domo stacionarii ad diversas vices [*blank*]
Solutum pro cirotecis & vino vicecomiti ad vices & in susceptione iuramenti sui[2] iiii s. ii d.
Solutum pro emendacione baculi bedelli inferioris in artibus xii s. viii d.
Solutum pro factura pali & pro hamis & pro potu Cancellario procuratoribus & bedellis post visitacionem Aularum in Quadragesima v s. x d.
Solutum pro reparatione orilogii sancte Marie Virginis, & pro cirotecis & vino dat' capellano ducis Bedfordie iiii s.

Summa omnium solutorum xxxiiii li. iii s. vii d. ob. & sic summa receptorum excedit summam solutorum xx s. ii d. ob., quam summam dicti computantes soluerunt iudicibus & sic recesserunt quieti.

[1] Perhaps this was when the Bull of Innocent VIII was received; see vol. i, p. 360.

[2] The last five words are an addition.

On the dorse.

Compotus magistrorum Thome Nayle & Iohannis Webe collectorum reddituum Universitatis anno domini MLXXXXII [*sic*].

In primis de doctore Churche pro scolis Canonistarum liii s. iiii d.
Item de Aula Bovina xliii s. iiii d.
Item de Nicholao Croke pro orto a dorso scolarum Canonistarum ii s.
Item de Aula Nigra xv s.
Item de Aula sancti Willelmi in Kiballestrete iiii s.
Item de Aula Mureligorum iiii s. viii d.
Item de Aula Tenchwike xiii s. iiii d.
Item de Aula adiacente Novo Hospicio vi s. viii d.
Item de Collegio Ballioli pro Aula Pascerina ii s.
Item de Iohanne Rede sklatter pro quodam orto iuxta ecclesiam sancti Egidii xvi d.

Summa reddituum vii li. v s. viii d.

Unde petunt allocari pro reparationibus factis in Aula Bovina & pro vacancia quarundam camerarum ibidem xxix s. iiii d.
Et de Aula sancti Willelmi propter defectum reparationum ii s.
Et de vacancia cuiusdam orti quem nuper tenuit Iohannes Rede xvi d.
Et pro stipendio collectorum xiii s. iiii d.
Et pro reparationibus Aule Nigre & pro orto vacante a dorso Aularum Canonistarum vii s. vi d. ob.

Summa allocatorum liii s. vi d. ob.

Et sic summa receptorum excedit summam allocatorum iiii li. xii s. i d. ob., quam summam coram iudicibus ad manus procuratorum tradiderunt & sic quieti recesserunt.

14.

[April 9, 1494—May 5, 1495.]

Compotus magistrorum Antonii Fisher et Roberti Dale procuratorum Uniuersitatis Oxonie de omnibus bonis per eosdem receptis et expositis a nono die mensis Aprilis anno gracie millesimo cccc nonagesimo quarto usque in quintum diem mensis Maii anni sequentis.

In primis dicti procuratores reddunt compotum de parte composicionis unius doctoris theologie, videlicet prioris de Duram xi lib. vi s. viii d.

Item de composicione duorum fratrum ordinis Minorum uidelicet Kyntone & Draper xiii lib. vi s. viii d.

Item de duobus doctoris iuris canonici, videlicet Keruer & Mumpesson xxvi lib. xiii s. iiii d.

Item de condicionibus graciarum hoc anno xii lib. vi s. iiii d.

Item de suscipientibus gradus hoc anno pro integris communis & dimidiis iii lib. vi s. x d.

Item de abbate & conuentu de Enysham pro scolaribus pascendis in die sancti Nicholai xvi s. viii d.

Item de abbate & conuentu de Osney pro distributione fienda inter regentes xxvi s. viii d.

Item de abbate & conuentu de Enysham pro consimili distributione fienda lii s.

Item de conuictis de perturbacione pacis hoc anno xxxi s. i d.

Item de oblationibus burgensium in festo sancte Scholastice iii s. iiii d.

Item de collectoribus reddituum Uniuersitatis hoc anno vii lib. v s. vi d.[1]

Summa totalis omnium receptorum lxxx lib. xv s. i d.

Soluciones & onera ordinaria una cum extraordinariis stipendiis reparacionibus & aliis hoc anno :—

In primis tabellioni Uniuersitatis pro stipendio suo liii s. iiii d.

Item capellano Uniuersitatis in complementum stipendii sui vii s. v d.

Item clerico Uniuersitatis pro custodia & mundacione domus congregationis, pro laboribus in vesperiis & in actibus & pulsacione hoc anno xx s.

Item clerico ecclesie beate Marie pro custodia orilegii & lectura epistolarum hoc anno vii s. x d.

Item clerico ecclesie sancti Petri in oriente pro pulsatione ad sermones in Quadragesima ii s. iiii d.

Item diaconis legentibus euangelia hoc anno & pro oblationibus factis missis Walteri de Grey trina[2] vice & in missa Reginaldi bidelli x s. xi d.

Item solutum in die sancti Nicholai in pascendo pauperes scholares xvi s. viii d.

[1] This is the full rental; the expenses were deducted afterwards; see the end of the roll.

[2] *bina* must be meant.

Item solutum in distribucione pauperum in die sancte Scholastice iii s. iiii d.
Item solutum in vigiliis sancti Iohannis Baptiste & sancti Petri in recreacione omnium graduatorum ex consuetudine laudabili, ut placet iudicibus vi lib. xiii s. iiii d.
Item pro cirpis consumptis in dictis vigiliis & certis reparacionibus factis in locis ubi tenebantur dicte recreaciones iii s.
Item pro consumptione luminum in eisdem noctibus et in obitibus dominorum Iohannis & Thome Kempe, ducis Glocestrie & episcopi Lincolniensis xvi s.
Item pro compositione luminum eorundem rectoribus ecclesie beate Marie in dictis dominorum obitibus vi s. iii d.
Item solutum pro preconizacione obitus ducis Glocestrie & domini Lincolniensis episcopi nuper Cancellarii per villam Oxonie viii d.
Item pro proclamationibus factis in Aula Gildarum & apud Carfox ad vices ii s.
Item solutum in custodia pacis & nocturnis vigiliis toto anno, ut placet iudicibus xlvi s. viii d.[1]
Item solutum priori sancte Frideswide pro quadam annua pensione iii s. iiii d.
Item solutum collegio Ballioli pro consimili pensione vii s.
Item solutum abbati de Enysham de redditu exeunti de Aula Bouina iii s.
Item solutum magistris scholarum in disputacionibus apud fratres Augustinenses xiii s. iiii d.
Item pro distributione fienda inter regentes iii lib. xviii s. viii d.
Item pro minutis expensis super diversos ad decorem & honestatem Uniuersitatis ad discrecionem iudicium xxx s.[2]
Item pro potu diversis magistris supervidentibus statum diversarum cistarum iiii d.
Item solutum pro papiro, membrana, cera rubea & pixidibus pro litteris vehendis hoc anno xxi d.
Item pro reparacione & conductione armorum hoc anno, ut placet iudicibus xl s.
Item solutum Bulcam bidello equitanti ad regem & ad Cancellarium diversis vicibus cum litteris Universitatis xiii s. iiii d.

[1] In the margin: 'magistro Antonio Fysher xxxiii s. iiii d., magistro Dale xiii s. iiii d.'

[2] In the margin: 'magistro Antonio xx s., magistro Dale x s.'

Item pro vectura sexaginta librarum in pecuniis in partem solucionis ciste de Phen [1] nuper fundate — xx d.

Item in regardis uni bacallario misso a doctore Fytziames cum litteris ad commissarium & procuratores pro certa materia concernente Uniuersitatem — xx d.

Item stacionario pro ligatura diversorum librorum & pro cathenacione eorum in libraria Uniuersitatis — xv s. iiii d.

Item pro reparacione duarum serarum ad cistam quatuor clauium & pro nova clavi ad unam earum — iiii d.

Item uni mundanti scholam theologie & gradus ad librariam & etiam schole [*sic*] Canonistarum — xiii d.

Item solutum uni lathamo & plumbario pro reparacionibus circa fenistram in domo congregationis & in scholis Canonistarum — xv d.

Item Henrico pictori pro reparacionibus factis circa fenistras vitrias schole theologie, librarie & schole Canonistarum — xxiiii s. ix d.

Item pro noua corda ad magnam campanam ecclesie beate Marie — ii s.

Item pro mutuacione caparum nigrarum & vestimentorum in diuersis exequiis & missis Uniuersitatis — viii d.

Item solutum procuratoribus ultimi anni Iolyff & Barnyngam de pecuniis debitis eis per Uniuersitatem in pede compoti eorundem ex decreto iudicum tunc temporis in partem solucionis — xl s.

Item pro vino dato Commissario & procuratoribus & bidellis pro eorum laboribus in visitacione Aularum — xvi d.

Item pro vino dato magistro Brey senescallo nostro [2] & pro vino Ypocratis cum confectis datis eidem cum primo accepit iuramentum in Uniuersitate — vi s. viii d.

Item pro cirotecis datis eidem, magistro Urswyke & aliis generosis secum tunc existentibus & certis sibi seruientibus — viii s. viii d.

Item pro vino & cerotecis datis magistro Wyllyby [3] venienti ad Uniuersitatem cum litteris regiis bina vice — ii s. xi d.

[1] Hugh Feen left £200 in 1489 to found a chest (*Ep. Ac.*, p. 555), but £60 of it was not obtained until 1494 (ibid. p. 615).

[2] Sir Reginald Bray was elected Steward of the University on June 4, 1494 (*Ep. Ac.*, p. 616).

[3] Edward Wyllyby came to Oxford Jan. 1495 (*Ep. Ac.*, p. 622).

Item pro vino cum ly waffyrs datis duci de Bokyngham & aliis dominis & militibus secum venientibus ad videndum Uniuersitatem — v s. vi d.

Item pro cirotecis datis eisdem in recessu eorum — iiii s.

Item pro vino & cirotecis datis magistro Schowrbone — ii s. viii d.

Item pro vino dato abbatibus de Wynchcombe, de Fowntayns, de Bylonde, de Stratforde, & abbati de Towrhyll[1] ad vices — ii s. x d.

Item pro vino & ly waffyrs datis filiis domini Markys[2] in primo aduentu eorum ad Uniuersitatem — ii s. vi d.

Item pro vino & cirotecis datis iudicibus domini regis — iii s. viii d.

Item pro expensis factis versus Langley per procuratores ad regem — iii s. v d.

Item pro scriptura priuilegiorum missorum ad dominum Cancellarium — iii s. viii d.

Item magistro North & magistro Sedner in portando litteras Uniuersitatis ad dominum Cancellarium — xi s. iiii d.[3]

Item pro vino magistro Hamsterley in recepcione pecuniarum de composicione prioris Dulmenensis — vi d.

Item pro vino dato Gulielmo Barkley militi, doctori Mydyltone & domino Thome Bowser militi — xviii d.

Item pro expensis factis per doctorem Veyse & procuratorem borialem equitando ad dominum Cancellarium, ut patet per billam — v lib. iiii s. vii d.

Item pro expensis magistri Scarbot equitando ad regem cum litteris Uniuersitatis, ut patet per billam — xxi s. v d.

Item pro expensis procuratorum apud Abindoniam pro uno scolari incarcerato per abbatem ibidem — xvi d.

Item pro refeccione facta iudicibus tempore huius compoti, ut placet iudicibus — l s.[4]

Item pro scriptura huius compoti & membrana eiusdem, ut placet iudicibus — ii s.

[1] Commonly called the Abbey of St. Mary de Graciis; it was at Tower Hill; a Cistercian abbey. We may assume that these abbots had brought donations for the rebuilding of St. Mary's; probably the same was the case with Barkley, Mydyltone, and Bowser, mentioned below. The University wrote to the Abbot of Fountains in 1490 (*Ep. Ac.*, p. 592).

[2] The Marquess of Dorset sent his sons to Oxford this year (*Ep. Ac.*, p. 620).

[3] In the margin: 'magistro North xvi d., magistro Sedner x s.'

[4] In the margin: 'ex certis causis nos in hac parte moventibus'.

Item pro tribus paribus cirotecarum datis domino Cancellario ac eius capellanis ac certis sibi seruientibus xiiii s. x d.
Item pro diuersis expensis domini Commissarii & certis pecuniis liberatis per eundem, ut patet per billam suam [*blank*]
Item Bulcam bidello alia vice equitanti ad regem & Cancellarium in negociis Uniuersitatis lix s. ii d. ob.
Item Commissario ex decreto auditorum compoti procuratorum superioris anni, ut patet in pede illius compoti xl s. xi d.
Item procuratoribus superioris anni viz. magistro Bernyngham & magistro Golyffe in plenam solucionem xxiiii s. viii d.

Summa solutorum xlix li. ix s. iii d. ob.

On the dorse.

Compotus magistrorum Iohannis Grede et Thome Drakys collectorum reddituum Uniuersitatis anno domini MCCCCLXXXXII [*sic*].
In primis de Aula Bouina xliii s. iiii d.
Item doctore Norton pro scola Canonistarum liii s. iiii d.
Item de magistro Trot pro Aula Nigra xv s.
Item de magistro Lloyd pro Aula Gulielmi yn Keballstrete iiii s.
Item de Aula Mureligorum iiii s. viii d.
Item de collegio Animarum pro Aula Tenchwyke xiii s. iiii d.
Item de orto adiacente Nouo Hospicio vi s. viii d.
Item de collegio Ballioli pro Aula Pascerina ii s.
Item de Ricardo Wottune bidello pro orto iuxta ecclesiam sancti Egidii xvi d.
Item pro orto a dorso scolarum Canonistarum ii s.

Summa reddituum vii lib. v s. viii d.

Unde petunt allocari pro reparacionibus factis in Aula Bouina hoc anno xvi s.
Item pro vacancia quarumdem camerarum ibidem viii s.
Item pro Aula Gulielmi ii s.
Item pro stipendio collectorum xiii s. iiii d.
Item pro certis reparacionibus factis in Aula Nigra in superiori anno non allocatis ut patet per billam x s. xi d.
Item pro orto iuxta ecclesiam sancti Egidii xii d.

Summa allocatorum li s. iii d.

Summa ciste quinque clavium imponenda xxviii lib. xiiii s. vi d. ob., quam summam in cistam quinque clavium imposuerunt, et sic quiete recesserunt.

15.

[April 15, 1496—April 8, 1497.]

Compotus venerabilium magistrorum Rowlandi Philipps et Thome Crakynthorpe huius alme Uniuersitatis Oxonie procuratorum anno domini millesimo cccc nonagesimo sexto a quintodecimo die mensis Aprilis usque ad octauum diem mensis Aprilis anno domini millesimo cccc nonagesimo septimo.

In primis reddunt compotum de compositione fratris ordinis Minorum doctoris in theologia vi lib. xiii s. iiii d.
Item de condicionibus graciarum hoc anno xiii lib. v s.
Item de suscipientibus gradus pro integris communis et dimidiis iiii lib. vi s. iii d.
Item de abbate et conuentu de Enysham pro pascendis scolaribus xvi s. viii d.
Item de abbate et conuentu de Enysham pro distributione fienda inter regentes lii s.
Item de abbate et conuentu de Osney pro simili distributione fienda xxvi s. viii d.
Item de transgressoribus et perturbantibus pacem hoc anno xxii s. viii d.
Item a collectoribus reddituum Uniuersitatis iiii lib. xiiii s. iiii d.
Item in oblationibus burgensium in die sancte Scolastice iii s. vi d.
Item de domino Vowell suam appellationem non prosequente ii s.
Item de cista Uniuersitatis liii s. iiii d.
Item de arte cissoria pro annuali pensione iii s. iiii d.

Summa omnium receptorum xxxvii lib. xviiii s. i d.

Soluciones :—

In primis capellano Uniuersitatis pro complemento stipendii sui vi s. viii d.
Item eidem pro diuersis missis ex statutis ix d.
Item tabellioni Uniuersitatis pro complemento stipendii sui liii s. iiii d.
Item diacono et subdiacono legentibus euangelia et epistolas in diuersis missis pro benefactoribus Uniuersitatis vii s. iiii d.
Item pro proclamationibus apud Quadriuium et in Aula Communi factis diuersis vicibus ii s.
Item clerico parochiali sancti Petri in oriente pro pulsatione in Quadragesima ad sermones ii s. iiii d.

Item clerico Uniuersitatis pro delatione scabellorum in quinque vesperiis artistarum & in duabus vigiliis Iohannis et Petri iiii s. iiii d.
Item solutum eidem pro delacione crucis in nouem processionibus Uniuersitatis et duabus in obviam Principis vii s.
Item eidem pro pulsatione ignitegii ii s.
Item eidem pro custodia & mundacione superioris domus congregacionis ii s. viii d.
Item eidem pro custodia & mundacione inferioris domus congregacionis ii s.
Item eidem pro laboribus in exequiis ducis Glowcestrie, Kempe et Lychfelde, qui hoc anno mortuus est iii s.
Item eidem pro pulsacione in crastino Natiuitatis beate Marie iiii d.
Item clerico beate Marie pro custodia horologii iiii s.
Item pro oblacionibus magistrorum et expensis bedellorum in duabus missis Grey et Reginaldi vi s. vii d.
Item pro recreacionibus factis in vigiliis sancti Iohannis Baptiste et apostolorum Petri et Pauli, quibus interfuerunt etiam Bacallarii iurium, ut placet iudicibus viii lib. xix s. iii d. ob.
Item pro cirpis in eisdem vigiliis iii s. iiii d.
Item pro cereis in eisdem iiii s.
Item pro expensis factis in nocturnis vigiliis pro custodia pacis, ut placet iudicibus iii lib.
Item pro conductura et reparacionibus armorum, ut placet iudicibus lvi s.
Item pro cereis in exequiis ducis Glowcestrie, Iohannis et Thome Kempe et Ricardi Lychefelde hoc anno defuncti vi s.
Item pro compositione inter rectores ecclesie beate Marie et Uniuersitatem pro eisdem exequiis vi s.
Item pro compositione obitus ducis Glowcestrie iiii d.
Item pro cerothecis datis Principi ac aliis proceribus in bino eius aduentu ix s. ii d.
Item pro vino dato episcopis Lincolniensi et Lichfildensi in terno eorum aduentu xi s. x d.
Item pro cirothecis datis episcopo Lincoln' in terno eius aduentu iii s. vi d.
Item pro cirothecis et vino datis iudicibus domini regis iiii s.
Item pro potacionibus factis cum seruientibus principis in

bino aduentu et dictorum episcoporum in terno aduentu, ut placet iudicibus xiii s. iiii d.

Item pro expensis duorum procuratorum cum duobus seruientibus equitantium ad Londinum ibique in negotiis Uniuersitatis permanentium per quindenam una cum stipendiis quatuor equorum [*blank*]

Item pro expensis factis cum diuersis dominis abbatibus, prioribus et generosis, ut placet iudicibus liii s. iiii d.

Item priori sancte Frideswide pro annua pensione iii s. iiii d.

Item pro refeccione facta pauperibus scolaribus in festo sancti Nicholai xvi s. viii d.

Item magistris superuidentibus scolas apud Augustinenses xiii s. iiii d.

Item pro distribucione fienda inter regentes iii lib. xviii s. viii d.

Item abbati de Enysham pro redditu exeunte de Aula Bouina iii s.

Item collegio Balielo [*sic*] pro annua pensione vii s.

Item in pecuniis distributis scolaribus in festo sancte Scolastice iii s. vi d.

Item pro delacione vestimentorum ad exequias ducis Glowcestrie et Kempe vi d.

Item pro pergameno et scriptura huius compoti, iudicibus ut placet ii s. viii d.

Item pro refeccione facta Commissario, doctoribus, et procuratoribus post visitaciones Aularum vii s. xi d. ob.

Item pro refeccione facta iudicibus tempore compoti, ut eisdem placet iudicibus xliii s. iiii d.

Item pro ligatura et reparacionibus librorum in libraria communi Uniuersitatis ii s. viii d.

Item pro funo [*sic*] ad campanam magnam Uniuersitatis ii s.

Summa solutorum xxxiiii lib. xix s. i d.; et sic summa receptorum exedit summam solutorum lix s. iiii d.; quam summam soluerunt in manus iudicum & sic recesserunt quiete ad hunc compotum.

Item in areragiis de condicionibus Waltiri [*sic*] Stone doctoris iuris ciuilis xl s.

Item in areragiis reddituum xxiii s. iiii d.

Summa totalis debita Uniuersitati, completo isto compoto, vi lib. ii s. viii d.

Compotus magistrorum Georgii Lassy et Richardi Sydnor collectorum reddituum Uniuersitatis anno domini MCCCC nonagesimo sexto.

Primo de Aula Bouina xliii s. iiii d.
Item pro orto a dorso scolarum Canonistarum iii s. iiii d.
Item a doctore Norton pro scholis [*sic*] Canonistarum liii s. iiii d.
Item a magistro Lloyde pro Aula sancti Willelmi ii s.
Item de Aula Nigra xv s.
Item de Aula Mureligorum iiii s.
Item de Aula Tencheweke xiii s. iiii d.
Item de Aula adiacente in Nouo Hospicio vi s. viii d.
Item de collegio Balioli pro Aula Pascerina ii s.
Item de Ricardo Wottune pro quodam orto iuxta ecclesiam sancti Egidii xvi d.

Summa reddituum vii lib. iiii s. iiii d.

Unde petunt allocari
In primis pro reparacionibus domorum et murorum Aule Bouine xvi s. viii d.
Item pro reparacionibus Aule Nigre iii s. iiii d.
Item petunt collectores allocari pro redditibus receptis a procuratoribus Uniuersitatis iiii lib. xiiii s. iiii d.
Item pro stipendio collectoris vi s. viii d.

Summa allocatorum vi lib. xii d.; et sic restant debita Uniuersitati ex summa reddituum xxiii s. iiii d.

In areragiis redituum xxx s.
Ex quibus areragiis restant in manibus principalis,[1] scilicet Edmundi Popley xxvi s. viii d.
Item in manibus magistri Willelmi Conway pro reditu Aule Willelmi ii s.
Item in manibus Ricardi Wottone xvi d.

[1] No doubt Principal of Beef Hall.

INDEX

Oxford Historical Society.

PUBLICATIONS.

1884.

1. **Register of the University of Oxford.** Vol. I. (1449–63; 1505–71), edited by the Rev. C. W. Boase, M.A., pp. xxviii + 364. (Price to the public, without discount, and prepaid, 16*s.*)

2. **Remarks and Collections of Thomas Hearne.** Vol. I. (4 July 1705—19 March 1707), edited by C. E. Doble, M.A., pp. viii + 404. (16*s.*)

1884–85.

3. **The Early History of Oxford (727–1100), preceded by a sketch of the Mythical Origin of the City and University.** By James Parker, M.A. With 3 illustrations, pp. xxxii + 420. (20*s.*)

1885.

4. **Memorials of Merton College, with biographical notices of the Wardens and Fellows.** By the Hon. Geo. C. Brodrick, Warden of Merton College. With one illustration, pp. xx + 416. (16*s.*, to members of Merton 12*s.*)

5. **Collectanea, 1st series,** edited by C. R. L. Fletcher, M.A. With 2 illustrations, pp. viii + 358. (16*s.*)

(Contents:—*a.* Letters relating to Oxford in the 14th Century, ed. by H. H. Henson; *b.* Catalogue of the Library of Oriel College in the 14th Century, ed. by C. L. Shadwell; *c.* Daily ledger of John Dorne, bookseller in Oxford, 1520, ed. by F. Madan; *d.* All Souls College *versus* Lady Jane Stafford, 1587, ed. by C. R. L. Fletcher; *e.* Account Book of James Wilding, Undergraduate of Merton College, 1682–88, ed. by E. G. Duff; *f.* Dr. Wallis's Letter against Maidwell, 1700, ed. by T. W. Jackson.)

1886.

6. **Magdalen College and King James II, 1686–89.** A series of documents collected and edited by the Rev. J. R. Bloxam, D.D. with additions, pp. lii + 292. (16*s.*, to members of Magdalen 12*s.*)

7. **Hearne's Collections** [as No. 2 above]. Vol. II. (20 Mar. 1707—22 May 1710), pp. viii + 480. (16*s.*)

8. **Elizabethan Oxford.** Reprints of rare tracts. Edited by the Rev. C. PLUMMER, M.A., pp. xxxii + 316. (10*s.*)

(Contents:—*a.* Nicolai Fierberti Oxoniensis Academiæ descriptio, 1602; *b.* Leonard Hutton on the Antiquities of Oxford; *c.* Queen Elizabeth at Oxford, 1566 [pieces by J. Bereblock, Thomas Nele, Nich. Robinson, and Rich. Stephens, with appendices]; *d.* Queen Elizabeth at Oxford, 1592, by Philip Stringer; *e.* Apollinis et Musarum Eidyllia per Joannem Sanford, 1592.)

1887.

9. **Letters of Richard Radcliffe and John James, of Queen's College, Oxford, 1749–83:** edited by MARGARET EVANS, with a pedigree, pp. xxxvi + 306. (15*s.*, to members of Queen's 10*s.* 6*d.*)

10. **Register of the University of Oxford, Vol. II (1571–1622), Part 1. Introductions.** Edited by the Rev. ANDREW CLARK, M.A., pp. xxxii + 468. (18*s.*)

1887–88.

11. **Ditto. Part 2. Matriculations and Subscriptions.** Edited by the Rev. ANDREW CLARK, M.A., pp. xvi + 424. (18*s.*)

1888.

12. **Ditto. Part 3. Degrees.** Edited by the Rev. ANDREW CLARK, M.A., pp. viii + 448. (17*s.*)

13. **Hearne's Collections** [as No. 2 above]. Vol. III. (25 May 1710—14 December 1712), pp. iv + 518. (16*s.*)

1889.

14. **Register of the University of Oxford, Vol. II, Part 4. Index.** Edited by the Rev. ANDREW CLARK, M.A., pp. viii + 468. (17*s.*)

15. **Wood's History of the City of Oxford.** *New Edition.* By the Rev. ANDREW CLARK, M.A. Vol. I. The City and Suburbs. With 3 Maps and several Diagrams, pp. xii + 660. (25*s.*, to citizens of Oxford 20*s.*; the two Maps of old Oxford separately, not folded, 1*s.* 6*d.*, to citizens 1*s.*)

1890.

16. **Collectanea, 2nd series,** edited by Professor MONTAGU BURROWS. With one diagram, pp. xii + 518. (16*s.*)

(Contents:—*a.* The Oxford Market, by O. Ogle; *b.* The University of Oxford in the Twelfth Century, by T. E. Holland; *c.* The Friars Preachers of the University, ed. by H. Rashdall; *d.* Notes on the Jews in Oxford, by A. Neubauer; *e.* Linacre's Catalogue of Grocyn's Books, followed by a Memoir of Grocyn, by the Editor; *f.* Table-Talk and Papers of Bishop Hough, 1703–1743, ed. by W. D. Macray; *g.* Extracts from the 'Gentleman's Magazine' relating to Oxford, 1731–1800, by F. J. Haverfield. Appendix: Corrections and Additions to Collectanea, Vol. I. (Day-book of John Dorne, Bookseller at Oxford, A.D. 1520, by F. Madan, including a 'Half-century of Notes' on Dorne, by Henry Bradshaw).)

17. **Wood's History of the City of Oxford** [as No. 15 above]. Vol. II. Churches and Religious Houses. With Map and Diagram, pp. xii + 550. (20*s.*, to citizens of Oxford 16*s.*; Map of Oxford in 1440, separately, not folded, 9*d.*, to citizens 6*d.*)

1890–91.

18. **Oxford City Documents,** financial and judicial, 1268–1665. Selected and edited by Prof. J. E. THOROLD ROGERS, pp. viii + 440 (+ 2 loose leaves for vols. 6 and 16). (12*s.*)

1891.

19. **The Life and Times of Anthony Wood, antiquary, of Oxford, 1632–1695, described by Himself.** Collected from his Diaries and other Papers, by the Rev. ANDREW CLARK, M.A. Vol. I. 1632–1663. With 7 illustrations, pp. xvi + 520. (20*s.*)

20. **The Grey Friars in Oxford.** Part I, A History of the Convent; Part II, Biographical Notices of the Friars, together with Appendices of original documents. By ANDREW G. LITTLE, M.A., pp. xvi + 372. (16*s.*)

1892.

21. **The Life and Times of Anthony Wood** [as No. 19]. Vol. II. 1664–1681. With 10 illustrations, pp. xxviii + 576. (20*s.*)

22. **Reminiscences of Oxford, by Oxford men, 1559–1850.** Selected and edited by LILIAN M. QUILLER COUCH, pp. xvi + 430. (17*s.*, to members of the University 10*s.* 6*d.*)

1892–93.

23. **Index to Wills proved and Administrations granted in the Court of the Archdeacon of Berks, 1508–1652.** Edited by W. P. W. PHILLIMORE, M.A. (Issued in conjunction with the British Record Society.) pp. viii + 200. (10*s.*)

1893.

24. **Three Oxfordshire Parishes. A History of Kidlington, Yarnton, and Begbroke.** By MRS. BRYAN STAPLETON. With a coloured map and 2 sheet-pedigrees, pp. xx + 400. (17*s.*, to residents in the three villages 10*s.*)

25. **The History of Corpus Christi College, with Lists of its Members.** By THOMAS FOWLER, D.D., President of the College. With 3 illustrations, pp. xvi + 482. (20*s.*, to members of Corpus 12*s.* 6*d.*)

1894.

26. The Life and Times of Anthony Wood [as No. 19]. Vol. III. 168½–1695. With 3 illustrations, pp. xxxii + 548. (21*s.*)

27. The Register of Exeter College, Oxford, with a history of the College, and illustrations. By the Rev. C. W. BOASE, M.A. Third edition, enlarged. pp. [8] + clxxxiv + 400. (*Presented to the Society by the author:* 15*s.*, to members of the College 10*s.*)

28. The Cartulary of the Monastery of St. Frideswide at Oxford. Edited by the Rev. S. R. WIGRAM, M.A. With illustrations. Vol. I. General and City Charters. pp. xx + 504 + 6 pages (loose) of corrections to vol. 24. (21*s.*)

1895.

29. The Early Oxford Press, a bibliography of printing and publishing at Oxford, '1468'–1640. With notes, appendixes, and illustrations. By FALCONER MADAN, M.A., pp. xii + 366. (Separate copies can be obtained only from the Clarendon Press, price 18*s.* The Society can only supply it in sets.)

30. The Life and Times of Anthony Wood [as No. 19]. Vol. IV. Addenda. With illustrations, pp. xii + 322. (24*s.*)

1896.

31. The Cartulary of the Monastery of St. Frideswide at Oxford. Edited by the Rev. S. R. WIGRAM, M.A. With illustrations. Vol. II. The Chantry and Country Parish Charters. pp. xii + 488 + 8 pages of additions and corrections (loose) to vol. 25. (21*s.*)

32. Collectanea, 3rd series, edited by Professor MONTAGU BURROWS. With illustrations, pp. xii + 450. (21*s.*)

(Contents:—*a.* Some Durham College Rolls, by Rev. H. E. D. Blakiston; *b.* Parliamentary Petitions relating to Oxford, by Miss L. Toulmin Smith; *c.* Poems relating to the riot between Town and Gown, 1355, by Rev. H. Furneaux; Tryvytlam de laude Univ. Oxoniae, by the same; *d.* Wykeham's Books at New College, by A. F. Leach; *e.* Correspondence of Henry Earl of Clarendon and James Earl of Abingdon, 1683–85, by C. E. Doble; *f.* Dr. Newton and Hertford College, by S. G. Hamilton; *g.* Charles Earl Stanhope and the Oxford University Press, by H. Hart.)

1897.

33. A History of Pembroke College, anciently Broadgates Hall. By the Rev. DOUGLAS MACLEANE, M.A. With 4 illustrations, pp. xvi + 544 + 4 pages of Addenda to vol. 32. (21*s*., to members of Pembroke 13*s*.)

34. Hearne's Collections [as No. 2 above]. Vol. IV (15 Dec. 1712—30 Nov. 1714). Edited by D. W. RANNIE, M.A., pp. x + 466 + [2], with a plate. (1898, 21*s*.)

1898.

35. Epistolae Academicae Oxon., a collection of letters and other documents illustrative of Oxford in the fifteenth century. Edited by the Rev. H. ANSTEY, M.A. With illustrations. Part I, pp. lii + 336. (21*s*.)

36. Ditto. Part II, pp. vi + 389. (21*s*.)

1899.

37. Wood's History of the City of Oxford [as No. 15 above]. Vol. III. Addenda and Indexes, with illustration, pp. x + 476 + [4]. (21*s*., to citizens of Oxford 16*s*.)

38. Old Plans of Oxford, by Agas, Hollar, and Loggan. A portfolio containing 15 plates. (21*s*., to citizens of Oxford 16*s*.)

1900.

39. Oxford Topography, an essay by HERBERT HURST, B.A. With sketch-map, pp. viii + 248. (A companion to No. 38: 21*s*., to citizens of Oxford 16*s*.)

40. The Life and Times of Anthony Wood [as No. 19]. Vol. V, completing the work. Indexes, pp. xvi + 402 + [4]. (21*s*.)

1901.

41. Studies in Oxford History, chiefly in the Eighteenth Century, by the Rev. J. R. GREEN and the Rev. GEO. ROBERSON, edited by C. L. STAINER, M.A. With illustrations, pp. *xx* + xxiv + 382. (21*s*.)

42. Hearne's Collections [as No. 2 above]. Vol. V (Dec. 1, 1714–Dec. 31, 1716). Edited by D. W. RANNIE, M.A., pp. viii + 402 + [6]. (21*s*.)

1902.

43. Hearne's Collections [as No. 2 above]. Vol. VI (Jan. 1, 1717–May 8, 1719). Edited under the superintendence of the Committee of the O. H. S. With an illustration, pp. viii + 432 + [6]. (31*s.* 6*d.*)

1903.

44. The Flemings in Oxford. Vol. I. Edited by the Rev. the PROVOST OF QUEEN'S COLLEGE, pp. xxiv + 592 + [8]. (31*s.* 6*d.*)

1903–4.

45. The Ancient Kalendar of the University of Oxford. Edited by the Rev. CHRISTOPHER WORDSWORTH, pp. xxxii + 294 + [8]. (31*s.* 6*d.*)

1904.

46. Oxford Silver Pennies. Edited by C. L. STAINER, M.A., pp. xlvi + 96 + [8]. With 15 plates. (21*s.*)

1905.

47. Collectanea, 4th series, edited under the superintendence of the Committee of the O. H. S., pp. xii + 346. (31*s.* 6*d.*)

(Contents:—*a.* Description of Oxford from the Hundred Rolls, ed. by Rose Graham; *b.* Oxford Church Notes, by Richard Symonds, 1643–4, ed. by Rose Graham; *c.* Three Consecrations of College Chapels (Lincoln, 1631; Brasenose, 1666; Queen's, 1717), ed. by A. Clark, F. Madan, and J. R. Magrath, D.D.; *d.* Thos. Baskerville's Account of Oxford, c. 1670–1700, ed. by Humph. Baskerville; *e.* Bill of Costs of Charles Ellis, agent in London to the Mayor of Oxford for the Coronation of George IV, 1821, ed. by F. Williams; *f.* Coaching in and out of Oxford, 1820–40, by William Bayzand.)

1906.

48. Hearne's Collections [as No. 2 above]. Vol. VII (May 9, 1719–Sept. 22, 1722). Edited under the superintendence of the Committee of the O. H. S., pp. viii + 428 + [8]. (31*s.* 6*d.*)

1906–7.

49. The Cartulary of the Abbey of Eynsham. Vol. I. Edited by the Rev. H. E. SALTER, pp. xxxvi + 441 + [8]. (31*s.* 6*d.*)

1907.

50. Hearne's Collections [as No. 2 above]. Vol. VIII (Sept. 23, 1722–Aug. 9, 1725). Edited under the superintendence of the Committee of the O. H. S., pp. viii + 443 + [8]. (31*s.* 6*d.*)

1908.

51. The Cartulary of the Abbey of Eynsham. Vol. II. Edited by the Rev. H. E. SALTER, pp. xcviii + 422 + [8]. (31*s.* 6*d.*)

1909.

52, 53. Brasenose College Monographs. Vol. I and Vol. II. Part I. [Only sold in sets of the Society's publications.*]

1910.

54. Brasenose College Monographs. Vol. II, Part II. [Only sold in sets of the Society's publications.*]

55. Brasenose College Register, 1509–1909. With Lists and Index. [*Presented to the Society by the Editor, Dr. Heberden.* Only sold in sets of the Society's publications.*]

* The two volumes of Monographs are published by Mr. B. H. Blackwell, Broad Street, Oxford, at 10*s.* 6*d.* each: and the Register by the same at 15*s.*

1910–11.

56. Liber Obituarius Aulae Reginae, printed in facsimile, with notes, pp. xliii + 153. [*Presented to the Society by the Editor, the Rev. the Provost of Queen's College.*] (42*s.*)

1911.

57. Catalogue of Oxford Portraits. Vol. I. By Mrs. R. L. POOLE, pp. xxxii + 278. (Additional copies can be obtained only through a bookseller in the ordinary way.)

58. Enactments in Parliament concerning Oxford and Cambridge. Vol. I (37 Ed. III—13 Anne), by L. L. SHADWELL, pp. xxxix + 360.

1912.

59–61. Enactments in Parliament, Vols. II–IV (1 George I—2 George V), by L. L. SHADWELL. Vol. II, pp. iv + 408; III, pp. iv + 420; IV, pp. iv + 384.

1913.

62. The Flemings in Oxford. Vol. II. Edited by the Rev. the PROVOST OF QUEEN'S COLLEGE, pp. xxviii + 418 + [8]. (21*s.*)

63. A Subsidy collected in the Diocese of Lincoln in 1526. Edited by the Rev. H. E. SALTER, pp. xvi + 348. [*Presented to the Society.*] (12*s.* 6*d.*)

64. Balliol Oxford Deeds. Edited by the Rev. H. E. SALTER, pp. xii + 388 + [8]. [*Presented to the Society.*] (21*s.*)

1914.

65. Hearne's Collections [as No. 2 above]. Vol. IX (Aug. 10, 1725–Mar. 26, 1728). Edited chiefly by the Rev. H. E. SALTER, pp. x + 424 + [8]. (21*s.*)

66. A Cartulary of the Hospital of St. John the Baptist. Vol. I. Edited by the Rev. H. E. SALTER, pp. xii + 492 + [8]. [*Presented to the Society by the President and Fellows of Magdalen College.*] (21*s.*)

1915.

67. Hearne's Collections [as No. 2 above]. Vol. X (Mar. 27, 1728–Dec. 16, 1731.) Edited by the Rev. H. E. SALTER, pp. 494 + [8]. (21*s.*)

68. A Cartulary of the Hospital of St. John the Baptist. Vol. II. Edited by the Rev. H. E. SALTER, pp. vii + 467 + [8]. [*Presented to the Society by the President and Fellows of Magdalen College.*] (21*s.*)

1916.

69. A Cartulary of the Hospital of St. John the Baptist. Vol. III. Edited by the Rev. H. E. SALTER, pp. lvi + 520 + [8]. [*Presented to the Society by the President and Fellows of Magdalen College.*] (21*s.*)

1917.

70. Mediaeval Archives of the University of Oxford. Vol. I. Edited by the Rev. H. E. SALTER, pp. xii + 382 + [8]. (21*s.*)

71. Munimenta Civitatis Oxonie. Edited by the Rev. H. E. SALTER, pp. xlviii + 308 + [8]. [*Presented to the Society by the Editor.*] (21*s.*)

1918.

72. Hearne's Collections [as No. 2 above]. Vol. XI (Dec. 9, 1731 to the death of Hearne). Edited by the Rev. H. E. SALTER, pp. xiii + 491 + [8]. (31*s.* 6*d.*)

1919.

73. Mediaeval Archives of the University of Oxford. Vol. II. Edited by the Rev. H. E. SALTER, pp. xix + 385 + [8]. (21*s.*)

WORKS IN ACTIVE PREPARATION.

The Flemings in Oxford. Edited by the Rev. the PROVOST OF QUEEN'S COLLEGE. Vol. III.

The Cartulary of Oseney Abbey. Part. I. The Town Properties. 2 vols. Edited by the Rev. H. E. SALTER.

The Merton 'Registrum Annalium', 1482–1508. Edited by the Rev. H. E. SALTER.